Ripley's Believe It or Not!®

Executive Vice President, Intellectual Property Norm Deska
Senior Director of Publishing Amanda Joiner

Editorial Manager Carrie Bolin
Editors Jessica Firpi, Jordie R. Orlando
Creative Content Manager Sabrina Sieck

Designer Luis Fuentes

ISBN 978-1-60991-251-2

For more information regarding permission, contact:
VP Intellectual Property
Ripley Entertainment Inc.
7576 Kingspointe Parkway, Suite 188
Orlando, Florida 32819
publishing@ripleys.com
www.ripleys.com/books

Manufactured in China in May 2018
First Printing

PUBLISHER'S NOTE
While every effort has been made to verify the accuracy of the entries in this book, the Publisher cannot be held responsible for any errors contained in the work. They would be glad to receive any information from readers.

WARNING
Some of the stunts and activities are undertaken by experts and should not be attempted by anyone without adequate training and supervision.

THE BEST OF

TWISTS EDITION

VOLUME 2

a Jim Pattison Company

INSIDE YOU'LL FIND:

Ripley's SPIDERS and scary creepy crawlies Believe It or Not!

fun, facts, and shudders...it's all about bugs... with a Ripley twist!

BOOK 1

BOOK 2

Ripley's WILD ANIMALS Believe It or Not!

fun, facts, and frights...it's all about animals... with a Ripley twist!

BOOK 3

BOOK 4

BOOK 5

BOOK 6

BOOK 7

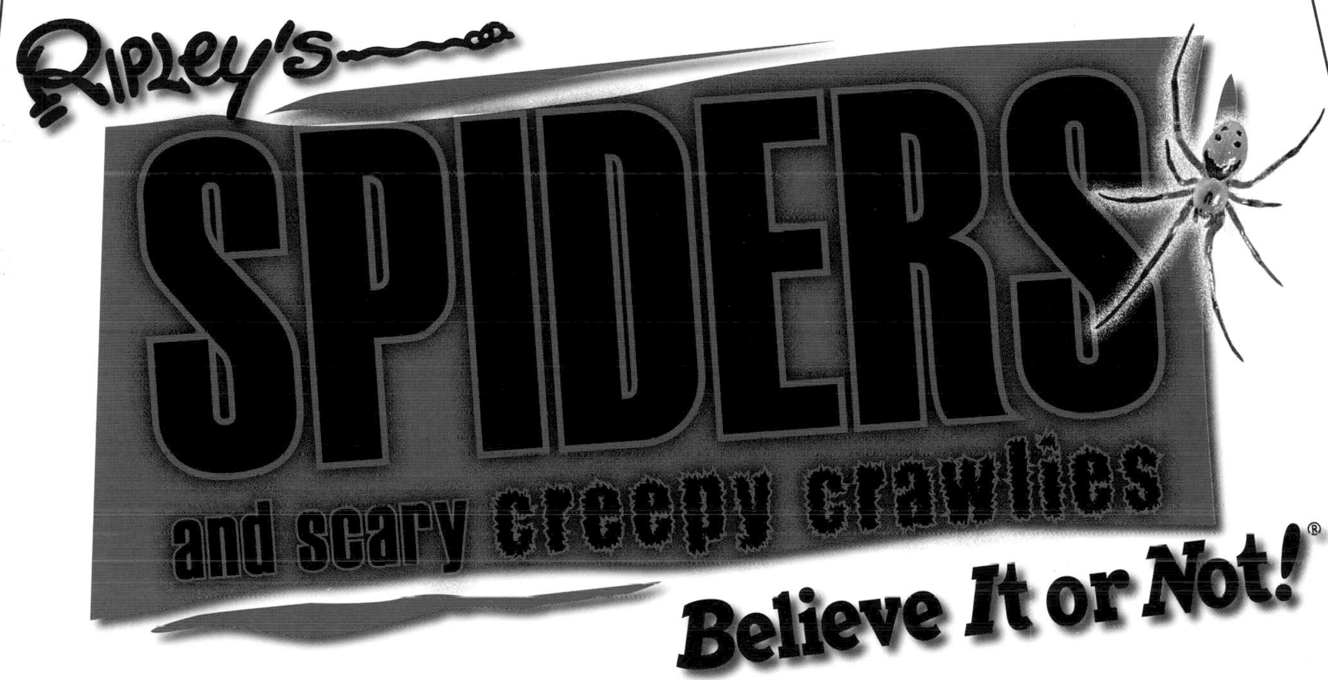

a Jim Pattison Company

Written by Camilla de la Bedoyere
Consultant Barbara Taylor

CONTENTS

Publisher Anne Marshall

Editorial Director Rebecca Miles
Project Editor Charlotte Howell
Picture Researchers Michelle Foster, Charlotte Howell
Proofreader Lisa Regan
Indexer Hilary Bird

Art Director Sam South
Senior Designer Michelle Foster
Design Rocket Design (East Anglia) Ltd
Reprographics Juice Creative Ltd

www.ripleybooks.com

First published in Great Britain in 2009 byYoung Arrow, Random House, 20 Vauxhall Bridge Road, London SW1V 2SA
www.randomhouse.co.uk

This edition 2014

Addresses for companies within The Random House Group Limited can be found at: www.randomhouse.co.uk/offices.htm

The Random House Group Limited Reg. No. 954009

ISBN 978-1-60991-234-5 (USA) | ISBN 978-009959-659-2 (UK)

10 9 8 7 6 5 4 3 2 1

A CIP catalogue record for this book is available from the British Library

Printed in China January 2018
2nd Printing

PAGE 43

PAGE 41

PAGE 11

MEGA MINI MONSTERS

They're scary!

This jumping spider may look scary, but its body actually measures just 0.5 cm long. These harmless spiders are capable of jumping up to 40 times their own length!

ACTUAL SIZE

You have got the world at your feet – and if you look closely you will see it is crawling with some bizarre beasts of the mini variety. There are billions of bugs, slithering slimy things, sinister spiders and creepy crawlies all around us, but how much do you know about them?

Join us on a trip into the dark dank soil, delve beneath plants, and peer into places you have never investigated before. We will show you the kingdom of the mini-monsters, where animals have giant crushing jaws, deadly venom and powerful pincers. These creatures have a way of life that is incredible, awesome and almost unbelievable!

These books are about 'Believe It or Not!' – amazing facts, feats, and things that make you go 'Wow!'

Ripley's Believe It or Not!®

Dr Mohamed Babu, from India, set up this ant experiment which shows their bodies changing colour as they drink from different coloured sugar water. Ants' abdomens are semi-transparent and absorb the colours they sip in the liquid.

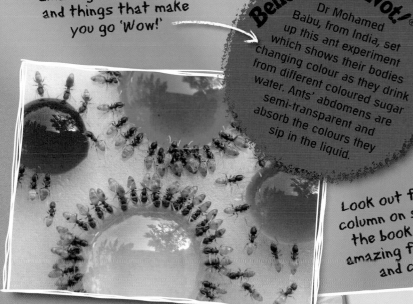

Found a new word? Big Word Alert will explain it for you.

Look out for the 'Twist It' column on some pages. Twist the book to find out more amazing facts about spiders and creepy crawlies.

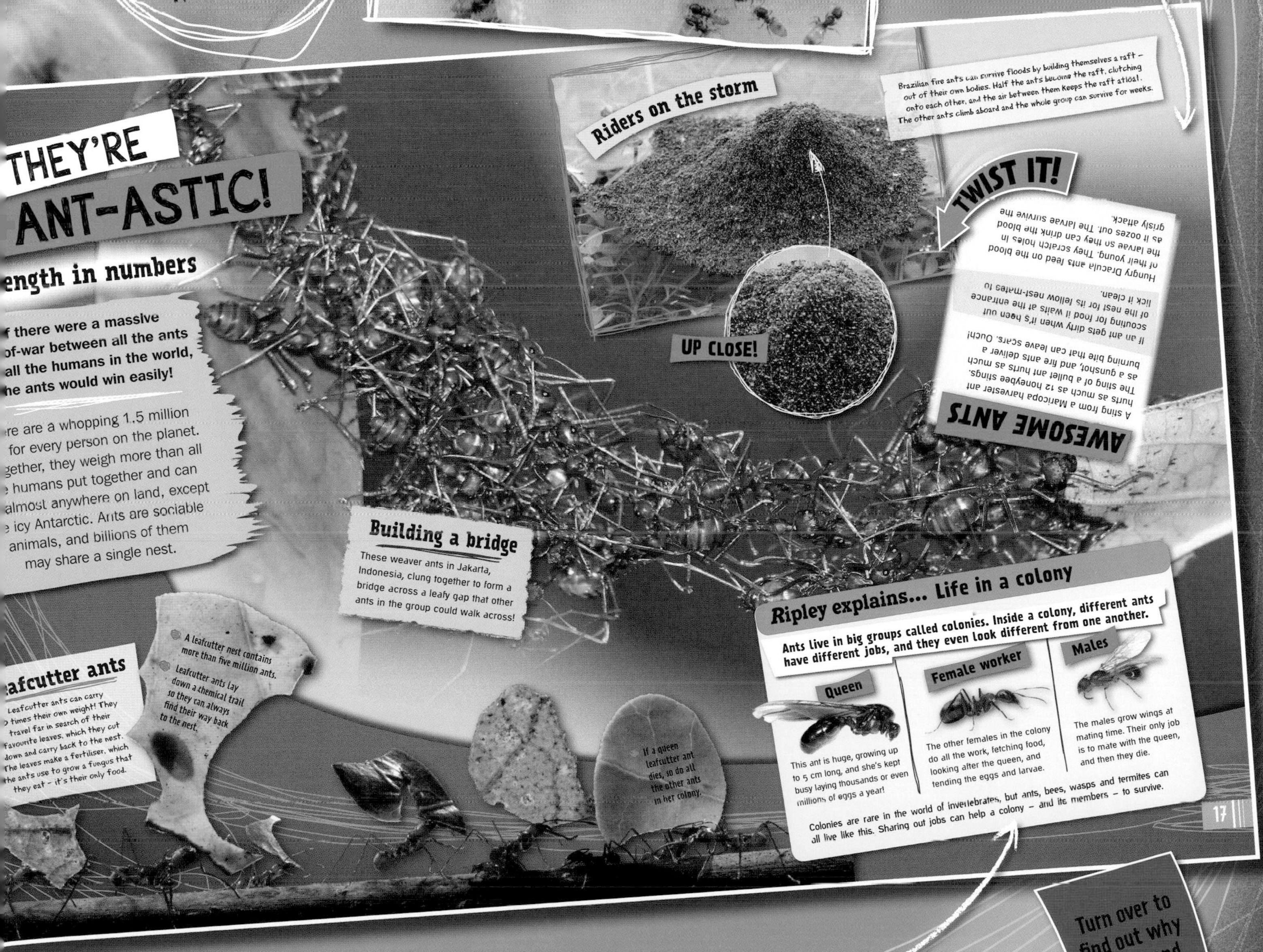

THEY'RE ANT-ASTIC!

…ength in numbers

…f there were a massive …of-war between all the ants …all the humans in the world, …he ants would win easily!

…re are a whopping 1.5 million … for every person on the planet. …gether, they weigh more than all … humans put together and can … almost anywhere on land, except … icy Antarctic. Ants are sociable animals, and billions of them may share a single nest.

Riders on the storm

Brazilian fire ants can survive floods by building themselves a raft – out of their own bodies. Half the ants become the raft, clutching onto each other, and the air between them keeps the raft afloat. The other ants climb aboard and the whole group can survive for weeks.

UP CLOSE!

TWIST IT!

AWESOME ANTS

A sting from a Maricopa harvester ant hurts as much as 12 honeybee stings. The sting of a bullet ant hurts as much as a gunshot, and fire ants deliver a burning bite that can leave scars. Ouch!

If an ant gets dirty when it's been out scouting for food it waits at the entrance of the nest for its fellow nest-mates to lick it clean.

Hungry Dracula ants feed on the blood of their young. They scratch holes in the larvae so they can drink the blood as it oozes out. The larvae survive the grisly attack.

Building a bridge

These weaver ants in Jakarta, Indonesia, clung together to form a bridge across a leafy gap that other ants in the group could walk across!

…afcutter ants

Leafcutter ants can carry …0 times their own weight! They travel far in search of their favourite leaves, which they cut down and carry back to the nest. The leaves make a fertiliser, which the ants use to grow a fungus that they eat – it's their only food.

A leafcutter nest contains more than five million ants.

Leafcutter ants lay down a chemical trail so they can always find their way back to the nest.

If a queen leafcutter ant dies, so do all the other ants in her colony.

Ripley explains… Life in a colony

Ants live in big groups called colonies. Inside a colony, different ants have different jobs, and they even look different from one another.

Queen
This ant is huge, growing up to 5 cm long, and she's kept busy laying thousands or even millions of eggs a year!

Female worker
The other females in the colony do all the work, fetching food, looking after the queen, and tending the eggs and larvae.

Males
The males grow wings at mating time. Their only job is to mate with the queen, and then they die.

Colonies are rare in the world of invertebrates, but ants, bees, wasps and termites can all live like this. Sharing out jobs can help a colony – and its members – to survive.

17

See the 'Ripley explains' panels for extra info from our bug experts.

Turn over to find out why spiders and bugs are so scary…

ARACHNOPHOBIA!

Fearsome or fabulous? You decide...

Most spiders are smaller than a coin and totally harmless, but they strike fear into the hearts of millions. What is it about these eight-legged creepy crawlies that freaks people out?

A fear of spiders is called arachnophobia and it is one of the most common fears that people suffer from. Here at Ripley we believe it is wise to find out more about animals that frighten us, so let's investigate these creatures and discover whether spiders are terrible, terrific or truly terrifying!

Hairy legs

Spiders don't need noses or tongues because their hairy legs can smell and taste things!

True or false?

	TRUE	FALSE
Almost all spiders live on land.	✓	
All spider venom is dangerous to humans.		✓
Some spiders have six legs.		✓
Spiders are hunters that feed on other animals.	✓	
Spiders inject venom into their prey to stun or kill it before eating it.	✓	

SPIDER TALES

Spiders are older than dinosaurs and have been crawling around Earth for at least 300 million years.

Spiders can probably see in colour, but like insects they probably can't see the colour red.

Water spiders are able to live underwater. They carry a bubble of air with them, to breathe.

TWIST IT!

...AND OTHER SCARY CREEPY CRAWLIES

LOUDEST

Some of the loudest animals in the world are cicadas – beetles that sing by vibrating a drum-like plate at the base of the abdomen. A group of cicadas can be louder than a drill!

FASTEST RUNNER

Tiger beetles can run at 9 km/h, which is faster than lots of humans can manage!

BEST SENSE OF SMELL

Male emperor moths can smell a female 11 km away.

Spinning machine

Spiders produce silk in the spinnerets at their bottom end, and use the silk to create extraordinary webs and traps.

The eyes have it

Most spiders have eight eyes in two or three rows at the front of their head. Their big eyes help them to see at night and focus on prey.

Huge brain

Small spiders have such a big brain that it spreads into their legs. They need a brain this size to be able to spin webs.

Mighty mouth

Spiders have pedipalps, which look like little arms, and chelicerae (say chell-is-er-ay), which are pincer-like jaws, to help them get food to their mouth.

WHAT'S THE VERDICT?

Do you give spiders the thumbs up? Do you agree with us that they are impressive animals with incredible powers and amazing lifestyles?

Do those long, spindly legs still give you the creeps, and are you still too scared to pick up a spider?

SMALLEST ANT

The tiniest ant in the world is less than 0.08 cm long.

GREEDIEST

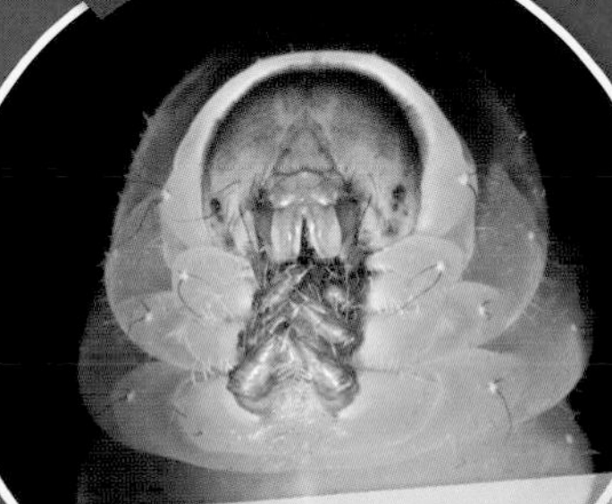

The caterpillar of a polyphemus moth eats 86,000 times its birth weight in the first two months of its life.

FASTEST JUMPER

Click beetles can shoot up into the air at a greater speed for their weight than any other insect. This action is measured as 'g-force'.

HIGHEST JUMPER

Cat fleas are the world's bounciest invertebrates, and – for their size – jump higher than any other creature. A cat flea can leap about 200 times its own length.

A WORLD OF CREEPY CRAWLIES

Endless invertebrates!

Spiders and super scary creepy crawlies are not like other creatures. Most of them are tiny, but they make up the largest group of animals on the planet – invertebrates!

Scientists think that there may be more than 10 million types of animal in the world, and that at least 8 million are invertebrates – a group of creatures without backbones that includes all insects and spiders. Let us introduce you to the inspiring invertebrates!

How many legs?

Most mammals, such as horses, have four legs. Birds have just two legs, and fish have none. Invertebrates, however, can have anything from zero to hundreds of legs!

Worms, slugs and snails

This group of invertebrates has no legs and soft skin. Earthworms live in the soil and breathe through their slimy skin. An earthworm has both male and female body parts.

Long slimy body

Slugs and snails belong to a group of animals called molluscs. Most molluscs live in the sea, but some of them enjoy life on the land.

Insects

Insects have six legs and a hard outer skin called an exoskeleton. Insects are the most successful animals on the planet and, so far, one million species have been discovered. Beetles, bees, flies, butterflies and ants are all insects.

An insect's body is divided into three parts.

A beetle has two pairs of wings. Its flying wings are tucked underneath a pair of hard, coloured wings for protection. These hard wings are called elytra, or wing cases.

Arachnids

Abdomen

Head and thorax

This wolf spider is a large and fast hunter.

Arachnids are a group of invertebrates that includes spiders, scorpions, mites and ticks. All arachnids have eight legs, and an exoskeleton. We know about 30,000 to 40,000 species of spider, but there are probably lots more lurking in dark corners.

Crustaceans

Crustaceans are invertebrates that mostly live in the sea, although a few species like to creep about on land. Some crustaceans have no legs, but others have 10, 14, or even more! Woodlice and beach hoppers are crustaceans.

The exoskeleton of a pill woodlouse (see left) is divided into many parts, or segments, so it can roll up and protect its softer underside.

BIG WORD ALERT

EXOSKELETON

A hard outer skin that protects the body.

Centipedes and millipedes

These creepy crawlies have an exoskeleton and one species has as many as 750 legs! It's odd, but the ones with more legs often run more slowly than those with fewer legs.

An African giant millipede (see right) can grow to 30 cm long. It looks scary, but it only eats dead leaves.

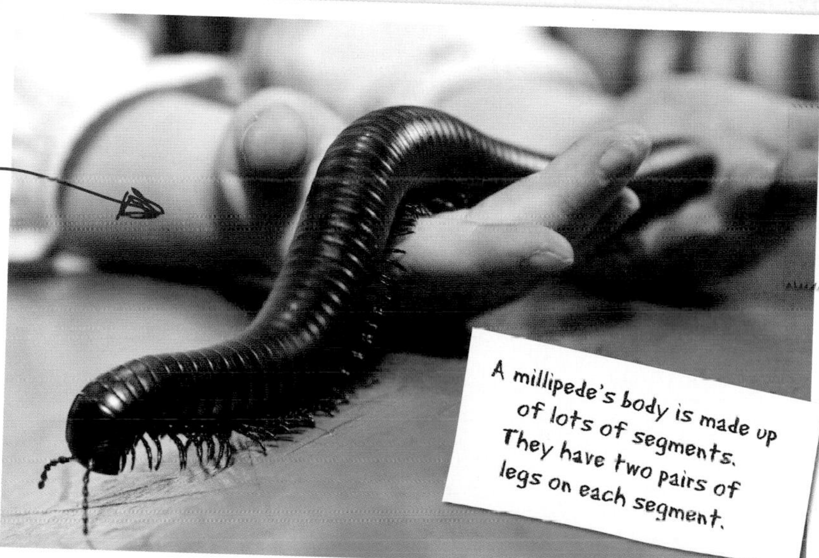

A millipede's body is made up of lots of segments. They have two pairs of legs on each segment.

Hard or squishy?

Invertebrates don't have a skeleton to keep their body strong, which is why they are small. Many of them do have an exoskeleton, though.

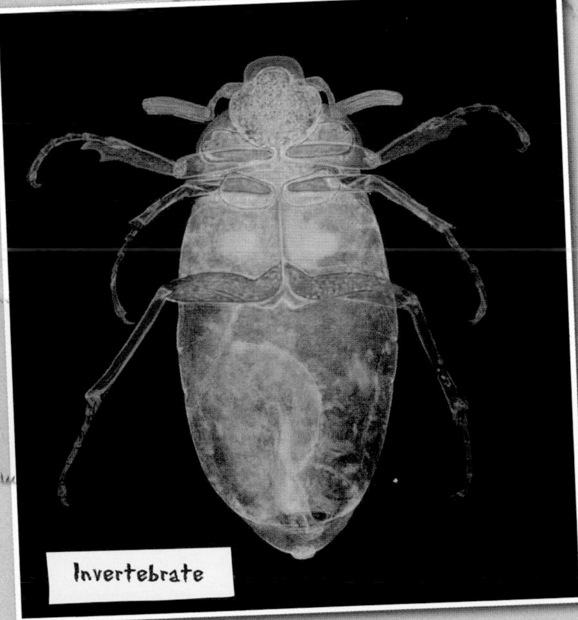

Invertebrate

This is an X-ray of a male cockchafer beetle, viewed from underneath. It has been coloured to show the different body parts. There are no dark solid areas inside the beetle's body because there are no bones, just soft organs. The animal's legs are attached to the outside of its body, on its thorax.

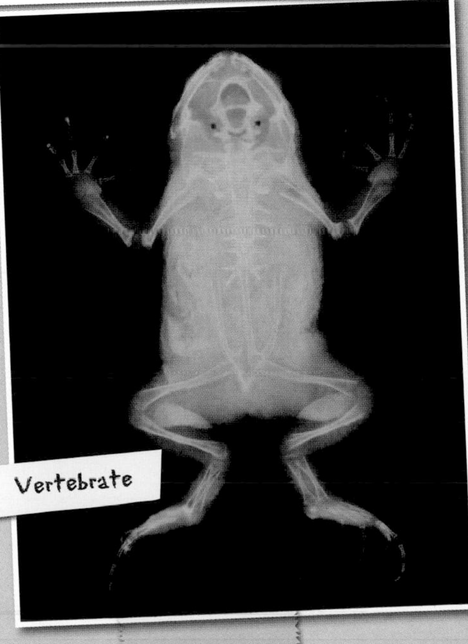

Vertebrate

This X-ray of a toad shows that it is a vertebrate – an animal with a backbone – as a bony skeleton is clearly visible inside its body. The long bone that runs from the head down the length of the body is called the vertebral column, or backbone. It protects the nerves that carry messages between the animal's brain and the rest of its body.

SLIME, SLITHER AND SLIDE

If you can't crawl, creep!

If humans didn't have legs, how would we get around? We'd probably have to slide along the ground coated in a thick layer of gloopy slime. It's a gross idea, and that's one reason why legless mini-beasts seem so gruesome.

Slugs and snails are slime movers! As they creep, these soft-bodied molluscs leave a thick trail of sticky, slimy gunge behind them. The slime stops them from drying out, helps them glide easily over rough ground and stick to trees and walls, and helps to deter predators.

Worms can slither because they are covered in thousands of tiny hairs and a slimy goo called mucus. When earthworms get dry they coat themselves in mucus and have a little nap until it rains.

HANG ON!

This is a no-win situation! A slimy ribbon worm might eat a cockroach, and a cockroach might fancy eating a worm (despite its foul flavour), but these two have got themselves into a desperately sticky state of affairs.

SLUDGY STORIES

Long ago, people boiled and mashed snails to make paste to treat burns, and even smeared snail mucus onto sore skin.

Snails, slugs and worms move by contracting and relaxing muscles in ripples, so their body moves forward.

Slime is so strong and stringy that a slug or snail can crawl along a sharp razor blade without being cut.

The world's longest worms can grow to 55 m or more!

Tiny Japanese landsnails are tough little things. If they get swallowed by a bird they can survive the journey through the digestive system, and come out the other end, alive and perfectly well!

Believe it or not, a slug's bottom is just behind its head!

Scientists hope that one day they can use slug slime to make a glue that can be used to stick open wounds together instead of stitches.

TWIST IT!

Ripley's Believe It or Not!®

A frog was peacefully snoozing when a slimy snail decided to take a short-cut – over its head! It took the snail eight minutes to slide over the frog, its only route across the branch.

Grub's up!

Some young bugs don't have legs and have to wriggle and wiggle to move. Called grubs or maggots, these supercreeps can't make a quick getaway, so they make a great meal for other animals. Witchetty grubs are baby moths, and they are big and juicy – so juicy that some people like to eat them!

BIG WORD ALERT

CONTRACT & RELAX

The way muscles change shape so animals can move.

MAKING MILLIONS

Taking over the world

Could bugs really ever take over the world? When one insect can produce thousands of offspring in just one year, are we at risk of drowning in a sea of spiders and scary creepy crawlies?

Spiders and insects usually live short, busy lives, and they don't often make caring parents. Their main aim is to eat and grow until they can produce young, and lots of them! They rarely spend much time looking after their eggs – they just hope that if they lay enough, some of them will survive.

Super spidermums

They may be in the minority, but some spiders make very good parents! Wolf spider mothers even carry their babies on their back for a week, while they grow bigger.

Baby spiders are called spiderlings. They look like their parents, but smaller. Their exoskeleton (outer skin) is soft, but it soon hardens.

Big one!

Unusually, for insects, female tsetse flies produce just one egg at a time, and keep it inside their body while it hatches and grows into a larva. It feeds from its mother's body until it is big enough to be born.

I'm a BIG BABY!

The mother can carry up to 100 spiderlings on her back at a time! They cling tightly to the little hairs on her body.

NASTY NUMBERS...

40,000,000 The number of humans who accidentally eat roundworm eggs every year. Roundworms live inside pigs, but humans can get infected with them by eating undercooked pork.

100,000 The number of eggs a tapeworm can produce every day. If an egg is eaten by an animal it will stay in the animal's guts and can grow into a worm measuring up to 30 m long!

10,000 The number of eggs some queen termites can lay in one day. The queen termite's job is to lay eggs for the colony every day for 15 years. When she gets old, the worker termites stop feeding her and she starves to death.

1 Queen's stomach with thousands of eggs inside

2 Queen's head

3 Worker termites ready to catch eggs

I'm a BIG MOMMA!

A queen termite is 100 times bigger than the 1–2 million termite workers that look after her and the eggs.

640 The number of baby aphids one aphid mum might produce in a summer. Female aphids are born pregnant. If all of their babies survive to have offspring there could be 1,560,000,000,000,000,000,000,000 new aphids in just one summer.

Egg-sac-tly!

Mother spiders usually wrap their eggs in a silken bundle, called a cocoon or egg-sac. They protect the eggs from animals, such as birds, that might want to eat them, and when the spiderlings are ready to hatch, the mother can help them out of the cocoon.

About three weeks after they are laid, 50 or so little spiderlings will hatch from the eggs of this huntsman spider.

EXTREME ARACHNIDS

A ferocious family

Spiders belong to the arachnid family, and they have some creepy cousins.

All arachnids have six pairs of 'limbs'. The first pair of 'limbs' are chelicerae, which are mostly used for feeding. The second pair – pedipalps – is used for touching and sensing. The other four pairs are legs. Many arachnids have venom (poison), and they are found all over the world.

Harvestmen

Some arachnids are extremely revolting! An enormous group, or 'cluster', of harvestmen with all those long, gangly legs is enough to make your skin crawl. They don't have venom but they do have foul stink glands that make a nasty smell to deter predators. It's thought they form massive clusters and use their combined stink to keep even big predators at bay.

A harvestman's legs are long and spindly and one pair is often used as a pair of 'feelers'.

A harvestman has just two eyes that are in the middle of its blobby body.

Ticks

Ticks may be tiny, but these arachnids are terrible pests that live on animals and spread disease. They can't move by themselves, so they wait for a victim, cling onto it, and use their mouthparts to suck its blood.

This tick has been feeding on a dog, and its body is swollen with the dog's blood.

A sun spider has huge chelicerae (jaws) for killing prey.
The long tail ends in a stinger, which is used for defence.
The body is shiny and black.
The pedipalps are large and strong and are used to kill prey.
ACTUAL SIZE

Sun spider

The sun spider's bite is deep, but not deadly. These arachnids have big jaws for crushing and killing, but they don't have venom. They use their pedipalps, which are equipped with suction pads, to grip onto their prey tightly.

Imperial scorpion

The imperial – or emperor – scorpion is the world's largest scorpion, although it is not the deadliest. An adult has a bulky body and can grow to more than 20 cm long. Prehistoric scorpions, however, could grow to four times that size!

THEY'RE F-ANT-ASTIC!

Strength in numbers

If there were a massive tug-of-war between all the ants and all the humans in the world, the ants would win easily!

There are a whopping 1.5 million ants for every person on the planet. Altogether, they weigh more than all the humans put together and can live almost anywhere on land, except the icy Antarctic. Ants are sociable animals, and billions of them may share a single nest.

Building a bridge

These weaver ants in Jakarta, Indonesia, clung together to form a bridge across a leafy gap that other ants in the group could walk across!

Leafcutter ants

Leafcutter ants can carry 20 times their own weight! They travel far in search of their favourite leaves, which they cut down and carry back to the nest. The leaves make a fertiliser, which the ants use to grow a fungus that they eat – it's their only food.

- A leafcutter nest contains more than five million ants.
- Leafcutter ants lay down a chemical trail so they can always find their way back to the nest.

Riders on the storm

Brazilian fire ants can survive floods by building themselves a raft – out of their own bodies. Half the ants become the raft, clutching onto each other, and the air between them keeps the raft afloat. The other ants climb aboard and the whole group can survive for weeks.

UP CLOSE!

TWIST IT!

AWESOME ANTS

A sting from a Maricopa harvester ant hurts as much as 12 honeybee stings. The sting of a bullet ant hurts as much as a gunshot, and fire ants deliver a burning bite that can leave scars. Ouch!

If an ant gets dirty when it's been out scouting for food it waits at the entrance of the nest for its fellow nest-mates to lick it clean.

Hungry Dracula ants feed on the blood of their young. They scratch holes in the larvae so they can drink the blood as it oozes out. The larvae survive the grisly attack.

*R*ipley explains... Life in a colony

Ants live in big groups called colonies. Inside a colony, different ants have different jobs, and they even look different from one another.

Queen

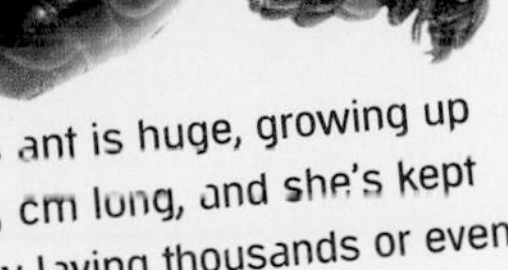

This ant is huge, growing up to 5 cm long, and she's kept busy laying thousands or even millions of eggs a year!

Female worker

The other females in the colony do all the work, fetching food, looking after the queen, and tending the eggs and larvae.

Males

The males grow wings at mating time. Their only job is to mate with the queen, and then they die.

Colonies are rare in the world of invertebrates, but ants, bees, wasps and termites can all live like this. Sharing out jobs can help a colony – and its members – to survive.

If a queen leafcutter ant dies, so do all the other ants in her colony.

WORLD WIDE WEBS

Silky strong

Spiders are nature's master builders. They not only build intricate and beautiful webs, they even manufacture their own building material!

All spiders make silk. They can use it to make a highly structured web, a messy flytrap, or to wrap up their lunch to keep it fresh. The most impressive webs are built around a central point. Lines of silken thread come out of the centre, like a bicycle's spokes, and spirals of silk are attached to them.

Stretchy net webs

The net-casting spider weaves a sheet of stretchy silk into a mini-web, or 'net'. The spider hides, holding the net, and waits for a victim. It then rushes out, throws the net over its prey, wraps it in silk, bites it, and feeds on it.

A net-casting spider has a long, slender, stick-like body so it can hide out of sight while it waits with its net.

*R*ipley explains... Web weaving

A web is made of three main types of silk thread – frame threads, radial threads and spiral threads. The frame and radial threads are made of strong silk, but the spiral is made of sticky elastic silk so it doesn't break when insects struggle to escape.

Step 1

The spider makes a long thread, which gets caught by the wind and sticks to a surface. It makes a second, looser thread attached to the first.

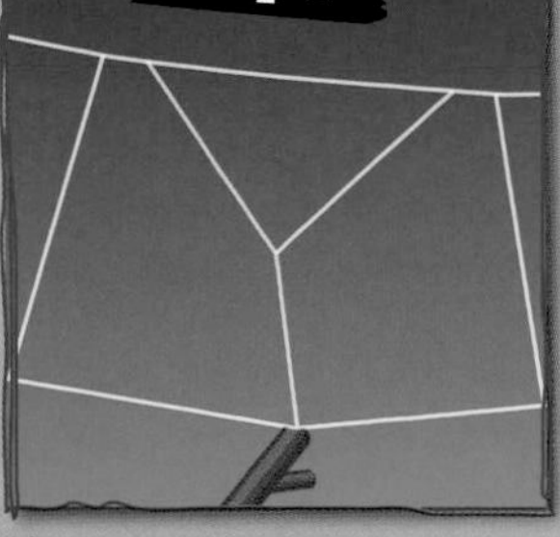

Step 2

Next, it makes a Y shape to create the centre of the web, and adds other threads to build the web's frame.

Step 3

The spider weaves radial threads from the hub to the frame, and then adds sticky spiral threads around the radial threads.

Spiders have special glands inside their abdomen that make liquid silk. The liquid silk comes out of the gland and into a spinneret. From here, it is forced through a tiny hole, called a spigot. The liquid silk is pulled through acidic silk glands that harden it and turn it into solid thread.

A spider guides the silk out of its body using its legs.

This nursery web spider is keeping guard over her newly-hatched spiderlings.

Big and tough

Giant orb-web spiders weave enormous webs that can span more than 1.8 m across. Females can be as big as a human hand, but the males are much smaller. The webs are strong enough to trap small birds and bats.

The spider taps the silken threads to make her web vibrate, and tempt prey to come closer.

Safety nets

Nursery web spiders hunt their prey rather than using a web to catch them. However, they do build large, messy, tent-like webs to protect their eggs.

SECRETS OF SILK

Silk is stronger and stretchier than any threads that humans have been able to make. It can stretch six times its own length before it snaps.

- Spiders can coat their silk with glue to make it extra sticky.
- Silk gets ten times heavier as it turns from liquid to solid.
- The best spider silk is stronger than human bone.

Giant web

Spiders in Texas spun an enormous web that stretched for over 180 m. Lots of different types of spider got in on the act and helped to make the massive bug trap.

BRILLIANT BUILDERS

And dastardly diggers

Spiders are wonderful with webs, but they are also good at creating other structures, as are lots of other creepy crawlies.

Birds build nests, foxes dig dens, and beavers build lodges out of sticks – but many creepy crawlies are also fantastic builders and diggers. Animals create homes to hide away from predators, protect their young or store food.

This cautious spider is carefully opening the trap door to its hidden burrow.

Trapdoor spiders

These clever spiders dig burrows to hide in, with silken lids and lots of silken 'trip-wires' around the entrance. If a bug moves the trip-wire, the waiting spider leaps out and grabs lunch.

Caddisflies

Caddisfly larvae live in ponds and rivers, and use silk to build themselves 'invisibility cloaks' and nets. Their silken nets are used to trap food, and their 'cloaks' are often strengthened with rock, sand and bits of plant. This larva has used tiny snail shells to build itself a disguise.

Paper wasps

A paper wasp chews up dead wood, and mixes it with spit to make a pulp for building its nest. The wasp constructs chambers, so an egg can be laid in each one. Each chamber is a hexagon, which is a great shape for building without wasting any space.

Mighty mound

Termites build mounds using soil. Inside a mound, there is a complex system of tunnels for the termites to move through. There are other tunnels that allow fresh air to move around – like an air-conditioning system!

Termites

Termites belong to the same family as bees and ants, and live in large colonies. They achieve some incredible building feats. One of the largest termite mounds found was 15 m tall. That's like us building a house a mile high!

Potter wasps

Potter wasps make nests out of mud, clay and spit. They capture a caterpillar and sting it, so it stops moving but does not die. The caterpillar is then put into part of the mud nest – or 'pot' – with an egg. When the egg hatches, it feeds on the caterpillar.

This potter wasp is carrying a ball of mud to add to its nest.

DRESSING UP

Masters of disguise

Many spiders and other creepy crawlies are kings of camouflage. One of these little creatures could be sitting right next to you – and you wouldn't even be aware of it.

Spiders and creepy crawlies are juicy treats for many animals, so some of them try their best to blend into the background to avoid being spotted and eaten. Some also use camouflage to catch unsuspecting bugs.

Disgusting disguise

If you really want to stop someone from eating you, then making yourself look like poo is a brilliant move! If you ever notice a bird dropping crawling along the ground, look a bit closer. It may be a **BIRD DUNG SPIDER!**

EWW!

Out of sight

Dressing up as a twig is a popular pastime in the animal world, which is no surprise given how many trees there are to hide in! Stick insects, birds, snakes, lizards, and caterpillars all have a go at this kind of disguise – but you need to be really eagle-eyed to spot a **STUMP ORB WEAVER SPIDER** such as this one.

Now you see me...

...now you don't!

Crafty crab

CRAB SPIDERS change their colour to match the plant or flower they are on. This crafty camouflage only lasts until it launches an attack, but by then it's too late. Its real identity is revealed and the bug realises it's on this pretty predator's menu.

Clever costume

Red signals danger. That's why ladybugs use this colour to warn predators that they taste foul. **LADYBIRD-MIMIC SPIDERS** take the trick one step further as their markings make them look like these toxic-tasting spotty bugs.

Berry surprise!

Birds love to eat caterpillars, they are so much nicer than a bitter, unripe berry. That's why a **NOLID MOTH CATERPILLAR** grows a big green part on its body that looks like a berry. And if a bird does get too close, the caterpillar vomits a foul green liquid that puts the bird right off its dinner!

MY LIFE STORY All change

Human children look like their parents – with two arms, two legs and a head. In the weird world of insects, however, adults and their young can look so different you might never guess they belonged to the same family.

The way that a young insect changes into an adult is called metamorphosis – and, for some insects, it's a time when their entire body may turn into a gloopy soup and rearrange to create a new stage in the life cycle.

The life cycle of a butterfly

A female lays her eggs on a leaf. An egg hatches and the butterfly larva (a tiny caterpillar) emerges, and eats and eats. A caterpillar can increase its body size 1,000 times in 2–4 weeks while it eats and grows. When it is done growing, it attaches itself to a branch.

The caterpillar becomes a pupa. Its body is protected by a hard skin

The caterpillar.

It becomes a pupa (a stage between larva and adult).

The life cycle of a ladybird

Females lay little eggs on the underside of leaves. The eggs hatch and tiny black larvae emerge. As they eat, the larvae grow and moult their skin. When the larvae are big enough, they pupate (turn into a pupa). The ladybird's metamorphosis takes about one week. A pale-coloured adult emerges, and as it begins to dry it turns red and its spots appear.

Before

An adult ladybird breaking out of its pupa.

After

Pupation

Some insects go through a stage called pupation, and become a pupa, when they are changing from a larva to an adult. This stage can take weeks, or even years.

Circle of life
Adult
Egg
Larva
Pupa

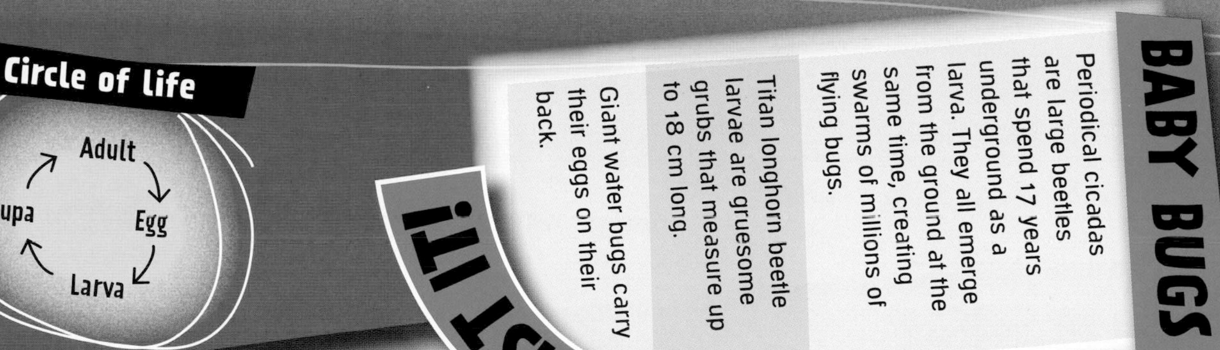

BABY BUGS

Periodical cicadas are large beetles that spend 17 years underground as a larva. They all emerge from the ground at the same time, creating swarms of millions of flying bugs.

TWIST IT!

Titan longhorn beetle larvae are gruesome grubs that measure up to 18 cm long.

Giant water bugs carry their eggs on their back.

while all the body parts break down and reform into the adult shape.

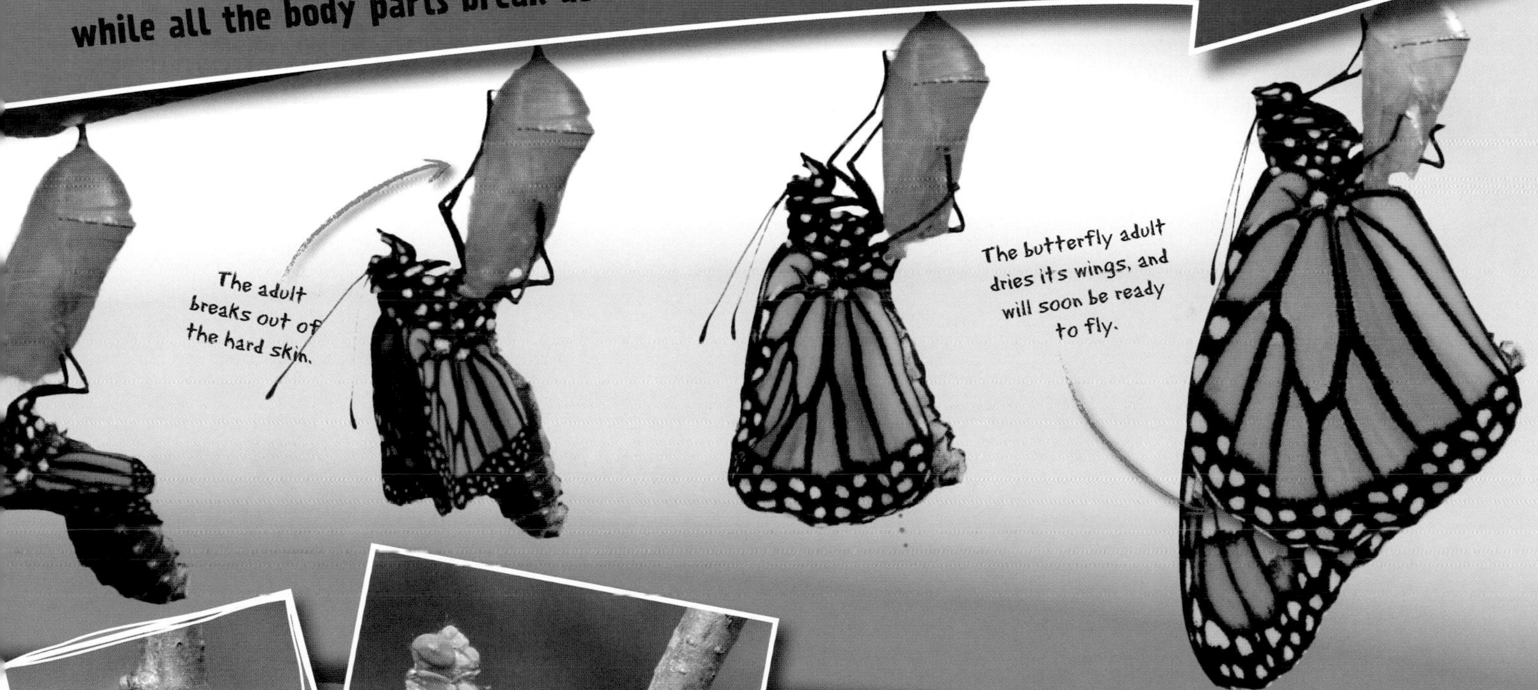

The adult breaks out of the hard skin.
The butterfly adult dries its wings, and will soon be ready to fly.

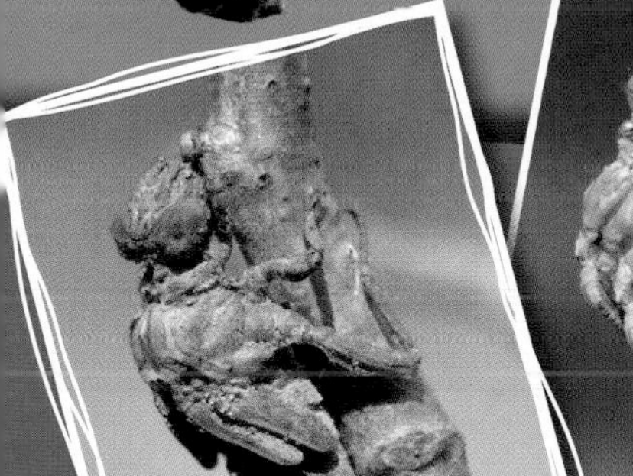

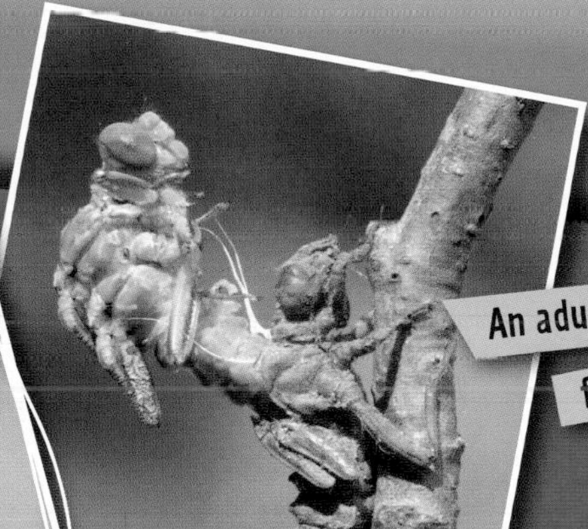

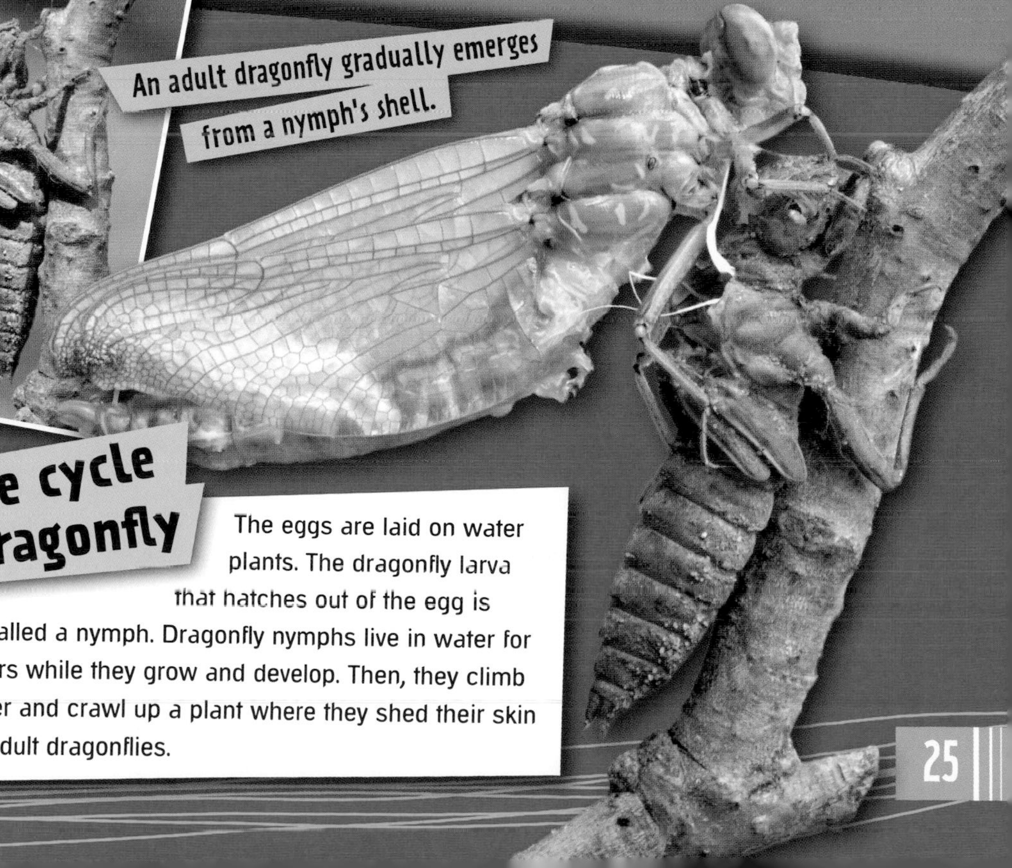

An adult dragonfly gradually emerges from a nymph's shell.

BIG WORD ALERT

LIFE CYCLE

The story of how an animal starts its life, grows, produces young, and then dies.

The life cycle of a dragonfly

The eggs are laid on water plants. The dragonfly larva that hatches out of the egg is called a nymph. Dragonfly nymphs live in water for about four years while they grow and develop. Then, they climb out of the water and crawl up a plant where they shed their skin and turn into adult dragonflies.

BEETLE MANIA

Tiny tanks of terror

Beetles are a very successful group of creepy crawlies – about one-third of all insects we know about today are beetles.

They have two pairs of wings, but the first pair has become hard and tough to protect the soft flying wings underneath.

Don't think I can't see you over there!

Giraffe weevils

Giraffe weevils have weird long necks, just like their namesakes. A male's neck can be three times its body length, and he uses it to fight other males when it's time to mate. The neck of the female isn't as long as the male, but they are still able to use it to help roll a leaf into a nest, where they can lay their eggs.

BIG WORD ALERT

WEEVIL

A type of small beetle with long mouthparts.

TWIST IT!

BEETLE BANTER

Some beetles can glow in the dark! They make light so that their mates can find them in the dark.

Beetles never suffer from smelly feet. Their feet make a liquid that keeps them fresh and clean.

Bombardier beetles spray a foul toxic mix of chemicals at their attackers.

Cochineal beetles are crushed to make a natural red dye that is used in food, drinks and make-up.

Bark beetles are no bigger than a grain of rice, but billions of them can destroy forests by munching through trees to lay their eggs. It is thought they have killed 30 billion trees in America alone.

ACTUAL SIZE

Not such a mini beast!

It's hard to believe, but titan longhorn beetles can grow bigger than a small dog, such as a Chihuahua! The largest giant titan beetle found measured a colossal 18 cm long!

CRUSHING JAWS

Despite those massive jaws, titan longhorn beetles do not feed as adults. After a long period as larvae, the adults fly around just long enough to find a mate and reproduce, and then they die. They use their jaws to fight, and the jaws are strong enough to snap a pencil in half or break a human finger.

Jewel beetles

Jewel beetles are so beautiful they were once commonly used to make sparkly, colourful jewellery. Some of them only lay their eggs in burnt wood, and they can detect the heat of forest fires 80 km away. They are also attracted to the sound of the wood crackling and burning.

Dung beetles

Dung beetles are fantastic at recycling. They collect animal dung (poo), roll it into balls, and lay their eggs in it. When larvae hatch from the eggs they find themselves safe and snug in a ball of delicious, smelly dung. It's a great place for a beetle to eat and grow.

Super strength

Taurus scarab beetles are a type of dung beetle known as the strongest beetle in the world. They can pull 1,141 times their own weight, which is like a man pulling six double-decker buses or lifting 80 tonnes.

TOP OF THE CLASS

The biggest and the best!

There are big spiders, little spiders, colourful ones, and those that are so well camouflaged you may never ever see one. But which ones are the best in the field of arachnid antics and eight-legged attacks?

Eye can see you!

This is a monster of a beast. It's a net-casting spider (see page 18), but is also known as an ogre-faced spider because of its fearsome face. It has such enormous eyes that when a torch is shone at them, they light up like the headlights of a car! These huge eyes help them to see better in the dark.

Spitting spiders win the prize for sticky surprises. Their venom glands have two parts – one part makes venom but the other part makes glue. When a spitting spider spots its prey, it fires two jets of superglue out of its fangs to fix the victim to the ground. Imprisoned by glue, the prey is finished off with a lethal jab of the fangs, and wrapped in silk to be eaten later.

Take aim, fire!

Longest legs

The prize for the spider with the longest legs goes to a type of huntsman spider with a leg span of up to 30 cm! Giant huntsman spiders live only in limestone caves in central Laos in Southeast Asia and they ambush their prey rather than build webs.

Big appetite

This goliath bird-eating spider will try to eat almost anything smaller than itself – and as it grows as big as a dinner plate that means lots of creatures find themselves on the menu! Female bird-eating spiders can live for 20 years and have a leg span of 25 cm or more. Even their fangs are 2 cm long.

SUPER SPIDERS

Widow spiders and funnel web spiders probably cause more serious bites to humans than any other spiders, but the most deadly of all are Brazilian wandering spiders. They are very aggressive and will bite rather than run away – and their venom can cause terrible pain and even death.

Bolas spiders don't waste their time building webs. They just hang a thread of sweet-smelling sticky silk beneath a branch and wait until a moth comes to investigate and gets stuck.

TWIST IT!

The fastest spiders in the world can cover 34 times their own body length per second when they run, but the golden wheel spider has a smarter way to get around. It somersaults its way across hot desert sand, covering a metre a second. If it gets too enthusiastic, it can die from exhaustion!

FLESH EATERS

Rotten rotters

Spiders may be scary, and creepy crawlies may look like ugly little monsters, but without them our world would be piled high with dead animals – and plants would die.

Spiders and bugs have some important jobs. Spiders eat the pests that would spread diseases to plants and animals. Worms, earwigs and woodlice chew up plant material into compost so plants can grow. Bugs also eat dead animals and poo. Imagine a world without them!

Super slimers

Slugs and snails usually feed on living or decaying plants, but giant Spanish slugs also munch on the bodies of dead animals. When a group of them slithers onto a road to feed on animals that have been run over, their slime is slippery enough to make cars skid!

FOUL FEAST

Maggots are fly larvae that feast on dead flesh and help dispose of animal bodies – it's nature's way of recycling. Unfortunately, lots of these maggots also like to eat our food. Let Ripley serve you up a delicious meal of unbelievable maggot grossness.

On the menu...

Casu Marzu is a traditional Italian cheese that is served with the live maggots of cheese flies wriggling around in it.

Really?

Yes. And what's more, the maggots eat the cheese, and their poo dissolves the cheese around them, making it soft and squishy.

And for dessert...

The maggots can settle down to life inside a person's gut, causing a nasty disease called myiasis.

Surprise!

The maggots can spring right out of the cheese and leap a distance of 12 cm towards your face as you eat!

TWIST IT!

KEY WORKERS

Up to one-third of the weight of a pillow can be made up of tiny arachnids called dust mites, their poo, and the bacteria that feeds on the poo. It sounds gross, but the dust mites do a great job of eating the dead skin that falls off your body while you sleep.

Everyone knows that bees fertilise plants so that the plants can make seeds, but lots of flies and beetles do this important job too.

Creepy crawlies and other animals that feed on dead animals and plants turn them back into nutrients such as nitrogen. These nutrients are important for growing plants, and the animals that eat them (including us!).

A sexton beetle can smell a dead animal a mile away.

Sexton beetles

Sexton beetles lead a very grave lifestyle. They dig a hole beneath a dead animal until it falls into their burrow. They roll it into a ball and bury it and a female then lays her eggs nearby. When the larvae hatch from the eggs, they feed on the dead body.

Seaside scrabble

Rotting seaweed doesn't just stink, it's also home to lots of bugs! Next time you are at the seaside, look out for kelp flies, tiny red mites, scarlet blood worms, beach pillbugs and creepy little beach hoppers.

BIG WORD ALERT

DECAY

When dead plants and animals rot and decompose.

Don't leaf litter!

The ground beneath a tree is usually smothered in a layer of rotting leaves, fruit and berries. Dig into leaf litter and you will find busy little beetles, bugs and worms devouring the plant matter and turning it into soil.

SUPERHERO SPIDERS

Super spider skills

You know about Spider-Man and his amazing arachnid abilities, but did you know that fact is often stranger than fiction?

Real spiders have their own collection of superpowers. Follow these intrepid superheroes as they put their best feet forward – all eight of them – to do battle.

SPIDERLINGS (YOUNG SPIDERS) MAKE SILKEN PARACHUTES AND DRAGLINES AND USE THEM TO FLY THROUGH THE AIR. IDEALLY, THEY WANT TO DISPERSE AS QUICKLY AS POSSIBLE BEFORE THEY ATTRACT THE ATTENTION OF PREDATORS. THE WIND CARRIES THE SPIDERLINGS SOME DISTANCE, BUT A SOFT LANDING IS NOT ALWAYS GUARANTEED!

FLY THROUGH THE AIR ON A ZIP WIRE!

ZIP!

VERY FEW ANIMALS CAN WALK ON WATER, BUT RAFT SPIDERS ARE ABLE TO STAY ON THE SURFACE OF A POND. THEY CAN FEEL MOVEMENTS UNDERNEATH THEIR FEET, AND GRAB ANY FISH THAT GETS TOO CLOSE. THIS RAFT SPIDER IS SINKING ITS JAWS INTO A STICKLEBACK FISH.

AAAARGHH!

WALK ON WATER!

WOW!

SUPER STRENGTH!
LATER, IN THE JUNGLE...
HEAVE!
SPIDERS DON'T NORMALLY EAT SNAKES, BUT IF ONE LANDS UP ON YOUR TABLE, WHAT ARE YOU TO DO? THIS GOLDEN ORB WEB SPIDER CAN MAKE THE MOST OF HER GOOD FORTUNE BECAUSE SHE HAS SUPERHERO STRENGTH. SHE EVEN MAKES EXTRA-STRONG SILK TO HOLD ON TO THE SNAKE, SO IT CAN'T ESCAPE OR FALL.

JUMPING SPIDERS ARE SUPERB ATHLETES. THEY CAN JUDGE DISTANCES EXTREMELY WELL, AND USE THEIR JUMPING SKILLS TO POUNCE ON PREY. A SPIDER THAT IS JUST 0.75 CM LONG CAN JUMP MORE THAN 20 CM – THAT IS LIKE YOU JUMPING ABOUT 25 M IN A SINGLE LEAP – OR SPIDER-MAN LEAPING BETWEEN TWO SKYSCRAPERS.
WHEEE...
JUMP INCREDIBLE DISTANCES!
POUNCE!

This Panamanian jumping spider is about to pounce on an unsuspecting cricket.

LONG AGO, ROMAN GLADIATORS TRAPPED THEIR ENEMIES IN NETS. SPIDERS DO THE SAME, BUT THEY USE INCREDIBLY STRONG SILK. IT'S LONG, BENDY AND STICKY – PERFECT FOR WRAPPING UP THEIR PREY.

TARANTULAS ARE VERY HAIRY AND WHEN THEY ARE SCARED THEY SHOOT HAIRS AT THE FACE OF AN ATTACKER – THE EFFECT IS LIKE BEING HIT BY A CLOUD OF POISONED ARROWS. THE HAIRS ARE EXTREMELY IRRITATING AND IF THEY GET INTO AN ATTACKER'S EYES AND SKIN THEY CAUSE PAIN.

SUPER SCARY SURVIVORS

Staying alive

Invertebrates fight to survive every day of their lives. Many things threaten them, but avoiding deadly predators is number one on their list of top survival tips.

Spiders and creepy crawlies have different ways of staying alive. Spiders hide or use venom to kill their attackers, and creepy-crawly insects use a range of crafty tricks to keep predators away.

Armoured cockroaches spray foul-smelling chemicals at attackers. The smell lingers for days.

Alien attack!

Praying mantids avoid attack by scaring their attackers with a fearsome pose – they look like scary, long-armed aliens! They raise their spiky forelimbs, which are equipped with crushing claws, and show off their big bug eyes and bright belly.

Mantids make a crunchy morsel for bats, who are not so impressed by their alien impressions. Luckily, mantids can hear the high-pitched sounds made by bats. They don't waste their time posing, they just dive for cover instead!

Strong suit

Creepy cockroaches are believed to be some of the most incredible survivors of the animal world. They can carry on living for months even if they have lost their head! They can eat all sorts of things, from other insects to paper, leather and hair. They can even go without food for months.

Gift giver!

Some female spiders take a fancy to males – but they don't just want to mate with the males, they quite like eating them too! Smart males give their female mate a gift of food so while she is busy eating they can make a quick escape.

Food parcel

This little male nursery web spider is hoping that his gift will make the female take pity on him, and get her lunch somewhere else today!

Promise you won't eat me?

TWIST IT!

SURVIVAL INSTINCT

Sow thistle aphids can sense an animal's hot breath. One whiff of it is enough to make an aphid leap off a plant and avoid being eaten!

The bright yellow and black stripes on a hornet warn other animals to stay clear – this mini-beast has a massive stinger! Hornets use their scary stingers for attack and defence.

Sexton beetle mothers lay too many eggs for the food she can give them, so when she gets hungry she just starts eating her 'extra' babies!

Squirting soldiers

Some termites can literally blow themselves up to protect the rest of their colony! Soldier termites stand guard outside the nest and if they are attacked they make a foul yellow liquid that they can spray at the attacker. It hardens into sticky glue when it makes contact, so the attacker can't move – but making the deadly liquid can cause the termite to explode!

Workers

Soldiers

Long nose termite soldiers are guarding workers in this nest. If any ants stroll by, the soldiers will spray glue at them.

VICIOUS WITH VENOM

Spine-chilling spiders

Almost every spider in the world is a deadly predator that feeds on the bodies of other animals.

Spiders are expert hunters, with speed, stealth and a powerful bite that delivers a lethal dose of venom. Just one spider in your living room will devour about 20 flies in a few months – but the good news is that most spiders are completely harmless to humans.

MONSTER JAWS

Bronzed tube web spiders have big jaws that appear to glow green in the dark!

Female spiders are more poisonous than males, except for the Sydney funnel-web spider.

Size isn't everything: furry bird-eating spiders – tarantulas – look like scary monsters, but they are quite peaceful spiders. Their bites may be painful, but they are not deadly to humans.

TWIST IT!

Scientists have found just one type of spider that eats plants. It lives on acacia trees and survives on tasty leaf tips and nectar from the tree's flowers.

Lunch!

Chelicerae

A spider assassin's long neck helps it to get its jaws closer to its prey.

Spider assassin

This spider belongs to a strange group of arachnids from the island of Madagascar. It's a member of the Archaeidae family, which all have extremely long chelicerae (jaws). The spider, known as a spider assassin, uses its chelicerae like spears and plunges them into its prey.

These spiders only hunt other spiders.

A spider's venom paralyses its prey – stopping it from moving.

Fangs!

At the end of some spiders' chelicerae are long fangs, which are connected to a venom gland. When the spider bites, venom flows through the hollow fang and into the victim's body.

Hands, jaws or claws?

All spiders have a pair of **chelicerae** – body parts that are positioned around their mouth. Chelicerae are sometimes described as a spider's hands because they can hold or move things. They are as powerful as jaws and are often lined with little 'teeth' so they can crush as well as bite. Some spiders use their chelicerae to mash their prey into a mush before they eat it.

Chelicerae

Fangs

Pedipalps

BIG WORD ALERT

VENOM

An animal poison that is injected by stinging or biting.

How spiders eat

- A spider grabs its prey with its arm-like pedipalps and moves it towards its jaw-like chelicerae.
- The spider plunges its fangs into the prey, and injects venom that paralyses the prey and stops it from moving.
- Once the prey is still, the spider vomits acid-like juices all over it.
- The juices dissolve the prey's insides, which the spider sucks out through the bite holes made by the fangs.

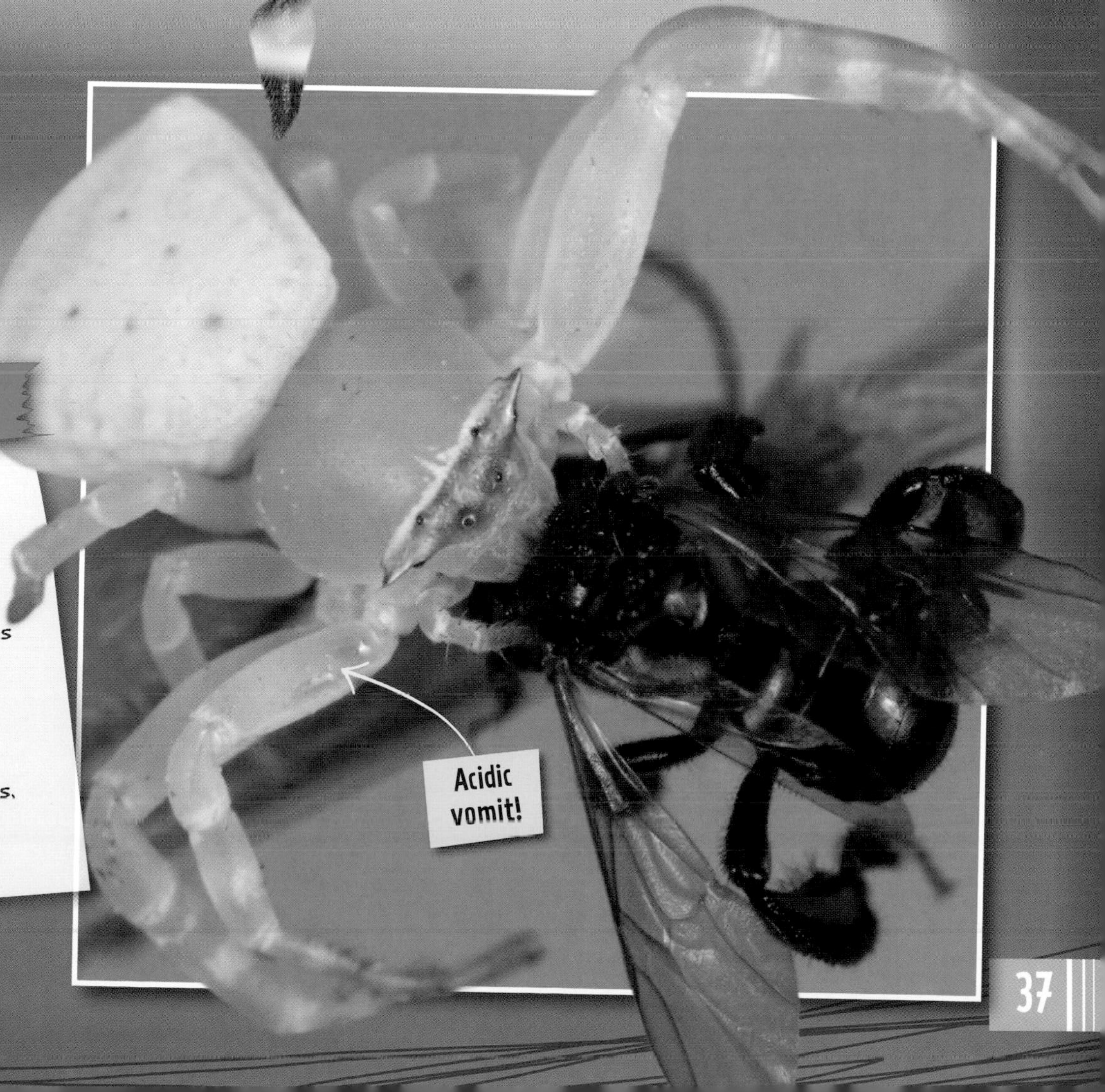

Acidic vomit!

IT'S UN-BEE-LIEVABLE

Workers unite!

Bees, wasps and hornets all belong to the same family of insects and most of them have a nasty stinger in the tail.

Honeybees live in colonies of up to 100,000 bees. Most honeybees are worker females that look after the queen and her young, tidy the hive, defend the nest, and collect nectar and pollen from flowers to feed the colony. Male bees are called drones, and their job is to mate with the queen to produce new bees for the hive.

Sweet treat

Bees make honey so they can store food over the winter. It is made from flower nectar (a sweet liquid made by flowers to attract insects), which mixes with chemicals inside the bee's stomach. The bees spit the nectar into wax cells inside the hive, and fan it with their wings to turn the paste into honey. Honey can last for many years!

TWIST IT!

BEE-LIEVE IT!

Some bees live in enormous colonies, making their homes in large hives. Paper wasps also live in groups, and make their nests out of chewed up wood and spit. Other bee and wasp species live alone.

A bee can visit up to 100 flowers during every trip out of the hive.

Paper wasps can recognise each other by their faces. Scientists think they might be as good at recognising faces as humans.

Super sting!

Only females have stings because each stinger is made from the part of the female's body that is used for laying eggs. Wasp stings are smooth, so they can be plunged into a victim and pulled out again without damaging the wasp itself. Honeybee stings are barbed (they have little hooks) so when the bee tries to pull the stinger out, it rips from its body. The bee dies soon afterwards.

Ripley explains... Wasp, bee or hornet?

They look similar, but they do have their differences.

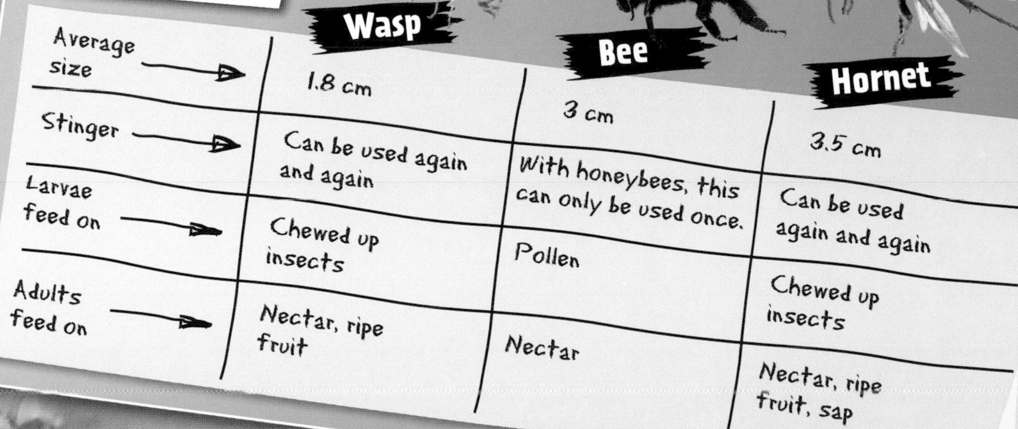

	Wasp	Bee	Hornet
Average size	1.8 cm	3 cm	3.5 cm
Stinger	Can be used again and again	With honeybees, this can only be used once.	Can be used again and again
Larvae feed on	Chewed up insects	Pollen	Chewed up insects
Adults feed on	Nectar, ripe fruit	Nectar	Nectar, ripe fruit, sap

Master mimic

Yellow and black stripes warn other animals that bees and wasps can sting. Some flies have copied the striped pattern as protection. When one animal pretends to be another it is called a mimic.

This neon cuckoo bee has a blue and black furry body.

BLUE BEE!

Not all bees are black and yellow. Some species, such as this cuckoo bee, are different colours. Cuckoo bees may look pretty, but they lead a nasty life. Instead of collecting their own pollen and making their own nests, they let others do all the work. A cuckoo bee lays its egg in another bee's nest and when the larva hatches, it eats the pollen that was intended for the host bee's larva, which starves to death soon after hatching.

A hexagon-shaped hole in a hive is a brood cell, where an egg is laid and a larva develops, or it is used for making and storing honey.

Ripley's Believe It or Not!®

Bees at a cluster of beehives in France produced honey in unusual shades of blue and green! Their keepers believe residue from containers of M&M's® sweets at a nearby factory was the cause.

BEAUTIES AND THE BEASTS

Look at me!

Feast your eyes on our catwalk of the world's most glamorous spiders in their gorgeous colours, but you might want to look away from some of their less attractive cousins!

Some of these spiders are eight-legged beauties, while others give us the creeps!

BEAUTIES

Most spiders like to hide, but these super stunner spiders have a good reason to show off. They are males that use their good looks to attract females, which are drab and dull by comparison.

Peacock spider

When handsome peacock spider males want a mate, they don't rely on just their looks to win a female's heart. They also like to wave their legs at her, and perform a little love dance!

Mirror spider

Mirror spiders look as if they are coated in shiny sequins. The dazzling patches on their body may be used to reflect light to confuse predators.

BEASTS

Beauty is in the eye of the beholder, but not even a mother could find these freaky faces attractive! Having an ugly mug doesn't bother these spiders, though. Who needs to look good when you have big fangs and deadly venom?

House spider

House spiders may be ugly up-close but they are harmless – except to the annoying flies that like to buzz around our food and spread diseases, which the spiders kill and eat! House spiders are the good guys in the spider world, keeping our homes pest-free.

Curved spiny orb weaver

Some spiders are show-offs and not shy. This spider is so bright and bold that predators are sure to spot it. Those colours and extremely long spines probably scare predators away.

Ripley's Believe It or Not!®

This spider is known as the happy face spider! Found in the rainforests of the Hawaiian Islands, the tiny spider is thought to be harmless to humans.

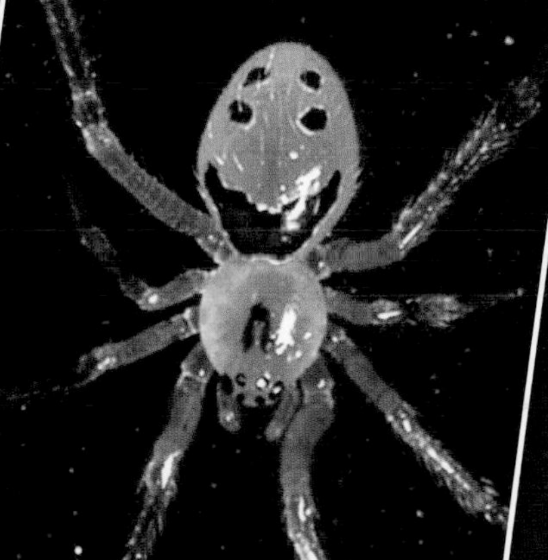

MORTAL COMBAT

Creepy-crawly killers

Most spiders and creepy crawlies may look scary, but they are, in fact, our friends not our enemies. However, there are some brutal beasties around, with lethal stings and bites, and dirty habits.

Watching bugs and spiders in action is fascinating. It is a great way to learn more about our natural world. Most are harmless, but avoid touching them unless you know what they are. There is no reason to kill most spiders and creepy crawlies – leave them alone and they will leave you alone! Here's our collection of some of nature's nasties.

Kiss of death

All assassin bugs, which are also known as kissing bugs, have sharp mouthparts that they use to pierce the skin of their victims. They carry the potentially deadly Chagas disease, which infects about 8 million people in the world.

Ant-snatching assassin bug

This is a particularly creepy insect that likes to keep safe by making itself a gruesome 'corpse cloak' out of dead ants! Scientists think that it covers itself with the stacked up bodies of dead ants to disguise it from predators such as spiders.

A mosquito can pierce its victim's skin and feed on their blood without being noticed.

Mosquitoes

The females of some types of mosquito feed on human blood when it is time for them to lay their eggs. As they feed, they can spread terrible diseases including malaria. Malaria kills about 660,000 people every year, most of them children.

Bluebottles and greenbottles are types of blowfly.

Blowflies

These flies have foul habits. They feed on dead animals and poo, and like to lay their eggs on our food. Blowflies can spread diseases that cause stomach upsets or more serious illness. Some even burrow into the flesh of animals and humans to lay their eggs.

TWIST IT!

SMALL BUT DEADLY

When a kissing bug bites, it injects a liquid into the victim's flesh, turning it into a soupy mixture that the bug can suck up.

The venom of a brown recluse spider is unlikely to kill a human, but it can destroy the flesh around the bite.

Not many scorpions can deliver a sting that kills people, but a deathstalker scorpion's venom is powerful enough to kill a child.

The venom of a black widow spider is 15 times more toxic than a rattlesnake's venom.

Black widows can be recognised by the 'hourglass' red markings on their abdomen.

Black widows

Black widows and funnel web spiders are two of the world's deadliest spiders. Funnel webs are very aggressive, especially when the males are hunting for a mate. Black widows are shy, so they are less dangerous.

BIG WORD ALERT

PARASITE

An animal that lives on, or in, another animal and does it harm.

These blood flukes have been removed from a person's intestine.

Fluke worms

Flukes are worm-like animals and parasites. They live in water, but burrow their way into the bodies of other animals to lay their eggs. Blood flukes infect about 200 million people around the world, causing diseases such as bilharzia, which make people very ill.

BUGS IN DANGER

BREAKING NEWS

Our planet needs its spiders and other creepy crawlies, but did you know that some of them are in danger of dying out? What is threatening the world of little animals, and what can you do to help them?

What's so great about all these bugs?

- Spiders eat flies that spread diseases.
- Bugs are food for bigger animals, such as birds.
- They clear up dead animals and plants.
- They pollinate plants.
- They can be a good source of food for humans.

What if we didn't have them?

- We'd run short of food pretty quickly, and so would lots of other animals.
- There would be no chocolate, fruit or honey!
- We'd be knee-deep in dead bodies and poo before long.
- The world would be bugless but BORING!

How you can help

If you have a garden, grow plants that encourage lots of different types of wildlife.

Who'll spot the last one?

This fluffy fellow is on his last legs, and having eight of them won't make his future any brighter. Ladybird spiders are so rare that scientists predict their days are numbered. The problem is that these gorgeous creatures live on heathland in northern Europe – a special habitat that humans have been destroying.

Can this precious spider keep its foothold on the future, or is it destined to go the way of the dodo and become extinct?

Why are bugs in danger?

There are some simple reasons that bugs and spiders are in danger, and we could deal with them all, if we wanted to:

- When farmers cover a large area with one type of crop, such as palm oil, the number of species of invertebrates falls. This means there is less BIODIVERSITY, which is a BAD THING.
- Pesticides may be useful for getting rid of pests but they often kill good bugs too. Pesticides can get into rivers, killing animals there as well.
- Habitat loss is a big problem for all animals. If we take away their homes, to farm or build on, they don't usually find another place to live – they die instead.

WHAT'S THE BUZZ ABOUT BEES?

Bees and flies pollinate flowers, which means they take pollen from one plant to another, so fruit and seeds can grow. The number of bees has fallen, and scientists and farmers are worried. No one knows why the bees are dying, but it is possible it is because of pesticides – chemicals used on crops to control insect pests.

HUMAN BEE-INGS!

In China, farmers have killed so many insects with their pesticides that there are large areas where there are none left to pollinate the fruit trees. Humans now have to do the job by hand!

BIG WORD ALERT

BIODIVERSITY
The variety of living things found in a particular place.

Time to say goodbye?

The dazzling peacock parachute spider can't rely on its good looks any more. This may be one of the most beautiful animals to walk the Earth, but it faces a bleak future. That's thanks to the destruction of its forest home, and 'pet traders' who capture spiders to sell as pets.

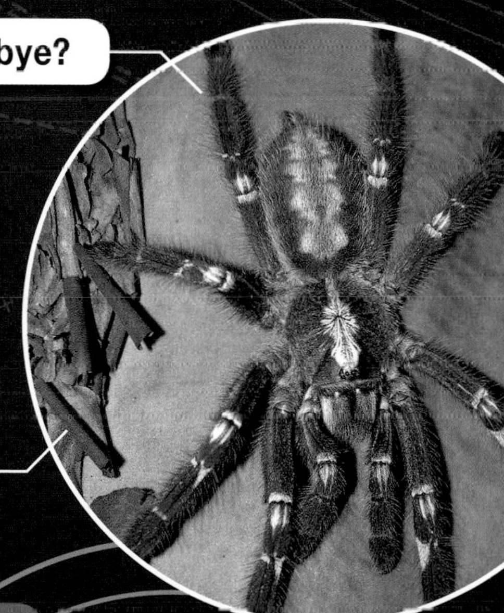

Found in just one Indian forest, the rare peacock parachute spider needs our help to survive.

What can we do to save our bugs?

- Take part in local wildlife watches, where you can learn more about the little animals, how to identify them, and keep records of when you see them.
- Don't disturb their habitat. Respect them and teach other people why they matter.
- Support businesses and places that protect the environment.
- Visit nature reserves where the land is being saved for all animals – big and small.

ACKNOWLEDGEMENTS

COVER (sp) Rex/Tomas Rax/Solent News, (t) Caters News Agency Ltd.; **2** (t/l) © spotwin - istock.com; **3** (t/l) Rex/F1 Online, (b/r) Rex/Lessy Sebastian/Solent News; **4** Rex/Tomas Rax/Solent News; **5** (t) Rex/Mohamed Babu/Solent News; **6** (b/l) © Dave Allen Photography - istock.com, (b/c) © tacojim - istock.com, (b/r) © johnandersonphoto - istock.com; **6–7** (dp) Nicky Bay, sgmacro.blogspot.com; **7** (c/r) © Serhiy Kobyakov - shutterstock.com, (b/l) April Noble/www.AntWeb.org, (b/c/l) © Barry Mansell/naturepl.com, (b/c/r) © Henrik_L - istock.com, (b/r) © cosmln - istock.com; **8** (l) © Raffalo - istock.com, (r) © alslutsky - shutterstock.com, (b) © Henrik_L - istock.com; **9** (t) © Hugh Lansdown - shutterstock.com, (c/r) Gustoimages/Science Photo Library, (b) Dave Roberts/Science Photo Library; **10–11** (dp) Nicky Bay, sgmacro.blogspot.com; **11** (t) AFP/Getty Images, (b) Rex/Lessy Sebastian/Solent News; **12** (b) © Kim Taylor/naturepl.com; **12–13** (dp) Brian Valentine; **13** (c/r) Mitshuiko Imamori/Minden Pictures/National Geographic Creative, (b) Nicky Bay, sgmacro.blogspot.com; **14** (b) © Visuals Unlimited/naturepl.com; **14–15** (dp) © Ingo Arndt/naturepl.com; **15** (r, t) © NHPA/Photoshot; **16** (b) © Bence Mate/naturepl.com; **16–17** (dp) Yanuar Akbar/Caters News; **17** (t) Jessica Dickson, (b/l) © Pan Xunbin - shutterstock.com, (b/c) © Henrik_L - istock.com, (b/r) © Antagain - istock.com; **18** (t/r) Nicky Bay, sgmacro.blogspot.com, (b/l) Rocket Design, (b/r) © Stephen Dalton/naturepl.com; **19** (t/l) Nicky Bay, sgmacro.blogspot.com, (t/r) © Nick Garbutt/naturepl.com, (b) © UPPA/Photoshot; **20** (c) Rex/Hans Christoph Kappel/Nature Picture Library, (b) © Stephen Dalton naturepl.com; **21** (t/l) © NHPA/Photoshot, (r) © nyiragongo - fotolia.com, (c) © Kim Taylor/naturepl.com, (b) © Nature Production/naturepl.com; **22–23** Nicky Bay, sgmacro.blogspot.com; **24** (b/l, b/r) © Rolf Nussbaumer/naturepl.com; **24–25** (dp) © stanley45 - istock.com; **25** (b/l, b/c, b/r) © vblinov - istock.com; **26** © Nick Garbutt/naturepl.com; **27** (t/l) © a-wrangler - istock.com, (t/r) © FourOaks - istock.com, (b) Natural History Museum, London/Science Photo Library; **28** (t) © Alex Hyde/naturepl.com, (b) Nicky Bay, sgmacro.blogspot.com; **29** (t) Nicky Bay, sgmacro.blogspot.com, (b) John Mitchell/Science Photo Library; **30** (t/r) Imagebroker/FLPA; **31** (t) © Dietmar Nill/naturepl.com, (c) © Jane Burton/naturepl.com, (b) © temmuz can arsiray - istock.com; **32** (t) Nicky Bay, sgmacro.blogspot.com, (b) © NHPA/Photoshot; **33** (t) Micky Lim, Singapore (http://www.flickr.com/photos/mickylim/), (c) Martin Dohrn Science Photo Library, (b/l) © CathyKeifer - istock.com, (b/r) Nicky Bay, sgmacro.blogspot.com; **34** (sp) © Jouan & Rius/naturepl.com, (b/l) Nicky Bay, sgmacro.blogspot.com; **35** (t) © Premaphotos/naturepl.com, (b) Emanuele Biggi/FLPA; **36** Paul Bertner; **37** (t) © Dietmar Nill/naturepl.com, (b) Nicky Bay, sgmacro.blogspot.com; **38** (b) © Alex Hyde/naturepl.com; **38–39** (dp) © tr3gin - shutterstock.com; **39** (t/l, t/r) © irin-k - shutterstock.com, (t/c) © paulrommer - shutterstock.com, (c) Nicky Bay, sgmacro.blogspot.com, (b) Reuters/Vincent Kessler; **40** (l) Nicky Bay, sgmacro.blogspot.com, (t/r) Jürgen Otto; **41** (t) Rex/F1 Online, (b/l) Nicky Bay, sgmacro.blogspot.com, (b/r) Caters News Agency Ltd.; **42** (c) Nicky Bay, sgmacro.blogspot.com, (b) © smuay - shutterstock.com; **43** (t) © Meul/Arco/naturepl.com, (l) © spotwin - istock.com, (r) Sinclair Stammers/Science Photo Library; **44** (t) © Hyena Reality - shutterstock.com, (b) © Ingo Arndt/naturepl.com; **45** (t/r) © Srabin - istock.com, (l) © ilfede - istock.com, (r) Rick. C West

Key: t = top, b = bottom, c = centre, l = left, r = right, sp = single page, dp = double page, bgd = background

All other photos are from Ripley's Entertainment Inc. All other artwork by Rocket Design (East Anglia) Ltd.

Every attempt has been made to acknowledge correctly and contact copyright holders and we apologise in advance for any unintentional errors or omissions, which will be corrected in future editions.

a Jim Pattison Company

Written by Camilla de la Bedoyere
Consultants Barbara Taylor, Joe Choromanski

Publisher Anne Marshall

Editorial Director Rebecca Miles
Project Editor Charlotte Howell
Picture Researchers Michelle Foster, Charlotte Howell
Proofreader Lisa Regan
Indexer Hilary Bird

Art Director Sam South
Senior Designer Michelle Foster
Design Rocket Design (East Anglia) Ltd
Reprographics Juice Creative Ltd

www.ripleys.com/books

ISBN 978-1-60991-231-4 (USA)

10 9 8 7 6 5 4 3 2 1

For information regarding permission, write to VP Intellectual Property, Ripley Entertainment Inc., Suite 188, 7576 Kingspointe Parkway, Orlando, Florida 32819
email: publishing@ripleys.com

Library of Congress Cataloging-in-Publication Data is available.

Printed in China
in January 2018
2nd Printing

PUBLISHER'S NOTE
While every effort has been made to verify the accuracy of the entries in this book, the Publishers cannot be held responsible for any errors contained in the work. They would be glad to receive any information from readers.

WARNING
Some of the stunts and activities in this book are undertak[en] by experts and should not be attempted by anyone without adequate training and supervision.

CONTENTS

PAGE 36

PAGE 23

WHAT'S INSIDE YOUR BOOK?

JAWS OF DEATH

DANGER IN THE DEEP SEAS

Is this a big grin that would welcome you in—or does this great white shark prefer juicy plump seals over swimmers? Find out on page 8.

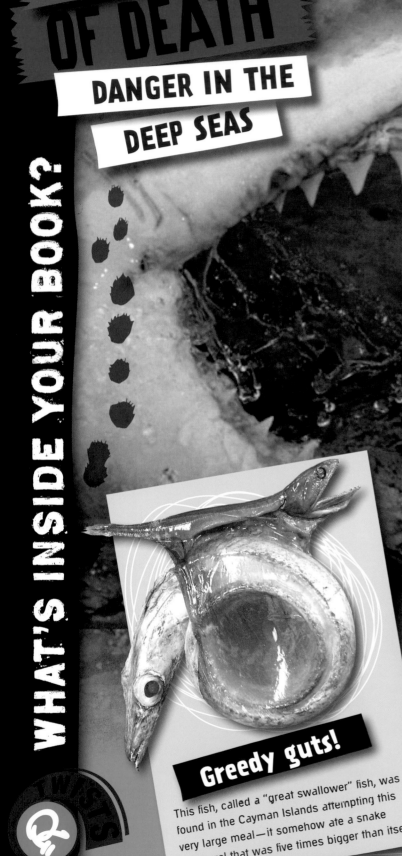

Everyone's scared of sharks, with their big mean mouths that are crammed with flesh-ripping teeth. But do these mighty sea beasts really deserve their reputation as monster marine killers?

Greedy guts!

This fish, called a "great swallower" fish, was found in the Cayman Islands attempting this very large meal—it somehow ate a snake mackerel that was five times bigger than itself!

Join us on an underwater journey into the exciting waters of the world's oceans. We reveal the truth behind the stories, the facts behind the fiction—and we will give you all the gory details of how sharks and other scary sea creatures really live their lives. Be prepared for some surprises—the oceans are home to some freaky, fast, and fabulous animals!

Ripley's Believe It or Not!®
This one-eyed albino shark is real! A Mexican fisherman found the rare baby cyclops shark by accident after cutting open a pregnant dusky shark in the Gulf of California, Mexico. It was one of nine babies, and the only one with one eye!
KEY FACTS

These books are about "Believe It or Not!"—amazing facts, feats, and things that make you go "Wow!"

Read more unbelievable facts when you spot a Key Facts box.

Look out for the "Twist It" column on some pages. Twist the book to find out more amazing facts about scary sea creatures.

SCARY SURPRISE
NASTY STINGING THINGS
Hunting prey is tiring, dangerous work, so some animals take a more laid back approach. They have exploding stinging cells that they fire at their prey.
Chasing, catching, and killing—that's all exhausting. It's dangerous, too! So why not sit back and relax, wait until lunch swims by—then fire a deadly stinging arrow straight into its flesh. It's so simple, it makes you wonder why all sea animals don't have stingers!
Portuguese man o' war
This bizarre beast looks like one animal, but it is actually a colony, made up of smaller animals called polyps (say pol-ips). Some polyps pack a powerful sting to catch prey, but others are in charge of digesting food.
Nomura's jellyfish
This giant is one of the largest jellyfish in the world and when fully-grown can measure more than the height of an average man in diameter. These jellies have killed at least eight people in Japan in recent times, and in their masses have affected fishermen's livelihoods by poisoning their catch and covering it with slime!
14
TWIST IT!
STINGY STUFF
The tentacles of a box jellyfish can dangle down 10 feet into the water.
Portuguese men o' war trail curtains of tentacles into the sea and can gather in huge groups to create a deadly threat to any living thing.
Anemones and jellyfish have just one hole that does the job of both mouth and bottom — that's disgusting!
Some anemones have lived for more than 80 years and, as these animals do not age, they could live forever (as long as nothing squashes or eats them!).
BIG WORD ALERT
COLONY
A group of animals of one kind that live close together.
Jellies
Jellyfish are not fish and they are not made of jelly! Their soft body is cup shaped and ringed with tentacles packed with stinging cells. Jellyfish can swim, but mostly drift with the currents. A fish swimming through the tentacles is stung and its lifeless body is moved toward the jellyfish's mouth.
Box jellyfish
The box jellyfish (above) is one of the deadliest of all animals. There are 15 long, dangling tentacles on each corner of its box-like body, or bell. The tentacles are covered in small stingers, each one delivering a tiny dose of venom that causes massive pain. A box jelly can kill a human in minutes.
Drop-dead gorgeous
Anemones are among the most beautiful of all sea animals, with their squidgy colorful body and tentacles that sway gently in the water. They use their tentacles to kill animals to eat, but they also sting hungry predators that come too close.
Venus flytrap?
This creature could be mistaken for a pretty Venus flytrap, but it is actually a deadly sea anemone that captures and stings prey with its tentacles.
15

Found a new word? Big Word Alert will explain it for you.

Turn over to find out why sharks and sea creatures are so scary...

FAST AND FURIOUS

WHY ARE SHARKS SCARY?

Dorsal fin
Fins help a shark to swim fast, and in the right direction.

Bendy bodies
Sharks have skeletons made of a bendy bone-like material called cartilage. Squish your nose and flap your ears—they are made of cartilage too.

The shortfin mako is the world's fastest shark. You wouldn't want to be chased by one of these hungry beasts—they can speed through the water at up to 50 mph, and even jump 20 feet out of the sea to catch animals!

Super sensor
This is called a lateral line. It can sense movements and chemicals in the water.

Swimtastic-body
A bullet-shaped body that is packed with muscles allows a shark to almost fly through water.

...AND OTHER SCARY SEA CREATURES

FASTEST SAILFISH

PAGE 11

This is one of the fastest animals on the planet, and the fastest in all the world's oceans.

MOST SURPRISING CUTTLEFISH

PAGE 38

Cuttlefish are able to change the look of their skin in a second, and hypnotize their prey by creating pulsing bands of color.

POISONOUS PUFFER FISH

PAGE 22

This fish avoids being eaten by filling up with water and turning into a large prickly ball. It contains enough poison to kill 30 humans.

UGLIEST VIPERFISH

PAGE 10

A fierce predator of the deep seas, viperfish can have teeth so big they don't fit inside its mouth!

If you had to design a perfect underwater killing machine what would it look like? Probably like a shark! There are few animals that inspire as much fear as sharks, but why do they have such a chilling reputation?

Sharks have been around for about 400 to 450 million years, so there must be some secret to their great success. Check out this shark's brilliant body to find some clues.

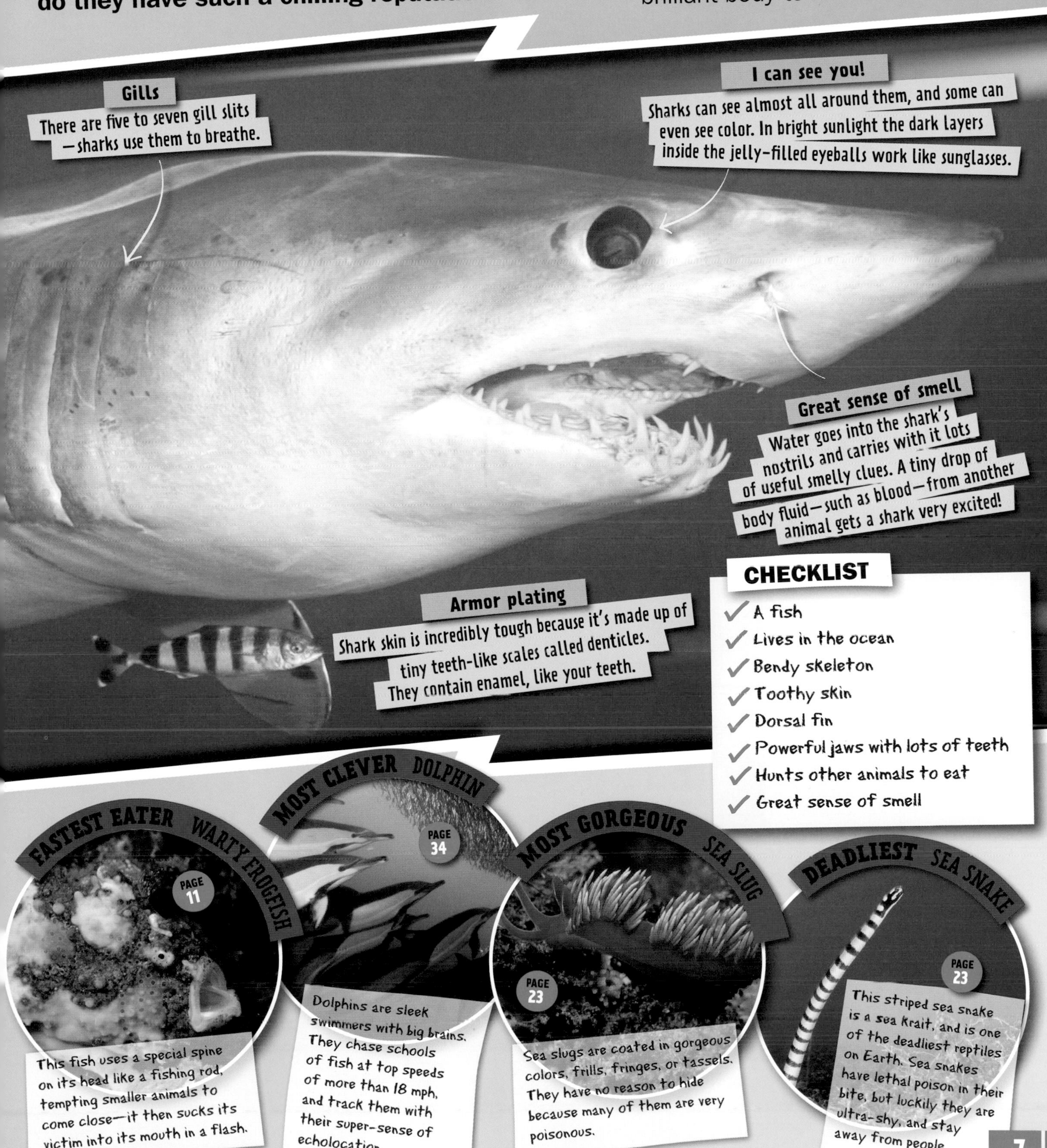

Gills
There are five to seven gill slits—sharks use them to breathe.
I can see you!
Sharks can see almost all around them, and some can even see color. In bright sunlight the dark layers inside the jelly-filled eyeballs work like sunglasses.
Great sense of smell
Water goes into the shark's nostrils and carries with it lots of useful smelly clues. A tiny drop of body fluid—such as blood—from another animal gets a shark very excited!
Armor plating
Shark skin is incredibly tough because it's made up of tiny teeth-like scales called denticles. They contain enamel, like your teeth.

CHECKLIST

- ✓ A fish
- ✓ Lives in the ocean
- ✓ Bendy skeleton
- ✓ Toothy skin
- ✓ Dorsal fin
- ✓ Powerful jaws with lots of teeth
- ✓ Hunts other animals to eat
- ✓ Great sense of smell

FASTEST EATER WARTY FROGFISH

PAGE 11

This fish uses a special spine on its head like a fishing rod, tempting smaller animals to come close—it then sucks its victim into its mouth in a flash.

MOST CLEVER DOLPHIN

PAGE 34

Dolphins are sleek swimmers with big brains. They chase schools of fish at top speeds of more than 18 mph, and track them with their super-sense of echolocation.

MOST GORGEOUS SEA SLUG

PAGE 23

Sea slugs are coated in gorgeous colors, frills, fringes, or tassels. They have no reason to hide because many of them are very poisonous.

DEADLIEST SEA SNAKE

PAGE 23

This striped sea snake is a sea krait, and is one of the deadliest reptiles on Earth. Sea snakes have lethal poison in their bite, but luckily they are ultra-shy, and stay away from people.

LEAN, MEAN, KILLING MACHINE

It's known as a great white, a man-eater, a white death, and a white pointer—but we call it the most incredible predator of the open oceans.

GREAT WHITE SHARK

Great whites use stealth and surprise to sneak up on their prey, and then speed up for the final attack. They have even been seen leaping out of the water to grab a snoozing seal on an ice floe.

Great whites are hot fish! Unlike most fish, they can keep their body warm, even in icy water.

NEAR MISS

Great white sharks don't always get it right. This 12-foot-long great white misjudged its attack on this seal, and it ended up perched on the end of its nose!

BIG WORD ALERT
HABITAT
The place where an animal lives.

Great whites have a big bite—about the same as a large saltwater crocodile.

KEY FACTS

Length: more than 21 feet—that's the same as one-and-a-half average-sized cars!

Habitat: coastal waters and open oceans

Found: in most oceans

Conservation status: rare

Ripley's Believe It or Not!®

Ron and Valerie Taylor from Australia were the first people to film great white sharks without the protection of a cage. They filmed the live underwater sequences of the shark for the 1975 film *Jaws*, and have dedicated their lives to protecting sharks.

Why are great whites so amazing?

They use some smart tactics for hunting:

- they are clever and plan their attacks
- they creep up on their prey, slowly and silently
- they can turn on the speed when it's time to attack
- they take a big bite, then leave their prey to bleed and weaken before returning for the kill
- they are strong enough to kill large animals, such as seals and dolphins
- they can live in warm, cool, or cold water
- and most importantly...

THEY HAVE LOTS OF REALLY, REALLY BIG, SHARP TEETH!

HOW TO FEAST LIKE A GREAT WHITE

DISH OF THE WEEK

You will need:
One plump day-dreaming seal

INSTRUCTIONS

- ★ *Slam headfirst, at top speed, into the seal.*
- ★ *Raise snout, drop lower jaw.*
- ★ *Push upper jaw forward to reveal rows of large gleaming teeth.*
- ★ *Move lower jaw forward and up, to impale seal on lower teeth.*
- ★ *Close mouth and chomp away. Enjoy!*

How deadly are great whites?

There is no doubt that seals and dolphins are in grave danger when there's a hungry great white nearby. These sharks are also responsible for one-third of all shark attacks on humans but, most of the time, humans escape an attack with their lives. We probably don't taste that good to a shark, and they may only bite to defend themselves, or because they mistake swimmers and surfers for seals.

FOUL FISH FILES

INCREDIBLE OCEAN PREDATORS

Fat, flat, fast, free-swimming, or floating—there are trillions of fish in the sea and most of them are hungry hunters.

Fish have some amazing ways to chase, catch, and eat their prey. If you were a fish, what type would you be?

MORAY EEL

Its skin may be pretty, but that face is ugly! Moray eels look like big-headed snakes and lurk in cracks in the rocks. They grab prey with a mouthful of deadly, sharp teeth.

FRIGHTFUL

WOLF FISH

This fish needs a huge head to house a mouthful of teeth that would put a bulldog to shame. In fact, this fish has been compared to a ferocious dog, because it can crunch big, shelled animals in half, and has even attacked people wading in shallow water!

FEROCIOUS

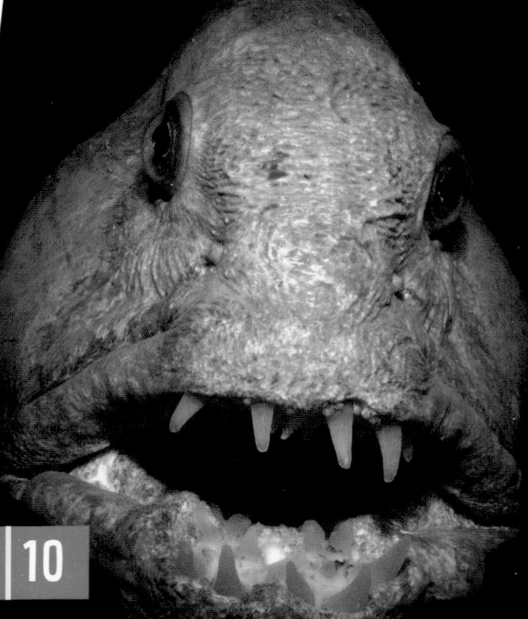

If you were a viperfish your teeth would be 12 inches long!

VIPERFISH

The deepsea viperfish lives where food is scarce, so it has a neat trick to keep its belly full. It can create light to entice swimming animals to come near, then it opens its mouth wide for a fang-tastic meal!

FANGED

HAGFISH

It looks like a giant worm, but don't be fooled. This is a fish to fear, with one of the most revolting lifestyles of any animal. A Pacific hagfish mostly munches dead animals, but it also happily swims into the mouth or bottom of a fish and eats it from the inside out. Eurgghhhh!

FIENDISH

Hagfish are covered in a gross, gloopy slime. When they get too slimy, the fish tie themselves in knots to remove the goo.

BIG WORD ALERT

PREDATOR

An animal that hunts other animals (prey) to eat.

FROGFISH

There are few fish quite as weird as frogfish. They sit motionless on the seabed, covered in warty or "hairy" skin that helps them stay hidden. When an unsuspecting fish swims past, the frogfish snatches it in a lightning-quick movement that lasts just 1/6,000th of a second—that's one of the fastest movements in the animal world.

FURTIVE

FAST

SAILFISH

A sailfish is not just the fastest fish in the sea, it's one of the speediest creatures on the planet. It can chase prey at speeds of 68 mph. Compare that to a cheetah, which reaches top speeds of about 60 mph. The sailfish's speed is an awesome achievement because it is much harder to move through water than through air.

FEARSUME AND FREAKY

UGLY MUGS AND ODD-BODS

Think you know what sharks look like? Think again! Forget the sleek, smooth body shape of a great white and prepare yourself for a short shark-shock!

There are over 500 species, or types, of shark in the world. They all have a head, body and tail—but apart from that basic body plan there are some surprising differences.

The classic shark shape is a long, slender body with a pointed snout and crescent-shaped tail. It's a perfect shape for fast swimming in the open ocean, but not all sharks share that lifestyle. You can sometimes learn a lot about how an animal lives and hunts by looking closely at its body shape.

Horn shark

My strange snout is really good for sniffing and smelling food, such as sea urchins and shellfish. Some people say that when I search for food I look like a snuffling pig, and that's why I'm sometimes called a pigshark (though my real name is "horn shark").

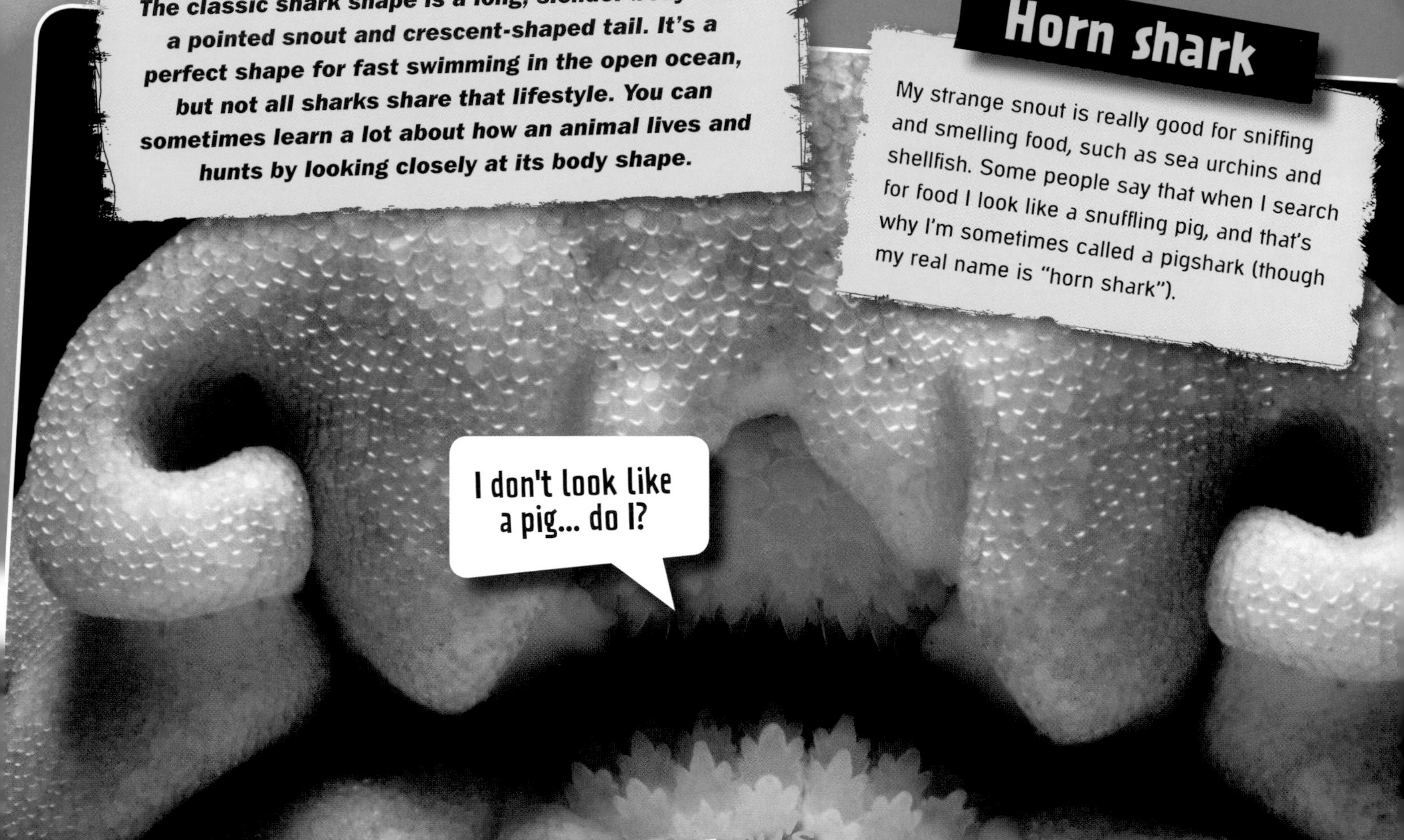

I don't look like a pig... do I?

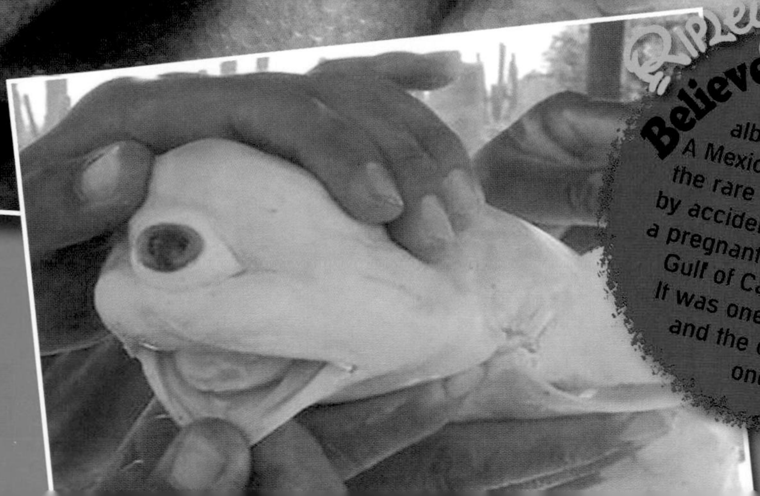

Ripley's Believe It or Not!®

This one-eyed albino shark is real! A Mexican fisherman found the rare baby cyclops shark by accident after cutting open a pregnant dusky shark in the Gulf of California, Mexico. It was one of nine babies, and the only one with one eye!

Anyone know a good orthodontist?

Goblin shark

Scientists think my peculiar snout may help me find prey. I live in the deep, dark sea where it is hard to find fish to eat, but electrical sensors on my huge honker help me sense anything swimming nearby.

FREAKY FACTS

TWIST IT!

Goblin sharks have catapult jaws that fly out of their mouth to grab prey. The jaws are attached by rubbery ligaments and can be pulled back into the mouth afterward.

Nurse sharks have been known to bite humans with such a vice-like grip that their jaws have had to be forced open using steel instruments.

Horn sharks are often fished for their two large spines, which are used to make jewelry. That's not very nice...

Frilled sharks are sometimes called "living fossils" because they are very similar to sharks that lived 350 million years ago.

Divers are often fascinated by horn sharks paddling along the seabed and have been known to pull their tail. Big mistake!

Who are you calling a sucker?

Nurse shark

My blunt snout is the perfect shape for feeding along coral reefs. I can get my mouth real close to crunchy snacks, such as crabs and lobsters, and I even gnaw on a bit of tasty coral from time to time. My top trick is to feed like a vacuum cleaner and suck in lots of water. With it comes lots of juicy fish!

Frilled shark

Do you like my lovely frilly gills and jaws? I have 25 "frills" in my mouth and each one is made up of five teeth, arranged in a pretty cluster. Each tooth has three long, pointy spikes. I live in the deep, deep ocean, so very few people have ever seen me. I can open my mouth wide enough to swallow a whole octopus.

Are you "frilled" to see me?

SCARY SURPRISE

NASTY STINGING THINGS

Hunting prey is tiring, dangerous work, so some animals take a more laid back approach. They have exploding stinging cells that they fire at their prey.

Chasing, catching, and killing—that's all exhausting. It's dangerous, too! So why not sit back and relax, wait until lunch swims by—then fire a deadly stinging arrow straight into its flesh. It's so simple, it makes you wonder why all sea animals don't have stingers!

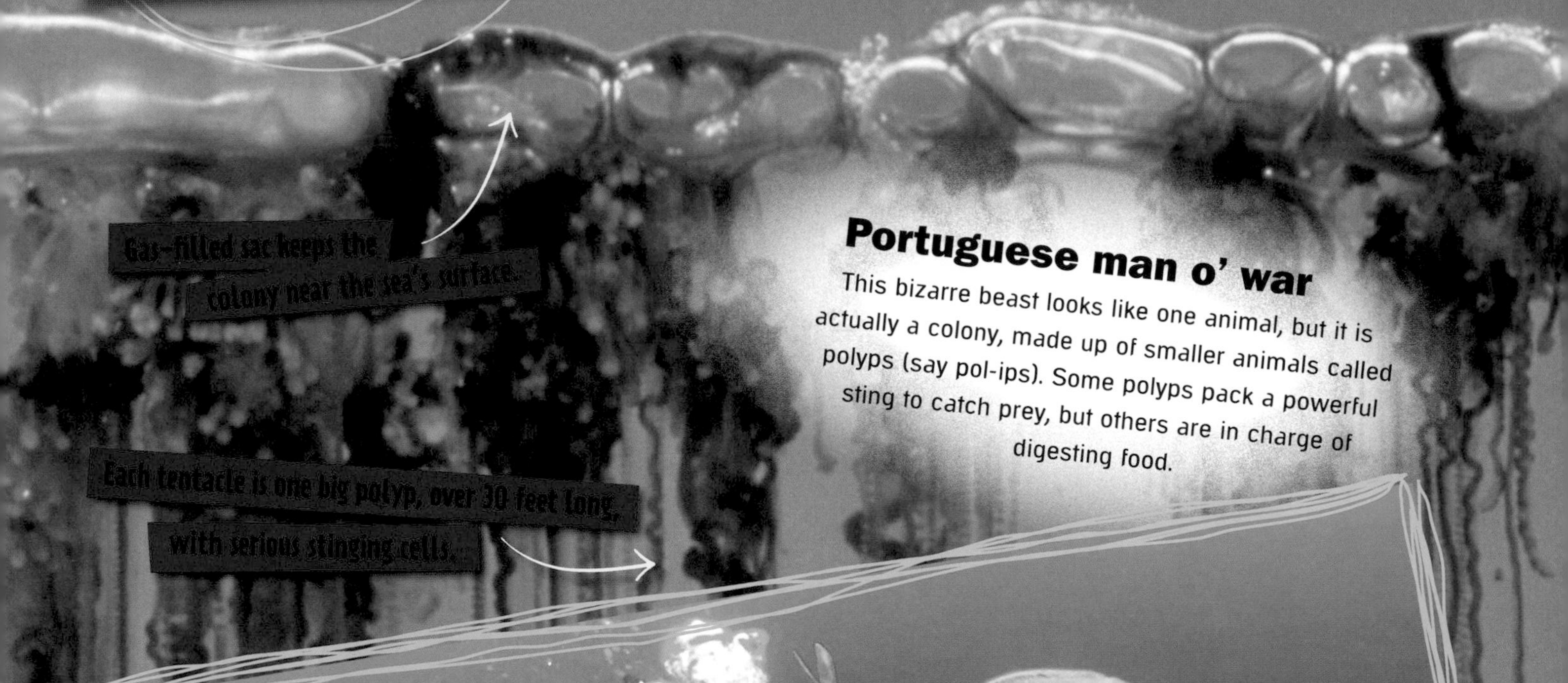

Gas-filled sac keeps the colony near the sea's surface.

Each tentacle is one big polyp, over 30 feet long, with serious stinging cells.

Portuguese man o' war

This bizarre beast looks like one animal, but it is actually a colony, made up of smaller animals called polyps (say pol-ips). Some polyps pack a powerful sting to catch prey, but others are in charge of digesting food.

Nomura's jellyfish

This giant is one of the largest jellyfish in the world and when fully-grown can measure more than the height of an average man in diameter. These jellies have killed at least eight people in Japan in recent times, and in their masses have affected fishermen's livelihoods by poisoning their catch and covering it with slime!

TWIST IT!

STINGY STUFF

The tentacles of a box jellyfish can dangle down to 10 feet into the water.

Portuguese men o' war trail curtains of tentacles into the sea and can gather in huge groups to create a deadly threat to any living thing.

Anemones and jellyfish have just one hole that does the job of both mouth and bottom—that's disgusting!

Some anemones have lived for more than 80 years and, as these animals do not age, they could live forever (as long as nothing squashes, or eats them!).

Jellies

Jellyfish are not fish and they are not made of jelly! Their soft body is cup shaped and ringed with tentacles packed with stinging cells. Jellyfish can swim, but mostly drift with the currents. A fish swimming through the tentacles is stung and its lifeless body is moved toward the jellyfish's mouth.

Box jellyfish

The box jellyfish (above) is one of the deadliest of all animals. There are 15 long, dangling tentacles on each corner of its box-like body, or bell. The tentacles are covered in small stingers, each one delivering a tiny dose of venom that causes massive pain. A box jelly can kill a human in minutes.

BIG WORD ALERT

COLONY

A group of animals of one kind that live close together.

Drop-dead gorgeous

Anemones are among the most beautiful of all sea animals, with their squidgy colorful body and tentacles that sway gently in the water. They use their tentacles to kill animals to eat, but they also sting hungry predators that come too close.

Venus flytrap?

This creature could be mistaken for a pretty Venus flytrap, but it is actually a deadly sea anemone that captures and stings prey with its tentacles.

HOW SHARKS HUNT

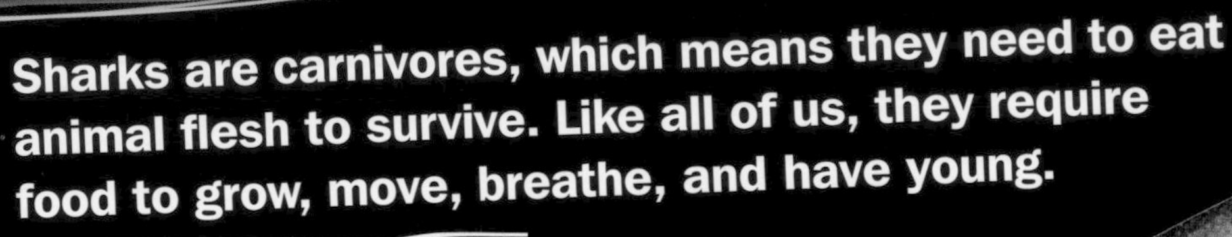

Sharks are carnivores, which means they need to eat animal flesh to survive. Like all of us, they require food to grow, move, breathe, and have young.

Hunting is a way of life for all sharks. They are the supreme hunters of the oceans, and can kill anything from fish and crabs to turtles and large mammals, such as seals and dolphins.

Sharks are successful predators because they have the body parts to find and catch food, and they are also very adaptable. There are sharks in all of the world's oceans, from shallow to deep water, from the icy cold northern seas to the warmest tropical bays.

SANDTIGER SHARK

Sandtiger sharks are able to move up and down in water in fast pursuit of prey —they manage it by gulping air (to go up), or burping (to go down)!

Aggressive attack

Every type of shark has varying behaviors to warn other creatures, and other sharks, that an attack is possible. These threat postures show the common positions of sharks when they are ready to attack.

Side view

Snout raised, back arched

Front view

Pectoral fins stiff and pointing down

Bird's-eye view

Tail curved to the side

A twist in the tail

Most sharks attack with their mouth, but threshers use their enormous tail instead, catching their prey completely unaware. Threshers swim ahead of, or beside, shoals of fish then wallop them hard with their curved tail fin.

Now that's what I call a tail!

Big nose

Sawsharks have electric noses! Their long snout can detect the electrical signals produced by other animals. They also work like swords, because they are lined with long, sharp teeth. When sawsharks are hungry they sweep their "sword" until they find food. A quick swipe with their deadly nose blade, and it's all over.

KEY FACTS

ATTACK STATS

In the last 500 years, about 800 unprovoked shark attacks have occurred around the world (unprovoked attacks are ones where humans have not attacked or annoyed the shark on purpose). Which types of sharks carried out the most unprovoked attacks on humans?

Great white	33.4%
Tiger	12%
Bull	11%
Requiem	4%
Sandtiger	5%

Thirty other types of shark were responsible for the remaining 34.6% of attacks. Out of 800 attacks, 160 people have died.

Gang fight

Most sharks live alone, but oceanic whitetips prefer to stick together. They can be spotted in the open ocean in groups of eight to 200 sharks. Oceanic whitetips often follow boats, and will eat whatever they can find, making them one of the most dangerous sharks.

BOAT!

Ripley's Believe It or Not!

In 1945, the US warship *Indianapolis* sank, with terrible results for the 1,196 men aboard. Most made it into the water, but were soon set upon by swarms of sharks. Five days later, when the rescue was finally complete, fewer than 330 men were still alive.

UNDERCOVER KILLERS

MASTERS OF DISGUISE

Cunning and camouflage are the tools of the trade for some marine predators. They take a smart approach to the art of hunting and stay hidden from view. It means they are invisible to their prey—and safe from attack by predators.

Smooth assassins are able to creep up on their victims, deliver a death-strike and disappear. The secret to success lies in the method, and these stealthy beasties know that a good disguise or hiding place is essential.

Secret snap!

Crocodiles may be famous for their ferocious attacks in rivers, but not many people know that some crocs hunt at sea, too. Saltwater crocs, with their darkly armored skin, lie motionless in the sea, near the shore, and blend into the rocky bottom—invisible to birds, fish, and turtles that pass overhead. The rock-like reptile bursts through the water to grab its prey with a single, quick snap with its giant jaws.

HIDE 'N' SEEK

Scientists were surprised to see a coconut shell sprouting legs and running across the sand—a closer look revealed a veined octopus was hiding inside. The shell proved to be a great disguise for the soft-bodied predator.

Toadfish have thick, slimy skin and hide in dens near the shore, leaving safety only to hunt. It's a lonely life, so the males make loud burping noises to help the females come and find them.

TWIST IT!

Some sea creatures can change color to blend in with their surroundings, and engineers are copying the way they do it to build robots that can change color, too!

King ragworms are happy to swim in the sea, or wriggle along in the sand, but when they want to hide away they quickly burrow down, covering themselves with slippery slime. All that is left is a small hole in the sand—don't stick your finger in though, they have huge jaws and they bite!

The skinny trumpetfish disguises itself by swimming upright among coral and seaweed, and then sucks up animals into its large mouth. It also swims alongside big, beefy fish, protecting itself by disappearing into the other creature's shadow, and then strikes its prey when least expected!

Take cover!

Hermit crabs have a crafty way of creeping around looking for prey—hiding inside old seashells. They can quickly withdraw into the shell, and no one knows they are inside. Impressed? That's nothing. Cloak anemones then drape themselves over a hermit crab's hideaway, protecting it and throwing stinging tentacles at any predator that comes too close.

The anemone has pink spots and its tentacles are under the hermit crab, where it collects leftover scraps of the crab's meals.

Something fishy!

Imagine you are taking a walk by the sea, and you spot a strange rock on the sand—don't tread on that rock! It could be a stonefish, equipped with 13 large spines, each attached to two large venom glands that can deliver one of the world's most deadly toxins straight into your foot. Stonefish can survive for 24 hours out of water, so even if it looks dead, it may not be.

Meet the whale shark, the world's largest fish. Whale sharks are special sharks: they are gigantic, spotty, and serene. They swim powerfully, but at a slow steady pace, while sucking in water. Whale sharks can even hang beneath a school of fish and "vacuum" them up!

They are giants in every way—even the fin on their back is 4 feet tall!

One whale shark was followed on an incredible journey across the Pacific Ocean. In 37 months it swam 8,078 miles.

MILD-MANNERED MONSTERS

GENTLE GIANTS OF THE OCEAN

Some giant sharks are described as harmless, but don't be fooled—these fish may not be interested in eating *you*, but they are able to catch and consume vast numbers of small animals. That makes them some of the most successful carnivores of the seas.

Near its surface, ocean water is like a soup—with lots of tiny tidbits floating about. Basking sharks, whale sharks, and megamouths scoop up these tasty creatures rather than hunting their prey. They are called filter feeders because of the unusual way they catch their food.

FILTER FACTS

Most whale sharks are about 32 feet long, but the largest ever seen was 44 feet—that's about the same as the length of a school bus!

Basking sharks are not usually dangerous, but their rough skin can hurt a diver—and they have been known to attack fishing boats after being harpooned.

Fewer than 60 megamouths have ever been seen. Nearly all of them were already dead when they were found, which is why we know so little about how they live.

BASKING SHARKS

Basking sharks swim near the surface of the ocean, with their large mouth agape. The shark's mouth can measure up to 3 feet 4 inches wide and contains around 1,500 tiny teeth.

Ripley's Believe It or Not!®

This diver was nearly sucked up into the mouth of the largest fish in the sea, the whale shark. Despite its size, whale sharks only eat plankton and if the diver had ended up in its mouth, the shark would have just spat him out!

BIG WORD ALERT

BIOLUMINESCENCE

say bio-loo-min-ess-ens

This is light that is made by living things. It is quite common in marine animals.

The megamouth is one of the world's most mysterious animals. It was first discovered in 1976, when a male got caught in the anchor ropes of an underwater research vessel. Its vast mouth led to its scientific name Megachasma pelagios, which means "Enormous cave of the sea."

IT'S MEGA!

Megamouths grow up to over 16 feet. They have flabby skin, deep-set eyes, and blunt heads, and are not fast swimmers. They feed on small animals, such as jellyfish and shrimps, which may be attracted to their gaping mouth by bioluminescent spots that surround their fleshy lips.

TOXIC TREATS

NATURE'S SILENT ASSASSINS

Substances that do harm are described as poisonous, or toxic. Every one of the animals here produces a toxic cocktail that can have lethal effects. Read on to find out about some of this planet's most dangerous animals.

Don't be fooled by these beasts. They may not be big but they have toxic power to knock out nerves, destroy muscles, inflict pain, stun, injure, and kill. Sometimes killing with toxins takes a lot out of an animal—check out the gross story about the sea cucumbers to discover exactly what we mean!

PUFFER FISH

In Japan, the flesh of a puffer fish—called fugu—is considered a fine food, but eating it can be very risky. These fish store a deadly toxin in their body, and many people have died from eating fugu. The first symptom of poisoning is a tingling of the lips, followed by feelings of warmth and happiness, but death can occur just six hours later. There is no known cure.

WOOAH!

CROWN OF THORNS

Most starfish have just five arms, but the crown of thorns starfish has up to 20—and each one is covered with poisonous spines. This starfish is doubly-deadly because it devours coral and has destroyed large areas of the Great Barrier Reef in Australia.

SEA SNAKE

The bite of a sea snake is painless, but the effects of its venom are not. Sea snakes may be shy but they have one of the most deadly snake venoms. These swimming serpents don't have very big teeth, so they grab hold of their prey and chew, forcing venom into the flesh. Thankfully, sea snakes are very shy and generally stay away from people.

TOXIC TALES

A crown of thorns starfish produces up to 60 million eggs a year.

Starfish make super glue that helps them stick quickly and firmly to rocks. When they want to get up and move about they make anti-glue to dissolve the sticky stuff in a flash.

Scientists think that seaweed contains some toxic treats that can be used to kill the bug that causes malaria—a terrible disease that affects millions of people.

Shellfish such as mussels and oysters feed on tiny toxic marine animals. The toxins can be stored in their flesh, and that is why people can sometimes get very ill after eating shellfish.

TWIST IT!

SEA CUCUMBER

This toxic tale is so bizarre it's hard to believe! When a sea cucumber is scared it forces its insides (entrails) out of its body and separates from them. The entrails expand and split into long sticky threads that attach to the attacker's body. The threads are coated with venom, which target the attacker's muscles, and can cause blindness. The sea cucumber is now safe, but it must survive for months without eating while it grows a new set of insides!

SEA SLUG

The color of a sea slug's skin serves as a warning—bright and bold means it's a bad little beastie with terrifying toxins. Known as nudibranchs (say new-dee-branks), these slugs either make their own toxins, or steal some off other animals. Nudibranchs that feed on toxic sea sponges, for example, are able to store the sponges' poisons in their own flesh. Their multi-colored skin warns predators that they contain a toxic treat.

SMASHING GNASHERS

SHARKS HAVE TERRIFYING TEETH!

A shark's top weapon is its mouthful of teeth. Its massive jaws are packed with row after row of slicers, shearers, snappers, and crushers.

Sharks are known as mean, keen, killing machines, but they would be harmless ocean fish without their teeth. A single bite can cut a seal in half, or crush a huge sea turtle. And if a shark breaks a few teeth, it's not a problem—these predators have a scary secret that means they are always ready to kill.

Gross, gruesome, and grisly

This shark is a gut-churning, flesh-gobbling marine monster! Cookiecutter sharks have sucker-like lips and grab hold of their victim with a sucking tongue. The top teeth stab the flesh and hold tight while the bottom teeth carve out a chunk of meat.

Humans have two sets of teeth, but sharks can keep growing new teeth all through their lives. Teeth are arranged in rows, and as teeth fall out, break, or wear out they are replaced. The new teeth grow forward from the rear of the mouth toward the front. Some types of shark may use as many as 20,000 teeth in their lifetime—we get just 52!

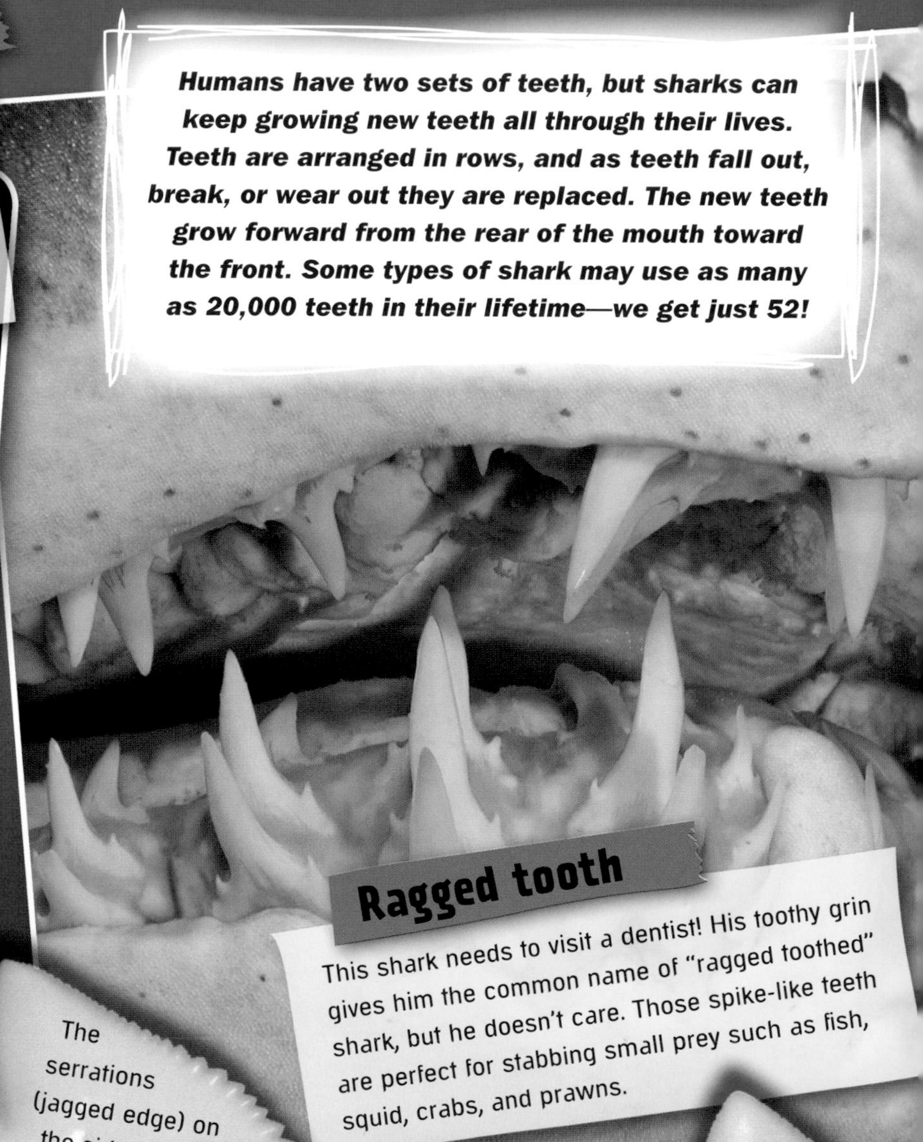

Ragged tooth

This shark needs to visit a dentist! His toothy grin gives him the common name of "ragged toothed" shark, but he doesn't care. Those spike-like teeth are perfect for stabbing small prey such as fish, squid, crabs, and prawns.

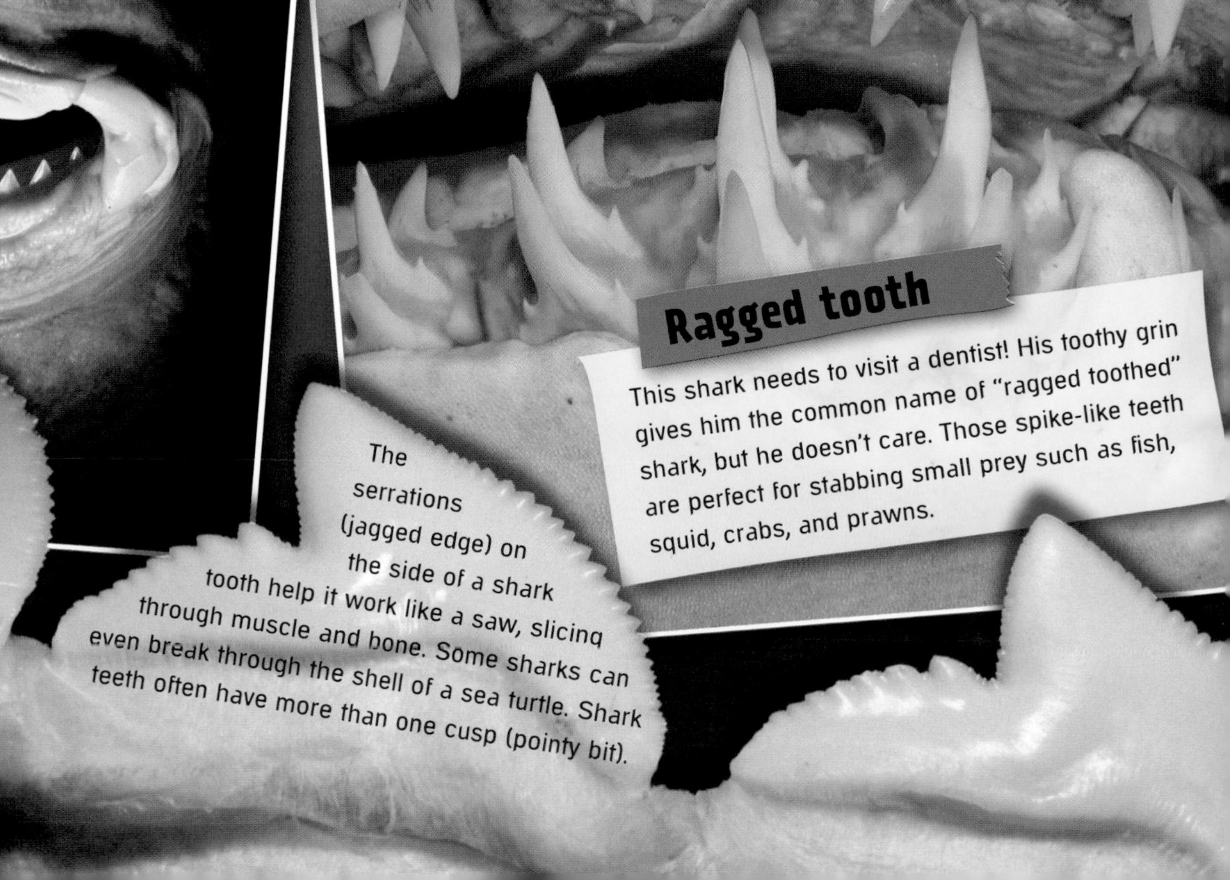

The serrations (jagged edge) on the side of a shark tooth help it work like a saw, slicing through muscle and bone. Some sharks can even break through the shell of a sea turtle. Shark teeth often have more than one cusp (pointy bit).

Big tooth!

On the left is the tooth of a great white shark and on the right is a tooth from an ancient shark called Megalodon. The Megalodon tooth is bigger than your hand! It was one of the largest fish to ever live.

Swell smile

This big mouth holds about 120 teeth and it belongs to a swell shark. This predator lies on the seabed at night with its mouth wide open, and waits for fish or other animals to be swept in by the currents. If it gets scared, a swell shark grabs its tail with its mouth and swallows water and swells up so it looks bigger than it really is.

KEY FACTS

THE BEST TEETH FOR THE JOB

Sharks need the right teeth for the type of animal they like to catch and eat.

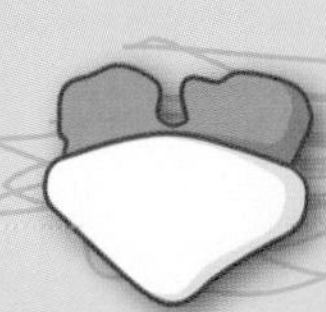

Thick, plate-like, and tough
Great for crushing crabs and other shellfish

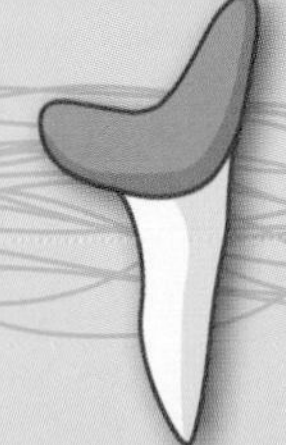

Long, narrow, and needle-like
Perfect for holding slippery fish and squid

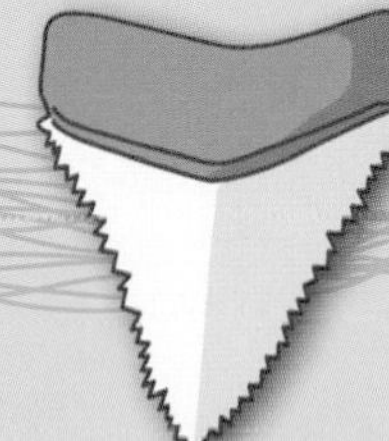

Big, sharp, cusped, and serrated
Ideal for big meat eaters

SUPERB ASSASSINS

KILLERS WITH SPECIAL SKILLS

Punching, walloping, crushing, and shooting—they are all good ways to stun your victim. Meet some of nature's most creative killers. Some of them look curious, some of them even look cute, but they are all pretty handy when it comes to delivering a death-blow.

Over millions of years, animals have developed crafty ways to protect themselves from attack. Predators have had to change to keep up, in a process called evolution. It has led to the appearance of some astonishing killing skills.

Orange fiddler crab

This orange fiddler crab likes to show off! One huge claw is half of his whole bodyweight, and painted in flashy colors. He waves it at other males to tell them to stay away, but if they don't take the hint then an "arm-wrestle" might follow.

Mantis shrimp

It's thought that mantis shrimps have the best color vision of any animal. Even more impressive, they can deliver a punch with as much force as a bullet! Each wallop is so powerful that it can kill a crab in less than a second, and can even shatter the thick glass of a fish tank.

Pistol shrimp

These little crustaceans can kill their prey while keeping a safe distance. They snap their claws shut with such speed that they fire out bubbles. As the bubbles collapse they reach a very high temperature, producing a flash of light and a cracking sound. This stuns the victim, so the shrimp can move in to eat.

Ripley's Believe It or Not!®

Japanese spider crabs are the giants of all crustaceans, with a leg span that can reach an amazing 12 feet. They mostly feed on dead animals, but can hunt too. Sailors used to believe that Japanese spider crabs dragged men from ships and pulled them underwater to eat!

Cone shell

This shelled animal may look as harmless as a garden snail, but looks can be deceptive. The cunning killer can fire a deadly harpoon at its prey. It carries fast-acting deadly venom that disables the victim, which is then pulled under the shell to be devoured.

Eaten alive

The gorgeous patterns on a harlequin shrimp's body tell predators that it is toxic to eat. It gets its poison from the bodies of starfish that it eats. These small shrimps have huge paddle-like legs, which they use to flip a starfish over, so they can reach the soft parts they like the best.

BOTTOM BITERS

FLAT FISH

Watch out below, there's a shocking surprise lurking on the seabed! Some sharks, and their close cousins rays, hover near the ocean floor to find the tastiest morsels to eat.

Living on the ocean floor requires a different body shape. These fish have flat bodies and are camouflaged, so they can lie still for hours waiting for their victims to come close. When the time is just right, they suddenly lunge forward to grab, bite, and swallow.

BIG WORD ALERT

CAMOUFLAGE

The colors or patterns that help an animal to hide.

What's eating you?

This poor bamboo shark was minding its own business when the ground seemed to open up and swallow it! A tasseled wobbegong shark was the culprit—these sharks are so well camouflaged they are almost invisible until they stir into action.

Wobbegongs belong to a group called the carpet sharks—and it is easy to see why, with their exotic skin patterns. The tassels around the shark's mouth look like seaweed, and really help it to blend in.

KEY FACTS

MEET THE FAMILY

Rays are closely related to sharks, and belong to the same family of fish. Like sharks, their skeletons are made of cartilage not bone.

- ☑ Flat bodies
- ☑ Eyes on the top of their head
- ☑ Fins are like "wings" and they "fly" through water

What's shocked you?

Electric rays have special superpowers. They find their prey by detecting the electricity made in the muscles of other animals. Even more shocking—they can create their own knock-out electrical charge. It is enough to stun animals, or to scare away predators.

Electric rays make a strong electric current in the two kidney-shaped organs near their eyes.

What's stabbing you?

A flick, a twist, and a quick, sharp stab—that's all it takes for a stingray to deliver a nasty toxic blow. These fish have sharp spines on their long tail, which are equipped with venom. Stingrays normally only use their sting to defend themselves.

Ripley's Believe It or Not!®

Australian TV star Steve Irwin loved animals, but his passion for wildlife led to his death in 2006. He was filming a program called *Ocean's Deadliest* when a stingray lashed out at him with its venomous tail, piercing Irwin in the chest. Sadly, this freak accident caused the star's death.

TWIST IT!

IT'S A SHOCKER

Large Atlantic torpedo rays can generate 220 volts of electricity in one go, but smaller rays can only generate about 40 volts.

Doctors in Ancient Rome liked to treat their patients with a quick electric shock from a stingray!

Warriors used to put stingray spines on their spears and daggers.

VIOLENT VISITORS

HUNGRY HUNTERS DROP IN FOR A FEAST

Danger overhead!

Ocean hunters don't just lurk on ice, or under the water's dark surface. Some of them attack from above, swooping down from the sky and grabbing wriggly fish in their terrible talons. White-tailed sea eagles can see fish from far away, and dive at speeds of 100 mph.

The ocean is one giant larder—stacked with protein-packed meals for hungry hunters. These predators enjoy a marine-style pick and mix from a tasty collection of fish, squid, seal, and jellyfish.

Not all ocean animals spend their lives underwater. Some of them swim on its surface, spend time on land as well as in the sea, or drop in for food then fly back to the sky above.

I AM THE WALRUS

Sharks are famous for their teeth, but the walrus has got to have some of the most impressive teeth found in the oceans. Both male and female walruses grow tusks up to 3 feet long. Walruses use their teeth to fight and pull themselves out of the water.

BIG WORD ALERT

MAMMAL

Animal with fur or hair that gives birth to live young, and feeds it milk.

Food chains

Big animals eat smaller animals. You can create links between animals that feed on one another to make a food chain. These diagrams show how all the animals and plants in a place need each other. It's called an ecosystem.

Tiny plants

Tiny animals

Bottom of the food chain

Sea bears

Most bears live on land, but polar bears live on the frozen Arctic Ocean, and love snow, ice, and being in the water. In fact, they are amazing swimmers and their scientific name, *Ursus maritimus*, even means sea bear. Polar bears mostly hunt ringed seals. They wait for the seals to pop their head up through holes in the ice then nab them with their massive paws and strong claws.

TWIST IT!

ATTACK-ATTACK

Polar bears hate being dirty. After eating, they dive in to the sea for a bath and often spend 15 minutes at a time washing the blood off their jaws and paws! If they are too far from water they clean themselves with snow instead.

A sea eagle's eyesight is thought to be six times sharper than a human's.

Fast-swimming walruses have been known to attack small boats, and use their tusks to wound those inside.

A female scientist in Antarctica was attacked and killed by a leopard seal in 2003. It was the first time one of these brutal beasts is known to have targeted a human.

Mean machines

Leopard seals are regarded as one of the meanest, deadliest, and most dangerous sea mammals. They are massive beasts—up to 10 feet long—with clawed flippers and sharp teeth. They hide in the water, underneath layers of ice, and wait for penguins to dive in—then pounce. They also hunt underwater, chasing squid through cold Antarctic seas.

Fish

Seal

Polar bear

Top of the food chain

HAMMERHEADS

BIG HEADS, SHY SHARKS

There is one way to describe this strange group of big-headed sharks—they're extraordinary! There are eight types of hammerhead shark, and they look like nothing else on Earth.

Long ago, an ordinary shark gave birth to a shark with a very wide head, and that shark probably became the ancestor of all modern hammerheads. It was a freak of nature, but its big head proved to be a bizarre boost to its hunting skills.

HEAD OF THE FAMILY

The eight different types of hammerhead shark:

* Great hammerhead
* Scalloped
* Smooth
* Smalleye
* Bonnethead
* Scoophead
* Mallethead
* Winghead

GREAT CANNIBALS

The great hammerhead can grow to 20 feet and its enormous size means it can hunt large fish, squid, octopuses, and other hammerheads! Its favorite meal is a stingray, and a hammerhead uses its huge head to pin a ray to the seabed while it begins to munch. Hammerheads are not bothered by a stingray's nasty weapon, and even eat its venomous tail. Hammerheads occasionally attack humans, but they are mostly shy sharks.

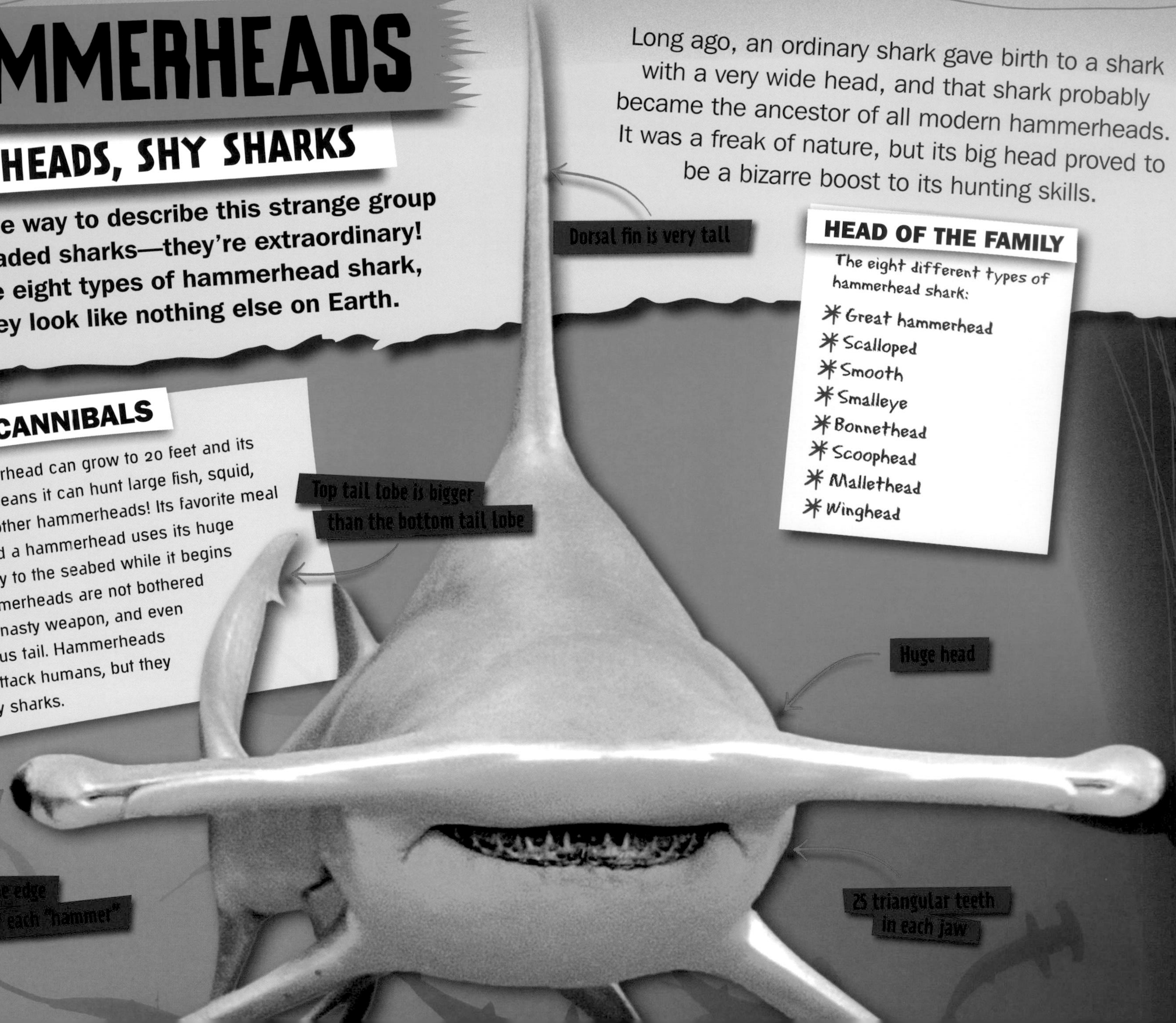

Dorsal fin is very tall

Top tail lobe is bigger than the bottom tail lobe

Huge head

Eyes on the edge of each "hammer"

25 triangular teeth in each jaw

Too cool for school

Enormous schools of scalloped sharks gather in the warm waters around California, but they don't seem to be doing any learning. In fact, they don't do much at all. They just swim slowly up and down. They even ignore tasty fish that swim by. No one knows why they do this, but the schools are mostly made up of females.

DANCING QUEEN

Female scalloped hammerheads love to dance and they like a clear dance-floor. They shake their head and twist their body in a move called the "shimmy." Then they do a super-fast full spin in the water—that's a "corkscrew." The dancers barge any other shark that gets too close!

KEY FACTS

Why does a hammerhead have a hammer head?

- Its wide head works like two wings. These "wings" have a flat bottom and curved top, like an airplane wing. This shape lifts the hammerhead through the water. The edges of each "wing" work like airplane wing flaps and the shark can change its shape, allowing it to make very sharp turns left or right.
- The hammerhead's organs of sense (for sight, smell, and electrical detection) are spread over a wider area, so the shark can find prey better than other sharks.
- The eyes are on the ends of the "wings." This helps the hammerhead focus well on prey, and it can even work out exactly how close its victim is.

GOING GOLD

One type of hammerhead turns bright yellow when it is a teenager! A small number of smalleye hammerheads feed on yellow catfish and golden shrimp, and the color of this food affects the sharks' skin.

DEADLY DOLPHINS

THESE GUYS ARE DANGEROUS

People tend to think of dolphins as cute, adorable, and friendly animals. In fact, they are marine hunters with big appetites, huge brains, jaws packed with rows of teeth, and a killer instinct. Dolphins are part of the whale family.

Echolocation—hunting by sound

Dolphins hunt in groups and use sound to find their prey of fish, shellfish, and crustaceans. As they swim, the dolphins make clicking noises—up to thousands of clicks per second. The sounds pass through water until they hit an object, like a fish, and are bounced back to the dolphin. These sounds ("echoes") give the dolphin information about the size, shape, and location of the object.

ORCA SLAUGHTER

Orcas love to spend time in groups, which are called pods. When one eagle-eyed orca spies a seal resting on an ice floe, he tells the rest of the gang, and together they hatch a cunning plan to catch it.

1 First, several orcas swim together towards the seal.

2 They create a large wave that washes over the ice.

The largest of all dolphins are orcas and they can grow up to 30 feet long. Orcas are also known as killer whales and they hunt almost anything, from turtles to sharks, seals, and even other dolphins and whales.

TWIST IT!

DAZZLING DOLPHINS

Orcas are not scared of great white sharks, and attack them from underneath. They often pull sharks out of the water—possibly to stop them from breathing.

A dolphin mother and her baby "talked" to each other using telephones hooked up in their separate tanks. Scientists say dolphins chat to each other just like humans!

Orcas sometimes force their way through slabs of ice to reach animals standing there. They can break slabs 3 feet thick!

Shhh! It may be a top secret, but there are rumors that dolphins have been trained to help countries during times of war. They have been taught how to find bombs underwater and seek out enemy swimmers.

KEY FACTS

BRILLIANT BRAINS

Dolphins are super smart animals. These are just a few of the clever things they can do:

- Follow instructions given by humans.
- Recognize the names for many objects, such as "ball."
- Copy human speech.
- Answer questions correctly.

NASTY NARWHALS

These dolphins only have one growing tooth, but it is a big one! It grows into a long tusk, up to 10 feet in length, and it is probably used for fighting rather than hunting, as females rarely have them.

3 This often plunges the seal into the water.

Unusually, however, on this occasion the seal catches a lucky break. A nearby huge humpback whale came along and frightened off the hungry orca.

CLOSE ENCOUNTERS

FACE TO FACE WITH SHARKS

The oceans are wide and deep, and millions of sharks live their lives without seeing a human being. Close to shore, however, the story is different—and risky. This is the conflict zone, where two top predators fight for space.

Sharks and people prefer to keep their distance from one another, but sometimes we have to share our habitats. Many people build their homes close to seas and rivers where sharks hunt. While some of those sharks do not pose any danger, some of them make bad neighbors!

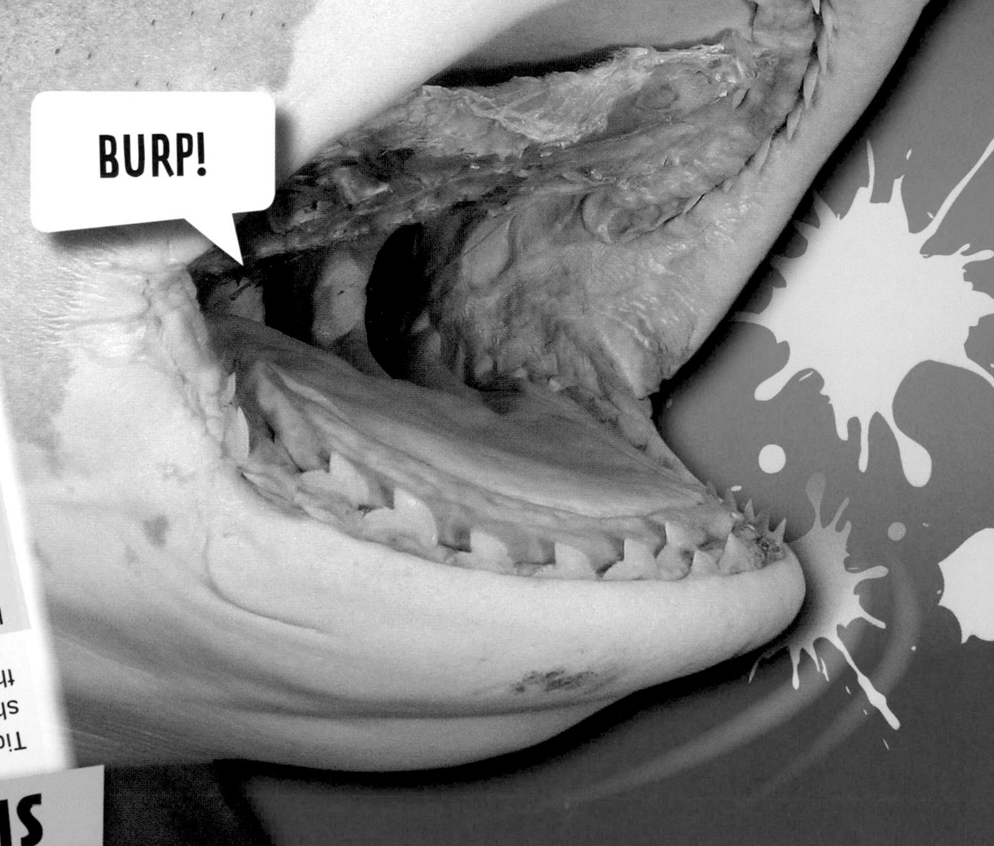

Tiger sharks are one of the most feared predators in the world. They are close to great whites in size and ferocity.

SHARK TALES

Tiger sharks often follow big ships, feasting on the waste that is thrown overboard.

In 2012, a huge shark tank in a Chinese shopping center cracked and exploded. The sharks weren't trying to escape: a drop in temperature and weak construction probably caused the accident.

It is hard for a shark to live in fresh water—their bodies are perfect for salty water. They cope with a fresh water environment by peeing in it, a lot!

TWIST IT!

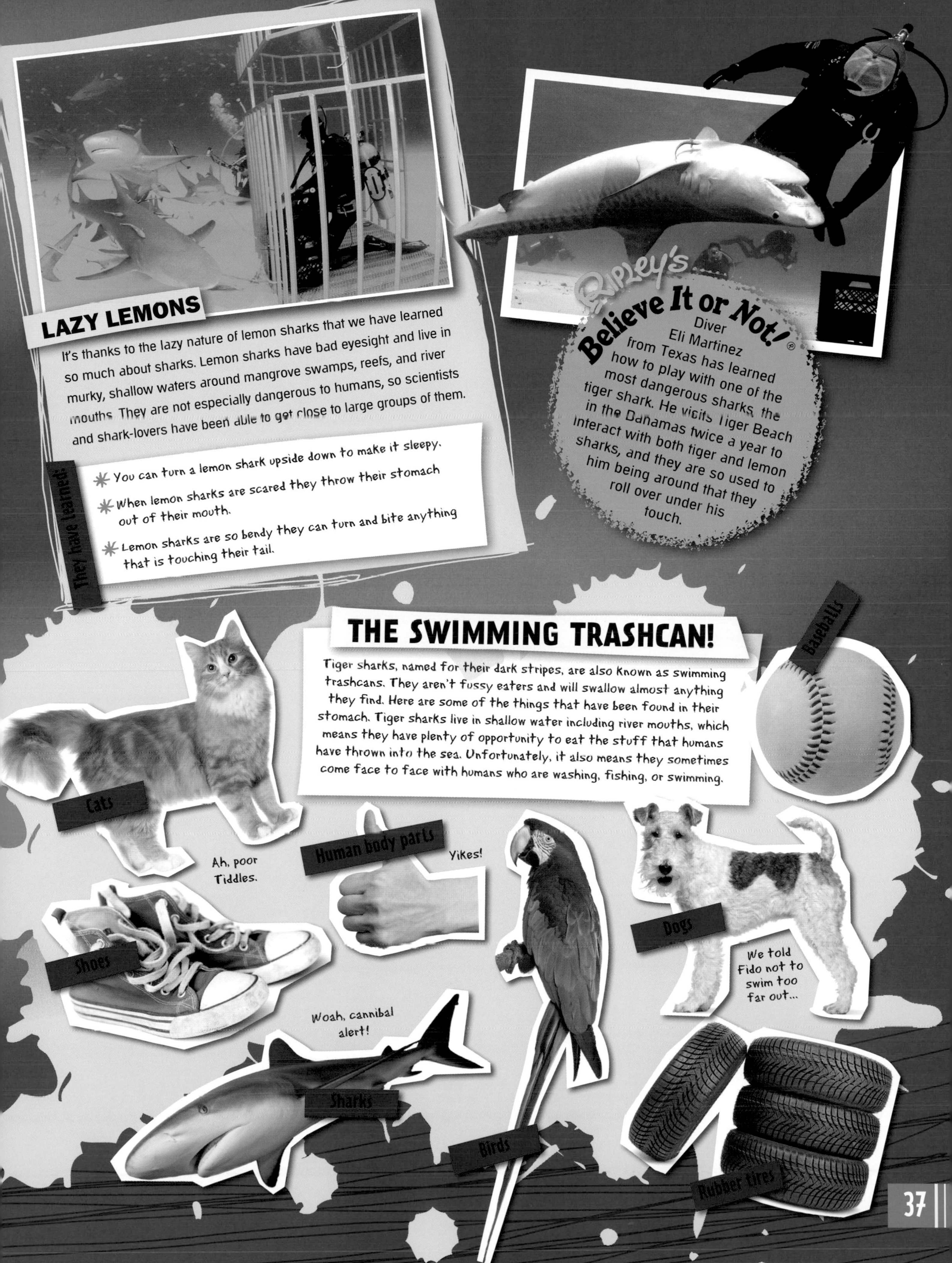

LAZY LEMONS

It's thanks to the lazy nature of lemon sharks that we have learned so much about sharks. Lemon sharks have bad eyesight and live in murky, shallow waters around mangrove swamps, reefs, and river mouths. They are not especially dangerous to humans, so scientists and shark-lovers have been able to get close to large groups of them.

They have learned:

- You can turn a lemon shark upside down to make it sleepy.
- When lemon sharks are scared they throw their stomach out of their mouth.
- Lemon sharks are so bendy they can turn and bite anything that is touching their tail.

Ripley's Believe It or Not!®

Diver Eli Martinez from Texas has learned how to play with one of the most dangerous sharks, the tiger shark. He visits Tiger Beach in the Bahamas twice a year to interact with both tiger and lemon sharks, and they are so used to him being around that they roll over under his touch.

THE SWIMMING TRASHCAN!

Tiger sharks, named for their dark stripes, are also known as swimming trashcans. They aren't fussy eaters and will swallow almost anything they find. Here are some of the things that have been found in their stomach. Tiger sharks live in shallow water including river mouths, which means they have plenty of opportunity to eat the stuff that humans have thrown into the sea. Unfortunately, it also means they sometimes come face to face with humans who are washing, fishing, or swimming.

TENTACLED TERRORS

SUPER SUCKERS A ID BITING BEAKS

The deep seas are home to some extraordinary animals, but these scary creatures look like nothing else on Earth. They have big bulging eyes, eight arms, and unusual ways to outsmart their enemies.

Octopuses and squid are the biggest and most intelligent animals without backbones in the world. Along with cuttlefish, they are related to shellfish, slugs, and snails but their amazing lifestyles and big brains set them apart from their relatives.

This broadclub cuttlefish is one of the largest cuttlefish.

Crazy creatures

Cuttlefish, squid, and octopuses are bizarre beasts: they have BLUE BLOOD that is pumped by THREE HEARTS. They swim by jet propulsion, and can walk or crawl with tentacles or arms that are covered with powerful suckers. Their toothless mouth is equipped with a tough beak—and some of them are venomous.

Magicians too!

These guys also have special skin, which can change color in the blink of an eye. They are shape-shifters, too, and can transform their body shape as well as the texture of their skin. These are all great ways to hide from predators and prey, but when those tricks don't work they simply disappear in a cloud of dark ink.

Its body is up to 20 inches long.

Squid and cuttlefish have eight arms and two tentacles. Octopuses have eight arms.

Copy cats

Meet the mimic octopus, the world's most astonishing quick-change artist. It can turn its hand—or tentacles—to creating almost any disguise it fancies. When danger threatens, it can change its color and shape to mimic (copy) other animals, such as flat fish, lion fish, jellyfish, shrimps, and sea snakes. If all that fails, a mimic octopus has a final trick up its sleeve, and dives into a hole in the seafloor where predators can't reach it.

Take a look at this clever octopus mimicking other sea creatures

Just me!

Starfish

Small but deadly

Most blue-ringed octopuses are smaller than your hand, and this one, the greater blue-ringed octopus, is the size of a golf ball, but they pack a lot of deadly venom in their skin and salivary (spit) glands. Some people have died, and many people have come close to death, after being bitten by this creature.

TENTACLE ALERT!

One octopus was seen to change color 1,000 times in just seven hours.

Paul the Octopus became famous during the 2010 Soccer World Cup when he correctly predicted the winners in eight matches.

Octopuses have learned how to open screw-top jars to reach food inside. They have mini brains in each of their eight arms.

Long ago, octopuses and squid ruled the seas—until fish and sharks evolved.

Humboldt squid are top of the menu in some parts of the world, but they get their revenge—often delivering nasty bites to divers and fishermen.

There is at least one report of an octopus coming to shore and wrestling with a man.

Red devils

Humboldt (or you can call them jumbo) squid are known as "red devils" because they flash bright red when they are about to attack. These marine monsters hide in the deep sea during the day, but swim upward at night to catch their prey near the water's surface. Sometimes they hunt in packs of hundreds! They are known as man-eaters and have razor-sharp beaks that can rip through flesh.

Sea snake

Conch shell

SCARY SECRETS

INTERNATIONAL FISH OF MYSTERY

Think you are a shark expert yet? Think again—even real shark experts admit they know very little about the way these secretive fish live. The best way to find out more is to swim alongside a shark, and watch everything it does. Fancy getting wet?

Sharks have been around for about 450 million years, but we've only been trying to find out about them for the last hundred. Today's sharks hold many secrets about their links to the past. It will be a long while before anyone can claim to really understand these mysterious fish.

Goblins and giants

Life in the ocean deep, where no light can ever reach, is tough and few animals brave the harsh conditions. It's a lonely place, where creatures wander through pitch-black water, endlessly searching for scraps of food. This is home for goblin sharks, which have odd-shaped heads and soft, flabby bodies (see page 13). Few have ever been seen, so how they live, and what they eat, is still a mystery.

Blue shark

Globe-trotters

Sharks often make incredible trips in search of food and mates. These journeys are called migrations. No one knows for sure how and why some sharks migrate, or even where some sharks disappear to for months at a time.

Blue sharks swim across the Atlantic Ocean when it is time to give birth to their pups, and go on journeys of up to 10,000 miles. They travel for longer and farther than any other sharks. Scientists track them around the world using a simple mapping system that sends messages from the sharks to satellites.

Can you solve this mystery?

Q. How do blue sharks know where to go?

A. They may be able to sense the Earth's magnetic field and use this to follow migration paths. They probably also use sounds to make a "sound map" of the oceans. It's incredible!

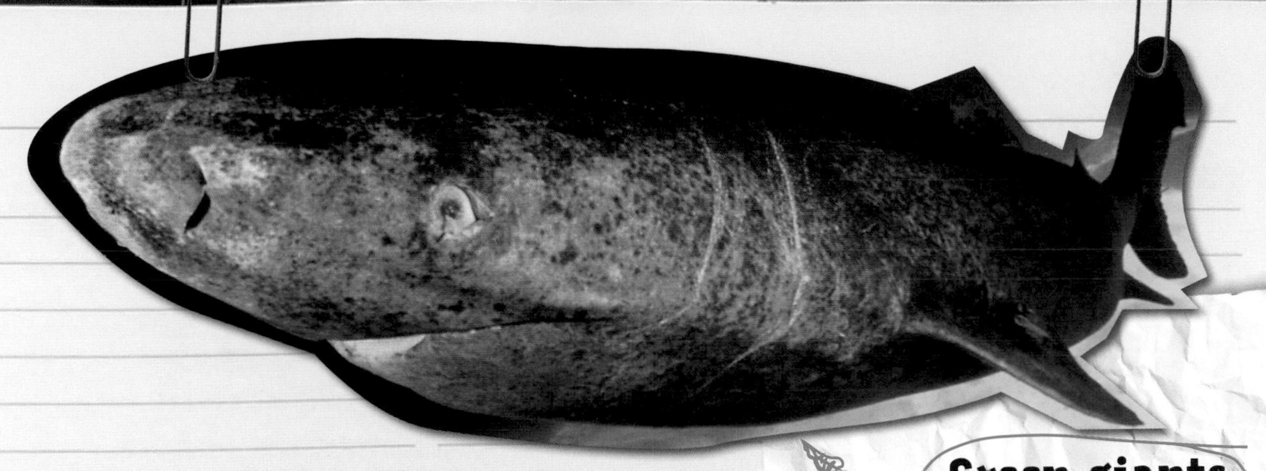

Some sharks lay eggs, but others give birth to live babies, which are called pups. Finding out how sharks find a mate and have their pups is still a big challenge to shark scientists. Sharks are shy creatures, and often go to secret places to lay eggs or give birth.

Shark eggs, however, are a common sight when they get swept up on to beaches. They are like little leathery pillows, and are often called "mermaid's purses." Look closely and you will see the growing pup inside. It can take ten months for a pup to grow to the right size for hatching.

Green giants

Greenland sharks are true giants of the deep, reaching 23 feet in length. They are the only sharks able to live under thick Arctic ice, coming up to shallow waters to hunt. They grow by less than the length of a fingernail every year, which means some Greenland giants may be hundreds of years old.

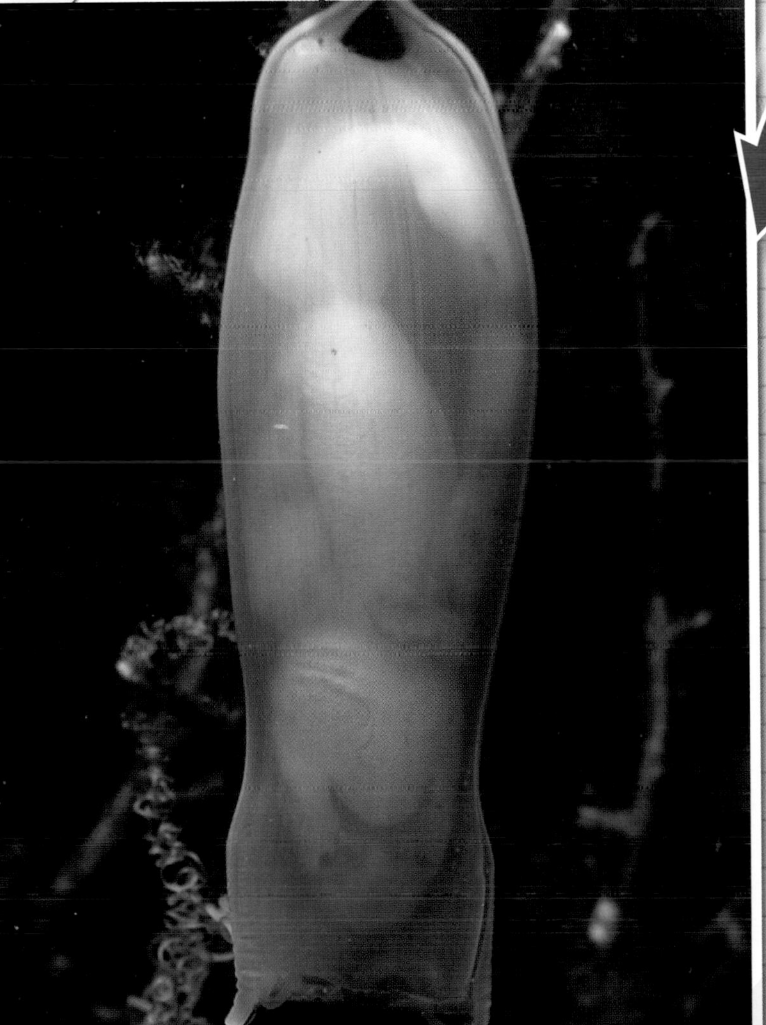

TOP SECRET

Greenland sharks are often blind. They can sniff out rotting food from far away, and are happy to feast on the long dead bodies of reindeer that have been washed out to sea.

Scientists always thought that a baby shark would need a mother and a father, but now they know that's not true. A female hammerhead in a shark tank gave birth to one pup, even though there was no male around!

Some sharks turn cannibal before they are even born—one pup might eat its brothers and sisters while still in its mother's tum!

No one knows why sharks don't stop growing, or just how big they can grow to. There may be many more types of shark hiding in the sea, waiting to be discovered.

TWIST IT!

A WHALE OF A TIME

NOBLE HUNTERS OF THE DEEP

Oooh, not now, I'm trying to sleep...

King carnivore

Who is the mightiest meat-eater on the planet? Not a crocodile, lion, or even a great white shark—it's a sperm whale. This is the world's largest carnivore (meat-eater), with a massive head that houses the largest brain of any animal. Males need about 2 tons of food every day—and they get most of that by diving to the seafloor and scooping up squid, octopuses, and fish.

Hungry humpbacks

Humpback whales (below) have some neat ways of getting a mouthful of food when passing through a school of fish.

* They whack the school with a fin, and scoop up any stunned fish.
* They slap the water with their tail to create foamy bubbles, which trap their victims.
* They dive down beneath the school then shoot upward, breathing out as they go. Their breath creates a circular curtain of bubbles that traps the school, and as the whale swims through the column of fish they open their mouth and swallow hundreds of fish at a time.

Woah—look at that tongue!

TWIST IT!

WHALE TALES

A sperm whale has no teeth on its upper jaw, and about 52 giant teeth on its long, slender bottom jaw—each one is up to 8 inches tall.

Whales breathe through blowholes on the top of their head. Humpback whales have two blowholes, but sperm whales have only one.

Blue whales are the biggest animals ever to have lived. The largest one seen was 110 feet long and weighed the same as 40 Asian elephants.

Whales are some of the most awesome predators on the planet. They have enormous appetites, and need large quantities of food to fuel their massive muscles and big brains, and to provide power for their incredible ocean journeys.

All whales are mammals, like us, which means they have to breathe air. They have poor eyesight, but find their way through the oceans using a superb sense of hearing, and can talk to each other using songs, clicks, and banging sounds.

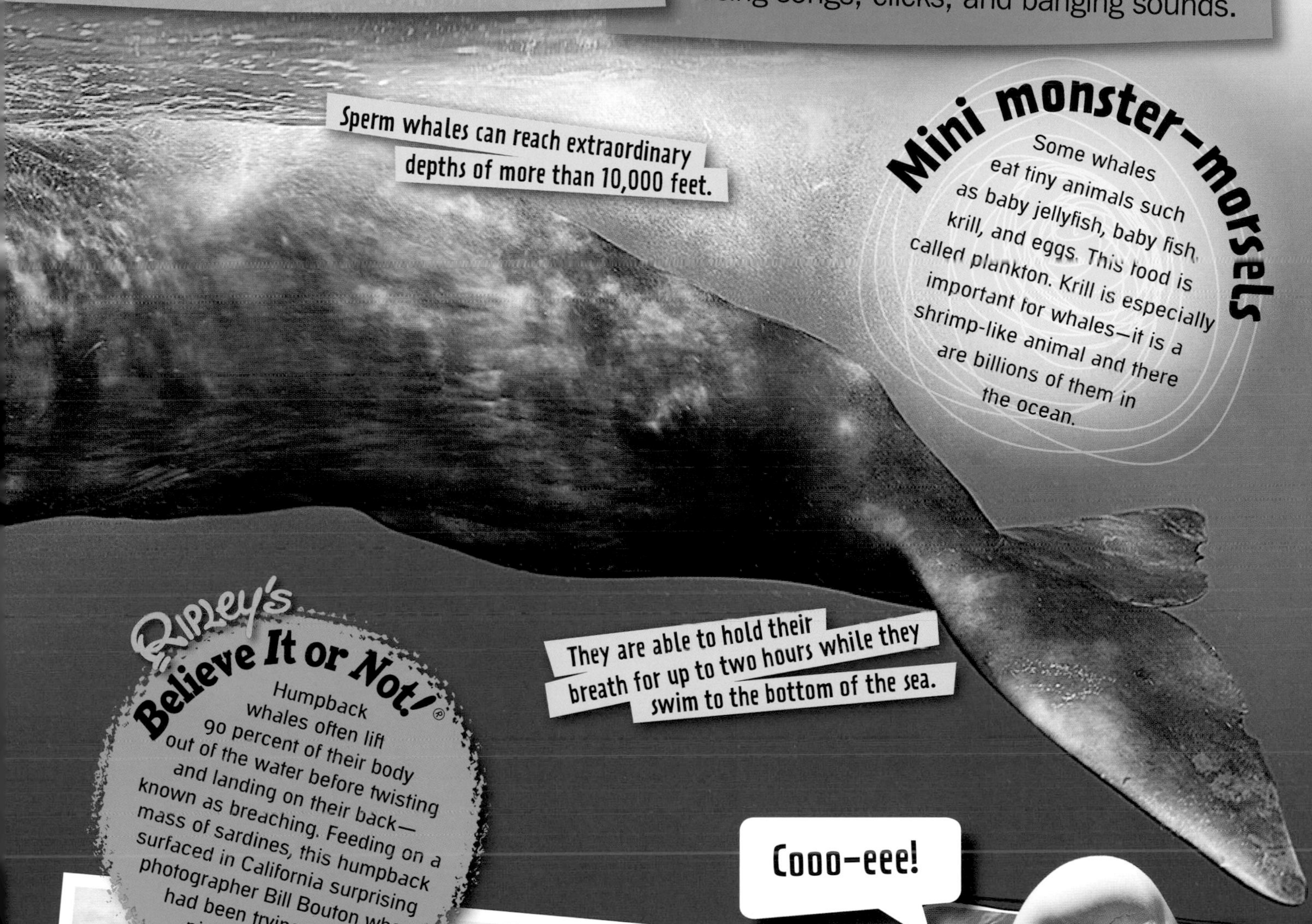

Sperm whales can reach extraordinary depths of more than 10,000 feet.

Mini monster-morsels

Some whales eat tiny animals such as baby jellyfish, baby fish, krill, and eggs. This food is called plankton. Krill is especially important for whales—it is a shrimp-like animal and there are billions of them in the ocean.

They are able to hold their breath for up to two hours while they swim to the bottom of the sea.

Ripley's Believe It or Not!®

Humpback whales often lift 90 percent of their body out of the water before twisting and landing on their back—known as breaching. Feeding on a mass of sardines, this humpback surfaced in California surprising photographer Bill Bouton who had been trying to take pictures of birds!

Cooo-eee!

Talking whale!

Beluga whales are also called sea canaries because they are chatterboxes that squeak, whistle, click, hum, and mew. One beluga, called NOC, managed to copy human voices!

IT'S AN OCEAN SOS

SAVE OUR SHARKS

SOS is the international code for "help," and right now the world's sharks need our help—and fast. Along with many other super-scary ocean creatures, they face a frightening future.

More than 100 types of shark are at risk of becoming extinct—dying out forever. That includes the most famous shark of all—the great white. Sharks are known as fearless predators, but humans have turned them from hunters to the hunted.

GOING HUNGRY

There is worldwide worry that people are taking too many fish from the sea. It's called overfishing, and it is a growing problem. If humans take too many fish, there are not enough left for ocean predators to eat. That could be why sharks come close to shore—to look for food.

Sharks in the soup

It is hard to believe, but millions of sharks are killed every year for their fins. These body parts are sliced off to be used in soup, which is a very popular dish in some parts of the world. Around 73 million sharks die every year in this way.

Fish food

Many sharks are caught by fishing boats. Sometimes, they are accidentally trapped in fish nets and then die, but they are also caught to be sold as food and souvenirs. Humans kill almost 100 million sharks each year.

Dirty water

Like all ocean animals, sharks suffer when the water is not clean. Humans often pour waste oil, sewage (that's poo!), and chemicals into rivers and the sea. Trash is thrown in too, including old fishing lines and hooks. This is all pollution—and it kills sea life.

SAFE HAVEN

Some countries are setting aside large areas of sea and turning them into marine parks, where no big boats can pass and no fishing can take place. The parks are safe places where animals can feed and have their young.

A large part of the Great Barrier Reef in Australia is protected by the Great Barrier Reef Marine Park, which helps to limit damaging activities, such as fishing and tourism. The Great Barrier Reef is the world's largest cluster of corals and other exotic marine life.

Telling the truth

When people understand how amazing sharks are, and that they belong in the ocean, they are more likely to leave them there. Teaching people about sharks is a great way to help save them from extinction.

Shark tourists

Lots of people are fascinated by sharks and want to see them. They travel to places, such as South Africa and Bimini in the Bahamas to watch sharks live free in the seas, often from the safety of a cage.

Watch and learn

Animals are happiest in their own homes, but keeping some sharks in large tanks, called aquariums, can be a good way to encourage people to learn more about them.

Studying sharks

Scientists find out more about sharks by using tags. A tag with a tracking device is attached to a shark, and scientists can follow its movements around the ocean. Scientists also watch sharks to find out how they behave.

ACKNOWLEDGMENTS

COVER (sp) © Brandon Cole/Naturepl.com,(r) Gavin Bernard/Barcroft Media; **2** (t/l) Phil Yeomans/Rex Features, (b) © Wesley Thornberry - Istock.com; **3** (t/r) © Stanislav Komogorov - iStock.com, (b/r) © Andrew Reid - Fotolia.com; **4** (sp) © Brandon Cole/Naturepl.com, (b) Gavin Bernard/Barcroft Media; **5** (t/l) Pisces Sportfishing Fleet/Rex Features; **6** (b/l) © FtLaudGirl - iStock.com, (b/c/l) © Georgette Douwma/naturepl.com **6–7** (dp) © Doug Perrine/naturepl.com; **7** (b/l) Birgitte Wilms/Minden Pictures/FLPA, (b/c/l) Alexander Safonov, (b/c/r) © Wesley Thornberry - iStock.com, (b/r) © Paul Cowell - Shutterstock.com; **8** (sp) Chris Fallows/apexpredators.com, (b) © Roman Sotola - Fotolia.com (and used throughout); **9** (t/l) © Valerie & Ron Taylor/ardea.com, (t/r) © Willtu - Fotolia.com, (r) © Oceans-Image/Photoshot; **10** (b/l) Fred Bavendam/Minden Pictures/FLPA, (b/r) Photo Researchers/FLPA, (t/r) © Joe Belanger - Shutterstock.com; **10–11** © tr3gi - Fotolia.com; **11** (t/l) Tom Mchugh/Science Photo Library, (r) Birgitte Wilms/Minden Pictures/FLPA, (b) © FtLaudGirl - iStock.com; **12** (c) © Biosphoto, Jeffrey Rotman/Biosphoto/FLPA, (b) Pisces Sportfishing Fleet/Rex Features; **13** (t/l) © Sea Life Park/Handout/Reuters/Corbis, (c) Gary Roberts/Rex Features, (b) © Photoshot; **14** (sp) Panda Photo/FLPA, (b) AFP/Getty Images; **15** © Jurgen Freund/naturepl.com, (b) Ian R. MacDonald, FSU (all rights reserved); **16** © Jeff Rotman/naturepl.com; **17** (t/l) © Nicolas.Voisin44 - Shutterstock.com, (t/r) © seapics.com, (b/r) © Shane Gross - Shutterstock.com; **18** (t) © Edwin Giesbers/naturepl.com, (b) © Jurgen Freund/naturepl.com; **19** (b/l) © Kristina Vackova - Shutterstock.com, (b/r) © PictureNature/Photoshot, (c/l) © Ekaterina Pokrovsky - Shutterstock.com, (t/r) © Amanda Nicholls - Shutterstock.com; **20** Reinhard Dirscherl/FLPA; **21** (b/r) © Bruce Rasner/Rotman/naturepl.com, (t/r) © Alex Mustard/2020vision/naturepl.com, (c) Mauricio Handler/Handlerphoto.com/Solent; **22** (t) © Beth Swanson - Shutterstock.com, (b) © David Fleetham/naturepl.com; **22–23** (c) © Paul Cowell - Shutterstock.com, (bgd) © Gastev Roman - Shutterstock.com, (boxes) © beholdereye - Fotolia.com; (t, b) © Lasse Kristensen - Fotolia.com; **23** (c) © Dr David Wachenfeld/Auscape/ardea.com, (b/r) © Wesley Thornberry - iStock.com; **24** (l) Bill Curtsinger/National Geographic Stock, (c) Marty Snyderman/Visuals Unlimited, Inc. /Science Photo Library; **24–25** © Doug Perrine/naturepl.com; **25** (r) Flip Nicklin/ Minden Pictures/National Geographic Stock, (t/l) © Jeff Rotman/naturepl.com; **26** (b) © Cuson - Shutterstock.com; **26–27** (c) © Nicolas Aznavour - Shutterstock.com, (dp) © Andrew7726 - Fotolia.com; **27** (b) © littlesam - Shutterstock.com, (r) Phil Yeomans/Rex Features, (c) © Island Effects - iStock.com, (t) © Bruce Coleman/Photoshot; **28** (sp) Tom Mannering/Rex Features, (c) © Jeffrey L. Rotman/Corbis; **29** (t/r) © Visuals Unlimited/naturepl.com, (b/l) Getty Images; **30** (t) © Roy Mangersnes/naturepl.com, (b) © BMJ - Shutterstock.com; **31** (t) © GTW/imagebroker/Corbis (r) © Doug Allan/naturepl.com; **32** (sp) © Oceans Image/Photoshot; **32–33** (dp) © Oceans-Image/Photoshot; **33** (r) © Seapics.com, (l) Tom Campbell/SplashdownDirect/Rex Features; **34** (sp) Alexander Safonov, (b) © Kathryn Jeffs/naturepl.com; **35** (b/r) © Kathryn Jeffs/naturepl.com, (c) Design Pics Inc/Rex Features; **36** (sp) © Andrew Reid - Fotolia.com; **37** (t) © Photoshot, (t/r) Caters News Agency, (t/l) © Nataliya Kuznetsova - iStock.com, (c/l) © Ivan Bajic - iStock.com, (b/l) © Rich Carey - Shutterstock.com, (c) © Malyugin - Shutterstock.com, (c/r, r) © Eric Isselée - iStock.com, (t/r) © Albo - Fotolia.com, (b/r) © MorePixels - iStock.com; **38** (c) © Georgette Douwma/naturepl.com, (b/l) © Stubblefield Photography - Shutterstock.com, (b/r) © Stephan Kerkhofs -Shutterstock.com; **39** (b/r) © Orlandin - Shutterstock.com, (b/l) © Jeff Rotman/naturepl.com, (r) © Doc White/naturepl.com, (t/r) © FrameAngel - Shutterstock.com, (t/l) Chris Newbert/Minden Pictures/FLPA; **40** (b/l) © Bioraven - Shutterstock.com, (b) © NHPA/Photoshot, (c/r) © Kanate - Shutterstock.com, (c/l) © MichaelJayBerlin - Shutterstock.com, (l) © Optimarc - Shutterstock.com; **40–41** © Netnut43 - Fotolia.com; **41** (t) © seapics.com, (t/r) © Kanate - Shutterstock.com, (b) © NHPA/Photoshot, (t/l, r) © Optimarc - Shutterstock.com; **42** (b) © Brandon Cole/naturepl.com; **42–43** (dp) © NHPA/Photoshot; **43** (b/l) Photo by Bill Bouton, (b/r) © Stanislav Komogorov - iStock.com; **44** (l) © Mark Carwardine/naturepl.com, (sp) © Cheryl-Samantha Owen/naturepl.com, (b/l) © kanate - Shutterstock.com; **45** (b) © Jurgen Freund/naturepl.com, (sp) © Tororo Reaction- Shutterstock.com, (b/l) © Kanate - Shutterstock.com

Key: t = top, b = bottom, c = center, l = left, r = right, sp = single page, dp = double page, bgd = background

All other photos are from Ripley's Entertainment Inc. All other artwork by Rocket Design (East Anglia) Ltd.

Every attempt has been made to acknowledge correctly and contact copyright holders and we apologize in advance for any unintentional errors or omissions, which will be corrected in future editions.

a Jim Pattison Company

Written by Camilla de la Bedoyere
Consultant Barbara Taylor

Publisher Anne Marshall

Managing Editor Rebecca Miles
Picture Researcher James Proud
Editors Lisa Regan, Rosie Alexander
Assistant Editor Amy Harrison
Proofreader Judy Barratt
Indexer Hilary Bird

Art Director Sam South
Design Rocket Design (East Anglia) Ltd
Reprographics Stephan Davis

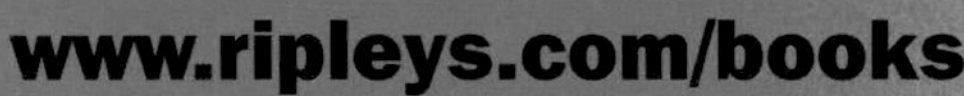

www.ripleys.com/books

First published in Great Britain in 2009 by Random House Books, Random House, 20 Vauxhall Bridge Road, London SW1V 2SA www.randomhouse.co.uk

This edition 2013

Addresses for companies within The Random House Group Limited can be found at: www.randomhouse.co.uk/offices.htm

The Random House Group Limited Reg. No. 954009

ISBN 978-1-60991-238-3 (USA) | ISBN 978-0-09956-816-2 (UK)

10 9 8 7 6 5 4 3 2 1

A CIP catalogue record for this book is available from the British Library

Printed in China
January 2018
2nd Printing

PAGE 9

PAGE 14

PAGE 18

PAGE 43

ALL CREATURES GREAT AND SMALL

WORLDWIDE WONDERS

WHAT'S INSIDE YOUR BOOK?

Aren't animals amazing? From tiny terrors to gentle giants, vicious predators to graceful grazers, our planet is home to over one million different species. Each one of these species has an important role to play in the way the world works. That's why it's so vital that we consider how our lifestyles affect the homes and habitats of every living creature today.

This book will open your eyes to the truly astonishing, the fearsomely frightening, and even the fantastically freakish members of the animal kingdom. Find out more about sea dwellers, microscopic marvels and endangered creatures, with special Ripley's fascinating facts and amazing 'Believe It or Not!' stories from around the world. Come on – read all about it!

Only male lions have a mane of long hair around their face. The males defend the pride (group) of lions and their territory, but the females are in charge of hunting and bringing home supper for the whole pride.

30

KEY FACTS

- A pride may cover up to 260 sq km as its territory.
- Lions learn to hunt when they are about a year old.
- A lion has a claw at the back of its leg, which it sometimes uses to pick leftovers from its teeth!
- The back teeth are used for cutting meat (rather than grinding food, like many other animals).

TWISTS

Do the twist

This book is packed with incredible creatures. It will teach you amazing things about wild animals, but like all Twists books, it shines a spotlight on things that are unbelievable but true. Turn the pages and find out more...

Twists are all about Believe It or Not: amazing facts, feats, and things that will make you go 'Wow!'

Ripley's Believe It or Not!®

The animal kingdom is full of creatures that sound like they're made up – but they're totally for real. Like this two-headed turtle, which has two heads, a pair of front feet on each side, one pair of back legs and one tail. It's actually conjoined twins, and is on display in an aquarium in Pennsylvania.

Found a new word? Big word alerts will explain it for you.

FAMILY MATTERS

GETTING TOGETHER

The multi-coloured peacock is a bird that dresses to impress. He can fan out his tail, in an eye-opening display of shimmering colours and stunning patterns.

It's an ingenious tactic; a show-off with perfect plumage is more likely to attract the attention of the watching peahens. The females admire bright colours and large 'eyespots' in the feathers – and the more eyespots the better! Once a female has picked her favourite male she will mate with him, and soon starts laying eggs. The most marvellous males win over a number of females to mate with, while shabby-looking peacocks remain alone.

BIG WORD ALERT

REPRODUCTION
The way that an animal has young is called reproduction. Some animals can have young all by themselves, but it's more common to have two parents: a male and a female.

LIFE STORIES

The story of how an animal lives, from birth to death, is a life-cycle.

If an animal can find a healthy and strong mate it is more likely to have youngsters that will survive. Some animals make a big effort to impress those they fancy – to show how fit they are. This is called a courtship.

Mammals are animals that give birth to live young and feed them with milk. Usually it's the mum who provides the milk, but in the job-sharing world of Dayak fruit bats, it's a job for the dads too!

The Virginia opossum is the USA's only naturally occurring marsupial.

After about 100 days, the babies climb onto their mum's back to hitch a ride.

The newborns crawl straight into their mother's pouch to grow.

An opossum mum usually has 13 babies at once.

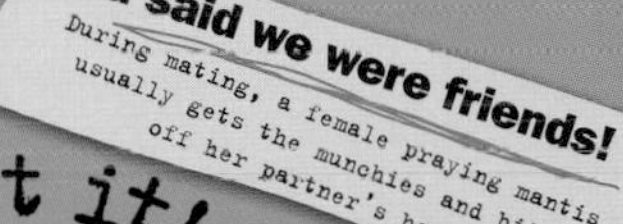

You said we were friends!
During mating, a female praying mantis usually gets the munchies and bites off her partner's head!

twist it!

TRUE LOVE

Sea horses are romantic, dancing for each other every day during the mating period. The female lays her eggs inside a special pouch on the male's body, and he cares for them until they hatch.

Female rhinos spray smelly urine, and males will fight each other, sometimes to the death, to mate with them.

Amphibians, such as frogs and toads, have to lay their eggs in water. Snakes and lizards are reptiles and lay their eggs on land.

A queen white ant, or termite, lays 30,000 eggs a day!

DADDY DAY-CARE

Male jawfish protect their eggs by keeping them inside their enormous mouths. Without their fatherly care, chances are that most of the eggs would be eaten before ever hatching.

31

Look for the Ripley R to find out even more than you knew before!

Learn fab fast facts to go with the cool pictures.

Don't forget to look out for the 'twist it!' column on some pages. Twist the book to find out more fast facts about amazing animals.

ARMED AND DANGEROUS

PREDATORS

If you are fitted out with killer claws, razor-sharp teeth, or toxic venom you could be a perfect predator – an animal that hunts to eat.

Which predator would you place at the top of a league for mean, keen killing machines? Sharks are a favourite for first place – after all, they've been prowling the oceans for around 400 million years. That means they were slicing, shearing and chomping through flesh 200 million years before the dinosaurs appeared on land! So are these hungry hunters the world's top predators? Since people kill around 100 million sharks every year – driving many types to the edge of extinction – that top spot might belong to us shame-faced humans instead.

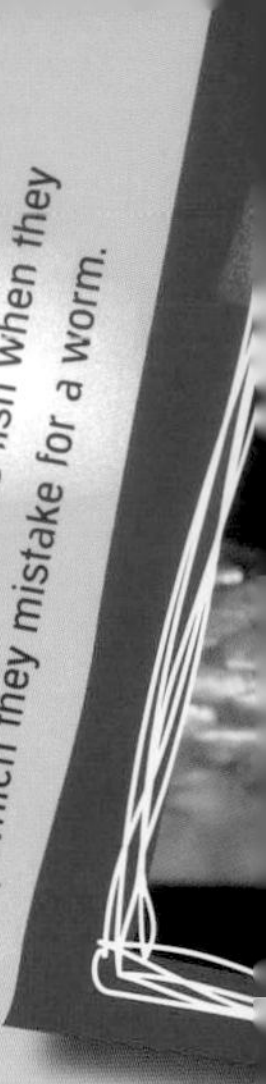

The alligator snapping turtle catches fish when they seize its tongue, which they mistake for a worm.

BIG WORD ALERT

PREDATORS Animals that kill and eat other animals. The animals they kill are called prey.

Tiger sharks attack almost anything, including people. One was found with cans, tyres, wood, half a dead dog and a tom-tom drum in its belly!

Open wide

The great white shark attacks ferociously, then retreats, letting the damaged prey grow weaker, only to return to finish it off. Each year 50 to 100 serious shark attacks are reported, with less than ten deaths on average.

THE FROG THAT FOUGHT BACK!

When this little tree frog got attacked by a cat-eyed snake he decided he wasn't going to give up without a fight. He grabbed hold of the snake's neck – and the predator and prey were still locked in mortal combat three hours later!

Just one bite!

In 1963, spearfishing champion Rodney Fox was attacked by a great white shark in the sea off Aldinga Beach, Australia. He had been virtually bitten in half and required 462 stitches. Less than three months later, however, he was back in the water, carrying a reminder of the attack embedded in his hand – a great white tooth.

FASCINATING FACT! FASCINATING FACT!

Knockout!

Mantis shrimps are a knockout! These crustaceans have the fastest and most powerful punch in the animal kingdom. They can wallop their prey with a force of 1,000 newtons – that's as deadly as a rifle bullet, and strong enough to smash glass. The shrimp's weapons are a pair of club-shaped legs that are tucked away under its head – until the time comes to lash out at a super-ballistic speed of up to 240 m/second!

A shrimp's weapons of smash destruction are folded under its head until it's time for lunch.

TINY TERROR

When it is worried, the blue-ringed octopus buzzes with colour. Its blue ring markings pulse brightly and its brown skin turns a vivid yellow. It measures only about 20 cm from armtip to armtip, but it has a deadly bite, which contains enough venom to kill at least seven people. In 1967, a man paddling in an Australian rock pool lived for just 90 minutes after being bitten.

TAKE A DIVE

DEEP DWELLERS

Oceans teem with animal life, from crystal-clear waters around coral reefs, to their darkest, inky depths. This may be where life on Earth began – simple creatures were burrowing in the slime of the ocean floor an unbelievable one billion years ago!

Oceans and seas are a mighty stash of food, and home to all sorts of critters, from ginormous blue whales with an average length of 27 m, to teeny-weeny rotifers – each one smaller than a grain of salt. From the shallow seashore to the deep ocean trenches, more than 10 km beneath the surface, animals are crawling, slithering, tunnelling, swimming, floating and drifting.

When the tiny male anglerfish mates, he grabs the larger female with his mouth, hangs on, and gradually fuses (joins) with her body.

In the vast, black ocean depths it can take time to find a breeding partner. The male deep-sea anglerfish becomes a part of the female. He shares her food via her blood supply, and in return fertilises her eggs.

Most of the male body disintegrates – his eyes, nostrils, everything – apart from what is needed to fertilise the female's eggs. Once this takes place, the male can never leave.

BIG WORD ALERT

PHYTOPLANKTON

The oceans are packed with phytoplankton (say: fie-toe-plank-ton). These mini plants get energy from sunlight, and are the favourite food of billions of animals.

WAY DOWN

Fish were the first animals with backbones to evolve on Earth and there are more than 30,000 species, or different types, of fish. Most of them live in the oceans or seas.

A shark's skeleton isn't made of bone – it's made of cartilage, which is the soft stuff you have holding your nose together. There are around 500 species of shark, of which only about 40 occasionally attack people.

Clownfish seek safety in the stinging tentacles of sea-anemones. The fish are immune to the stings, and clean the anemone in return for a safe place to live.

If you spot puffer fish on a menu, give it a wide berth! Although these fish are sometimes served in Japanese restaurants, they contain enough poison to kill a person in 20 minutes. Chefs have to train for years to learn how to remove all the deadly body bits. But would you risk it?

Coral reefs are ocean wildlife hotspots. They are formed from living creatures, called coral polyps, and are home to thousands of other types of water beasties. Many coral reefs are dying, due to pollution and human activity.

twist it!

This red handfish looks grumpy – maybe that's because he has to get around by walking on his 'hands', which are really just fins.

Many ocean-going creatures crunch on krill. These little animals swim in giant groups called swarms.

Oceans and seas are salty, but rivers and lakes have much less salt in the water. Animals usually live in one or the other habitat, but rarely both.

Ripley's Believe It or Not!®

Slithering sea slugs lost their shells millions of years ago. They don't need them, because these soft-bodied creatures have toxins (poisons) and stinging cells in their skin. Their bright colours are a bold signal to keep clear – or prepare for pain!

YIKES!

Deep in the oceans, where sunlight never reaches, there's a small army of weird creatures. Deep-water fish, such as this vicious viperfish, usually have dark bodies, huge mouths and hundreds of light organs called photophores. These are parts of the body that can actually make light, helping the fish to find food in the murky depths. The viperfish's teeth protrude far beyond its mouth and eyes, giving it – in proportion to its head – the longest teeth of any animal. If your teeth were this big, they would stick out a massive 30 cm!

Most animals that live in the seas and oceans are able to take oxygen from the water. Don't try this at bath time – we're equipped with air-breathing lungs, not gills.

If you were an animal, would you choose to crawl like a caterpillar or fly like a moth? Flying wins every time – can you imagine the thrill of swooping and soaring through the air?

Only birds, bats, and insects use their own mighty muscle power to truly fly. That little problem hasn't put off other creatures, such as flying squirrels and frogs, from taking a brave leap and trusting the wind to carry them along. Gliding is great if you're lazy, but animals that soar through the air can't always control how they travel, and where they end up. So it's fingers crossed for a soft landing!

Eagle-eyed ospreys soar over water looking for fish. They plunge, feet first, and grab their prey with talons that are covered in slippery-fish gripping spikes. They can even close their nostrils when they dive, so they don't get water up their nose.

KEY FACTS

- Flying can be a great way to get beyond the reach of predators. Plus, while you're flying past that tree, you might just spot some juicy fruits to eat too...
- ...which is just as well, because flying is hard work. It takes a great deal of energy – flying animals have big appetites.
- A bird's flapping wings create an up-force, which lifts the animal into the sky.

A HEAD FOR HEIGHTS

It flies, it hums, and it sips nectar. Is it a hummingbird? No, this is a hummingbird hawk moth. When it flies, this insect's orange hindwings beat so fast they look like flickering flames, giving the impression that the moth is on fire.

Hummingbirds have trough-shaped tongues and long, skinny beaks. They work like a drinking straw – perfect for sipping sweet nectar and the occasional insect, too.

FASCINATING FACT! FASCINATING FACT!

The heart of a ruby-throated hummingbird beats around 600 times a minute.

twist it!

FLY BY

Want to know the funny thing about flying lemurs? They can't really fly, and aren't really lemurs! These furry mammals live in Southeast Asia and have kite-shaped membranes of skin stretched between their limbs. They leap off trees, spread out the skin, and glide for up to 136 m.

It's almost impossible to swat a fly – they move quickly, have great eyesight that allows them to see in virtually every direction, and can sense the air moving in front of your hand long before it reaches them.

When a tropical two-wing flying fish needs to escape a predatory dolphin it flaps its enormous fins to gain lift-off, and sails out of the water and through the air for up to 40 seconds.

Bats are the only mammals that can fly, rather than glide. Their wings are made from double layers of skin that stretch from fingers to ankles.

Wallace's flying frog is an amphibian with an ambition to fly! It may not have wings, but this animal has got wide webbed feet and skin flaps that catch the air. When a frog jumps from a tree it can glide for up to 15 m.

WOW!

The hummingbird has the biggest heart and wings in proportion to body size of all warm-blooded animals!

>> HIGH-FLYERS >>

- Some bats chase moths to heights of 3,000 m.
- Alpine choughs (a type of bird) fly at 8,500 m in the Himalayas.
- Queen of Spain Fritillary butterflies have been found at 2,700 m.

ON THE FAR SIDE

EXTREME SURVIVORS

Animals have to cope with extremes of temperature and all sorts of difficult conditions. If you're thirsty, you get a glass of water. If you're cold, you put on more clothes. It's all about controlling what's going on inside, and outside, so your body can reach maximum performance levels. And that's what animals do, too.

FISH ON THE ROCKS

The blood of an icefish contains chemical antifreeze, which stops it from turning solid in the chilly waters of the Antarctic.

warm wallow

Japanese macaques make the most of the cold weather by enjoying a dip in the warm waters of a hot spring. They have even been known to make and throw snowballs, rolling them along the ground to get bigger and better ones!

BIG WORD ALERT

HABITAT The place an animal lives. Some animals have evolved to be able to live in extreme habitats.

KEY FACTS

- It's worth being an extreme survivor if you can find safety or food in a place where few other animals venture.
- Animals living in very hot, cold, dry, or wet places often need super-adapted body parts.

BIG BULLY!

Frogs like it damp, so when there is no rain, large African bullfrogs bury themselves underground. They can survive for several years, wrapped in a cocoon so they don't dry out.

This African frog has seized its prey – a small mouse!

WHO'S THE COLDEST?

- Arctic foxes can survive at −30°C if well fed.
- Snow buntings nest nearer to the North Pole than any other bird.
- Ptarmigans can survive sub-zero temperatures for six weeks.
- Himalayan yaks survive at a height of 6,000 m on ice-fields.

EXTREMES!

twist it!

Less than 1 cm of rain falls in the Namibian Desert every year. Desert adders living there don't drink water – they get all they need from the lizards they eat.

Some animals snooze their way through the worst weather of winter. Little Siberian birch mice hibernate for up to eight months of the year.

Black grouse spend up to 95% of the winter hidden deep in snow burrows. The only time they emerge is to have a snack!

Musk oxen have been around since the Ice Age, and they still use thick woollen coats to keep them warm in Alaska. Their fur reaches to the ground, and is the longest growing hair of any animal.

Little baby ears are perfect for keeping in body heat.

Two layers of thick fur help to keep out the cold.

You won't see a polar bear putting on a coat! This extreme survivor has got a body that can cope with sub-zero temperatures. In fact, polar bears get too hot sometimes, and roll around in the snow to chill out! They are the largest predators on land.

Who's the biggest?

This enormous individual was a real giant amongst elephants. He was an African bush elephant and was shot in Angola in 1974. He measured 4.16 m to the shoulder and was thought to weigh 12.25 tonnes, which makes him about twice the length and weight of an average bull elephant. The elephant was stuffed and you can now see him in the Smithsonian Museum of Natural History, Washington DC, USA.

HORN OF PLENTY

FASCINATING FACT!

Lurch, an African Watusi steer, had horns that were an incredible 2.3 m across and 97 cm around! His parents had perfectly normal horns.

Tallest animal!

The giraffe has a tongue almost 50 cm in length!

MEGA!

Millipedes have more legs than any other creature – but they don't really have 1,000 of them. The most ever counted on one millipede was 750 legs.

Gaboon vipers have hollow teeth that pump venom into the snake's victim. They have the longest fangs of any snake and one bite contains enough venom to kill ten people.

For its size, the rhino beetle is the strongest animal on the planet, and can move an object 850 times its own weight!

The world's biggest earthworms can grow to 5 m long, and are as thick as your arm. They are not as long as bootlace worms, found in coastal areas of Britain, which can measure 55 m!

Deep in the oceans whales talk to each other using grunting and moaning sounds. Some of these sounds are the loudest animal noises ever recorded – they are about as loud as a rocket taking off!

Spotted skunks stink – and that's official. They are the smelliest animals alive, and even perform headstands when they spray their foul liquids, to get the best results.

twist it!

BIG, REALLY BIG!

A colossal squid is a giant in anyone's book. This one turned up in the nets of a fishing boat in the Ross Sea, near Antarctica. It was the first intact specimen ever seen, measured around 10 m in length, and had eyeballs bigger than dinner plates. They probably gave this creature great vision deep underwater, where very little light can penetrate.

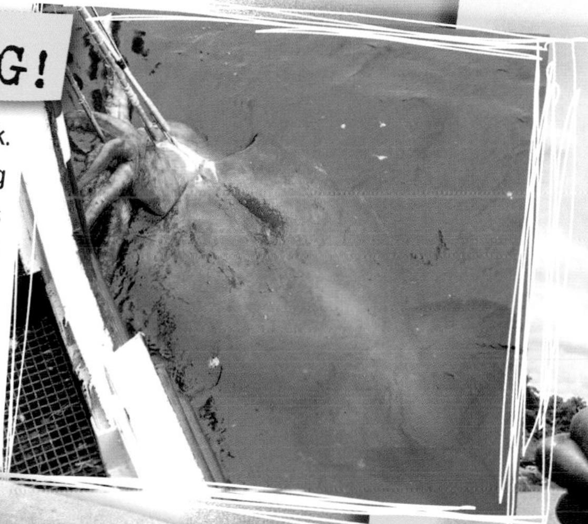

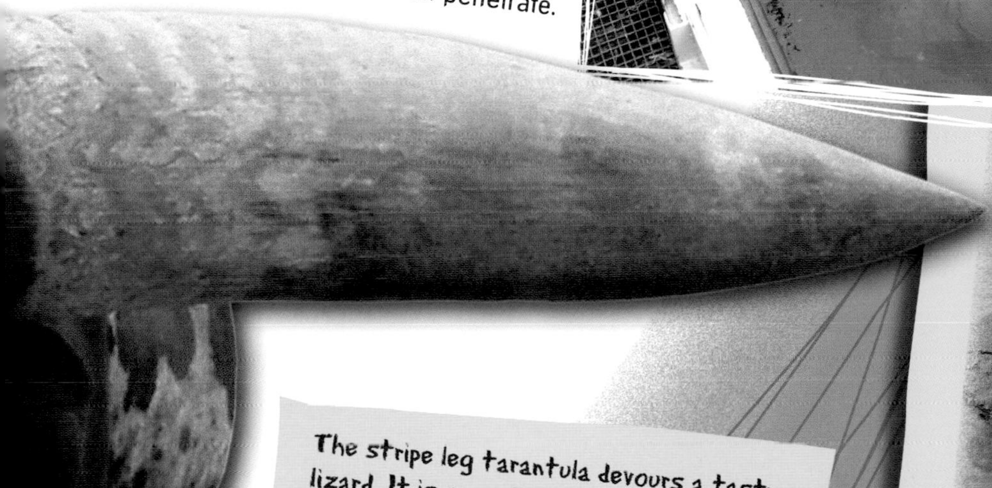

The stripe leg tarantula devours a tasty lizard. It is one of the largest spiders in the world and lives in the Amazon area of South America.

ACTUAL SIZE!

OVERSIZE JUMPER

This goliath frog must be hopping mad he got caught! These bulky amphibians live in West Africa and can measure 40 cm from nose to tail.

BLACK-OUT

Tiny tarsiers live in the rainforests of Southeast Asia. They spend most of their time scampering through trees, using their long, slender fingers to grip to branches. Tarsiers can turn their heads right round, to check what's going on behind them, and use their enormous eyes and excellent hearing to listen for prowling predators.

Little fennec foxes have enormous ears. They live in the desert and come out to hunt when the sun goes down. Their large ears help them listen out for prey, but they also help the foxes to lose heat during the boiling desert days.

A mole 15 cm long can dig a tunnel almost 70 m long in a single night.

A single dingo – a species of Australian wild dog – can kill 50 sheep in one night.

Oilbirds spend their entire lives in darkness, inhabiting the caves of South America. They venture out at night to feed on fruit and find their way around using echolocation.

twist it!

A barn owl, upon hearing a mouse, can take off in half a second, fly 3.8 m/second and adjust its talons to the size and shape of its prey – in the dark!

The barn owl catches more mice than 12 cats!

Watch this!

An owl's eyes take up about half of the space in its head.

WHOO'S THERE?

NOCTURNAL HUNTERS

When the sun slips down in the sky, stealthy stalkers begin to stir. Millions of animals, from wolves to wombats, join the wide-awake club and get active under the cover of night.

On the up side, night workers should be hard to see, so they might avoid being eaten. The downer is that lots of other wide-awakers have got crafty methods for seeking out prey at night.

Suckers!

Blood-drinking vampire bats feed on other animals and, occasionally, humans too. Here they are feeding on a cow's foot, slicing through flesh, and sucking up the oozing blood. Chemicals in their spit stop the wound from healing.

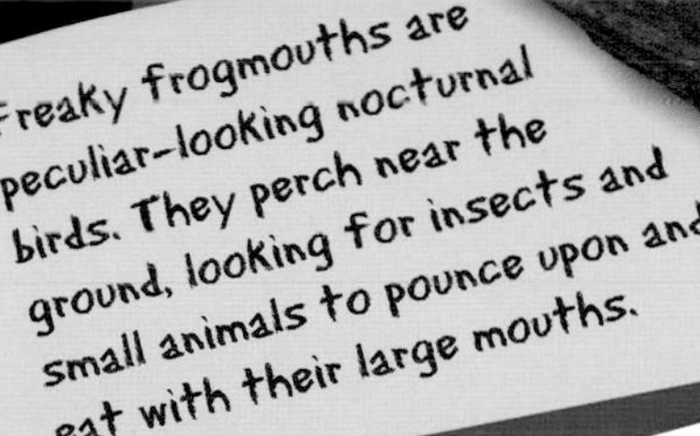

Freaky frogmouths are peculiar-looking nocturnal birds. They perch near the ground, looking for insects and small animals to pounce upon and eat with their large mouths.

If a frogmouth is frightened it clings to a tree, stays still, and pretends to be a broken branch!

Ouch!

Barn owls usually swallow their small prey whole. Creatures such as mice, birds, lizards, and frogs are eaten, feathers, bones, and all!

Ripley's Believe It or Not!® Night beast

A strange hairless animal was found dead outside Cuero, Texas, in August 2007. It was thought to be a chupacabra, a mythical nocturnal beast. The chupacabra gets its name (Spanish for goat-sucker) from its habit of attacking and drinking the blood of livestock. Descriptions of a chupacabra vary: a hairless dog-like creature; a spiny reptile that hops and has red glowing eyes. As for this animal: some believed it was a fox with mange...or was it?

KEY FACTS

- Around half of all the animals that live on land are nocturnal. That means they head out and about at night, but sleep in the day.
- Nocturnal creatures often need super senses, so they can find their way around in the dark.
- Animals that live in hot places often stir at night, because it's easier to keep cool once the sun has set.

MIGHTY MUNCHERS

DINNER TIME

Feeling a bit empty inside? Are you hungry enough to eat 2,500 hamburgers? If you were a furry shrew, that's the same amount of food you'd have to find and eat every day of your life! Except it wouldn't be burgers you'd be eating, it would be nearly your own body weight in bugs, slugs and grubs. Tasty!

YUK!

Spotted hyenas are the most powerful scavengers in the world with jaws and teeth that can exert enough pressure to smash rocks, and can crush, and then digest, bone, horn, hooves and hides.

It's tough, but true: some animals need to eat all day long to stay alive. Take a swarm of desert locusts: each insect weighs only 2 g, but when you've got 16,000,000,000 of them devouring any crops in their path, that's a whopping 32 million kg of food every 24 hours.

really?

Big animals need lots of food. Most blue whales reach about 27 m long and eat 1,000 kg of krill every single day to survive. Krill are shrimp-like creatures – each one is no bigger than your little finger!

Faddy diets are common in nature. Giant anteaters, for example, are fussy eaters that devour tens of thousands of ants and termites daily. They can't eat anything else. Vampire bats live on a diet of blood.

Some animals swallow food whole, others mash it with their teeth first. Flies, however, vomit burning juices on to their lunch before sucking it up like soup. Yum!

Ripley's Believe It or Not!®

One sand tiger shark in the 'womb' kills and eats all of its brothers and sisters. A scientist was dissecting a dead female sand tiger and had his finger bitten by the one surviving baby shark!

BIG WORD ALERT

OMNIVORE – Eats anything

HERBIVORE – Nature's vegetarians

CARNIVORE – Mighty meat eater

PISCIVORE – Loves a fish dinner

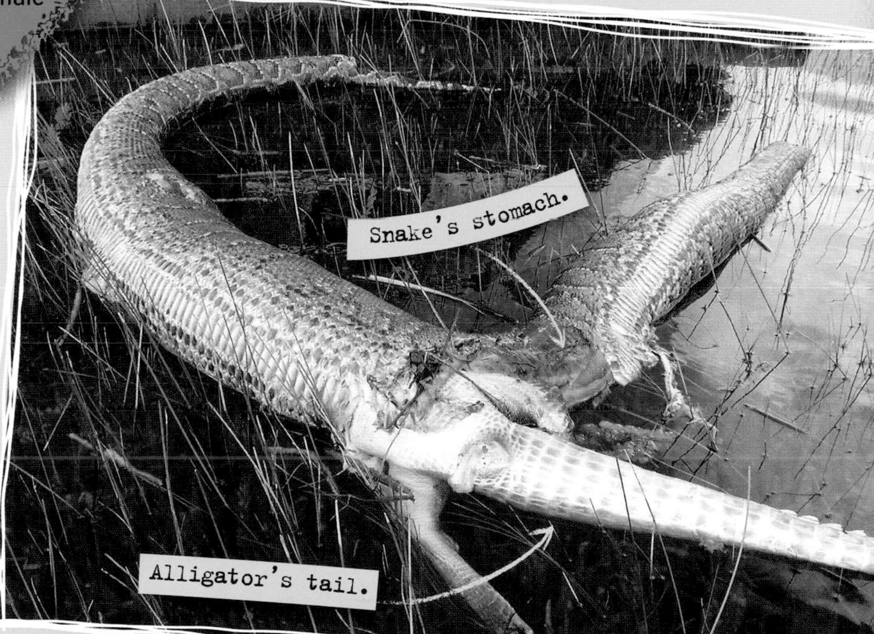

This 4-m Burmese python bit off more than it could chew when it tried to swallow whole a 1.8-m American alligator. Both animals were found dead, floating in the water. Experts think the alligator was still alive when the snake swallowed it, snout-first, and that repeated kicks from its hind legs made a hole in the snake's stomach wall.

OPEN WIDE

Pets, like people, are getting bigger and unhealthier. Lack of exercise and over-feeding are causing pooches and pussycats to pile on the weight. The world's biggest domestic cats weigh as much as a five-year-old child!

The caterpillar of the polyphemus moth is a record-breaking mighty muncher. It eats 86,000 times its own birthweight in just 56 days. That's like a baby eating 273 tonnes of food!

When Kyle, a small collie/Staffordshire bull terrier, got peckish, he swallowed a bread knife measuring 38 cm. Amazingly, Kyle survived his deadly snack attack!

Tiny dust mites make a meal from dead skin and hair. Thousands can live in just 1 g of dust, causing asthma and other allergic symptoms.

twist it!

When a Nile crocodile was killed in 1968 its stomach was found to contain the remains of a woman, two goats and half a donkey!

SPEED MERCHANTS

THE FASTEST

In the nasty world of nature there's one golden rule to staying alive: run for it! Whether you're chasing lunch, or on the menu yourself, speed is a vital survival skill. When a pronghorn antelope smells the hot breath of a coyote nearby, it springs into action. Within just a few seconds, these graceful grazers turn into powerhouses that can reach breathtaking speeds of 67 km/h for 1.6 km, making them the world's fastest long-distance runners. How do humans compare? Even the world's speediest 100-metre runner can manage only a measly 37 km/h for ten seconds.

BIG WORD ALERT

ACCELERATE
When an animal increases its speed it accelerates.

A very flexible spine helps the cheetah make enormous strides.

Grippy claws dig in to accelerate.

Whoooosh!

Cheetahs are the fastest land animals over a short distance. They can achieve top speeds thanks to their light and muscular bodies. Their spine is incredibly flexible, which means these big cats can take enormous strides. Their claws grip the ground as they run, just like the spikes on a human sprinter's running shoes.

>> WHO'S THE FASTEST? >>

Peregrine falcon 200 km/h

Sailfish 109 km/h

Cheetah 96 km/h

Pronghorn 67 km/h

Speed freaks

<< Killer crabs

Ghost crabs are crusty crustaceans with ten legs, two of which are claws. They live by the sea, and burrow into soft sand along the beach. At night, they come out to feed (this one is about to snack on a dead turtle) but the slightest disturbance will send them racing back to their tunnels. Ghost crabs run sideways very fast and can cover 2 m in just one second.

Living torpedoes >>

All penguins are clumsy waddlers on land, but watch them in the ocean and their funny-looking bodies are perfect for being propelled through water. They have torpedo-shaped bodies and wings like flippers that cut through water, reducing water resistance. Gentoo penguins of the Antarctic region are the fastest of all.

KEY FACTS

- Speed – it's brilliant for getting you out of trouble, but it takes a lot of energy, and a body that's built for rapid action.
- Being able to move fast is handy if you're a predator – as long as you can move quicker than your prey.
- If you belong to a speedy species you may find you become someone else's lunch when you can't move so fast. Most at risk are newborns and injured or elderly animals.
- Speedy creatures need to eat plenty of food to replace all the energy they burn.

twist it!

A GOOD RUN

Three-toed sloths prefer slo mo. It would take them an hour to walk 120 m, if they could be bothered!

Animals on land can usually move more quickly, and easily, than animals under water. That's because water exerts a greater force (water resistance) than air. Peregrine falcons are the fastest animals of all when they fall into a dive because gravity helps them on their way.

Boffins at the University of Washington, USA, wanted to find out which reptile can move fastest, so they set up a racetrack! As the lizards raced they passed through light beams that triggered a timing device. The spiny-tailed iguana won the race, reaching an impressive 34.9 km/h!

Despite their huge and bulky bodies, elephants can thunder along the African plains at speeds of 25 km/h.

Man 37 km/h

Iguana 34.9 km/h

Elephant 25 km/h

Sloth... 120 METRES per hour!

JOURNEYS

MIGRATION

Turtles have been swimming through the oceans for 220 million years. But it's hard to find any of them, because they are always on the move!

These shelled reptiles are a blast from the past, and have a weird creature feature: they go on mega-marathons. When a newly hatched female loggerhead turtle emerges from her egg, she is just 5 cm long. She wades into the sea and begins a lonely journey that will take up to ten years and cover nearly 15,000 km. The adult turtle then returns to the same place where she hatched, to lay her own clutch of eggs.

DIAMOND RAYS

WHEN THOUSANDS OF GOLDEN RAYS SET OFF ON THEIR ANNUAL TRIP ALONG THE EASTERN COAST OF MEXICO, THEY TURN THE SEA INTO AN AWESOME DIAMOND-PATTERNED SPECTACLE. EACH FISH MEASURES UP TO 2 M ACROSS, AND SWIMS BY FLAPPING ITS ENORMOUS TRIANGULAR-SHAPED FINS LIKE WINGS.

WILDEBEEST VACATION
This is me!
Look mum, I can fly!

get off the line!
Sadly, my best friend Bob didn't make it.
Asking the lions for directions was not the best idea.
Ahhhh, the green, green, grass of home

COAST TRIP

Every year, 120 million red crabs crawl out of their burrows on Christmas Island and head off to the coast. But this is no summertime spree... these brave crabs are marching off to mate. They have to make it past roads, railways and farms to reach the Indian Ocean.

MIGRATION

BIG WORD ALERT

A long journey is called a migration. These incredible trips usually happen at certain times of year, and often following the same routes. Animals migrate to get to more food, or to find a better place to mate. Many migrations happen from places that are cold in winter to ones that are warm in summer. It's a bit like going on holiday.

When wily wildebeest travel they make a big deal of it, migrating for seven months in search of food. They follow the rains north, and can hear thunderstorms 30 km away. They know that where there's rain there is juicy green grass – yum!

Get up close and personal with the hairy, scary side of nature. All you need is a microscope – all these creatures are magnified many times. Scary!

KEY FACTS

- Microscopes magnify things, which means that they look bigger and you are able to see much more detail.
- Scientists can use Scanning Electron Microscopes (SEMs) to get brilliant pictures of tiny things. SEMs can magnify something 250,000 times!
- Without microscopes we wouldn't know much about bacteria, viruses and other tiny living creatures.

Ant

Journey to OUTER SPACE!

No, it's not an alien, but this ant's cousins have been to space. Fifteen ant astronauts were sent into space so scientists could see how they coped with life there. The ants went crazy, digging tunnels!

Wasp
This flying insect has a sting in the tail and a tough, hairy skin called an exoskeleton.
SHARK
FISH
Sharks have rough skin and tooth-like scales, which are made from material similar to the white enamel on your teeth! The scales of most fish, however, are made of bone and are smooth and shiny.
FASCINATING FACT
Butterfly wing
When light hits the rows of tiny scales on this butterfly wing, the wing appears to turn a brilliant, shimmering blue.
Tapeworm
His nasty little hooks attach to the inside of your gut where he can absorb your juices!
Gecko
Wall-climbing geckos have lots of super-sticky hairs on their feet.

HOW CLEVER!

PROBLEM SOLVING

Imagine someone has put a wad of banknotes in a jar, and sealed it shut. If you can get the money out of the jar, it's yours. What would you do?

You'd quickly put your thinking cap on, of course! You use your brilliant brain to think up ways to tackle every problem you come across. That makes you one of the most intelligent animals on the planet, despite what your teachers might say! Maybe humans are the *most* intelligent species, but who knows? There are plenty of other clever creatures, and being a problem solver is a top survival skill in the competitive world of animals.

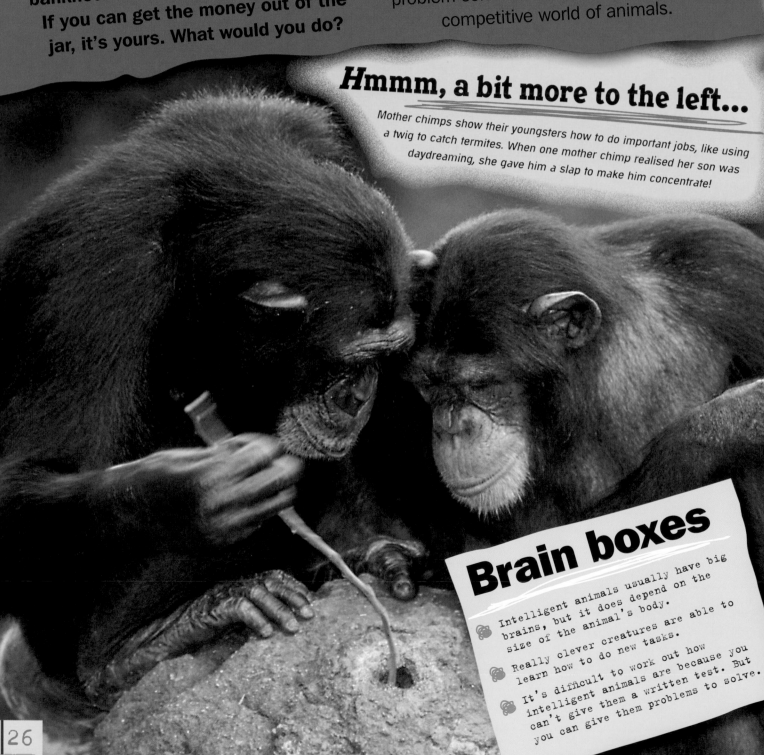

*H*mmm, a bit more to the left...

Mother chimps show their youngsters how to do important jobs, like using a twig to catch termites. When one mother chimp realised her son was daydreaming, she gave him a slap to make him concentrate!

Brain boxes

- Intelligent animals usually have big brains, but it does depend on the size of the animal's body.
- Really clever creatures are able to learn how to do new tasks.
- It's difficult to work out how intelligent animals are because you can't give them a written test. But you can give them problems to solve.

HEY, I KNOW EWE

Sheep can recognise the faces of up to 50 other members of the flock!

twist it!

Are you left- or right-handed? It's thought that octopuses also have a favourite 'arm', though, of course, they have eight to choose from. Scientists have given them toys such as bricks, balls and puzzles to see whether there is a pattern to how they pick them up.

FISH FOOD

An archerfish shoots a jet of water at its insect prey to knock it down and gobble it up. Adult archerfish usually hit their target with the first shot, and this can be up to 1.5 m away. If the prey is close to the water, however, the fish will leap out to grab it with its mouth.

Big baby!

This clever cuckoo has conned a mother wren into bringing it up in place of her own babies. Mum's the word!

BRAIN BOX

Orangutans sometimes use large leaves as umbrellas. They have even been seen to use leaves as napkins and 'toilet paper'.

Scientists have discovered that fish can tell the time, and they also have great memories, remembering stuff for up to three months.

Sea lions can remember tricks they learned ten years earlier. Trainers have taught sea lions that certain hand gestures have meaning and they can understand a whole sentence of gestures, such as 'fetch the large white ball'.

Pigs have been trained to detect explosive mines in the field of war. Their trainers say they are better than dogs, because they are not only more intelligent, but also have a better sense of smell.

HIDE AND SEEK

CAMOUFLAGE

More than 1.5 million types, or species, of animal have been found so far – but scientists are still looking for the other 28.5 million they think exist. Why can't these eagle-eyed boffins find them? Well, many creatures are either masters of disguise, or hide from view to survive!

It's a dog-eat-dog world out there and these clever defenders blend in with their surroundings to avoid becoming lunch. It's a cunning trick known as camouflage – and many animals, especially insects, are experts.

Camouflage isn't all about defense. Prowling predators, like striped tigers and spotted leopards, disappear among the dappled shadows of their forest homes. Becoming invisible is a handy trick when you're a hungry hunter!

CHAMELEON

Male panther chameleons live on the island of Madagascar and are famous for their fabulous displays of colour. Their skin can turn from red to blue or green in seconds. A sudden flush of colour impresses the ladies!

THORN BUGS

Cunningly disguised as sharp thorns, these female thorn bugs suck sap from a tree. Any keen-sighted bird that sees through the camouflage and takes a bite will quickly discover that these fancy fakers taste foul.

KEY FACTS

- Black, yellow and red are nature's code for stranger-danger. Wearing stripes or spots in these colours can keep predators at bay, even if you're a totally harmless beastie.
- It doesn't matter how cleverly camouflaged you are if you stink. That's why smelly animals aren't usually camouflaged.
- Leaf-eating insects are so well disguised that there are probably thousands of species that have never been spotted.

They may be yellow, but they're not cowards! Frightened yellow-bellied toads flip onto their backs, showing brightly coloured undersides. The yellow warns predators: 'Danger: poison!'

Ripley's Believe It or Not!®

- **Chameleons** use their colour-changing skills to scare off love rivals rather than as camouflage. They can also change colour when the temperature or light changes, or they are unwell.
- **Cuttlefish** are eight-armed sea creatures that can send waves of shimmering colour down their bodies, changing shades and patterns in seconds.
- **Stick insects** stay still and make like a twig. If their cunning disguise isn't working they drop all their legs off for maximum effect. Luckily, the legs grow back!
- **Sleepy sloths** hang upside down in trees and sleep for 18 hours out of 24. Green plants grow in the sloths' fur, providing perfect camouflage in their rainforest homes.

LEAF INSECT

Leaf insects are one of nature's most extraordinary sights – if you ever get to see one, that is! This is Phyllium giganteum, the world's largest leaf insect, and it grows to more than 13 cm long.

BARK MANTID

Don't challenge a bark mantid to a game of hide and seek – unless you're happy to lose! They're quite common creatures in Australia, but you're only likely to see one if it's moving.

FAMILY MATTERS

GETTING TOGETHER

The multi-coloured peacock is a bird that dresses to impress. He can fan out his tail, in an eye-opening display of shimmering colours and stunning patterns.

It's an ingenious tactic; a show-off with perfect plumage is more likely to attract the attention of the watching peahens. The females admire bright colours and large 'eyespots' in the feathers – and the more eyespots the better! Once a female has picked her favourite male she will mate with him, and soon starts laying eggs. The most marvellous males win over a number of females to mate with, while shabby-looking peacocks remain alone.

The Virginia opossum is the USA's only naturally occurring marsupial.
After about 100 days, the babies climb onto their mum's back to hitch a ride.
The newborns crawl straight into their mother's pouch to grow.
An opossum mum usually has 13 babies at once.

LIFE STORIES

The story of how an animal lives, from birth to death, is a life-cycle.

If an animal can find a healthy and strong mate it is more likely to have youngsters that will survive. Some animals make a big effort to impress those they fancy – to show how fit they are. This is called a courtship.

Mammals are animals that give birth to live young and feed them with milk. Usually it's the mum who provides the milk, but in the job-sharing world of Dayak fruit bats, it's a job for the dads too!

BIG WORD ALERT

REPRODUCTION

The way that an animal has young is called reproduction. Some animals can have young all by themselves, but it's more common to have two parents: a male and a female.

You said we were friends!

During mating, a female praying mantis usually gets the munchies and bites off her partner's head!

twist it!

TRUE LOVE

Sea horses are romantic, dancing for each other every day during the mating period. The female lays her eggs inside a special pouch on the male's body, and he cares for them until they hatch.

Female rhinos spray smelly urine, and males will fight each other, sometimes to the death, to mate with them.

Amphibians, such as frogs and toads, have to lay their eggs in water. Snakes and lizards are reptiles and lay their eggs on land.

A queen white ant, or termite, lays 30,000 eggs a day!

DADDY DAY-CARE

Male jawfish protect their eggs by keeping them inside their enormous mouths. Without their fatherly care, chances are that most of the eggs would be eaten before ever hatching.

NATURAL BORN KILLERS

PROGRAMMED TO KILL

Imagine you are swimming in the beautiful clear waters of Australia when you feel something long and smooth glide over your leg. It's time to start counting: if you've been stung by a box jellyfish you've got about four minutes to live.

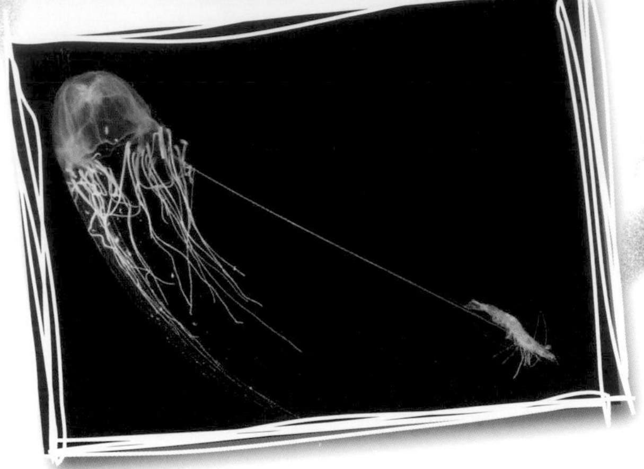

These animals, which are also known as sea wasps, are almost see-through and have long trailing tentacles that are covered in rapid-fire stingers. If you haven't got any anti-venom tucked into your swimming costume you're in hot water! The poison from those stingers will give you excruciating pain, a burning feeling and a one-way ticket to death.

Brown bears are dangerous, and do kill people!

BIG KILLERS

Brazilian wandering spider: there are more than 30 types of deadly spider, but this feisty beast has a bad temper and attacks anyone, and anything.

Black mamba: this skinny snake is a super-speedy assassin. It lurks in trees or crevices before attacking and can slither faster than you can run! Its deadly venom acts quickly, but kills slowly and painfully.

Cape buffalo: this curly-horned bruiser is the bully of the African plains. Get in its way, and one of these big beasts will run you down like a tank at full speed.

Golden poison-dart frog: don't touch this little fella, or you'll croak! Its highly poisonous skin can cause instant death.

Plasmodium: this tiny creature lives in the spit of mosquitoes and causes the deadly disease malaria. Malaria is spread when mosquitoes bite people, and is responsible for around one million human deaths every year in Africa alone.

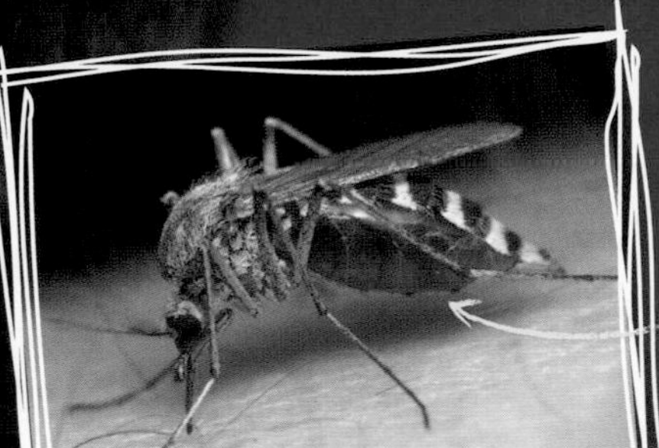

STAY SAFE

- Animals normally kill people only if they are very hungry or scared.
- Humans are in the most danger from deadly creatures when they move into those animals' natural habitats.
- The most dangerous animal on the planet is the human – that's us! Unlike most other animals, we are able to destroy entire environments, and totally wipe out other species.

The Brazilian wandering spider's venom causes unbelievable pain before death.

GRUESOME TALES

Ripley's Believe It or Not!®

One day, a Brazilian man found his six-year-old son in the jaws of an anaconda – that's an enormous South American snake. The poor boy had been nearly entirely swallowed. With no time to spare, the man picked up a wooden oar and belted the snake with it, until it coughed the boy out – he was still alive!

Scott MacInnes is un-bear-ably unlucky. He lives in Alaska and has been attacked and savaged twice by brown bears. On the plus side, he did survive both attacks, despite major wounds.

Saltwater crocodiles don't kill people out of fear, but out of hunger. When a riverboat sank in Indonesia, in 1975, more than 40 passengers were set upon and eaten by saltwater crocs.

Ants are more deadly than they look. Bulldog ants and jumper ants inject painful acid into their prey, which can sometimes kill humans. There are rumours that columns of army ants and driver ants can climb all over a human victim, stinging and then eating them!

DEAD END

More people die from bee stings each year than from shark attacks or snake bites.

Gustave is a cold-blooded killer from Burundi. This giant African crocodile is rumored to have killed around 300 people.

Hippos kill more people in Africa than any other large animal. They are herbivores, but can attack humans to protect their calves and defend their territory.

Every year, 10,000 Indians lose their lives after being bitten by cobras.

One box jellyfish has enough venom to kill 60 people.

Twist it!

KILLING MACHINE

Saltwater crocodiles are the world's largest living reptiles, and unfortunately they've got big appetites, too. They are known as Australia's most dangerous animals.

SEE ME IN ACTION ON PAGE 23!

MEET THE UGLIES!

NATURE'S TOP 5

NAKED MOLE-RAT

Good looks don't matter to these burrowing mammals. They're nasty to look at, and nasty by nature: males kidnap youngsters from other colonies and keep them as slaves, forcing them to dig new tunnels.

1st

JUDGES' COMMENTS

It's put me right off my breakfast!

JUDGES' COMMENTS

Unspeakably ugly – looks like my old maths teacher!!

2nd

GIANT SUNFISH

A giant sunfish starts life as a teeny-weeny tiddler, but increases its weight 60 million times until adulthood – when it looks like a giant floating head and is the size of a car!

THORNY DEVIL

This Australian lizard is no shrinking violet. It feeds during the day, relying on camouflage and its armory of spines to keep it safe. A thorny devil can eat 2,500 ants in one meal!

JUDGES' COMMENTS

Good effort, we particularly like the big spiky boil on the back of the neck.

MARINE IGUANA

Seaside life and salty water don't suit any lizards – except marine iguanas of the Galapagos Islands. These giant salt-covered sunbathers dive for food in the sea, or graze on seaweed in rocky pools nearby.

JUDGES' COMMENTS

Godzilla's ugly brother.

PROBOSCIS MONKEY

You've got to feel sorry for this fella. If he looks up too quickly his giant schnoz will flop back and smack him in the eyes! His pot belly and big nose are a hit with the ladies though.

JUDGES' COMMENTS

We felt the nice haircut really sets off the big flappy nose!

ANIMAL TALK COMMUNICATING

Dolphins whistle to each other, chimps bang tree trunks like drums, and a honeybee shakes its rear end in a weird wiggle dance. Animals may not be able to talk like us, but they can certainly get their messages across.

Communication is crucial. If you can talk to your friends you can warn them when a predator is nearby, tell them where they can find food, or declare your love! Stick a few bright and bold stripes or spots on your skin and you could be telling predators to stay away because you taste vile, or have vicious venom up your sleeve.

HISTLE

Dolphins call each other by whistling. Amazingly, a group of dolphins gives each dolphin a name – which has its own special whistle.

RUMBLE

IGGLE

When a honeybee has found a good patch of flowers it flies back to the hive and starts dancing. By running up and down, and wiggling its body, the bee tells the others exactly where to find the flowers!

Elephants can communicate over many kilometres using very low rumbling sounds, which travel through the ground. Other elephants pick up these signals through their feet. This way, females can let adult males know they would be welcome to visit the herd!

YOU LOOKING AT ME?

SHRIEK

When a chimpanzee shrieks, he is telling the rest of the gang that he's found food. Chimps also use their faces to show emotions such as anger and playfulness.

The bold colours on a male mandrill's face tell other members of his troop just how strong and important he is. When he bares his enormous teeth he's saying, 'Don't mess with me!'

QUICK, SCRAM!

Gunnison's prairie dogs are smarter than they look. With one call they warn their friends of an impending hawk attack – and the group looks up before scarpering. A different call signals 'coyote' and the gang make for the safety of their burrows.

UNWELCOME GUESTS

PARASITES

Welcome to the world of the meanest, most selfish of all creatures – the pathetic parasites. These lazy lowlife take their food directly from other, living animals – often hurting them.

Once settled upon, or inside, another animal (called the host), pesky parasites have got an easy life, absorbing food and making a comfortable home for themselves. The problem comes when it's time to reproduce. Getting eggs or babies from one host to another can be a challenge, especially if home is someone's gut, liver or even brain. Despite those difficulties, there are parasites aplenty out there, mostly invisible to our eyes.

The body swells with blood.
A female louse can lay up to 300 eggs.

A human body louse feeds on human blood.

Bed fellows

Dust mites join you in your bed at night, but don't complain. These little creatures munch their way through all your dead skin cells. You could count about two million of them in one bed! Bed bugs, however, are not such helpful bedfellows – they feed on human blood!

Ripley's Believe It or Not!®

That's disgusting!

The larvae of the botfly burrow into live flesh and eat it. They often attack horses but can target humans. Aaron Dallas had five botfly larvae removed from his head, where he could hear and feel them moving around.

BIG WORD ALERT

INVERTEBRATE

Many parasites are invertebrates – that is animals without backbones, such as worms and fleas.

ONE AND ALL

The candiru is a parasitic fish of the Amazon. It swims up a person's wee-hole and settles down in the bladder, where wee, or urine, is stored. The poor host will need surgery soon, or face death.

Sinus flukes, which are similar to leeches, burrow into whales' brains.

One of the most dangerous parasites in the world is a rat flea that carries bubonic plague – a disease that was common long ago, and caused around 25 million human deaths in Europe alone.

Roundworms, or nematodes, are some of the most abundant animals on the planet. There are more than 20,000 species and many of them are parasites, living in the guts of other animals.

A cat flea can jump 34 cm – that's like a human jumping to the top of a skyscraper in a single bound. Fleas can also keep jumping for days without taking a break.

Twist it!

Eaten from the inside out!

Parasitic wasps make sure their babies have plenty to eat, by laying their eggs inside, or on, a caterpillar's body! When the eggs hatch, the tiny larvae don't have to bother searching for fresh food.

The wasp lays its eggs all over the poor caterpillar.

Gross!

After eating the caterpillar's guts and juices, a wasp larva bursts out of its skin!

TERRIBLE TICKS!

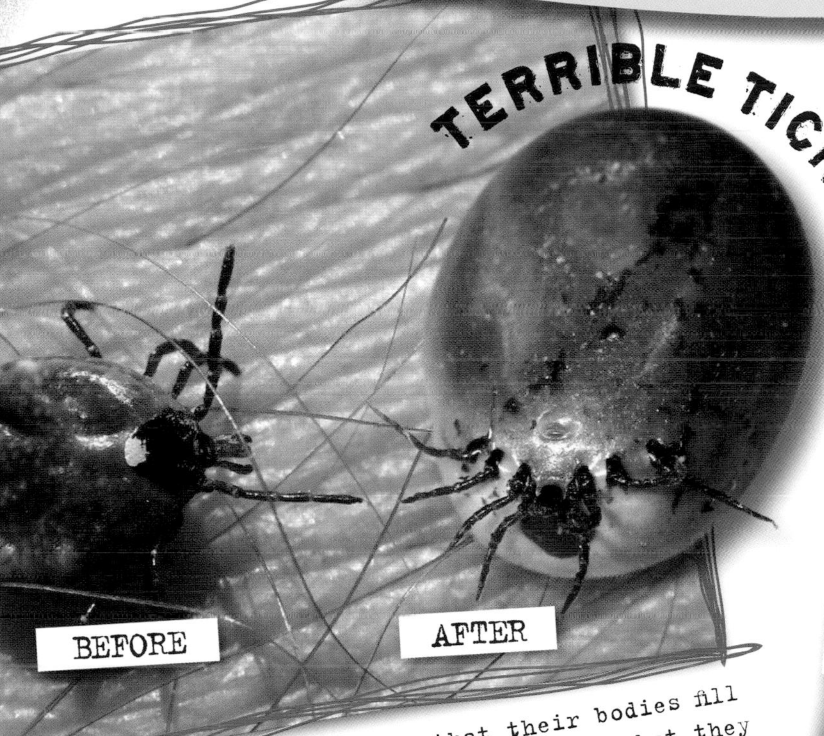

Ticks suck up so much blood that their bodies fill up like a balloon. They can't fly or jump, but they carry many diseases that are deadly to humans.

Vile!

This putrid sight is actually lice feeding on the skin of a giant grey whale.

SWARM!

SAFETY IN NUMBERS

Desert locusts are loners, until they run out of food. Then, their brains produce a special friendship chemical called seratonin.

The locusts get an urge to hang out together – often in their billions! The giant gang then guzzles its way through millions of tons of food.

When a bunch of animals all get together they are called a swarm. Swarming happens because there is safety in numbers. When birds or fish gather in their thousands they buddy-up like one mighty monster. Each animal copies what its neighbour is doing, and the giant mass of moving flesh is more than a match for most predators.

KEY FACTS

- The time of year, the season and weather conditions can all play a part in swarming behaviour.
- Swarming is a good idea if lots of your favourite food is ripe and ready to eat for just a short time. You can gobble it all up!
- Some swarms have bosses. These leaders communicate with the rest of the gang, telling them where to go and what to do.

BIRDS OF A FEATHER FLOCK TOGETHER

Never was that more true than in the case of red-billed queleas. These seed-eating African birds number more than half a billion, and one flock can hold hundreds of millions of birds. When they settle on trees to strip off the fruit, the queleas' combined weight can break branches.

IT'S A STING THING

Giant swarms of stinging jellyfish, like these thimble jellyfish, are bad news for swimmers. They are becoming more common as seas warm up.

Dr Norman Gary is an insect scientist who tours the world with his Thriller Bee Show. While he plays the 'bee flat' clarinet as many as 100,000 bees swarm all over him, even entering his mouth. Dr Gary is a bee expert who has written hundreds of scientific papers on his favourite subject, and has even trained bees to act in movies.

BEE FLAT

Locusts in a feeding frenzy can cause terrible food shortages and misery for humans as they strip crops bare.

ONE AND ALL

Millions of salmon-pink flamingos gather at Lake Nakuru in Kenya to feed on the bacteria that live in the water. The birds get their pink colour from their food.

King penguins can live together in enormous groups that number 600,000 or more.

In 1981, a swarm of 10 million krill, which are shrimp-like creatures that live in the sea, collected near Antarctica. There were so many of them, the swarm could be seen from space! It was the largest swarm of any animal that has ever been known.

Periodical cicadas are bugs that survive for 17 years underground, then all emerge at the same time to breed. Males have a drum-like part of the body, which can be used to create a loud noise, to impress the females. When millions of cicadas swarm, the noise is so loud it's painful to the human ear.

Killer bees were created when scientists got different types of honeybee to mate. Twenty-six of the new, ferocious type of bee escaped from the laboratory and 40 years later had become established in the wild, creating enormous swarms. Although each sting is no worse than an ordinary bee sting, the killer insects are much more aggressive and likely to sting in large numbers, which can prove deadly.

twist it!

BEAST BUDDIES

ANIMAL FRIENDS

BAILEY THE BUFFALO

Bailey the buffalo is not just a pet, he's treated like one of the family and is allowed to watch TV. He even eats at the kitchen table!

LION LOVER

Animal scientist Kevin Richardson loves lions, and is happy to cuddle up with them. He reckons it's easy to be mates with a lion, as long as you hang out with them while they are still cubs.

THE COBRA KING

King cobras are one of the world's most deadly snakes, but the Thai people of King Cobra Village keep them close to their hearts – literally! Most households keep a live cobra in a wooden box beneath their home, and get it out once a year for the village's three-day snake festival – when men fight the snakes and women dance with them.

HOTEL TRUNKS

Elephants are creatures of habit - and not particularly frightened of people. So they weren't bothered when a hotel was built across their route to some mango trees. Now hotel staff and guests stand back and watch while the elephants march through the hotel lobby to get to the ripe fruits!

THERE'S A HIPPO IN THE HOUSE!

How would you feel about adopting a wild animal? That's what a South African couple did when they found a newborn hippo, stranded and orphaned by floods. They named the cute little baby Jessica, and cared for her in their home while she grew, and grew and GREW! Adult hippos weigh up to 3.2 tonnes, and can reach 3.5 m long, so Jessica had to leave home, and take up with a group of wild hippos that lived nearby!

WOLF MAN

Shaun Ellis is so comfortable in the company of wolves that he knows how to interact with them. He has studied their body language, facial expressions and eating habits for years.

Going, Going, Gone

Evolution and Extinction

One quarter of all mammals and one third of all amphibians (frogs, newts and toads) are threatened with extinction, partly because humans are destroying animal habitats faster than ever before.

When people turn forests into farms or towns, and pollute natural environments, like the oceans and rivers, more and more animals die. Some species are killed for their skins and body parts, which are used in some traditional remedies. Other creatures are simply hunted for food or collected as pets.

LONESOME GEORGE

GIANT TORTOISE

GHARIAL

BIG WORD ALERT

EXTINCT
When every last animal of a species has died, it has become extinct. Dinosaurs, dodos, and carrier pigeons are all extinct.

10 of the most endangered species

Scientists believed Lonesome George was the last of his kind: a type of GIANT TORTOISE from the Galapagos Islands. However, after his death in 2012 scientists think there might be at least 17 other tortoises on the Islands that are similar to him.

In the last ten years, the number of GHARIALS has halved, plummeting to just 200 or so. These fish-eating crocodiles live in India and Nepal. They were once hunted for their skins, but are now critically endangered because their river habitats are being destroyed by humans.

All rhinos are in danger of extinction, but there are only about 50 JAVAN RHINOS left. Once there were thousands of these grass-grazers in Southeast Asia, but nearly all of them have been killed for their horns.

There are just 90 KAKAPOS left, and they are looked after by a group of scientists. Kakapos are the world's biggest parrots, and longest-living birds. They can't fly, which is why they nearly died out when people brought predators to their New Zealand home.

Gorillas are peaceful, plant-eating apes that live in African forests. All gorillas are endangered, but CROSS RIVER GORILLAS are especially rare because farms and roads are destroying their habitats. There are about 250 to 300 left.

The IBERIAN LYNX will probably be the first big cat to become extinct for at least 2,000 years. There are no more than 38 adult females left in the wild, and only around 110 wild Iberian lynxes altogether.

In 2004, a new species, the RAMESHWARAM PARACHUTE SPIDER, was discovered, but there are only a few hundred of these eight-legged creatures, and they live in a handful of plantations on an island near India.

SUMATRAN TIGERS are poisoned, hunted, trapped, and snared, and now there are less than 400 left in the wild. Also, the forests where they live are being turned into farms.

All over the world, the GIANT PANDA is used as a symbol for saving animals. There are about 1,500 pandas in the wild and they mostly eat bamboo. A panda baby is 1/900th the size of its mother, making it one of the smallest mammal babies.

A SOUTHERN BLUEFIN TUNA can live for 40 years and reach over 2 m in length, if it doesn't get caught and eaten first. So many have been killed for food that they are now in serious danger of becoming extinct.

ACKNOWLEDGEMENTS

COVER (l) Matt Rourke/AP/PA Photos, (r) © Gabriela Staebler/zefa/Corbis; **2** (c) © Olga Khoroshunova – fotolia.com, (b) Courtesy of Janice Wolf; **3** (t) © Eric Isselée – istockphoto.com, (r) Linda Cowen/Wolfpack Management; **4** © Gabriela Staebler/zefa/Corbis; **5** (t/r) Matt Rourke/AP/PA Photos; **6** © Tobias Bernhard/zefa/Corbis; **7** (t) NHPA/Photoshot, (c) Used by permission of Rodney Fox, (b/r) © Oceans Image/Photoshot, (b) © Jeffrey L. Rotman/Corbis; **8** (sp) Neil Bromhall/www.photolibrary.com; **9** (t/l, b/l) Peter Scoones/ Science Photo Library, (r) © Olga Khoroshunova – fotolia.com, (b/r) Gregory Ochocki/Science Photo Library; **10** © NHPA/Photoshot; **11** (c) © ktsdesign – fotolia.com, (t) Adrian Bicker/Science Photo Library, (r) © NHPA/Photoshot; **12** © Shusuke Sezai/epa/Corbis, (r) Oceans-Image/Photoshot; **13** (t/l) Karl H. Switak/Science Photo Library, (t/r) Tom McHugh/Science Photo Library, (b) © Larry Williams/Corbis; **14** (t) © N & B – fotolia.com, (b) © NHPA/Photoshot; **14–15** (l) Courtesy of Janice Wolf; **15** (c) Ministry of Fisheries via Getty Images, (b, r) © NHPA/Photoshot; **16–17** Jim Zipp/Science Photo Library; **17** (r) © NHPA/Photoshot, (t) Rexford Lord/ Science Photo Library, (b) Eric Gay/AP/PA Photos; **18** (b) © Eric Isselée – istockphoto.com, (sp) © Remi Benali/Corbis; **19** (l) © filip put – istockphoto.com, (r) Reuters/Ho New; **20** © DLILLC/Corbis; **20–21** (b) © N & B – fotolia.com; **21** (t) © Anthony Bannister/Gallo Images/Corbis, (b) Andy Rouse/Rex Features; **22** (b/l) © John Anderson – fotolia.com, (sp) David B Fleetham/www.photolibrary.com, (t, t/r) © NHPA/Photoshot; **23** (t/c/l, t/c/r, t/r) © NHPA/Photoshot, (b) © Roger Garwood & Trish Ainslie/Corbis; **24** Eye Of Science/ Science Photo Library; **25** (bgd) George Bernard/Science Photo Library (t/l) Mark Fairhurst/UPPA/Photoshot, (b/l) Cheryl Power/Science Photo Library, (t/c) Eye Of Science/Science Photo Library, (t/r) Alan Sirulnikoff/Science Photo Library, (b/r) Pasieka/Science Photo Library; **26** Manoj Shah/Getty Images; **27** (t/l) © Paul Stock – fotolia.com, (t/c, t/r) Satoshi Kuribayashi/www.photolibrary.com, (c) Bournemouth News/Rex Features, (b/r) Maurice Tibbles/www.photolibrary.com; **28** (l) © NHPA/Photoshot, (r) © sunset man – fotolia.com; **29** (l, r, t, t/c) © NHPA/Photoshot; **30** (t) © Eky Chan – fotolia.com, (r) Frank Lukasseck/Getty Images; **31** (t, b) © NHPA/ Photoshot; **32** (l) James Balog/Imagebank/Getty Images, (b) © Yaroslav Gnatuk – fotolia.com, (t) David Doubilet/National Geographic/ Getty Images; **33** (t) © Holger Mette – fotolia.com, (b) © NHPA/Photoshot; **34** (b) Mark Newman/FLPA, (t) Hiroya Minakuchi/Minden Pictures/FLPA; **35** (l) © NHPA/Photoshot, (b/r) Michael K. Nichols/National Geographic/Getty Images, (t) John Beatty/Science Photo Library; **36** (l) © Kitch Bain – fotolia.com, (c) © Karen Roach – fotolia.com, (b/l) © The physicist – fotolia.com; **37** (t/l) Michael Nichols/National Geographic/Getty Images, (c) Gail Shumway/Taxi/Getty Images, (r) © RebeccaAnne – fotolia.com; **38** (l) © NHPA/ Photoshot, (r) Darlyne A. Murawski/National Geographic/Getty Images; **39** (l) © Dwight Davis – fotolia.com, (b/l) Ken Lucas/Getty Images, (c) © Heinz Waldukat – fotolia.com, (t) © Henrik Larsson – fotolia.com, (c/r) © Stephen Bonk – fotolia.com, (b/r) Robert F. Sisson/National Geographic/Getty Images; **40** (l) Oceans-Image/Photoshot, (r) Bildagentur RM/www.photolibrary.com; **40–41** (bgd) David Shale/www.photolibrary.com; **41** (t/r) Sipa Press/Rex Features; **42** (l) Carlo Allegri/Getty Images, (b) Photograph by Falise Thierry/Gamma/Eyedea/Camera Press London, (c) Zoom/Barcroft Media; **43** (t/l, r) Zoom/Barcroft Media, (b) Linda Cowen/Wolfpack Management; **44** (l) © siloto – fotolia.com, (c) Reuters/Guillermo Granja; **45** (t/l) Tony Camacho/Science Photo Library, (l) Sue Flood/ Getty Images, (b/r) © Timothy Lubcke – fotolia.com, (c/r) © ImagineImages – fotolia.com, (t/r) © dzain – fotolia.com

Key: t = top, b = bottom, c = centre, l = left, r = right, sp = single page, dp = double page, bgd = background

Every attempt has been made to acknowledge correctly and contact copyright holders and we apologise in advance for any unintentional errors or omissions, which will be corrected in future editions.

Ripley's
SPORTS
Believe It or Not!®

Ripley
PUBLISHING

a Jim Pattison Company

TWISTS

Written by Geoff Tibballs

Consultant Stewart Newport

Publisher Anne Marshall

Editorial Director Rebecca Miles
Project Editor Lisa Regan
Editor Rosie Alexander
Assistant Editor Charlotte Howell
Picture Researchers James Proud, Charlotte Howell
Proofreader Judy Barratt
Indexer Hilary Bird

Art Director Sam South
Senior Designer Michelle Cannatella
Design Rocket Design (East Anglia) Ltd
Reprographics Juice Creative Ltd

www.ripleys.com/books

First published in Great Britain in 2010 by Random House Books, Random House, 20 Vauxhall Bridge Road, London SW1V 2SA
www.rbooks.co.uk

Addresses for companies within The Random House Group Limited can be found at: www.randomhouse.co.uk/offices.htm

The Random House Group Limited Reg. No. 954009

ISBN 978-1-60991-235-2 (USA) | ISBN 978-0-09954-4-425 (UK)

10 9 8 7 6 5 4 3 2 1

The Random House Group Limited supports The Forest Stewardship Council (FSC), the leading international forest certification organisation. All our titles that are printed on Greenpeace approved FSC certified paper carry the FSC logo. Our paper procurement policy can be found at www.rbooks.co.uk/environment

A CIP catalogue record for this book is available from the British Library

Printed in China January 2018
2nd Printing

WARNING
Some of the activities in this book are undertaken by experts and should not be attempted without adequate training and supervision.

PUBLISHER'S NOTE
While every effort has been made to verify the accuracy of the entries in this book, the Publishers cannot be held responsible for any errors contained herein. They would be glad to receive any information from readers.

CONTENTS

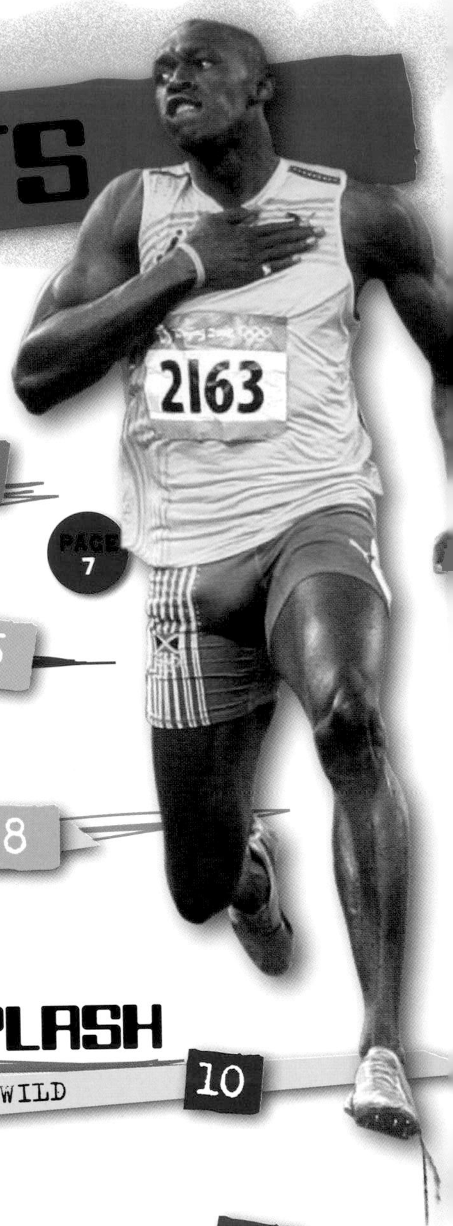

PAGE 7

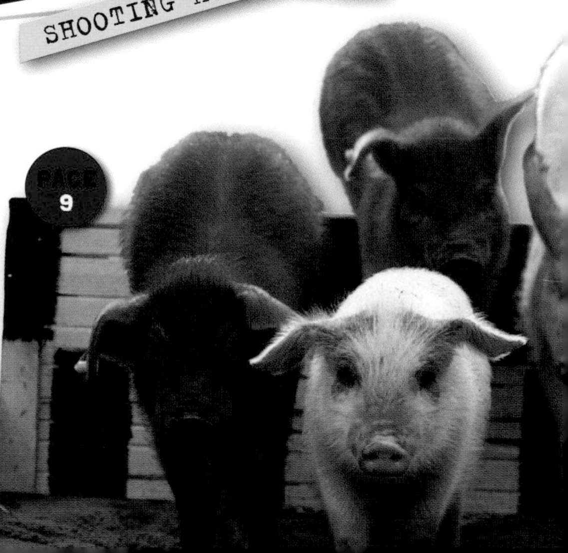

PAGE 9

TWISTS

PAGE 13

WORLD OF SPORT

PLAY TIME!

WHAT'S INSIDE YOUR BOOK?

So you think you know about sport? Well, prepare to learn even more! Top sports attract millions of spectators and billions of pounds, and bring together countries across the globe to play, watch and shout about their favourite games and competitions.

Sport isn't just about big money, clubs and players. Some sports are played and watched by only a few people, but are just as much fun. So, if you're not into ball games, this book will introduce you to tug-of-war, BMX racing, and even worm charming. There's something here for everyone...

Do the twist

Take a look...each page is packed with sporting superstars, amazing achievements, and of course, crazy pastimes that don't get a mention in other sports books. That's what a Twists book is all about!

Don't forget to look out for the 'twist it!' column on some pages. Twist the book to read snappy sports stories from all around the world; if you're feeling super sporty then read it standing on your head!

TWISTS

twist it!

...EE KICKS

Some football matches are decided by penalty shoot-outs, where eight kicks are often enough to get a result. At the end of a 2005 Namibian Cup tie in Africa, the penalty contest went on for an incredible 48 kicks and lasted nearly an hour!

Important football matches often attract crowds of over 70,000 people, but the 1950 World Cup final between Brazil and Uruguay was watched by nearly 200,000 spectators.

An annual football match called the Calcio takes place in Florence, Italy, between two teams of 27 players dressed in 16th-century costume. It is a rough game, and players are allowed to elbow, kick, and even head butt each other!

Welsh footie fan Steve Thatcher named his son after all the players in his favourite team, Cardiff City. It means young Sam has 12 middle names!

SPEEDY SPORTS

Sport isn't all about speed – but speed certainly makes sport exciting! See what's fastest in the world of sport...

Motorbike 580 km/h

Formula 1 Car 414 km/h

Learn fab fast facts to go with the cool pictures.
Ripley explains some of the science and know-how behind your favourite sports.
Say what? Oh, so that's what that word means...
SURF'S UP
RIDING THE WAVES
It's not only waves that are a danger to surfers. Each year as many as 80 surfers are attacked by sharks.
Ripley explains...
You catch a wave by pushing the water toward the back of the surfboard with your hands, moving you forward. As you ride on the wave the water rises beneath you and pushes you forward faster and faster. All the time gravity is trying to push you down, while buoyancy is pushing you up.
RIDING HIGH
Kite surfers use wind power to help them speed across the water and soar up to 162 feet in the air. They stand on a board and hold on to a large controllable kite. The aim is to do tricks such as jumps, spins, and even somersaults, and to see how high and long they can jump off waves.
SAY WHAT?
CATCH A WAVE
This is when you launch yourself into the path of a suitable wave.
surfers rode the same wave at the same time off the coast of Brazil in 2007.
Have you ever wished you could ride a wave on a surfboard? Some waves are huge—up to 70 feet high. That's more than four times the height of an adult giraffe! That just makes it even more
rfer. You can surf a
or lying down—and some
on the same wave for half an
just do what you enjoy.
PLAIN SAILING
Windsurfers attach a sail to their surfboards. When the wind blows into the sail from behind, it makes the board go faster: sometimes up to 60 mph! Windsurfers can perform amazing stunts, jumps, and spins.
Kite surfers can go great distances when the wind is behind them. In 2006, UK kite surfer Kirsty Jones traveled 140 miles from Lanzarote in the Canary Islands to Morocco.
Donald "D.J." Dettloff has created a colorful fence from more than 700 surfboards near his home in Hawaii.
Ripley's Believe It or Not!
Lauren Miller's dog Auggie liked to do tricks with tennis balls. He could pick up five in his mouth at the same time!
Twists are all about 'Believe It or Not!' – amazing facts, feats, and things that will make you go 'Wow!'
Look for the Ripley 'R' to find out even more than you knew before!
Motorbike Wheelie 225 km/h
Ostrich 72 km/h
Camel 64 km/h
Racehorse 64 km/h
Human (sprinter) 37 km/h

SPEED KINGS

FAST AND FURIOUS

The cars reach speeds of nearly 400 km/h on the straights.

Imagine flying a plane at over 3,000 km/h. Or riding a motorbike at 600 km/h. Or driving a speedboat at 500 km/h. Wow! Ever since vehicles were invented, people have wanted them to go as fast as possible. We love speed. That's why we dream of one day racing in NASCAR or driving in a Formula-1 race. The cars there can go from 0 to 160 km/h and back to 0 in under five seconds.

Three drivers (AJ Foyt, Al Unser and Rick Mears) have won four Indy 500s.

Jamaica's Usain Bolt doesn't need an engine to go fast. He can run at amazing speeds. In 100-metre races he averages just under 40 km/h but for a few strides he actually reaches 50 km/h. That's the speed limit for a car in most towns!

The Indy 500 is probably the most famous motor race in the world. About 400,000 people turn up to watch, and millions more see it on TV in more than 160 countries. The 500-mile (805-kilometre) race takes place every year at the oval-shaped Indianapolis Motor Speedway in Indiana.

CRAZY CORNERING

As they go round corners, motorbike racers lean their machines at almost impossible angles of 50 degrees without falling off. The riders have their knee just a few centimetres off the ground to work out how much they can lean before their bike loses balance and topples over.

HIGH SPEED FURNACE

Formula-1 drivers need to be amazingly fit. The temperature in the car reaches 50°C and drivers get very hot beneath their fire-proof overalls. They lose an average of 2 kg in body weight during each race. When braking and cornering, the pull on the driver's neck is so great that it feels as if their head wants to roll off their shoulders!

When the Indy 500 was first raced in 1911, the track was made up of 3.2 million bricks, earning it the nickname 'The Brickyard'.

MOTORHEADS

The first car race was run in France from Paris to Rouen in 1894. The average winning speed was just over 17 km/h!

English farmer George Shields drives a garden shed that can do 90 km/h. He once drove it all the way from one end of Britain to the other. That's nearly 1,300 km.

CG Mouch of Los Angeles fitted the front end of a 750cc Honda motorcycle to the rear end of his lawn mower to create a 'chopper mower' that could mow the lawn at up to 15 km/h.

The 1972 Bandama Car Rally in West Africa was so tough that none of the 52 starters finished the race.

In 2005, Australian Matt Mingay did a motorbike wheelie at a speed of 225 km/h.

Twist it!

FASCINATING FACT

LIGHTNING BOLT

Jamaican runner Usain Bolt won the 100 metres at the 2008 Beijing Olympics in an incredible 9.69 seconds – despite slowing down to celebrate and having his left shoelace undone!

ON FOUR LEGS

ANIMAL ATHLETES

Racehorses are bred for speed. These thoroughbreds, as they are known, can gallop at up to 65 km/h. Horse-racing dates back nearly 3,000 years to the ancient Greeks who added the spectacular sport of chariot racing to the Olympics in 680BC. Horse-racing is so popular today that in Switzerland there is even a horse race on ice, run on a frozen lake.

There are also races for animals that you might not think are built for speed, such as camels, armadillos, pigs and sheep. Whatever the animal, there is probably a race for it somewhere in the world. We don't only race animals. We wrestle them, we ski behind them, and in parts of Asia polo is played on elephants instead of horses.

HORSE POWER

In the Palio, which takes place twice each summer, horses race at breakneck speed three times around the main square in Siena, Italy – and the riders don't even have saddles to sit on. No wonder so many fall off!

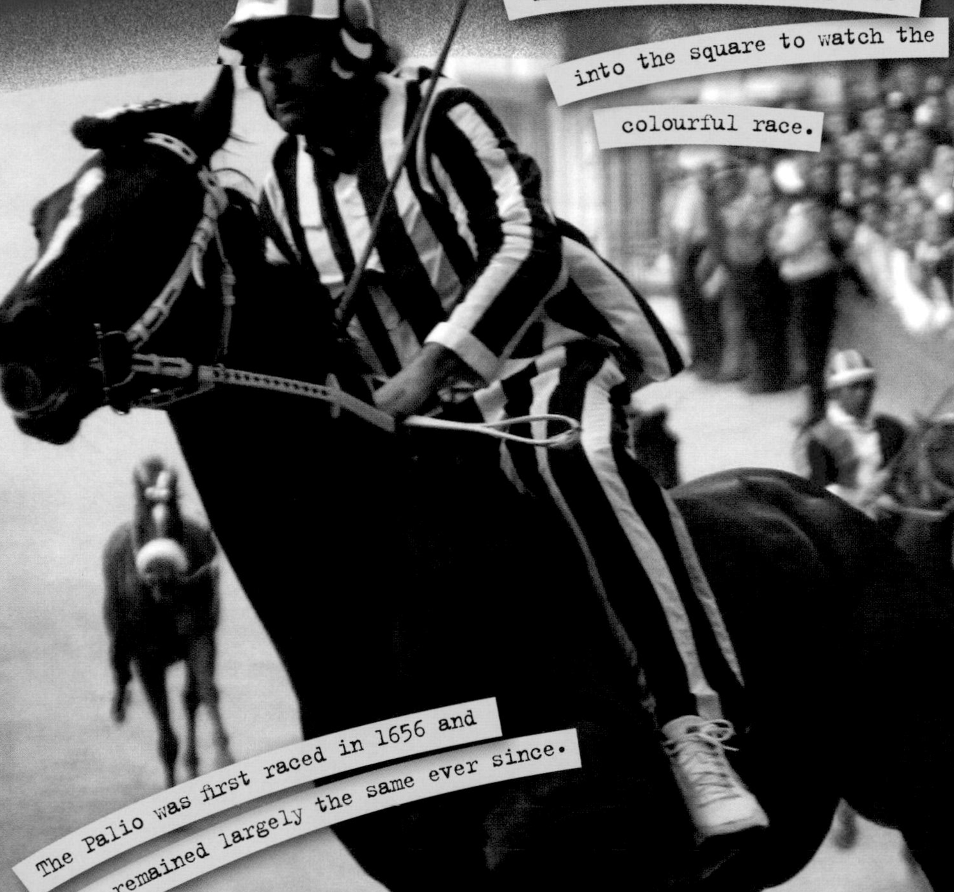

Around 60,000 people squeeze into the square to watch the colourful race.

The Palio was first raced in 1656 and has remained largely the same ever since.

A bank of mattresses is positioned to protect the horses and riders from the walls of a café at a turn known as the 'corner of death'.

Jockeys are usually small, but they also have to be strong, because racehorses can weigh up to 700 kg.

SAY WHAT?

DERBY

A derby is a type of race. The original derby was a horse race run in Epsom, England, and was named after the Earl of Derby who founded the event in 1780.

JUMBO POLO

Polo is usually played on horseback but in countries such as Nepal, India and Thailand they play it with elephants. Two people ride each elephant – one to steer the elephant, the other to hit the ball. The mallet used to strike the ball is made of bamboo and can be up to 3.7 m long, depending on the height of the elephant. If a player falls off, it's a long way down!

RACING AROUND

The Frog Derby takes place in Rayne, Louisiana, where kids dress frogs in miniature jockey uniforms! By tapping the ground behind the frogs, they encourage them to hop along the course in leaps and bounds.

At an annual round-up in Stephensville, Wisconsin, participants try to wrestle slippery, squirming pigs to the ground in thick mud.

You may have heard of greyhound racing. Well, in Oklahoma City, they have a dog race with a difference – it's for little dachshunds and it's called the Dachshund Dash.

Back in 1937, a man in England tried to stage cheetah racing as an alternative to greyhounds. The cheetahs showed no interest in running, however, and often just stood still.

twist it!

<< PIG OLYMPICS >>

It's not only humans that have their own Olympics. There is also an Olympic Games for pigs! Miniature pigs run over hurdles, compete in swimming races and play a version of football called pigball, where they chase a ball covered in fish oil with their snouts.

A racehorse named Camarero won 56 races in a row in Puerto Rico between 1953 and 1955.

DESERT DERBY

In the Middle East and Australia, camel racing is a serious sport with big prize money. Top racing camels sell for up to £30,000. Camels can run as fast as 65 km/h in short sprints and can maintain a speed of 30 km/h for an hour. Jockeys need nerves of steel because the camels can sometimes suddenly stop mid-way through a race without warning!

MAKING A SPLASH

WET AND WILD

Water isn't a person's natural element: our lungs need air, we don't have webbed feet or hands, and we aren't designed for speed in the way that a shark or a seal is. That hasn't stopped us from taking the plunge, though.

Free divers plummet to depths of more than 180 m using only their finely tuned athlete's bodies. Marathon swimmers race over distances of up to 25 km in lakes, rivers or the ocean. Competition divers perform graceful gymnastics before hitting the water at around 55 km/h. They're all spectacular.

PROFESSOR SPLASH

From heights of up to 25 m, Darren Taylor, of Denver, Colorado, dives into tiny, shallow pools, some containing just 30 cm of water! He says the secret is to make a real splash when he lands – that way his fall is cushioned. The impact still leaves his body so bruised that it hurts him to laugh for weeks afterwards.

Taking a dive

Competitive divers perform twists or somersaults in mid-air after jumping from a platform up to 10 m above the pool. They have just a split second to get everything right. They must enter the water with their body in a vertical position and their arms extended forward – and without making much of a splash.

SAY WHAT?

FREESTYLE

In a freestyle race swimmers can use any style – front crawl, butterfly, backstroke or breaststroke. Most use the front crawl, because it's the fastest.

DIVE IN!

Once a diver has left the board, his or her body must be held in one of four positions.

STRAIGHT:
no bend in either
the hips or knees
PIKE:
knees straight and
the body bent at
the waist
TUCK:
the body is curled up
in a tight ball
FREE:
a combination
of straight,
pike or tuck
with the legs
together

HIGH DIVE

Tom Daley became the world 10-metre platform diving champion in 2009 at the age of just 15. That made him the youngest diver ever to win a title in men's platform diving. He started diving at age seven and was Britain's youngest competitor at the 2008 Olympic Games.

Absolutely nuts

Twiggy the grey squirrel is nuts about water-skiing. Her Florida trainer, Lou Ann Best, taught her to be towed around an inflatable paddling pool by a remote-controlled model boat at speeds of up to 10 km/h. Twiggy has demonstrated her skills at boat shows across America.

SLOW STARTER

It's never too late to start a sport. As a child, Australia's Ian Thorpe was allergic to chlorine (the chemical used in swimming pools), so he didn't swim in his first race until he was seven. Even then the allergy forced him to swim awkwardly with his head out of water.

His nickname was 'the Thorpedo' because of his speed in the water.

By age 14 Ian Thorpe was representing his country.

TRIALS OF STRENGTH

FEEL THE FORCE

Some people are so strong they can bend iron bars with their head or pull trains with their teeth. Others can lift cars off the ground, tear thick books with their bare hands or pull trucks with their hair. For centuries, people have demonstrated their strength by taking part in competitive combat sports such as boxing, sumo wrestling, judo, taekwondo and karate.

If you don't want to be a real-life muscle man, you could take part in some wackier trials of strength. How about having a go at fish tossing, welly hurling or mobile-phone throwing?

It took Rev. Fast 1 minute 16 seconds to pull the plane 8.8 m with a rope.

The Globemaster weighed a huge 187 tonnes.

The previous record for pulling a plane was 186 tonnes and had stood for 12 years.

He trains for his strong-man challenges by pulling his pickup truck up hills.

PLANE CRAZY

In 2009, Reverend Kevin Fast, of Cobourg, Ontario, Canada, managed to pull an enormous military CC-17 Globemaster airplane across the tarmac at Canadian Forces Base Trenton.

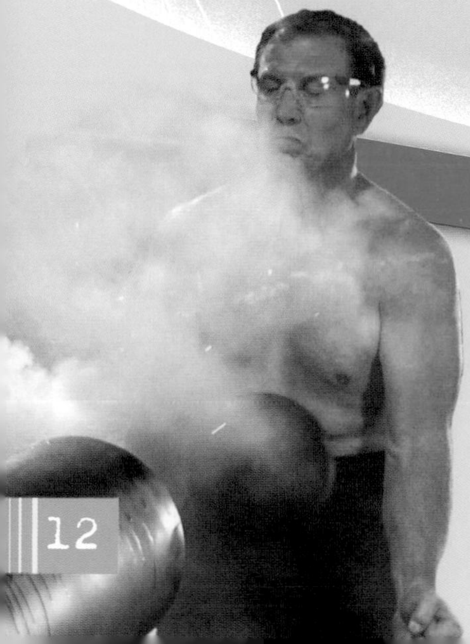

Strong stomach

Fitness instructor Ken Richmond has such a sturdy stomach he lets people fire cannon balls at it! He can also survive a cannon ball being dropped on his head and withstand the force of a massive 18,000-kg wrecking ball slamming through a concrete wall and into his amazing abdomen.

FAST MOVER

Ripley's Believe It or Not!®

American martial arts movie star **Bruce Lee** moved his arms and feet with lightning speed. He was so fast he could snatch a coin off a person's open palm before they could close it, and leave a different coin behind.

- To toughen the skin on his fists, he used to regularly thrust his hands into **buckets of rocks** and gravel up to 500 times.
- He could **break wooden boards** that were 15 cm thick with a single punch.
- He could perform **one-handed push-ups** using only his thumb and index finger.
- He could **thrust his fingers** through unopened fizzy drink cans.
- He practised his **high kicks** by jumping up and tapping people on the ear with his foot.

Ripley explains...

In the Japanese martial art of karate, you can punch or kick but the most famous technique is the knifehand or karate chop. Some people can smash over 30 slabs of concrete with just a single karate chop.

EARS!

Zafar Gill, from Pakistan, can lift 55 kg with one of his ears.

EYES!

Dong Changsheng, from China, once pulled a 1,700-kg minibus carrying two adult passengers... with his eyelids!

TOUGH TEETH

Luxembourg's Georges Christen can do just about anything with his teeth. He has towed a 95-tonne ship with them, and bent 368 nails with them in an hour. One stunt saw him stop three 110-horsepower Cessna Sport airplanes from taking off at full power – one with his teeth and two with his arms.

STRONG STUFF

twist it!

Ed Byrne from England used his bare hands to karate chop through 55 concrete blocks in less than five seconds...and it didn't even hurt!

The first Mobile Phone Throwing World Championships were held in Finland in 2000. One of the sport's top throwers is the UK's Chris Hughff who can hurl a phone 95.7 m. That's a real long distance call!

In Michigan in 1997, Samoan heavyweight boxer Jimmy Thunder knocked out Crawford Grimsley after just 1.7 seconds of their fight.

In New Zealand, there is an annual contest to see who can throw a gumboot (wellington boot) the farthest. At the end of the competition, the winner is presented with a Golden Gumboot!

ON COURT

More than 46 million Americans play volleyball and there are around 800 million players worldwide. In fact, football is the only sport that more people play across the globe. Like basketball, tennis, squash and badminton, volleyball is played on a court. All of these sports require you to be able to run about, have quick reactions, and be very fit. Tennis players can cover 8 km during a match!

Tennis players can also earn a lot of money. The winners of the singles titles at Wimbledon in London (the world's oldest tennis tournament) receive £1 million. Basketball players can earn even more. Some get paid over £13 million a year!

Michael was so feared that opponents would put two or even three men to cover him every time he touched the ball.

GROWTH SPURT

At high school, **Michael Jordan** was considered too short to play basketball. Then he grew 10 cm one summer, and began the path to superstardom that saw a 1996 sports magazine name him the greatest athlete of the past 50 years. He finished with an incredible career total of 32,292 points, the third highest in league history.

High court

Top tennis players Roger Federer and Andre Agassi needed a head for heights when they played on this court. It was marked out on the helipad of a Dubai hotel 210 m above ground. If a ball sailed out, nobody went to fetch it!

PLAYING BALL

America's Andy Roddick can serve a tennis ball at 250 km/h – that's as fast as an express train.

A game of volleyball that took place in Amstelveen, the Netherlands, in 2008 lasted 60 hours. That's 2½ days!

Basketball-crazy Mike Campbell made 1,338 free throws in an hour (faster than one throw every three seconds) and over 90 per cent of his shots were successful.

Twin brothers Ettore and Angelo Rossetti played a continuous tennis rally that lasted nearly 15 hours, with a total of 25,944 shots.

Joseph Odhiambo dribbled a basketball through the streets of Houston, Texas, for 26 hours in 2006.

You have to be really fit to play squash. A squash player can burn up to 1,000 calories during a one-hour game. That's almost twice as many than if you were doing push-ups non-stop for the same amount of time. Phew!

Ripley's Believe It or Not!®

Lauren Miller's dog Auggie liked to do tricks with tennis balls. He could pick up five in his mouth at the same time!

twist it!

IN A SPIN

Using his hands, feet, knees, and even his mouth, American Bruce Crevier can spin up to 21 basketballs at the same time. He has also spun a single basketball on his fingers for more than 22 hours – that's nearly a whole day!

SISTER ACT

Venus Williams and her younger sister Serena have dominated women's tennis in the 21st century. Between them they have won over 30 Grand Slam titles.

Venus was docked a point at the 1999 Australian Open tennis tournament when a string of beads fell from her dreadlocked hair and scattered around the court.

At the 2007 US Open, Venus served at 208 km/h – the second-fastest woman's serve ever recorded.

SMASHING!

Badminton is played by hitting a shuttlecock made either from goose feathers or plastic. Shuttlecocks can be hit very hard and very fast. A smash by China's Fu Haifeng was recorded at 370 km/h.

SNOW AND ICE

CHILLS AND THRILLS

If you've ever sped down a hill on a sledge, you'll know how exciting snow can be. Wherever there is suitable snow and ice, sportspeople can be found competing on it. Speed skiers can hit a breathtaking 240 km/h, ski jumpers leap 180 m while sailing through the air at 105 km/h, and teams on bobsleighs hurtle around a steep course of solid ice at 145 km/h. They all know that the slightest mistake could result in a bad injury.

It's not all about speed. There's the gracefulness of ice skating, the elegance of snowboarding, and the rough and tumble of hockey. So if you thought the best thing about snow was building a snowman, you might have to think again.

SNOW TRICKS

Snowboarding is like surfing on snow. Boarders perform lots of tricks. In a U-shaped trench called a halfpipe, they do acrobatic spins and flips and even a trick where they grab their board in mid-air.

DOWNHILL RACERS

Slalom skiers speed down a steep mountain, weaving their way between a series of poles called gates. Nets are placed alongside the course at the most dangerous places but the skiers still have spectacular falls.

LOONY LUGE

Luge is one of the most dangerous sports. Competitors lie down on a fibreglass sledge and hurtle feet-first down an icy track at speeds up to 145 km/h. They wear little protection, their bodies are just centimetres from the ice, and the luge has no brakes!

ICE BOWLING

The coolest game of bowling takes place in Japan. Players roll a bowling ball made of ice along a frozen 5-m lane towards 17-cm-high ice pins.

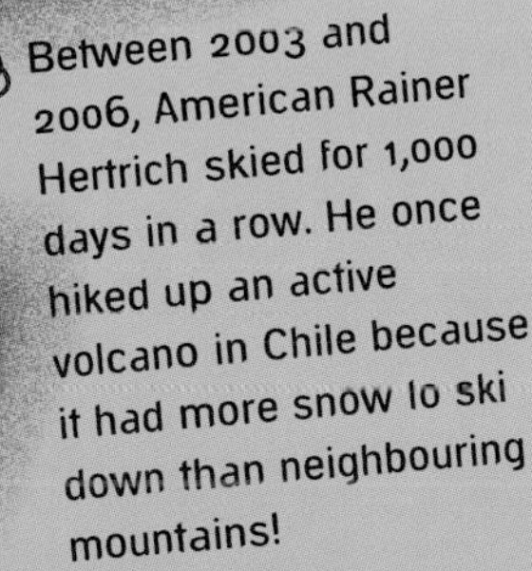

Between 2003 and 2006, American Rainer Hertrich skied for 1,000 days in a row. He once hiked up an active volcano in Chile because it had more snow to ski down than neighbouring mountains!

WAYNE'S WORLD

Canadian Wayne Gretzky is the only National Hockey League player to total over 200 points (goals and assists) in a season, and he did it four times. He scored over 100 points in 14 consecutive seasons and was so popular that he used to receive 1,000 fan letters every month.

At the Montreal Ice Cup, riders race bicycles over a course of sheet ice. They get a grip on the slippery surface by putting up to 400 screws into the rubber tyres.

OFF THE WALL

UNUSUAL SPORTS

The World Games is held every four years and features several unusual sports that aren't in the Olympics. These include canoe polo, dragon boat racing, climbing, tug of war, roller hockey, and even dancing. If you prefer your sports a little less energetic, have you ever thought about taking up worm charming or cherry pit spitting? There are many weird and wonderful sports that you can try wherever you live.

PULLING POWER

In tug of war, two teams of eight grip tightly on to either end of a 35-m-long rope and use their combined strength to pull their opponents over a line. Tug of war was practised as early as 500BC by Greek athletes and was an Olympic sport until 1920.

MIGHTY MUSCLES

A Japanese bodybuilder flexes her muscles at the 2009 World Games. Nearly 3,000 athletes from 84 countries took part in the Games.

PIE IN THE SKY

A Canadian and two Australians battle to catch the Frisbee during the flying disc competition at the World Games. The sport can be traced back to the Frisbie Pie Company in Connecticut, where workers played a game in which they threw empty pie tins to one another!

SPORTS CRAZY

At the World Flounder Tramping Championships in Scotland, people catch fish using their bare feet. They wade into the river and when they feel the flat fish wriggling between their toes, they pick it up. The person who catches the most fish is declared the winner.

If you've got something to shout about, you can do it at the National Hollerin' Contest, held each year at Spivey's Corner, North Carolina. Contestants yell as loud as they can for four minutes – you might want to take ear plugs!

At the Sheep Counting Championships of Australia, several hundred sheep are encouraged to run across a field while competitors try to count them.

twist it!

SPIT THE PIT

Like many established sports, cherry pit spitting started as a casual pastime and has developed into a popular event in which people compete at national and international competitions. At the 2006 World Championship in Germany, Franz-Wolfgang Coersten spit a pit an impressive 19.3 m.

THE EARLY BIRD

The World Worm Charming Championships have taken place since 1980 in Willaston, Cheshire, England. Competitors coax earthworms to the surface by wiggling garden forks in the soil or by pouring water on it. The winner is the person who brings the most worms to the surface in half an hour. In 2009, 10-year-old Sophie Smith won the first prize with a grand total of 567.

POLE POSITION

To be crowned pole-sitting champion, you need a head for heights and a lot of patience. In 2002, Daniel Baraniuk won $20,000 (about £13,000) after spending 196 days and nights (over six months) on top of a 2.5-m-high pole. His closest rival fell off a month earlier!

COW PATTY BINGO

In some rural areas of North America you can play cow patty bingo. A field is divided into numbered squares, and contestants bet on which square the cow will take a poop!

TOUCH DOWN

CATCH AND KICK

Each year American football's biggest game, the Super Bowl, is watched on US TV by nearly 100 million people. American football grew out of the sport of rugby, which was invented in the UK in the early 19th century. Both American football and rugby use an oval-shaped ball. When the ball hits the ground, its odd shape means that it can bounce in any direction.

To play American football or rugby, you need to be strong or fast – better still if you are both. American football is played in other parts of the world, too, including Japan, Mexico and Europe.

Ripley explains...

NFL players have had to wear helmets to protect their head since the 1940s.

Shoulder pads are made of shock absorbing foam with a hard plastic cover. These protect the players and also make them look much bigger than they really are!

Plastic knee pads fit into pockets inside the football trousers. They protect the players' knees when they crash to the ground.

ROUGH AND TUMBLE

American football is fun and fast but also very physical with a lot of body contact. Around 40,000 high-school players suffer concussion (a mild head injury) every year playing football. Quarterbacks or running backs, who are tackled most often, rarely get through a season without being injured.

SCHOOLBOY ERROR

Rugby began in 1823 when William Webb Ellis, a student at Rugby School in England, caught the ball during a game of football and ran towards the other team's goal. It is now played in over 100 countries worldwide.

twist it!

END ZONE

David Withoff, a young Green Bay Packers' fan, was so excited by his 2003 Christmas gift – a Packers' jersey with Brett Favre's No 4 – that he wore it every day for over four years.

The boys' American football team at De La Salle High School, Concord, California, won 151 games in a row from 1992 to 2004.

Willie McQueen was a great defence tackler for Flint Southwestern Academy High School team, Michigan, despite being only 0.9 m tall. He had been left with no legs after a railway accident.

Jim Purol of California sat in all 92,542 seats at the Pasadena Rose Bowl over a period of five days in 2008. He sat for 12 hours each day and took a cushion to stop him from getting a sore behind.

American footballer Roy Riegels became famous for running the wrong way! When playing for the California Golden Bears in the 1929 Rose Bowl, he picked up a fumble, lost his sense of direction, and ran 70 yards towards his own end zone. He was finally grabbed by one of his team-mates on his own one-yard line.

GRRRRR

<<THE FRIDGE>>

William Perry, a popular defensive lineman for the Chicago Bears, was known as 'The Fridge' because of his 1.88-m, 173-kg square body. Yet at high school he could leap high enough to dunk a basketball!

Rooster booster

The French national rugby team have a live cockerel as their mascot. Sometimes he even attends the team's training sessions. It gives them something to crow about!

PEDAL POWER

PUSHING IT

Riders can pedal forwards and backwards for tricks.

Wheels can have up to 48 spokes to help deal with bumpy landings.

The handlebars can spin in a circle.

BMX magic

BMX (Bicycle Motocross) began in southern California in the 1970s, but is so popular that in 2008 it became an Olympic sport. The bikes are designed for performing tricks and for racing on hilly dirt tracks. Riders must wear a full-face helmet, elbow pads, knee pads and shin guards. Yet even the best riders sometimes get hurt. American Mat Hoffman has had over 50 operations and 500 stitches, and broken almost every bone in his body.

There are so many different sports you can do on a bike. Racing cyclists zoom around a track at nearly 80 km/h. Cyclo-cross competitors ride through woods and across such rough land that they have to get off and carry their bikes up steep hills. BMX bikers are able to perform fantastic jumps and acrobatic twists in mid-air. In 2008, Kevin Robinson of the USA soared 8.2 m into the air on a BMX bike – equal to jumping over a three-storey building.

There are endurance races, too. At the Lotoja race in the USA, riders cover 330 km in a single day. Other people ride bikes down glaciers and mountains, and even ride them backwards – sometimes playing a musical instrument at the same time!

In the Netherlands there are more bicycles (16 million) than there are people.

ROUND AND ROUND

Austrian Marcus Stoeckl rode a mountain bike down a snow-covered mountain in Chile, reaching a speed of 210 km/h.

At the Down the Hill bike race in Taxco, Mexico, competitors ride mountain bikes through a house! They go in through a door, ride down a flight of stairs, and exit through another door.

Jumping from a ramp, Australian Nathan Rennie cleared over 36 m on his mountain bike in 2005.

At the 2009 X Games in Los Angeles, Anthony Napolitan performed two complete somersaults in mid-air to land the first-ever double front flip on a bicycle.

During the 1904 Tour de France – the world's most famous cycle race – French spectators sprinkled broken glass on the road so that the leaders would get punctures and allow their local favourite to win.

TWIST IT!

Balancing act

Ripley explains...

When you pedal a bike, you use your muscles to create a force. You are like the engine for your bike. Bicycles are so efficient they can convert 80 per cent of the energy you supply at the pedals into energy that powers you along. To compare, a car engine converts only 25 per cent of the energy in petrol into useful power.

It's scary enough riding a bike around volcano craters or on cliff tops, but Canada's Kris Holm does it on a unicycle! The one-wheeled daredevil has ridden on the rail of a 60-m-high bridge, the edge of a 805-m-high cliff, and within 10 m of red-hot, bubbling lava on a volcano in Hawaii.

COASTING ALONG

With an oxygen tank on his back, Maaruf Bitar of Lebanon practises his favourite hobby – underwater cycling – off the coast of the Mediterranean city of Sidon. Underwater cyclists have ridden at depths of over 60 m beneath the sea, that's 30 times the depth of an Olympic swimming pool.

EXTREME ACTION

NO LIMITS

Who would think you could play Scrabble underwater or iron a T-shirt at the top of a mountain? You can, thanks to a new range of extreme sports designed to make gentle pursuits or boring jobs much more exciting.

Instead of doing their ironing in the living room, some people do it in caves, in a canoe, on top of a statue, in the middle of a forest, or while snowboarding. It has become so popular that now you can even play Wii extreme ironing – back in your living room!

If only Jim were as keen to iron at home!
Don't look down!

Ironing on the roof of a car, Sahara Desert

Extreme housework! Sahara Desert

Cliff ironing – not for the faint hearted

Underwater ironing – poor results

Mountain ironing (note the use of crossed skis for an ironing board)

Extremely silly

Extreme ironing was thought up by Englishman Phil Shaw in the 1990s and became so popular that the first Extreme Ironing World Championships took place in Germany in 2002. Eighty competitors from ten countries had to think up peculiar places for doing the ironing.

Ripley's Believe It or Not!®

BOUNCE

Fred Grzybowski of Los Angeles, California, can jump over a car on a pogo stick. The extreme pogo rider is able to bounce 2.4 m into the air and can also perform an incredible nine consecutive pogo backflips. The world championship called Pogopalooza attracts over 60 riders from the USA, Canada and the UK. The best riders can perform over 220 bounces in a minute.

INSANE IRONING

- **Two South Africans** ironed while hanging from a rope across a 30-m-wide mountain gorge.
- **A British pair** did some ironing at a height of 5,425 m on Mount Everest.
- In 2007, **Henry Cookson** dragged his iron and ironing board 1,770 km across the frozen wastes of Antarctica.
- **Australian Robert Fry** threw himself off the side of a cliff in the Blue Mountains with an iron, a board, some laundry and a parachute!
- In 2009, **86 British scuba divers** ironed underwater at the same time – in water as cold as -2°C.

EXTREME SCRABBLE

To celebrate the 60th anniversary of Scrabble in 2008, extreme enthusiasts played in some crazy places. Skydivers Nicole Angelides and Ramsey Kent played Scrabble at 4,000 m above Florida. With each move, they had to glue the tiles to the board to stop them blowing away.

twist it!

ABOVE AND BEYOND

American Peter Jenkins has started a new sport – extreme tree climbing. He and his friends climb trees and perform acrobatic stunts. These include balancing on the branches and running across the canopy (the top) of the trees. They also tree surf, where they go high into the tree on a windy day and ride the branches like waves.

On a 2006 tour, extreme cello players Clare Wallace, Jeremy Dawson and James Rees carried their musical instruments on to the roofs of 31 different cathedrals in England and played a short concert on each.

In 2008, while orbiting in the International Space Station at 8 km a second, Canadian astronaut Greg Chamitoff played a game of extreme chess against a team of US students on Earth.

Running wild

Free running, or parkour, is a form of urban acrobatics. You run through towns and cities, vaulting walls and railings as stylishly as possible, adding spins or twists in mid-air. You can use ledges, handrails or steps to perform handstands and somersaults. You just make it up as you go along.

SHOW SOME MUSCLE

BODY POWER

Some people can do amazing things with their body. They can squeeze it through the head of a tennis racquet – with the strings taken out, of course. They can balance on their head on a high wire just a couple of centimetres wide, thousands of metres up in the air without a safety net.

Back on the ground, in 1980 a Japanese man did more than 10,000 push-ups nonstop, and free-running experts can jump between the roofs of buildings, just like in the movies.

IN A SPIN

Kareena Oates from Australia is able to rotate 100 hula hoops around her body at the same time. She has also spun 41 hula hoops around her waist while suspended in the air by her wrists.

UP, UP, UP...

At the Tarragona Castells festival in Spain, acrobats climb over each other to form amazing human towers. There have been as many as ten levels of people standing on each other's shoulders, but sometimes the whole thing just comes crashing down.

HUMAN FLAG

Canadian gymnast and acrobat Dominic Lacasse held himself horizontally on a bar as a 'Human Flag' for 39 seconds, a display of incredible strength.

Twist it!

ENERGY BUZZ

American Don Claps can perform more than 1,200 consecutive cartwheels, and he can even carry on doing them while drinking water from a paper cup!

In 2009, Davit Fahradyan of Armenia completed 354 arm-aching turns on a horizontal bar.

New Yorker Ashrita Furman hula hooped underwater for 2 minutes 20 seconds at a Florida dolphin centre in 2007. He used a special metal hoop and was able to breathe air through scuba-diving equipment.

Olga Berberich completed 251 jumps with a rope in just one minute in Germany in 2007.

Contortionist Daniel Browning-Smith, of Los Angeles, California, is so flexible he can squeeze his entire body into a box the size of a microwave oven.

Working in shifts of two people at a time, eight boys, aged between eight and 11, bounced nonstop on an inflatable castle in Michigan for 24 hours in 2008.

GET YOUR SKATES ON

HEELS ON WHEELS

American skater Rob Dyrdek once did 215 ollies in a row.

In 2006, Welshman Dave Cornthwaite spent 90 days on a skateboard, riding it all the way across Australia – a distance of more than 5,600 km! Skateboarders love to try new challenges. One man jumped over four cars on a skateboard, and another built a skateboard so big that nearly 30 people could stand on it at the same time.

Dude!

The ollie is one of the most popular aerial skating tricks. You bend down, push your back foot down on the tail end of the board and then allow the board to pop back up. As you leap into the air, the board appears to be stuck to your feet, as if by magic.

There are now more than 18 million skateboarders in the world. You could also try roller hockey, speed skating, or if you can really stretch your arms and legs, the latest Indian craze of limbo skating!

GREAT SKATES

Skateboarding was born when Californian surfers wanted something to surf on when the waves in the sea were flat. Believe it or not, top skaters have reached speeds of nearly 100 km/h.

DANNY'S WAY

In Mexico City in 2006, American skater Danny Way landed a sensational backflip, which he called El Camino ('The Way'). He sped down a 23-m-high ramp and leaped 21 m through the air at a speed of 80 km/h. The previous year he had jumped over the Great Wall of China on a skateboard. Not bad for someone who says he is afraid of heights!

Roller skates first became popular in the 1880s.

The lowdown

Limbo skaters have to be strong and flexible to skate under more than 50 parked cars at a time. They practise for months to get their body into the right position. Young limbo skater Aniket Chindak can roller-skate under cars that are just 24 cm off the ground.

TURNING HEADS

At the 1999 X Games, American Tony Hawk became the first skater to land a 900: that's 2½ rotations in mid-air.

Bingo, a Border collie, used to ride through the streets of Winnipeg, Canada, on a skateboard picking up litter.

In 2000, Richie Carrasco completed 142 dizzying 360-degree spins on a skateboard without stopping.

A roller skate invented by Frenchman M Mercier in the 1900s was powered by a two-cylinder petrol engine. This enabled the skater to zoom along at speeds of 30 km/h.

Around 280 roller skaters held on to the waist of the person in front of them to form a giant skating chain that snaked through the streets of Singapore City in 2006.

Rohan Ajit Kokane is so good at limbo skating he can do it under cars while blindfolded!

twist it!

SPEED SKATER

German inline skater Dirk Auer reached incredible speeds of nearly 300 km/h while being dragged behind a high-powered motorbike. Dirk is used to extreme skating and has also managed to skate along the roof of an airborne plane and down a rollercoaster.

Ripley's Believe It or Not!®

ROLLER MAN

Frenchman Jean-Yves Blondeau wears a special plastic suit with sets of rollers attached. It means he can roll down the motorway at nearly 100 km/h. He can even overtake motorbikes!

GOAL CRAZY

FANTASTIC FOOTBALL

About 3.5 billion people either play or watch football, making it the world's most popular sport. Every country plays the game, right down to tiny islands. On the Isles of Scilly, off the southwest coast of England, the league is made up of just two teams who play each other every week! It does mean the draw for the cup is not very exciting...

Football is fast and skilful. Some people love the game so much they name their children after their favourite players, dye their hair in their team's colours, or travel thousands of miles just to watch their team. The best players are treated like superstars and are paid over £100,000 a week. Boys and girls play football, but you need to be fit to be a professional, as some top players run up to 10 km during a match.

GOAL CRAZY

Freezing Footie

Jungfrau Mountain — Switzerland

International footballers staged a 2007 exhibition match on an artificial pitch laid out on a glacier. It took place in the shadow of Switzerland's 4,160-m Jungfrau Mountain. The high-altitude air was so tiring that the teams played just five minutes each half.

GOAL CRAZY

Dan Magness — Britain

Using his feet, thighs, chest and head, Britain's Dan Magness kept a football in the air for 24 hours. He touched the ball around 250,000 times, knowing that the smallest lapse in concentration would mean he would have to start all over again!

FREE KICKS

Some football matches are decided by penalty shoot-outs, where eight kicks are often enough to get a result. At the end of a 2005 Namibian Cup tie in Africa, the penalty contest went on for an incredible 48 kicks and lasted nearly an hour!

Important football matches often attract crowds of over 70,000 people, but the 1950 World Cup final between Brazil and Uruguay was watched by nearly 200,000 spectators.

An annual football match called the Calcio takes place in Florence, Italy, between two teams of 27 players dressed in 16th-century costume. It is a rough game, and players are allowed to elbow, kick, and even head butt each other!

Welsh footie fan Steve Thatcher named his son after all the players in his favourite team, Cardiff City. It means young Sam has 12 middle names!

It's true!

GOAL CRAZY
Tiny Field
Microscopic
Created by technology, this football pitch is so tiny that 20,000 of them could fit on the tip of a single human hair. It has all the markings of a full-sized pitch but can only be viewed using a really powerful microscope.
GOAL CRAZY
GOOOAAALLL!!!
Portugal
Nani
Portuguese football star Nani performs his famous backflip celebration after scoring a goal for Manchester United. The fans love it – as long as he doesn't injure himself doing it.
GOAL CRAZY
The Legendary Pelé
Pelé
Brazil
The great Brazilian footballer Pelé scored 1,281 goals in his career – more than any other professional player. He helped his country to win the World Cup three times, and scored the opening goal in the 1970 final when Brazil beat Italy 4–1.
GOAL CRAZY
Brainy Ball
Adidas
Germany
Adidas has designed a clever football. It contains a chip that sends a radio signal to the referee's watch in less than a second of the ball crossing the goal line. So there should be no more arguments about whether or not a shot was a goal.
GOAL CRAZY
On the Head
Manoj Mishra
India
Indian footie fan Manoj Mishra won a competition by balancing a ball on his head for 14 hours. He practised yoga exercises so that he could get used to keeping still for so long. Afterwards he dedicated his success to his hero, Argentinian football legend Diego Maradona.

FLYING HIGH

TAKING TO THE SKIES

Many humans love to fly. As we don't have wings like a bird, we try the next best thing and take up sports such as hang gliding, paragliding, ballooning, gliding and skydiving. American skydiver Don Kellner has made over 36,000 jumps, and Jay Stokes once made 640 jumps in a single day! Skydivers free fall at 200 km/h before the safety parachute opens and they descend gently to the ground.

YEEE-HAAAA...

Although skydiving looks dangerous, in the USA there is only one death for every 100,000 jumps.

If you are worried about heights, you don't have to go up alone. You could always take your dog with you. Brutus, a miniature dachshund from California, made more than 70 jumps with his owner!

WAA-HOOOO...

JUMP!

Skydivers jump from airplanes, helicopters and even hot-air balloons. Once their parachutes are open, they control their direction by pulling toggles on the end of steering lines attached to the chute. That's how they can land on a small cross marked on the ground after jumping from 4,000 m.

Mike Howard, an airline pilot, walked blindfolded along a 5.8-m-long pole from one balloon to another, 1,200 m above Bristol, England, in 2004. When he had completed the daring tightrope walk, he parachuted to the ground.

<<human bird>>

American Jeb Corliss comes as close as any human has to flying. Wearing a special winged jumpsuit, he takes part in the scary sport of proximity wingsuit flying. He jumps from a helicopter or off a cliff edge thousands of metres up and flies terrifyingly close to mountain faces. Jeb once flew down the 4,478-m-high Matterhorn Mountain in Switzerland, within just 1.5 m of the jagged cliff-face, and reached speeds of 160 km/h.

SUPERFLY GUYS

Holly Budge from England skydived over Mount Everest in 2008. She jumped from a plane at 8,990 m and reached speeds of 225 km/h and braved temperatures of −40°C.

In 2004, Bob Holloway flew 4,152 km in a powered paraglider from Astoria, Oregon, to Washington, Missouri.

Vijaypat Singhania flew a hot-air balloon to an incredible altitude of 21,027 m over India in 2005.

In just eight days, Englishman Martin Downs skydived on six continents: Africa, Europe, South America, North America, Australia and Asia.

twist it!

In Japan they stage kite fights. Competing teams tie sharp razor blades and broken glass to the tail strings of their kites and fly them against one another. The aim is to rip the opposing kite to shreds so that it can no longer fly.

Ripley's Believe It or Not!®

Buddy the Labrador and his owner, Bill Kimball of San Diego, California, went hang gliding together for more than eight years. Buddy joined Bill on over 75 flights.

Ripley explains...

Hang gliders can stay thousands of metres in the air for hours, soaring through the skies like an eagle. A hang glider has a lightweight aluminium frame, a big nylon wing, and no engine. The pilot is attached to the frame by a harness. There are no switches or buttons to worry about. Pilots steer by shifting their body weight on the frame, then all they have to do is relax and admire the views.

SURF'S UP

RIDING THE WAVES

Ripley explains...

You catch a wave by pushing the water towards the back of the surfboard with your hands, moving you forwards. As you ride on the wave the water rises beneath you and pushes you forwards faster and faster. All the time gravity is trying to push you down, while buoyancy is pushing you up.

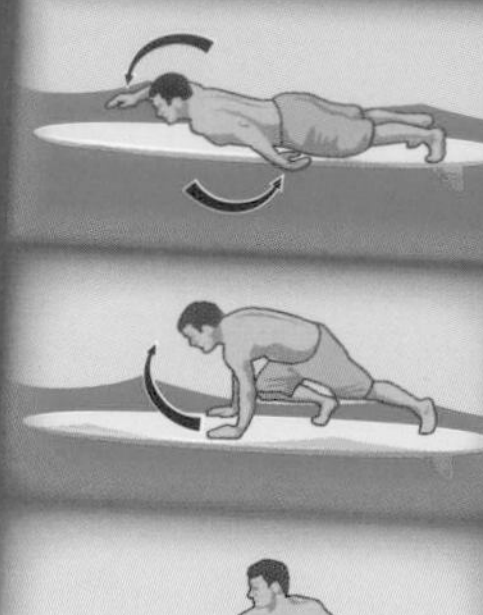

It's not only waves that are a danger to surfers. Each year as many as 80 surfers are attacked by sharks.

84 surfers rode the same wave at the same time off the coast of Brazil in 2007.

Have you ever wished you could ride a wave on a surfboard? Some waves are huge – over 20 m high. That's more than four times the height of an adult giraffe! That just makes it even more of a challenge for a surfer. You can surf a wave standing up, crouching or lying down – and some surfers have managed to stay on the same wave for half an hour. There are no rules, you just do what you enjoy.

The first surfers – in Tahiti in the 18th century – used planks of wood, but today's surfboards are made of lightweight polyurethane foam. Surfing is really popular in places like California, Florida and Hawaii, where the shape of the seabed and strong winds create big waves.

RIDING HIGH

Kite surfers use wind power to help them speed across the water and soar up to 50 m in the air. They stand on a board and hold on to a large controllable kite. The aim is to do tricks such as jumps, spins and even somersaults, and to see how high and long they can jump off waves.

SAY WHAT?

CATCH A WAVE
This is when you launch yourself into the path of a suitable wave.

Kite surfers can go great distances when the wind is behind them. In 2006, UK kite surfer Kirsty Jones travelled 225 km from Lanzarote in the Canary Islands to Morocco.

PLAIN SAILING

Windsurfers attach a sail to their surfboards. When the wind blows into the sail from behind, it makes the board go faster: sometimes up to 100 km/h! Windsurfers can perform amazing stunts, jumps and spins.

Donald 'DJ' Dettloff has created a colourful fence from more than 700 surfboards near his home in Hawaii.

Ripley's Believe It or Not!®

In California they have a surfing contest that's just for dogs. Four-legged surfing dudes show their style on their own and with human partners. The winner receives a basket full of dog treats.

IN THE RUNNING

MARATHONS

People can't run as fast as cheetahs, but they can run much further. They need great stamina to do this. The longest running race in the Olympics is the marathon at just over 26 miles (42 km).

Just running a marathon is exhausting, but some athletes need greater challenges. So they run extreme (ultra) marathons that are a mega 160 km long. Occasionally, someone will even run all the way around the world – with lots of stops, of course!

The first marathon

In 490BC, Pheidippides, a Greek soldier, ran about 25 miles (40 km) from the town of Marathon to Athens to announce that the Greeks had defeated the invading Persians in battle. The route was exhausting, and shortly after arriving in Athens Pheidippides fell to the ground dead.

In 1896, the first modern Olympic Games in Athens held a race of roughly the same length in his honour. It became known as the marathon.

MARATHON FACT FILE

- More than **400,000 people** in the USA compete in marathons annually.
- More than **800 marathons** are run in the world each year. The biggest marathons can have tens of thousands of runners.
- A marathon runner will go through **two pairs of trainers** while training for the race.
- Top marathon athletes will run **160 km** a week in training.
- It takes the average woman **51,214 steps** to complete a marathon.
- In 2008, 64-year-old Texan Larry Macon ran **105 marathons.**

Sand marathon

A competitor climbs a sand dune during the 2009 Marathon des Sables in the Sahara Desert. This desert marathon is considered the hardest in the world.

COOL RUNNING

Runners tackle rough mountain trails in the 2006 Everest Marathon. The starting line is at 5,180 m near Mount Everest Base Camp in Nepal, making it the highest marathon in the world.

Bringing up the rear >>

Englishman Lloyd Scott walked the 2002 New York and London marathons wearing a 55-kg antique diving suit. In London, it took him five days and eight hours. In 2003, he wore the same suit to complete a marathon underwater!

HAVING A BALL

There are many ways to complete a marathon. This man at the 2008 Berlin Marathon was running in a sphere!

STAYING POWER

Dave Heeley from England ran seven marathons on seven continents in seven days in 2008, even though he is blind.

Michal Kapral, from Toronto, Canada, ran a marathon in 3 hours 7 minutes in 2005 while juggling three balls at the same time.

Between 1997 and 2003, England's Robert Garside ran 48,000 km around the world in 2,062 days.

US soldier Jake Truex ran 5,000 m in just over 22 minutes in Germany in 2006 with a heavy 18-kg backpack strapped to his back.

Charlie Engle (USA), Ray Zahab (Canada) and Kevin Lin (Taiwan) ran the same distance as two marathons a day for 111 days to cross the 6,400-km Sahara Desert on foot in 2007. They had to cope with temperatures that were over 37°C by day, but below freezing at night.

Twist it!

DID YOU KNOW?

At the London Marathon...

They use 710,000 bottles of water, 950 portable toilets, 500 stretchers and 68 ambulances.

The blue paint that marks out the course is steam-cleaned off as the last runner passes, so the streets of London can be quickly returned to normal.

Australia's Kurt Fearnley completed the 2009 race in a wheelchair in a record 1 hour 28 minutes 56 seconds.

The London Marathon was the first to be run over 26.2 miles. This is because at the 1908 Olympics the Royal Box lay 385 yards (350 m) beyond the 26-mile finish line. The race was extended so it could finish beneath the Royal Box.

RISKY BUSINESS

Cave divers plunge to depths of up to 30 m underwater in total darkness at the risk of losing their way or running out of air. Kayakers ride over the world's highest waterfalls, hitting terrifying speeds of 110 km/h on the way down. Bungee jumpers leap from bridges high above raging rivers with one end of an elastic cord tied to their ankles and the other end tied to the jumping-off point. For some people sport is only fun if they are putting their life at risk.

Over the past 30 years, dozens of dangerous sports have been introduced that are exciting to do but, when things go wrong, can result in serious injury, even death. Only really physically fit people should attempt these sports – and even then they must have the right equipment, or the consequences could be fatal.

In the balance

This is not a trick photo. Eskil Ronningsbakken really is performing a one-handed handstand while balancing on the edge of a ladder attached to a 300-m-high cliff in Norway. He was able to do this by adding 150 kg of weights at the balancing end. It still looks pretty scary though.

DEATH DEFYING

SAY WHAT?

BASE JUMPING

BASE jumping is named after the places you jump from: Buildings (skyscrapers, statues), Antennas (radio masts, cranes), Spans (bridges), and Earth (cliffs).

READY TO ROLL

Have you ever wondered what it is like to be a hamster in a wheel? Well, the sport of Zorbing lets you find out. Zorbanauts roll down hills inside large transparent plastic spheres, reaching speeds of over 50 km/h.

CRAZY KAYAKING

One of the world's top extreme kayakers is fearless Jesse Combs from Oregon. Jesse risks life and limb by taking his kayak over steep crashing waterfalls such as this 20-m drop at the Mesa Falls in Idaho.

A NEED FOR SPEED

David Kirke, founder of England's Dangerous Sports Club, adapted a medieval rock-throwing device called a trebuchet so that humans could be catapulted 17 m into the air in under two seconds.

Bull running takes place in several Spanish towns, most famously in Pamplona. Participants have to run in front of a herd of angry bulls that have been let loose in the streets. Fifteen people have been killed in the Pamplona event since 1910.

Tyler Bradt paddled a kayak down the raging waters of the 33-m Alexandra Falls in Canada, and didn't flip once.

In 1991, John Kockelman made a bungee jump of 300 m from a hot-air balloon 1,500 m above California.

In BASE jumping, people hurl themselves from tall structures with just a parachute to save them from certain death. The thrill is to wait as long as possible before pulling the parachute cord. Here, leaping 280 m from the Menara Kuala Lumpur Tower in Malaysia, this jumper will have six seconds of freefall before he has to use his parachute.

- *People have* ***BASE jumped*** *from San Francisco's Golden Gate Bridge, the Eiffel Tower in Paris and New York City's Empire State Building.*
- *In 2006, Australians Glenn Singleman and Heather Swan jumped off a* ***6,500-m-high*** *precipice on Meru Peak, India, and landed on a 5,000-m-high glacier.*
- *In 2006, Dan Schilling made* ***201 BASE jumps*** *in 24 hours off a bridge 14 m above the Snake River Canyon, Idaho. He kept jumping even after fracturing his wrist.*
- *An average of* ***15 people*** *are killed while BASE jumping every year.*

twist it!

HAVING A BALL

CATCHING ON

Believe it or not, golf was the first sport to be played on the Moon. Astronaut Alan Shepard hit a couple of shots on the 1971 *Apollo 14* Moon mission. Ball games such as golf, bowling, pool and table tennis are played all over the world. Baseball also has a wide following, and an amazing 42 million people play it in the USA alone. Cricket is played in the UK, Australia, South Africa and Asia.

Most of these sports are over 100 years old, and some have their origins in ancient history. A form of bowling was played in Egypt as far back as 3200BC. The game was outlawed in England in 1366 because King Edward III wanted his soldiers to concentrate on archery practice instead.

The odds of a spectator being hit by a ball at a Major League game are 300,000 to 1.

Nearly 80 million people pay to watch Major League baseball in a season.

Big teams like the New York Yankees average attendances of over 50,000 per game.

The athletic **Nomar Garciaparra** first starred for the Boston Red Sox in the 1990s. He is one of only a handful of players in Major League baseball history to have hit two grand slams (a home run hit when there are runners at three bases) during a single game.

UPSCALE BALL

Instead of being covered in leather, this cricket ball is covered in 2,704 diamonds. Made in Sri Lanka, it is said to be the first life-sized diamond-and-gold cricket ball in the world.

CRICKET ODDITIES

- Cricket is played by two teams of 11 players. One team bowls and fields while the other bats. A team is in (at bat) until ten of its batsmen are out. Then the other team is in!
- Batsmen try to score runs by hitting the ball a long way. If a batsman is out for no runs, he has scored a duck – because zero is shaped like a duck's egg.
- The bowlers aim at three wooden stumps in the ground known as the wicket. They take it in turn to bowl 'overs', which consist of bowling six balls at the batsman. If no runs are scored off an over, it is called a maiden.
- There are ten ways a batsman can be out, including bowled, caught and leg before wicket (lbw).

twist it!

PLAY BALL

English golfer Andrew Winfield teed off from the summit of Africa's Mount Kilimanjaro in 2008, 5,895 m above sea level.

Table tennis was first played in Victorian England in the 1880s on a dining room table, often using a cigar box lid as a bat, a champagne cork as a ball, and a row of books as a net!

In 2007, English golfer David Huggins hit his third hole-in-one...and he was only eight years old.

Playing baseball for Portsmouth High School, Ohio, in 2008, triplets Howard, John and Matt Harcha all hit home runs, in the order of their birth from oldest to youngest.

Every Thanksgiving, Cincinnati, Ohio, hosts a Turkey Bowl, where competitors bowl frozen turkeys instead of bowling balls!

BILLION-DOLLAR MAN

American golfer Tiger Woods became the first ever athlete to earn a billion dollars. He has won more than 70 tour events and when he was only three years old he shot an amazing score of 48 over nine holes at a golf club in California. He usually wears a red shirt on the final round of tournaments because he believes it helps him to win.

Perfect pitch

Jim Abbott was a Major League baseball pitcher in the 1990s even though he was born with only one hand. In 1993, playing for the New York Yankees, he even pitched a no-hitter (where the opposing team has no hits in an entire game) against the Cleveland Indians. This was a fantastic achievement because on average just two no-hitters a year have been thrown in Major League baseball since 1875.

WACKY RACES

FUN RUNS

You don't need an engine to take part in a wacky race, just a daft sense of humour. In various places across the world people push, pull or carry beds, toilets, coffins, even their wives – all in the name of sport.

For serious athletes who like a fun run, there is the mad dash up the stairs of the Empire State Building in New York. Germany's Thomas Dold won in 2006, 2007, 2008 and 2009, and he also excels at another crazy form of racing – running backwards!

BIRDS IN FLIGHT

Lightweight jockeys ride ostriches in a race in Shanghai, China. Ostrich racing is also popular in South Africa and in several locations in the USA. Ostriches can run at 72 km/h, the fastest running speed of any bird. Ostriches are harder to steer than horses, so although the jockeys have special saddles and reins, they still regularly fall off.

STEP UP THE PACE

Each year more than 300 runners take part in the race up the stairs of the Empire State Building. The climb to the observation deck is up 320 m, 86 floors, and 1,576 stairs. It takes most of the runners about 15 minutes to reach the observation deck. The building's elevator can get there in less than a minute.

DEAD FUNNY

Every year in Manitou Springs, Colorado, teams race coffins with a living female occupant. Around 40 coffins take part. They are rerunning the legend of Emma Crawford, who died in 1890 and was buried on top of Red Mountain, only to have her coffin slide down the canyon in 1929 after heavy rains.

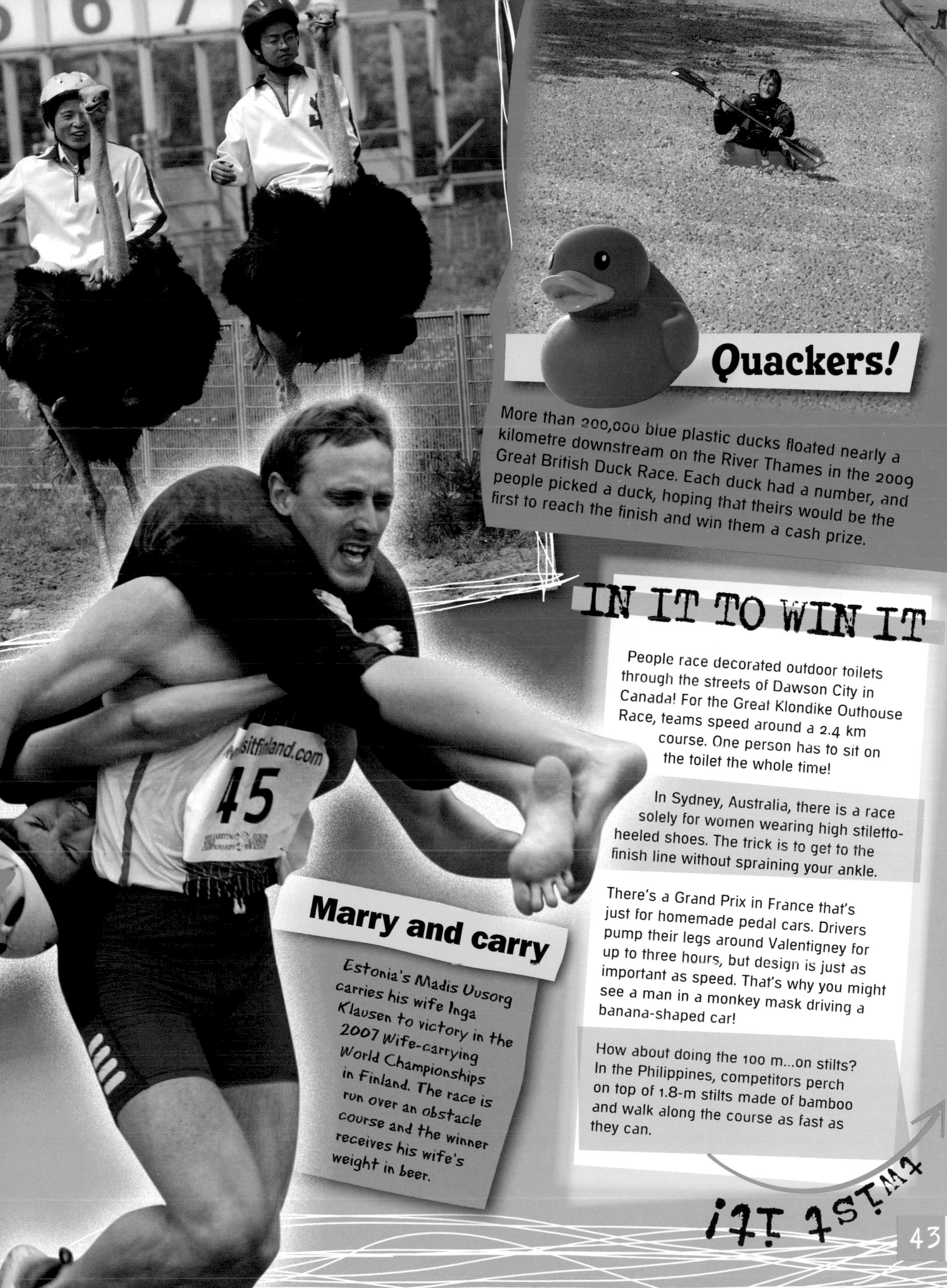

Quackers!

More than 200,000 blue plastic ducks floated nearly a kilometre downstream on the River Thames in the 2009 Great British Duck Race. Each duck had a number, and people picked a duck, hoping that theirs would be the first to reach the finish and win them a cash prize.

IN IT TO WIN IT

People race decorated outdoor toilets through the streets of Dawson City in Canada! For the Great Klondike Outhouse Race, teams speed around a 2.4 km course. One person has to sit on the toilet the whole time!

In Sydney, Australia, there is a race solely for women wearing high stiletto-heeled shoes. The trick is to get to the finish line without spraining your ankle.

There's a Grand Prix in France that's just for homemade pedal cars. Drivers pump their legs around Valentigney for up to three hours, but design is just as important as speed. That's why you might see a man in a monkey mask driving a banana-shaped car!

How about doing the 100 m...on stilts? In the Philippines, competitors perch on top of 1.8-m stilts made of bamboo and walk along the course as fast as they can.

Marry and carry

Estonia's Madis Uusorg carries his wife Inga Klausen to victory in the 2007 Wife-carrying World Championships in Finland. The race is run over an obstacle course and the winner receives his wife's weight in beer.

¡7I 7ST₄

FUN AND GAMES

OLYMPIC DREAMS

The Olympic Games are the greatest sporting show on earth. The ancient Olympics were held in Greece starting in the 8th century BC – nearly 3,000 years ago. Sports included the javelin, long jump, running in armour, and even kissing! After a long break, the Olympics were brought back in 1896 and are now held every four years. An incredible 4.5 billion people watched the 2008 Olympics in Beijing, China, either on TV or online.

In Beijing, more than 11,000 athletes from around 200 countries competed in more than 300 events, from athletics to wrestling. The Winter Olympics are just as exciting, featuring sports such as skiing, ice skating and bobsleigh. The winner of each event receives a gold medal, second place gets a silver medal, and third place gets a bronze medal. These are the most important prizes in sport.

STEVE REDGRAVE

A powerful rower, Britain's Steve Redgrave (second from left) in 2000 was one of only four Olympians to have won a gold medal at five consecutive Olympic Games.

Fan-tastic

To celebrate the 2008 Olympics in Beijing, a Chinese man, Dr. Wei Sheng, pierced his head, face, hands and chest with 2,008 needles in the five colours of the Olympic rings.

4,200 athletes from 148 countries took part in the 2008 Paralympics. These Games are for athletes with a physical disability or vision impairment. Sports include wheelchair basketball and wheelchair tennis.

EDWIN MOSES

Edwin Moses of the USA won gold in the 400 metres hurdles at both the 1976 and 1984 Olympics. Between 1977 and 1987 he was undefeated, winning a record 122 consecutive races.

US swimmer Michael Phelps won eight gold medals at the 2008 Beijing Olympics. It was the first time that this had been achieved by a competitor at a single Olympic Games.

Live pigeon shooting was an event at the 1900 Olympics. Nearly 300 birds were killed. It was the first and only time in Olympic history that animals were killed on purpose.

twist it!

GOING FOR GOLD

At the 1904 Olympics, George Eyser (USA) won six gymnastics medals, including three gold, despite having a wooden left leg.

Women were not allowed to compete in track and field events at the Olympics until 1928. However, so many collapsed at the end of the 800 metres in that year that the event was banned until 1960.

A 1956 Olympic water-polo match between Hungary and the USSR (modern-day Russia) was abandoned after the teams started fighting underwater.

After winning a rowing gold medal at the 1956 Olympics, 18-year-old Russian Vyacheslav Ivanov quickly lost it. He threw the medal into the air in celebration, but it landed in the lake. He dived in but was unable to find it.

The USA are the reigning Olympic rugby champions. That's because rugby was last featured in the Olympics in 1924 when the USA beat France 17–3 in the final.

Party time

The opening ceremony at the 2008 Beijing Olympics featured over 15,000 performers and a spectacular display of 35,000 fireworks. The four-hour ceremony cost £70 million – that's nearly £5,000 per second – making it the most expensive in Olympic history.

CLARA HUGHES

Canada's Clara Hughes is one of only a few athletes to win medals at both the Summer and Winter Olympics. She succeeded at both cycling and speed skating.

MICHAEL PHELPS

ACKNOWLEDGEMENTS

COVER (t/l) © Speedfighter – Fotolia.com, (c) © Diego Cervo – Fotolia.com, (c/l) © Feng Yu – Fotolia.com, (t) © Albo – Fotolia.com, (b/r) www.jw-sportfoto.de; **2** (b) Reuters/Claro Cortes, (t) Anja Niedringhaus/AP/Press Association Images; **3** Georges Christen; **4** (b/l) © Michael Lawlor – Fotolia.com, (b/c) © kamphi – Fotolia.com, (t) iStock.com, (b/r) © Terry Morris – Fotolia.com; **5** (t/r) © Thomas Lammeyer – iStock.com, (b/l) © Michael Lawlor – Fotolia.com, (b/cl, b/c, b/cr) N & B – Fotolia.com, (b/r) Pawel Nowik – Fotolia.com, (r) © Feng Yu – Fotolia.com; **6** (b/l) Reuters/United Photos; **6–7** (dp) Reuters/Stringer USA; **7** (r) Anja Niedringhaus/AP/Press Association Images; **8** Reuters/Stefano Rellandini; **9** (t/l) Reuters/Fahad Shadeed, (b/r) Reuters/Claro Cortes, (b) Reuters/Chaiwat Subprasom; **10** (l) Phil Walter/Getty Images, (t/r, c) Michael Martin/Barcroft Media Ltd, (b/r) © Chepko Danil – iStock.com; **11** (r) John Chapple/Rex Features, (t/l) Tony Gentile/Reuters, (b/r) Reuters Photographer/Reuters; **12** William Tremblay wl_tremblay@hotmail.com; **13** (t/l) Archive Photos/Getty Images, (b/r) Georges Christen; **14** (b/r) Mike Hewitt/Getty Images; **14–15** (t) Nathaniel S. Butler/NBAE/Getty Images; **15** (b/l) © Thomas Lammeyer – iStock.com, (b/r) Toby Melville/Reuters, (c) David E. Klutho/Sports Illustrated/Getty Images; **16** (t) © Pierre Jacques/Hemis/Corbis, (b) Gary Caskey/Reuters; **17** (t/r) Reuters/Yuriko Nakao, (t/l) © Reuters/Corbis, (r) S Levy/Getty Images; **18** (l) Sam Yeh/AFP/Getty Images, (t/l) Reuters Photographer/Reuters; **18–19** Sam Yeh/AFP/Getty Images; **19** (t/l) Heribert Proepper/AP/Press Association Images, (b/r) © Julien Rousset – Fotolia.com; **20** (l) David Purdy/Landov/Press Association Images, (r) © George Peters – iStock.com; **20–21** (dp) © Peter Baxter – Fotolia.com; **21** (t/l) Lynne Cameron/PA Wire/Press Association Images, (l) Jonathan Daniel/Getty Images, (b/r) Damien Meyer/AFP/Getty Images; **22** Lester Lefkowitz/Corbis; **23** (l) seanwhite.net/Sean White Photography, (r) AFP/Getty Images; **24** (t/l, t/r, c, b, r) Rex Features; **25** (t/l) Barcroft Media via Getty Images, (t/r) Barcroft Media Ltd; **26** (t) © Maxym Boner – iStock.com, (l) © Arturo Limon – iStock.com, (b/r) © Bart Sadowski – iStock.com; **27** (l) Alfaqui/Barcroft Media Ltd, (t/r) Samantha Sin/AFP/Getty Images, (r) Ermann J. Knippertz/AP/Press Association Images; **28–29** (c) Doug Pensinger/Getty Images, (b) Anthony Acosta; **29** (b/l) www.jw-sportfoto.de, (b/r) ChinaFotoPress/Cheng Jiang/Photocome/Press Association Images, (t/r) © Simon de Trey-White/Barcroft Pacific; **30** (t/l) Reuters/Christian Hartmann, (c) Johnny Green/PA Wire/Press Association Images; **30–31** (dp) Stephen Pond/Empics Sport; **31** (t/l) Wenn, (t) Kin Cheung/AP/Press Association Images, (t/r) © Reuters/Corbis, (b/r) © EuroPics [CEN], (b/l) Rex Features; **32** © Daniel Ramsbott/epa/Corbis; **33** (b/l, b) © Axel Koester/Corbis, (t/l) Sam Barcroft/Rex Features, (r) © Daniel Cardiff – iStock.com; **34** Neale Haynes/Rex Features; **35** (l) Warren Bolster, (r) © Don Bayley – iStock.com, (b/l) Denis Poroy/AP/Press Association Images, (b/r) John Hugg: mauisurfboard.com; huggsmaui.com; **36** Pierre Verdy/Getty Images; **37** (l) Getty Images, (t) Reuters/Str New, (c) Reuters/Pawel Kopczynski; **38** (sp) Sindre Lundvold/Barcroft Media, (b/r) Sipa Press/Rex Features; **39** (l) Photograph by Darin Quoid, (t/r) © Jörg Hackemann – Fotolia.com; **40** (sp) Paul Spinelli/MLB Photos via Getty Images, (b/r) Sena Vidanagama/Stringer/Getty Images; **41** (t/r) iStock.com, (b/l) John Zich/AFP/Getty Images, (b/r) Dave Martin/AP/Press Association Images; **42** (b/l) Reuters/Brendan Mcdermid, (b/r) Andra DuRee Martin; **42–43** (t) Reuters/Nir Elias; **43** (l) Reuters/Lehtikuva Lehtikuva, (t/r) Jonathan Hordle/Rex Features, (t) © Michael Flippo – iStock.com; **44** ((b/l) Sipa Press /Rex Features, (c) ChinaFotoPress/Photocome/Press Association Images; **44–45** (dp) © Luc Santerre Castonguay – iStock.com, (t/r) Bob Jones/Rex Features; **45** (b) Reuters/Staff Photographer, (l) Rex Features, (b/r) Reuters/Max Rossi

Key: t = top, b = bottom, c = centre, l = left, r = right, sp = single page, dp = double page, bgd = background

All other photos are from Ripley's Entertainment Inc. All artwork by Rocket Design (East Anglia) Ltd.

Every attempt has been made to acknowledge correctly and contact copyright holders and we apologise in advance for any unintentional errors or omissions, which will be corrected in future editions.

TWISTS

a Jim Pattison Company

Written by Clint Twist, Lisa Regan, Camilla de la Bedoyere

Consultant Barbara Taylor

Publisher Anne Marshall

Editorial Director Rebecca Miles
Project Editor Lisa Regan
Assistant Editor Charlotte Howell
Picture Researchers James Proud, Charlotte Howell
Proofreader Judy Barratt
Indexer Hilary Bird

Art Director Sam South
Senior Designer Michelle Cannatella
Design Rocket Design (East Anglia) Ltd
Reprographics Juice Creative Ltd

www.ripleys.com/books

First published in Great Britain in 2010 by Random House Books, Random House, 20 Vauxhall Bridge Road, London SW1V 2SA
www.rbooks.co.uk

Addresses for companies within The Random House Group Limited can be found at: www.randomhouse.co.uk/offices.htm

The Random House Group Limited Reg. No. 954009

ISBN 978-1-60991-228-4 (USA) | ISBN 978-0-09954-444-9 (UK)

10 9 8 7 6 5 4 3 2 1

The Random House Group Limited supports The Forest Stewardship Council (FSC), the leading international forest certification organisation. All our titles that are printed on Greenpeace approved FSC certified paper carry the FSC logo. Our paper procurement policy can be found at www.rbooks.co.uk/environment

A CIP catalogue record for this book is available from the British Library

Printed in China January 2018
2nd printing

WARNING
Some of the activities in this book are undertaken by experts and should not be attempted without adequate training and supervision.

PUBLISHER'S NOTE
While every effort has been made to verify the accuracy of the entries in this book, the Publishers cannot be held responsible for any errors contained herein. They would be glad to receive any information from readers.

CONTENTS

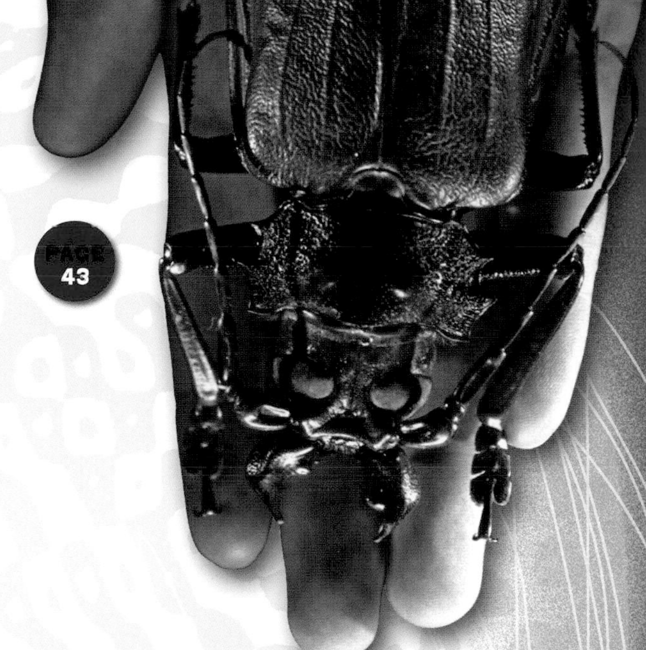
PAGE 43

PAGE 29

WHAT ON EARTH!

OUR HOME

WHAT'S INSIDE YOUR BOOK?

Welcome to your world! It's easy to spend your time on this planet, making the most of its rich resources, without stopping to think about what the Earth is really like. It's home to over six billion people, and provides all we need: food, water, shelter, energy, and even the air that we breathe is safe because of Earth's atmosphere.

Take a look around and you'll see amazing features of breathtaking beauty. Earth is the only planet in our Solar System to have our spectacular combination of mountains, oceans, volcanoes, deserts and rainforests. So read on and prepare to be amazed at our world.

Do the twist

This book is packed with superb sights created by nature. It will teach you amazing things about our planet, but like all Twists books, it shines a spotlight on things that are unbelievable but true. Turn the pages and find out more...

Learn fab fast facts to go with the cool pictures.

HOT AND COLD

These Japanese macaques like it hot – even when it's cold. They keep warm in winter temperatures of –15°C by bathing in natural hot springs. Macaque babies also roll snowballs, just for fun!

EARTH EXTREMES...

Coldest
Antarctica
–90°C

Hottest
El Azizia, Ethiopia
57.8°C

Windiest
Antarctica
306 km/h

Wettest (average)
Mount Wai-'ale-'ale, Kauai, Hawaii, about 1,270 cm a year

Found a new word? Big word alerts will explain it for you.

Ripley explains some of the geographical know-how behind features on our planet.

Don't forget to look out for the 'twist it!' column on some pages. Twist the book to find out more fast facts about the world we live in.

ROOF of the WORLD

MIGHTY MOUNTAINS

Majestic mountain ranges are nature's way of showing off! Their spectacular peaks are capped in clouds and mist and cloaked with snow and ice.

Mountains are created by the slow-moving forces that cause the Earth's plates to collide. Over time, rock is thrust upwards, crumpling and folding into beautiful shapes. It takes millions of years, but as soon as mountains form, erosion and weathering start to wear them down. As ice freezes and thaws near the peaks, rocks split and break away, leaving sharp pyramid-like tops, while running water and glaciers produce softer, more rounded edges. Eventually, the mountains will be completely worn away!

BIG WORD ALERT: SUMMIT A summit is the highest part of a mountain.

New Zealand's highest peak is Mount Cook. In 1991 the top 10 m fell off in an avalanche.

Mount Everest is known as Sagarmatha in Nepalese.

...o the world's second highest mountain. It is nearly 250 m ...orter than Everest.

The tallest peaks are in the Himalayas in southern Asia. The world's highest mountain, Mount Everest in Nepal, is here and measures 8,850 m. The Himalayas were formed when the Indian and Eurasian plates collided about 45 million years ago.

Ripley explains...

When two continental plates collide, the rocks on both plates become compressed (squashed) and folded. Over millions of years, the folds are forced higher and higher above the surrounding surface. Mountains are formed in this way.

twist it!

A US expedition to the Himalayas in the 1960s was followed by a pilgrim from Nepal, who trekked barefoot through the snow and slept outdoors in temperatures as low as -29°C wearing just a shirt, trousers and an overcoat.

Mona Mule Pati and Pem Dorjee Sherpa were the first couple to get married at the top of Mount Everest, the world's highest peak. They exchanged their vows there in May 2005.

The highest mountain in the USA (outside Alaska) is Mount Whitney, California. It is less than 130 km from Zabriskie Point in Death Valley – the lowest point in the USA.

HIGH HOPES

The Caledonian Mountains of Scotland were once part of the Appalachian Mountains in North America, until they became separated by the Atlantic Ocean as plates moved apart.

...en Summits are a collection of the ...mountains on each continent. The ...on to climb all seven was Canadian ...ow in 1986.

...merica: Denali (6,194 m)
...merica: Aconcagua (6,959 m)
... Elbrus (5,642 m)
...Kilimanjaro (5,895 m)
...erest (8,850 m)
...sia: Carstenz Pyramid (4,884 m)
...c: Vinson Massif (4,897 m)

There are two 'base camps' on Everest, both at around 5,200 m. Climbers camp there on their way up and down the mountain, eating, resting, and acclimatizing (getting used to being so high up).

ICED TEA

Seven people sat down to eat a five-course meal that they had prepared on a mountain in Tibet. They carried their food, plus table, chairs, silver cutlery, wine, flowers and candles to a height of 6,700 m, and even dressed the part with top hats and smart suits and ties.

Mountain memorial

A giant face in the rocky mountainside of the Black Hills, South Dakota, USA, is part of a memorial to the area's Native Americans. The sculpture was begun in 1948 and still has lots of work to be done – eventually the mountain will show a whole figure riding a horse. It is being blasted out of the rock to honour Chief Crazy Horse.

172 m HIGH!

13

Ripley's Believe It or Not!®

RARE ROCK

A stone covered with long white 'hair' is so rare it has been valued at over a million dollars. The hair is strands of fossilized fungus formed over millions of years.

Twists are all about Believe It or Not: amazing facts, feats, and things that will make you go 'Wow!'

Look for the Ripley R to find out even more than you knew before!

Driest Atacama Desert, Chile, no rain since records began

Tallest Mount Everest 8,850 m

Deepest Pacific Ocean (Mariana Trench) 10,923 m

Iciest Antarctica has 90 per cent of Earth's ice

OUR PLACE IN SPACE

Welcome to planet Earth, a spinning ball of hot rock that flies through space at more than 107,000 km/h. The world is our home and we love it! Earth is one of eight planets that circles the Sun, and the Sun is just one of billions of stars in our galaxy – the Milky Way. What makes Earth so special? So far, it's the only place in the entire Universe we know of where life exists.

Feeling dizzy? You should be, because you're not only flying around the Sun, you're also spinning at 1,600 km/h as the Earth turns. It's the way the Earth spins on its own axis, and orbits the Sun, that gives us measurements of time, including our 24-hour days, our 365-day years and our seasons.

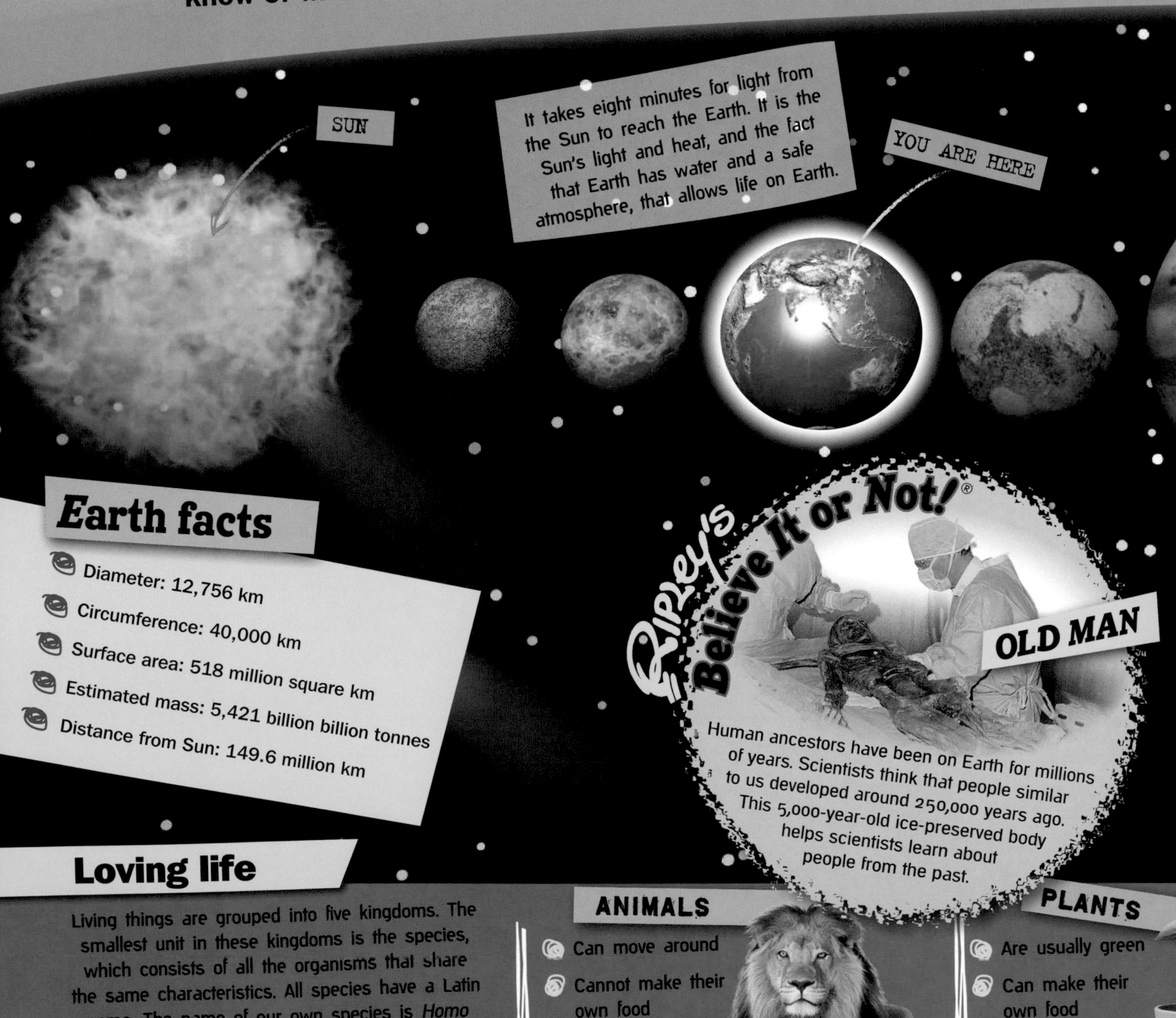

It takes eight minutes for light from the Sun to reach the Earth. It is the Sun's light and heat, and the fact that Earth has water and a safe atmosphere, that allows life on Earth.

Earth facts

- Diameter: 12,756 km
- Circumference: 40,000 km
- Surface area: 518 million square km
- Estimated mass: 5,421 billion billion tonnes
- Distance from Sun: 149.6 million km

Ripley's Believe It or Not!®

OLD MAN

Human ancestors have been on Earth for millions of years. Scientists think that people similar to us developed around 250,000 years ago. This 5,000-year-old ice-preserved body helps scientists learn about people from the past.

Loving life

Living things are grouped into five kingdoms. The smallest unit in these kingdoms is the species, which consists of all the organisms that share the same characteristics. All species have a Latin name. The name of our own species is *Homo sapiens* (which means 'wise man'). Which kingdom do you think we fit into?

ANIMALS

- Can move around
- Cannot make their own food
- Have more than one cell

PLANTS

- Are usually green
- Can make their own food
- Have more than one cell

Ripley explains...

Tilted axis

Sun

Earth's orbit

Winter in southern hemisphere

The Earth is tilted in relation to the Sun. As the Earth makes its 365-day journey around the Sun, different parts of it are tilted towards, or away from, the Sun's light and heat. The Sun's light and heat hit the different places on Earth at different angles, giving some places more sunlight in summer and less in winter.

SUPER PLANET

The largest animal species that has ever lived is alive today. A full-grown blue whale can reach 30 m in length and weigh 135 tonnes.

Scientists estimate there are about 20 million different living species on Earth, of which only about 10 per cent have been identified and described.

A mushroom fossil found in Myanmar, Asia, is thought to be as much as 100 million years old.

The Earth is slowing down! It is spinning on its axis less quickly, and scientists say it may be significant enough for days in the future to have 25 hours instead of 24.

Fossils of sea creatures have been found near the top of Mount Everest.

twist it!

AXIS
Imaginary line drawn through the centre of the Earth from the North Pole to the South Pole.

Fossil finds

Fossils are living things that have been turned to rock over millions of years. They provide evidence of creatures that lived long ago, and allow scientists to work out what has been happening with life on our planet.

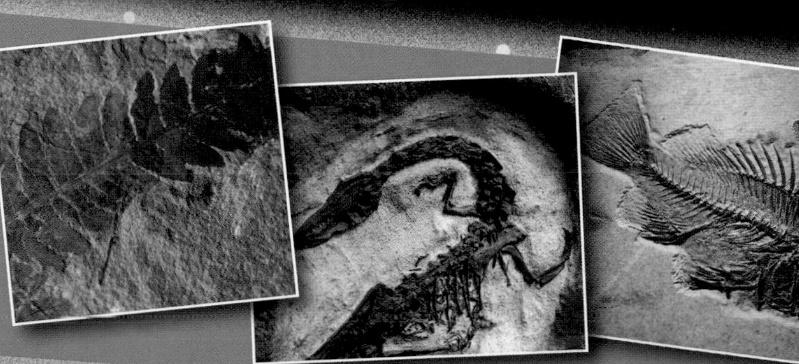

FUNGI

- Cannot make their own food
- Produce spores, not seeds eg yeast, mould
- Have more than one cell

PROTISTA

- Have only one cell
- Often live in soil or water eg amoeba

MONERA

- Have only one cell
- Very simple eg bacteria

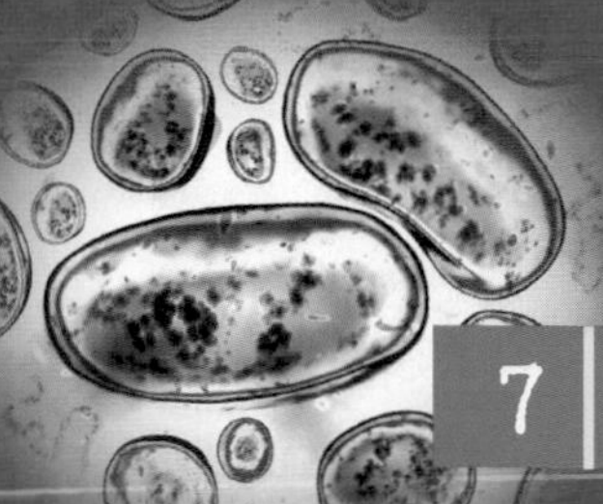

CRACKING UP

A LOOK INSIDE

There are 14 large plates and 38 smaller plates. Seven of the larger plates roughly match up to the continents of the world.

The plates carrying North America and Europe are moving away from one another at a speed of about 1.8 m every 75 years. That means the two continents are getting farther away from each other at about the same rate your fingernails are growing!

The world is cracking up! The planet's outermost layer is a thick band of rock, called the crust – and it's in pieces. These pieces, known as plates, fit together like a giant jigsaw puzzle.

Strangely, plates are always on the move, stretching and squashing into one another as their edges grow or get sucked down into a super-hot layer of molten rock below. This whole fantastical process is called plate tectonics, and these crusty clashes are to blame for volcanoes, rift valleys, mountains and earthquakes.

About 250 million years ago, all of today's landmasses were joined in one super-continent called Pangaea. As the Earth's plates moved, at maximum speeds of just 12 cm a year, it was pulled apart.

The Earth has three layers: the crust, the mantle, and the core. The mantle is a thick layer of molten (liquid) rock with temperatures up to 3,200°C. Below is Earth's core where temperatures rise above 5,000°C. The outer core is liquid, but the pressure keeps the inner core solid.

The supercontinent of Pangaea was surrounded by a single ocean called Panthalassa. Look carefully at this map and you might see some familiar continent shapes.

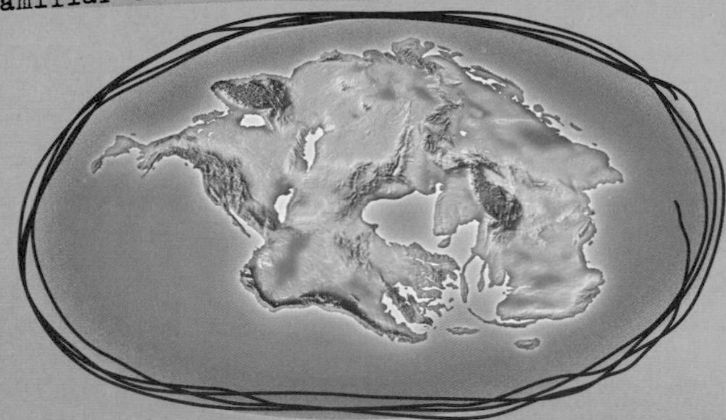

Hot stuff

It's your fault

Some of the world's worst earthquakes happen along fault lines. The San Andreas Fault in California marks the boundary between the Pacific and North American plates. The fault line extends at least 16 km into the Earth, and stretches for over 1,100 km from north to south.

AROUND THE WORLD

The interior of the Earth is kept hot by heat from when the planet first formed, heat produced by radioactive elements, and heat from small dense particles colliding as they sink towards the centre of the Earth.

Although the Earth's crust is made of rock and is solid, it is actually nearly 50 per cent oxygen.

The South Pacific island of Niuafo'ou is the fastest-moving place on Earth, moving at 25 cm a year.

Margaret Hegarty of Concord in North Carolina, USA, is the oldest woman to run a marathon on each of the seven continents. She was 76 when she completed the task, but has carried on running well into her 80s.

Lava lover

Volcanic craters are a kind of window to the inner Earth. The hot, molten rock (called magma) in the mantle can push its way to the surface, where it comes out as lava.

Patrick Koster from the Netherlands has spent ten years photographing volcanoes and loves them so much that he proposed to his wife at the edge of a crater. He even reorganised his honeymoon so that he didn't miss a major eruption.

SHOCKS AND SHAKES

Hold on tight – the Earth's moving! For a few terrifying seconds the ground shakes and quakes. Buildings topple and great cracks appear in the Earth's surface as it rips open – this is the awesome power of an earthquake.

These mighty Earth movements happen in an instant, but they build up over a long time. As the Earth's plates grind against one another they build up tension. One sudden slip is all it takes for all that stored energy to be released, with ferocious force. Entire cities may be destroyed in an earthquake, bringing misery, chaos and death.

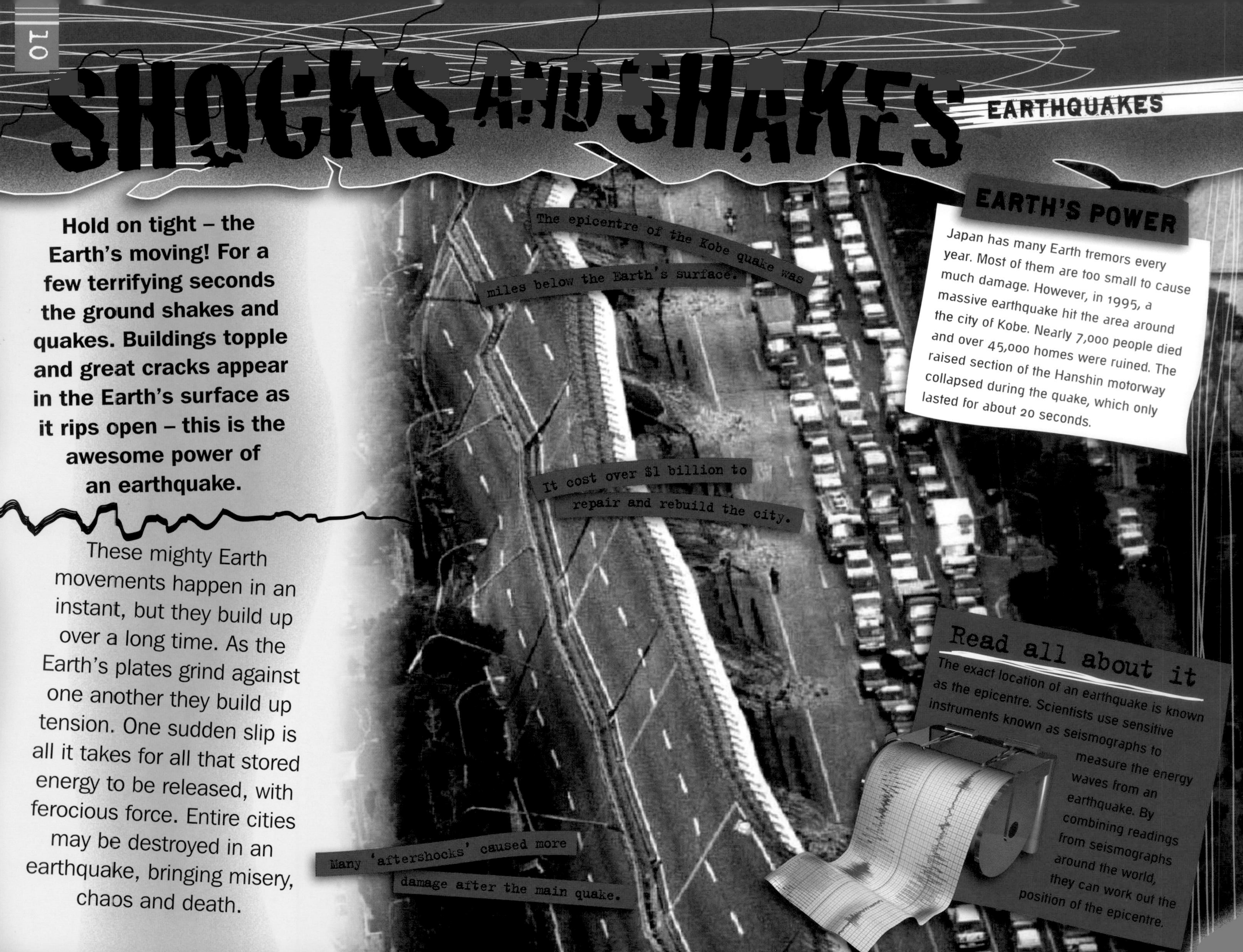

The epicentre of the Kobe quake was miles below the Earth's surface.

It cost over $1 billion to repair and rebuild the city.

Many 'aftershocks' caused more damage after the main quake.

EARTH'S POWER

Japan has many Earth tremors every year. Most of them are too small to cause much damage. However, in 1995, a massive earthquake hit the area around the city of Kobe. Nearly 7,000 people died and over 45,000 homes were ruined. The raised section of the Hanshin motorway collapsed during the quake, which only lasted for about 20 seconds.

Read all about it

The exact location of an earthquake is known as the epicentre. Scientists use sensitive instruments known as seismographs to measure the energy waves from an earthquake. By combining readings from seismographs around the world, they can work out the position of the epicentre.

18 April, 1906

DISASTER STRIKES SAN FRANCISCO

An earthquake lasting only a minute struck San Francisco at 5:12 this morning, and has caused the worst damage seen in this nation's history. Fires are raging through the city, leaving people without homes, work, belongings and loved ones.

Eyewitnesses report seeing buildings crushed like a biscuit in your hand, the ground moving in waves like the ocean, and the earth slipping from beneath their feet. Some streets have sunk by over a metre; others have been pushed up to form 1.5-m-high waves of rubble.

One result of earthquakes is that the shaking can cause some soils to behave like liquids, so that buildings sink into the ground.

Clever creatures

Japanese scientists believe the deep-sea oarfish, which usually lives at depths of up to 200 m, helps them to predict earthquakes by appearing at the surface before tremors are felt.

30 April, 1906

QUAKE UPDATE:

The fires in San Francisco burned for three days. Over a quarter of a million people were made homeless, and at least 3,000 people were killed. Nearly 500 city blocks – at least 25,000 buildings – were destroyed.

ALL SHOOK UP

The island of Ranongga in the South Pacific was lifted out of the water by over 3 m in 2007, by an earthquake that measured 8.1 on the Richter scale.

An earthquake in Mexico in 1985 was strong enough to shake water out of a swimming pool 2,000 km away in Tucson, Arizona, USA.

Hundreds of hibernating snakes came out from their underground hideaways in China, just before an earthquake struck in 1975.

A 2007 earthquake was powerful enough to throw back a torpedo boat that had sunk in World War II.

The shock waves forming an earthquake can travel between 6 km a second and 11 km a second, depending whether they are in the Earth's core or near the surface.

>>Double disaster<<

The mountainous province of Sichuan in southwest China was hit by an earthquake in May, 2008. Nearly 90,000 people were either killed or reported missing. A year later, a landslide destroyed this bridge – part of a main road used while trying to rebuild the devastated area – killing even more people.

Twist it!

ROOF of the WORLD

MIGHTY MOUNTAINS

Majestic mountain ranges are nature's way of showing off! Their spectacular peaks are capped in clouds and mist and cloaked with snow and ice.

Mountains are created by the slow-moving forces that cause the Earth's plates to collide. Over time, rock is thrust upwards, crumpling and folding into beautiful shapes. It takes millions of years, but as soon as mountains form, erosion and weathering start to wear them down. As ice freezes and thaws near the peaks, rocks split and break away, leaving sharp pyramid-like tops, while running water and glaciers produce softer, more rounded edges. Eventually, the mountains will be completely worn away!

New Zealand's highest peak is Mount Cook. In 1991 the top 10 m fell off in an avalanche.

Mount Everest is known as Sagarmatha in Nepalese.

K2 is the world's second highest mountain. It is nearly 250 m shorter than Everest.

The tallest peaks are in the Himalayas in southern Asia. The world's highest mountain, Mount Everest in Nepal, is here and measures 8,850 m. The Himalayas were formed when the Indian and Eurasian plates collided about 45 million years ago.

The Seven Summits are a collection of the highest mountains on each continent. The first person to climb all seven was Canadian Pat Morrow in 1986.

- North America: Denali (6,194 m)
- South America: Aconcagua (6,959 m)
- Europe: Elbrus (5,642 m)
- Africa: Kilimanjaro (5,895 m)
- Asia: Everest (8,850 m)
- Australasia: Carstenz Pyramid (4,884 m)
- Antarctic: Vinson Massif (4,897 m)

There are two 'base camps' on Everest, both at around 5,200 m. Climbers camp there on their way up and down the mountain, eating, resting, and acclimatizing (getting used to being so high up).

BIG WORD ALERT

SUMMIT A summit is the highest part of a mountain.

Ripley explains...

When two continental plates collide, the rocks on both plates become compressed (squashed) and folded. Over millions of years, the folds are forced higher and higher above the surrounding surface. Mountains are formed in this way.

twist it!

HIGH HOPES

The Caledonian Mountains of Scotland were once part of the Appalachian Mountains in North America, until they became separated by the Atlantic Ocean as plates moved apart.

The highest mountain in the USA (outside Alaska) is Mount Whitney, California. It is less than 130 km from Zabriskie Point in Death Valley – the lowest point in the USA.

Mona Mule Pati and Pem Dorjee Sherpa were the first couple to get married at the top of Mount Everest, the world's highest peak. They exchanged their vows there in May 2005.

A US expedition to the Himalayas in the 1960s was followed by a pilgrim from Nepal, who trekked barefoot through the snow and slept outdoors in temperatures as low as −29°C wearing just a shirt, trousers and an overcoat.

Mountain memorial

A giant face in the rocky mountainside of the Black Hills, South Dakota, USA, is part of a memorial to the area's Native Americans. The sculpture was begun in 1948 and still has lots of work to be done – eventually the mountain will show a whole figure riding a horse. It is being blasted out of the rock to honour Chief Crazy Horse.

172 m HIGH!

ICED TEA

Seven people sat down to eat a five-course meal that they had prepared on a mountain in Tibet. They carried their food, plus table, chairs, silver cutlery, wine, flowers and candles to a height of 6,700 m, and even dressed the part with top hats and smart suits and ties.

VIOLENT ERUPTIONS

VOLCANOES

When a mountain comes to life, and starts spouting smoke and spewing lava, it's clearly no ordinary mountain. Mighty volcanoes sit on top of the Earth's hot spots.

Super-heated rock bubbles quietly beneath the surface until its energy can no longer be contained – and an explosive force erupts. Boiling liquid rock, poisonous gases, ash and volcanic bombs all spew out of active volcanoes, spelling tragedy and devastation for people living nearby. When volcanoes are quiet, between eruptions, they are described as dormant, and when they are no longer active at all, volcanoes are said to be extinct.

The temperature of lava inside a crater can reach 1,480°C. That's nearly one third the temperature of the Sun's surface.

The 1883 eruption of Krakatoa created a tsunami that was 40 m high.

The Indonesian volcano Krakatoa killed over 36,000 people when it erupted in 1883. 165 towns and villages were destroyed and another 132 were badly damaged. Debris was blown 35 km into the sky, and the noise of the eruption could be heard over 7,200 km away in Sri Lanka. In 2009, the volcano began erupting again.

Bubbling under?

The mud-filled crater of Totumo volcano in Colombia is a popular bathing spot! The hot mud is supposed to have beneficial effects on the human body.

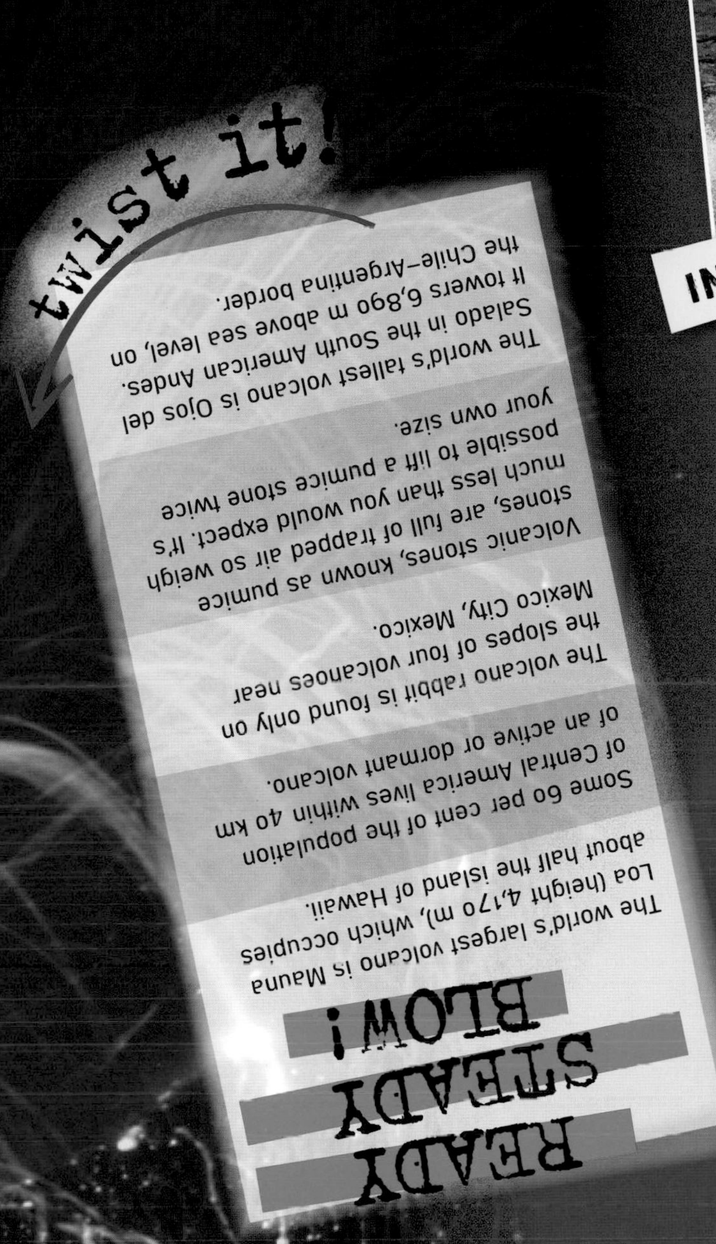

twist it!

READY STEADY BLOW!

The world's largest volcano is Mauna Loa (height 4,170 m), which occupies about half the island of Hawaii.

Some 60 per cent of the population of Central America lives within 40 km of an active or dormant volcano.

The volcano rabbit is found only on the slopes of four volcanoes near Mexico City, Mexico.

Volcanic stones, known as pumice stones, are full of trapped air so weigh much less than you would expect. It's possible to lift a pumice stone twice your own size.

The world's tallest volcano is Ojos del Salado in the South American Andes. It towers 6,890 m above sea level, on the Chile–Argentina border.

IN HOT WATER

Extreme surfer CJ Kanuha surfed within 6 m of the lava flow from Kilauea volcano on Hawaii's Big Island. The molten rock heats the sea to 200°C and it melted the wax on his surfboard.

Ripley explains...

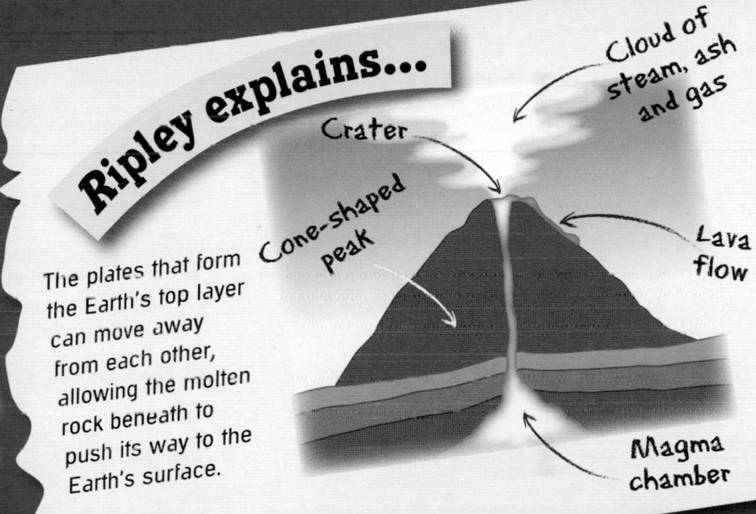

The plates that form the Earth's top layer can move away from each other, allowing the molten rock beneath to push its way to the Earth's surface.

Buried in ash

In 79 AD Mount Vesuvius erupted and buried the Roman town of Pompeii under 6 m of ash. Archaeologists discovered casts of the bodies of some of the unfortunate inhabitants who were buried as they tried to hide or escape.

Blown sky high

This photograph is of Sarychev Peak, next door to Russia and Japan. It erupted in 2009, blowing an 8-km tower of smoke, ash and steam into the air and through a hole blown in the clouds by the force. The picture was taken from the International Space Station, orbiting the Earth.

MAGMA

The molten rock from deep inside the Earth. It is called lava once it has made its way to the surface.

WELLHARD

ROCKS AND MINERALS

Think rocks are dull? Think again, because some of them are shiny or colourful, and a few even contain precious minerals and gems, such as diamonds! There are three main types of rock: igneous, metamorphic and sedimentary.

The type of rock that forms in the Earth's crust depends on three things: temperature, pressure, and the recipe of minerals it contains. When these three factors play their part, a soup of minerals can be transformed into different rocks, such as a smooth, sparkling white marble, or a salt-and-pepper patterned granite. And if rocks get very hot and squashed again, they melt back into a mineral magma soup!

FIRE ROCKS

Igneous rocks form from magma that has cooled and turned hard when it came close to, or burst through, the Earth's surface. The Giant's Causeway on the coast of Northern Ireland is made up of about 40,000 columns of the igneous rock basalt that were pushed up millions of years ago.

Igneous rocks are sometimes called fire rocks because they were formed from volcanic material.

SET IN STONE

Sedimentary rocks are formed from sediments, such as sand and clay, that are deposited by wind and water. These amazing sandstone stripes are part of the Coyote Buttes and are known as The Wave. They were formed around 190 million years ago on the border of Arizona and Utah, USA. Over time, the sandstone has been eroded into the fascinating swirling shapes.

Rock formation

These may look just like piles of stones – very cleverly balanced, you must admit – but they're more than that. They are 'inukshuk', stone landmarks built by many Arctic people. Enukso Point on Baffin Island, Canada, is a national historic site containing more than 100 of these stone structures.

ROCK 'N' ROLL

Certain types of the sedimentary rock limestone are composed entirely of the compressed shells of prehistoric sea creatures.

In 1906, a miner named Lindsay Hicks was buried inside Granite Mountain, California, after a mine cave-in. He was covered by thousands of tonnes of rock, but was rescued unharmed after 15 days.

Rocks have been forming and changing for millions of years. If you climb the Guadalupe Mountains in Texas you will be touching limestone that was once a tropical reef, about 250 million years ago.

twist it!

BIG WORD ALERT

GEOLOGISTS Scientists who study rocks.

Ripley's Believe It or Not!®

RARE ROCK

A stone covered with long white 'hair' is so rare it has been valued at over a million dollars. The hair is strands of fossilised fungus formed over millions of years.

ALL CHANGE

Metamorphic rocks are rocks that have been metamorphosed (changed into something else) by volcanic heat and pressure. Slate, for example, is metamorphosed shale, and limestone turns into marble. Many of the world's mountain ranges contain metamorphic rocks. These rocks in the Swiss Alps have been changed further by glacier movement smoothing and scratching them.

GOING UNDERGROUND

CAVES AND MINES

Hidden from view, below the ground, are some of the Earth's most amazing natural wonders. Enormous caves and labyrinths of tunnels weave between solid rocks, carved out by the powerful force of water.

The crystals are made of gypsum and are translucent.

Rainwater and river water can seep through the cracks in rocks to form underground rivers. Water also dissolves some rocks, such as limestone, turning it into a liquid that drips and hardens again, to create amazing stalactites and stalagmites.

Some tunnels and caves owe more to people power. Valuable minerals such as coal form deep underground, and miners remove them by cutting into the rock, creating tunnels and caves.

The biggest crystals are 12 m long.

CRYSTAL CAVE

These crystal daggers are as long as a bus! They were found by miners in 2000, around 300 m below the ground. They are part of the Naica Mine in Mexico, which has other caves containing smaller – but still spectacular – crystal formations.

Miners had to pump water out of the cave to clear it.

Light up, light up

Cave tours in New Zealand let you see in the dark! The roof of this cave is covered with glowing fireflies. The creatures are actually beetles and can flash their lights to attract other fireflies. They make the light on their abdomen by allowing air to mix with a special substance they produce.

MILES UNDERGROUND

The world's longest system of underground caves is the Mammoth Cave complex below Kentucky, USA, which extends over 565 km (about the distance from Los Angeles to San Francisco) and has a maximum depth of 115 m.

COOL DOWN

Temperatures in Coober Pedy, in the Australian outback, reach an uncomfortable 49°C, and so the people there have moved somewhere cooler: underground. There are a range of houses to choose from here, plus shops, museums, churches and hotels.

DEEP THOUGHTS

The deepest oil well ever drilled is the Tiber well that goes 10,685 m below the seabed in the Gulf of Mexico. This means that the bottom of the well is more than 11,800 m below sea level, and deeper than Mount Everest is high.

Blackwater rafting is a thrill-a-minute sport that takes participants through the caves of New Zealand – on an inner tube! Underground rivers carry along the tubes through dark passages that can be full of eels.

Starting in 1906, William Schmidt spent 38 years digging an underground passage through the El Paso Mountains of California. He burrowed for 630 m and through more than 2,350 tonnes of rock.

twist it!

SPELEOLOGY
The science of exploring underground spaces.

COMFORT BLANKET

THE ATMOSPHERE

The atmosphere around our planet keeps it nice and cosy! This thick layer of air is a rich mix of gases that protects us from the burning rays of the Sun, and keeps the heat in at night, like a comforting blanket.

That's not all we have to thank the atmosphere for: one of its top jobs is creating climate. The bottom layer of the atmosphere is called the troposphere and this is where weather happens. Liquid water spends part of its time as water vapour, high in the sky, and some of the water that falls today as rain was once drunk by dinosaurs!

SKY LIGHTS

Amazing light displays appear in the highest layers of the atmosphere and can be seen near the North and South poles. They are called the aurora borealis (say or-ora bor-ee-ar-lis) in the north and aurora australis (say or-ora os-trar-lis) in the south. The lights are created by a reaction between atoms from the Sun and gases in the Earth's atmosphere.

The auroras are sometimes called the Northern Lights or Southern Lights.

Sometimes the lights move and dance or shimmer.

Ripley's Believe It or Not!®

All hail

Hailstones can grow really big – like these ones found after a hailstorm in Kansas, USA, in 1999.

HEAD IN THE CLOUDS

Clouds form different shapes at different heights, and depending how much water or ice they contain. Thin, wispy clouds high in the sky are known as cirrus clouds. This one, seen over Wellington in New Zealand, has been blown into the shape of a deer!

Ripley explains...

Water in the oceans – or even in a puddle – evaporates (turns to gas) and mixes with the air. It is carried by the wind until it condenses (turns back to water), making clouds. It falls back to the ground as precipitation and the cycle starts all over again.

>> Blown away <<

This house was damaged by a tornado. It had one end blown off completely, but the inside was left intact. The dishes in the pantry weren't even broken!

Twists it!

RAIN OR SHINE

Within the troposphere, the air temperature drops by about 6.5°C per 1,000 m of altitude.

Mount Waialeale, on Kauai in Hawaii, has rain nearly every day of the year. Only a few miles away on the coast, they get as little rain as 50 cm in a whole year.

NASA satellites have shown that the two sunniest places in the world are patches in the Pacific Ocean, south of Hawaii, and in the Sahara Desert in Niger.

Up to 100 tonnes of space dust falls into the Earth's atmosphere every day. That's about the same weight as 20 African elephants.

BIG WORD ALERT

PRECIPITATION
Any kind of wetness coming from the sky: rain, snow, sleet, hail, and even fog.

FUNNEL VISION

A tornado is a whirling funnel of air formed in some thunderstorms. They can travel at high speeds of 400 km/h and cause chaos and destruction. They happen in many parts of the world, but are frequent and famous in the central states of the USA, which are known as 'tornado alley'.

BEND IT

A rainbow is formed by sunlight being refracted (bent) by raindrops. You will only see a rainbow if the sun is behind you.

UP IN THE AIR

WILD WEATHER

Take a look outside – is the weather looking wild or mild? Right this moment there are about 2,000 thunderstorms and 100 flashes of lightning zapping through the sky, all over the world. Just one flash of supercharged lightning contains enough energy to light 150 million light bulbs!

Extreme weather might get you off school, but it can play havoc with people's lives. In the globe's cold spots, temperatures dip below a supercool –15°C in winter, while coastal areas can be hit by storm surges, gale force winds, and heavy rains that bring cliffs crashing to the ground.

- An average lightning storm can discharge sufficient power to supply the entire USA with electricity for 20 minutes.
- In 1998, during a soccer game in the Democratic Republic of Congo, all 11 players on one team were killed by lightning. None of the other team was struck.
- A single lightning strike in Utah, in 1918, killed 504 sheep in one blast.
- Ray Cauldwell, a baseball pitcher for the Cleveland Indians, was struck by lightning while playing. He was knocked unconscious but came to and carried on playing – and was on the winning side!

Kenneth Libbrecht of California has found a way to take photos of snowflakes. The results are beautiful, and show the six-sided formation of each individual flake.

CRYSTAL CLEAR

If the air in the atmosphere is cold enough, the rising water vapour (see Ripley explains, page 21) freezes instead of turning to liquid. This forms six-sided crystals: snowflakes. The air near the ground needs to be below freezing, too, or the crystals will turn to rain as they fall.

FREAKY FREEZE

Residents near Lake Geneva were shocked by scenes in January 2005. Gale-force winds carried water droplets from the lake, which froze on anything in their path because of −12°C temperatures.

Really wild

A hurricane is the most awesomely powerful of all weather events. The largest hurricanes extend 1,000–1,600 km in diameter and produce winds up to 320 km/h. They are caused by rising warm air over the ocean. As the storm reaches land, it begins to die out – but can still last for days and cause devastating damage.

SNOW DONUTS

These amazing snow rollers, or snow donuts, are formed naturally when a clump of soft snow falls into hard snow at the top of a slope. They are quite rare, but Mike Stanford found these ones in Washington State in 2007 that were big enough to poke his head through!

HOME ALONE

A hurricane raged across Texas in 2008 and completely flattened buildings and trees. The only house left standing in one area was that of Warren and Pam Adams. They had lost a previous home to a 2005 hurricane, so had wisely built their new one on 4-m-high columns to withstand the storms.

>> Fenced in <<

A 2008 hurricane in Texas left these fish high and dry! The storm caused huge floods, which carried these fish over a metre high and left them stuck in the links of a fence.

WATERWORLD

We call our planet Earth, but a better name might be Water, because more than 70 per cent of the world's surface is actually covered by oceans and seas.

OCEAN COMMOTION

The biggest and deepest ocean is the Pacific and it contains more than half of the entire planet's seawater. While lakes and rivers have fresh water, which we can drink, oceans and seas are salty. There are five main zones, or layers, in the oceans, from just below the surface to the darkest depths.

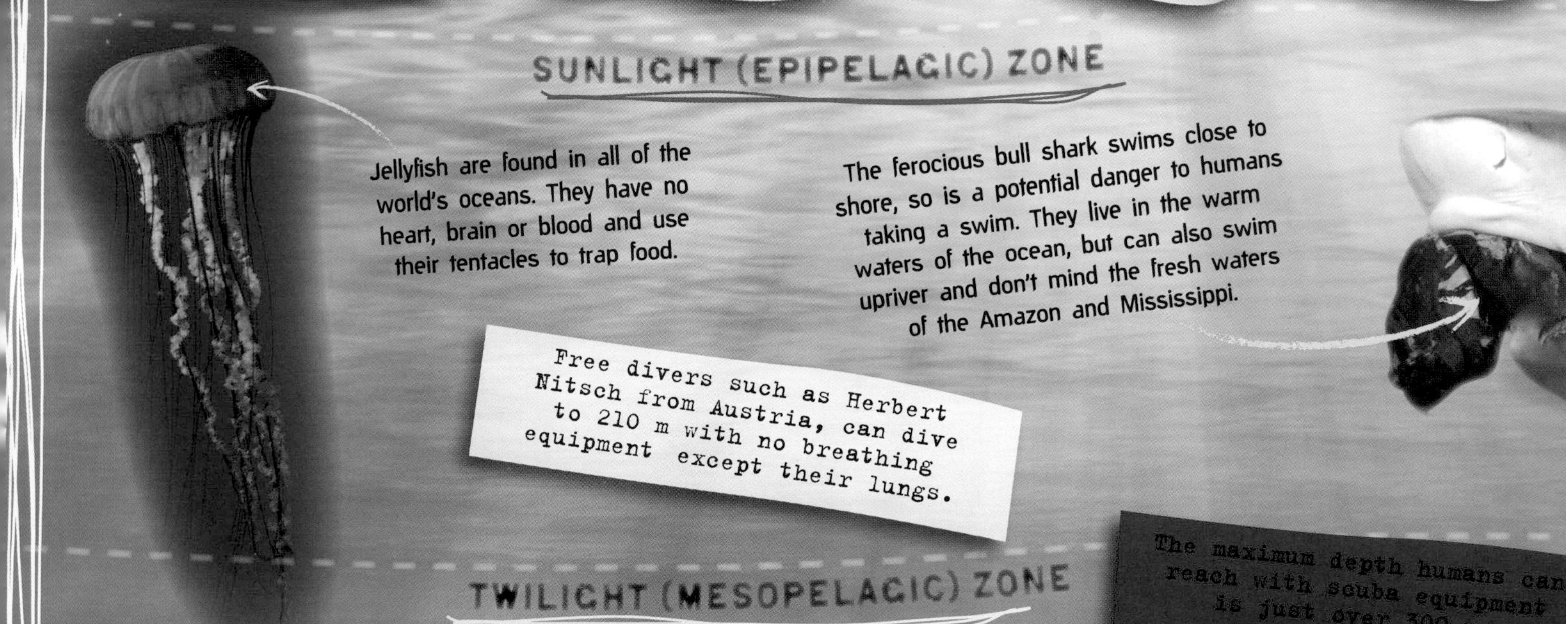

SUNLIGHT (EPIPELAGIC) ZONE

Jellyfish are found in all of the world's oceans. They have no heart, brain or blood and use their tentacles to trap food.

The ferocious bull shark swims close to shore, so is a potential danger to humans taking a swim. They live in the warm waters of the ocean, but can also swim upriver and don't mind the fresh waters of the Amazon and Mississippi.

Free divers such as Herbert Nitsch from Austria, can dive to 210 m with no breathing equipment except their lungs.

TWILIGHT (MESOPELAGIC) ZONE

The maximum depth humans can reach with scuba equipment is just over 300 m.

The menacing-looking fangtooth fish only grows to about 15 cm, but its teeth are the largest of any ocean fish compared to its body size.

MAKING A SPLASH

Scientists have calculated that there are about the same number of molecules in a spoonful of water as there are spoonfuls of water in the Atlantic Ocean.

The Atlantic Ocean is still growing at a rate of 3.8 cm per year. This means it was about 20 m narrower when Columbus landed in America in the 15th century.

From the top of Mount Irazu in Costa Rica you can see both the Pacific Ocean and the Atlantic Ocean.

In 1990, ocean adventurer Tom McClean sailed across the Atlantic in a boat shaped like a bottle. Onboard he had a four poster bed!

twist it!

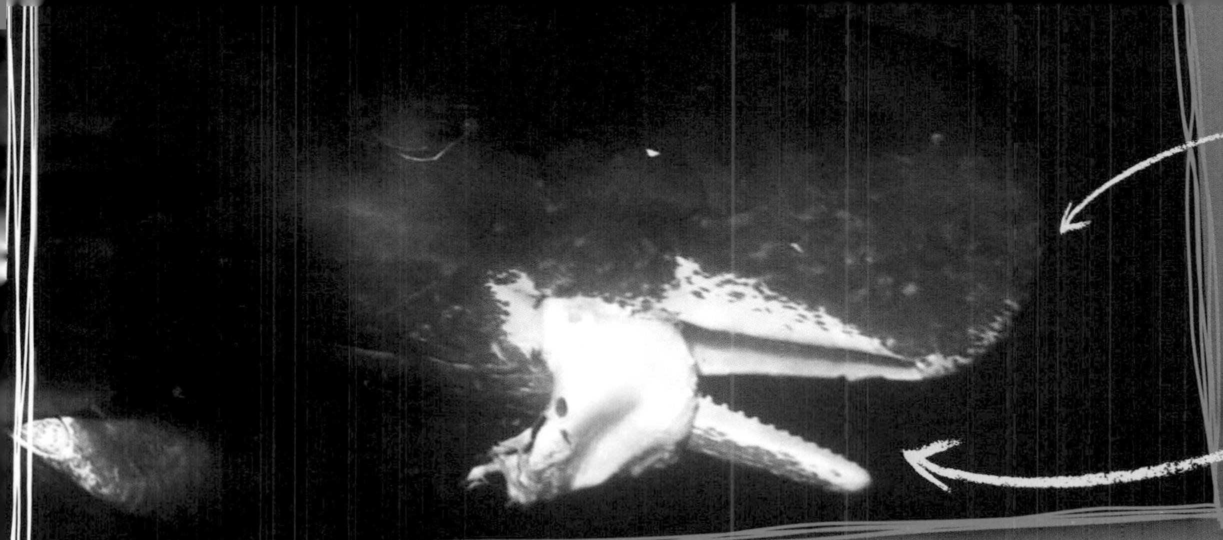

MIDNIGHT (BATHYPELAGIC) ZONE

1,000–4,000 m

The sperm whale can dive deeper than most other whales – probably as deep as 2,500 m. The water pressure is so great that it squashes its rib cage, but the whale's ribs are designed to fold up so they stay unhurt.

Giant squid are so big they can eat fish, crabs and even sharks. They catch their prey by coiling up their tentacles around their victim. The squid must watch out, though – they are the chosen food of the sperm whale.

ABYSS (ABYSSOPELAGIC) ZONE

4,000–6,000 m

Manned submersibles such as the US *Alvin* dive to depths of around 4,500 m to study ocean life.

The dumbo octopus gets its name from its ear-shaped fins that make it look like an elephant. It moves by flapping these fins to push itself through the water.

TRENCH (HADALPELAGIC) ZONE

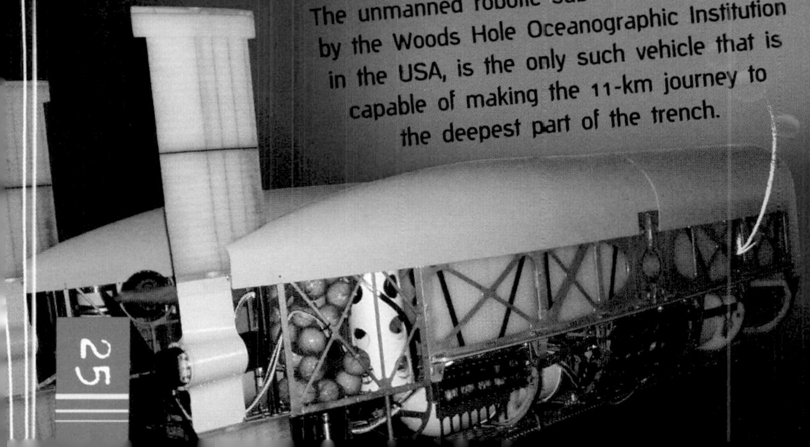

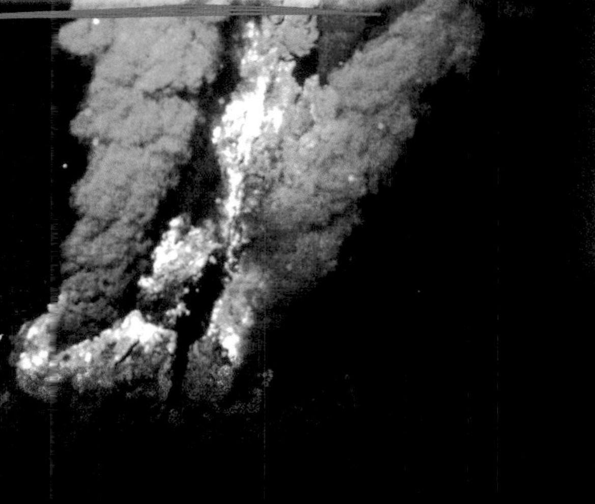

Hydrothermal vents appear at plate boundaries on the ocean floor. Water seeps into the Earth's crust and into the Earth's crust and is heated by the magma, then shoots back up through cracks in the ocean floor.

The unmanned robotic sub *Nereus*, developed by the Woods Hole Oceanographic Institution in the USA, is the only such vehicle that is capable of making the 11-km journey to the deepest part of the trench.

REMARKABLE REEFS

CORAL AND THE TROPICS

Coral reefs can grow enormous, but they are built by tiny animals that are no bigger than your fingernail!

Reefs are rocky structures that are home to little squashy polyps, which are related to sea anemones and jellyfish. The polyps use minerals from the water to create rocky cups around themselves. Over many years, thousands of polyps add to a reef, and it grows bigger. Lots of other animals find refuge in the reef and become part of a precious ecosystem. Polyps grow best in warm, shallow and clean water in the tropics just north and south of the Equator.

Many of the species living in reefs look like plants, but are animals that feed on fish and animal scraps.

400 species of coral make up the Great Barrier Reef.

Around 1,500 species of fish live on the Great Barrier Reef.

The world's largest reef is the Great Barrier Reef, which runs some 2,000 km along the eastern coast of Australia and covers an area of about 207,000 square km.

Reef-building corals need sunlight and cannot live below about 60 m. They are also very sensitive to water temperature and cannot tolerate changes of more than about 1°C. Coral polyps can be as small as 3 mm, but they form colonies up to 1.5 m across.

Hideaways

Many reef-dwellers use camouflage to keep them safe in the sea. They may choose bright colours and hide in the coral itself, or disguise themselves with sandy colours and burrow into the seabed.

COMMON OCTOPUS

Ripley's Believe It or Not!®

Toothy monsters

Moray eels cannot swallow their prey. Instead, they have a second set of teeth in their throat, which move forward to grab the prey and pull it into their body to digest.

DIVE IN!

Coral reefs are very fragile, and each year boat propellers, anchors, fishing nets and careless divers damage large areas of reef.

Beware of the attractive red fire coral – if touched with bare skin the coral polyps will deliver a nasty sting.

Coral reefs sometimes form ring-shaped islands, known as atolls, around the craters of undersea volcanoes.

The shallow waters off Palm Beach, Florida, are home to an unusual reef: an artificial commemorative reef, made from concrete cases containing the cremated remains of dead people.

The Great Barrier Reef is longer than the west coast of the USA.

twist it!

Cleaning up

Certain small fish have an important job on the reef: cleaning up. Larger fish allow them to swim into their mouth, without eating them, to nibble at the parasites that pester them. Some turtles even visit special 'cleaning stations' to get rid of unwanted hitchhikers on their shells and soft undersides.

ON THE EDGE
COASTLINES

Coasts are the world's most popular places to live, but they are also among the most dangerous. Crashing waves, storm surges, collapsing cliffs, and terrible tsunamis mark out the seashore as a place of potential peril!

The ebb and flow of the oceans also make their mark on coastal life and landforms. Twice a day, the water level at a shore rises and falls in a freaky phenomenon we call tides.

High tides and low tides are the result of big bulges in seawater that are caused by the Moon! As our near neighbour orbits Earth, and Earth spins, the Moon's gravity pulls on the water, forcing it to move in and out at coastlines.

Many mountaineers climb up the stack to reach the top.

The Old Man of Hoy is still being eroded and getting weaker at its base.

This tall rock is called the Old Man of Hoy. It is 137 m high and is found in the Orkney Islands, Scotland. Rocks like this one are called sea stacks and are made when the waves crash against the coast. Eventually enough rock is worn away to leave a tower standing on its own.

The rock was probably part of the coast as little as 400 years ago.

Along steep rocky coasts, the action of the tide and waves often forms vertical cliffs. The world's tallest sea cliffs are on Canada's Baffin Island and rise some 1,370 m above the sea.

Jim Denevan's sand art

Sand artist Jim Denevan spends up to 7 hours creating his pictures. He uses a stick washed up from the sea to draw with, and walks up to 50 km up and down the beach. When the waves come, his work is washed away.

FIX STAMP HERE

P. Mariner
Lighthouse Road
Norfolk

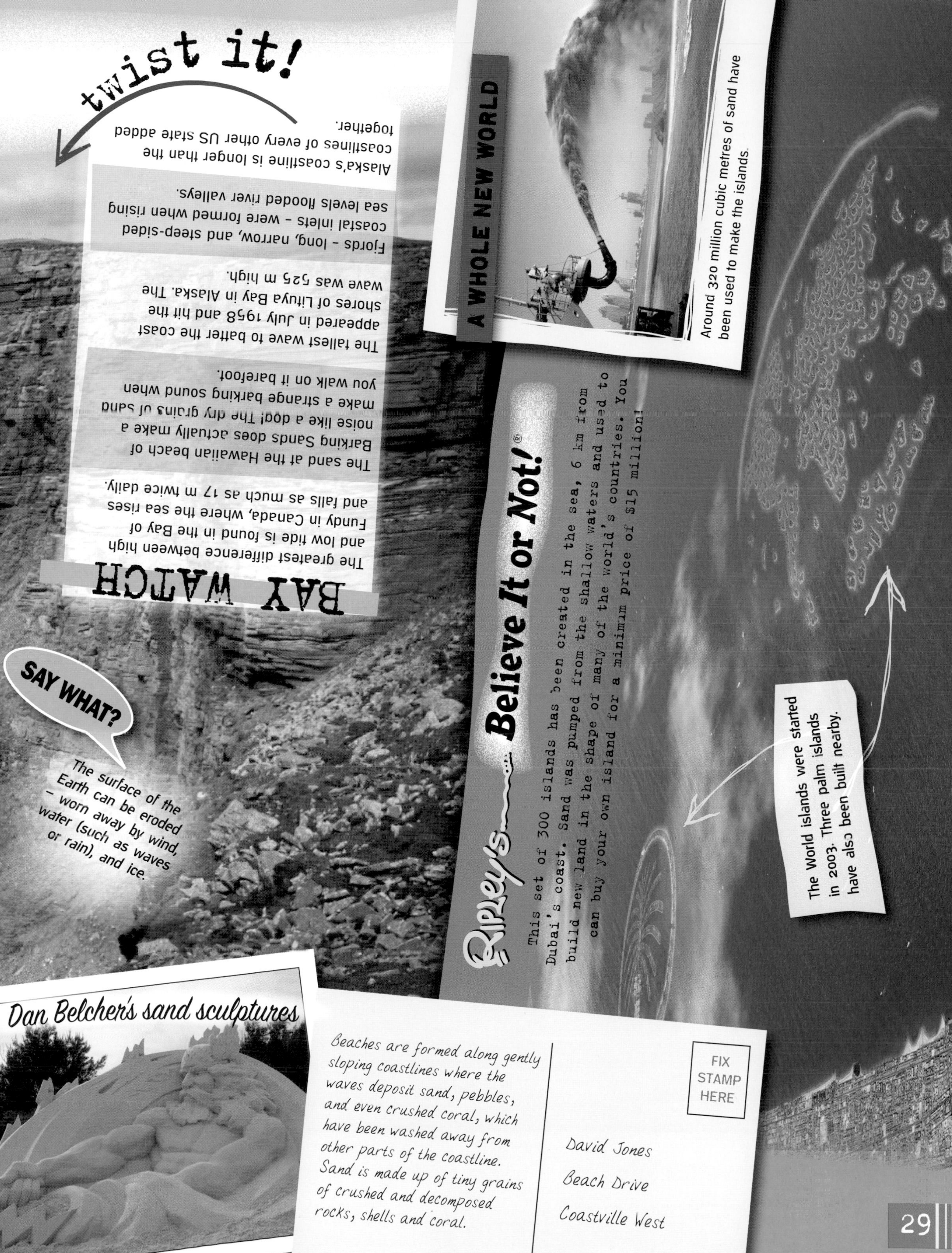

twist it!
BAY WATCH
The greatest difference between high and low tide is found in the Bay of Fundy in Canada, where the sea rises and falls as much as 17 m twice daily.
The sand at the Hawaiian beach of Barking Sands does actually make a noise like a dog! The dry grains of sand make a strange barking sound when you walk on it barefoot.
The tallest wave to batter the coast appeared in July 1958 and hit the shores of Lituya Bay in Alaska. The wave was 525 m high.
Fjords – long, narrow, and steep-sided coastal inlets – were formed when rising sea levels flooded river valleys.
Alaska's coastline is longer than the coastlines of every other US state added together.
A WHOLE NEW WORLD
Around 320 million cubic metres of sand have been used to make the islands.
Ripley's Believe It or Not!®
This set of 300 islands has been created in the sea, 6 km from Dubai's coast. Sand was pumped from the shallow waters and used to build new land in the shape of many of the world's countries. You can buy your own island for a minimum price of $15 million!
The World islands were started in 2003. Three palm islands have also been built nearby.
SAY WHAT?
The surface of the Earth can be eroded – worn away by wind, water (such as waves or rain), and ice.
Dan Belcher's sand sculptures
Beaches are formed along gently sloping coastlines where the waves deposit sand, pebbles, and even crushed coral, which have been washed away from other parts of the coastline. Sand is made up of tiny grains of crushed and decomposed rocks, shells and coral.
FIX STAMP HERE
David Jones
Beach Drive
Coastville West

COOL WATERS

RIVERS, WATERFALLS AND LAKES

Water, water, everywhere! Get the umbrella out and put your boots on – more than 500,000 cubic km of water is expected to fall on Earth in the next year.

Thirsty plants will suck up most of it to make food, but about one third will flow, in streams and rivers, back to the sea. The source of a river is usually high in the mountains, and the water flows downwards fast; full of energy, it carves valleys into the rock. By the time a river reaches its mouth, it's worn itself out and flows more slowly, depositing sand, mud and silt in a flood plain, as it meanders towards the sea.

Niagara Falls are the most powerful waterfalls in North America.

The falls are separated by Goat Island.

>> Fall guy <<

The first person to walk across Niagara Falls on a tightrope was Jean-François Gravelet, also known as 'The Great Blondin', of France. In 1859, he used a 400-m rope and walked from bank to bank, dressed in a wig, purple tunic, and pantaloons. He also crossed on a bicycle, in the dark, on stilts, carrying a man on his back, with a wheelbarrow, and on one trip he carried a table and stopped in the middle to eat cake.

There are two waterfalls on the Niagara River: Horseshoe Falls and the American Falls.

Take a drop

Niagara Falls, on the US-Canadian border, are unusually wide, with terrific amounts of water flowing over them. If temperatures drop low enough, an ice bridge may form across the river.

Amazing Amazon

The world's mightiest river is the Amazon, which flows for 6,430 km across South America. Enough fresh water pours from the Amazon into the Atlantic Ocean every day to provide the USA with the water it needs for five months – ten times the amount of water carried by the Mississippi River.

At its widest point, the Amazon is 11 km wide during the dry season. During the rainy season, it grows to around 40 km across. Where the Amazon opens at its estuary, the river is over 325 km wide!

Going to great lengths

Slovenian Martin Strel has swum some of the world's greatest rivers. His most amazing achievement, in 2007, saw him swim the length of the Amazon River in only 66 days. He had to swim for up to 12 hours each day to cover the distance, in muddy waters that hide flesh-eating fish, poisonous spiders and dangerous snakes, wearing a homemade mask to protect his face against sunburn.

twist it!

HIGH AND FLOW

The world's longest river is the Nile, which flows 6,648 km from lake Victoria in central Africa to the Mediterranean Sea.

Mountain streams in Valais, Switzerland, are home to hungry snakes, which lie in wait and grab trout that jump above the water.

In the southwestern USA, the Colorado River has slowly cut down through solid rock to create the 446-km-long Grand Canyon, which has an average depth of 1,660 m.

An incredible sight was reported at Florida's Gasparilla Lake in August 2003. Despite the lake being totally landlocked, with no links to the sea, locals saw a dolphin swimming there!

The world's largest lake is the Caspian Sea, which borders Russia, Iran and Turkmenistan, with a total area of about 371,000 square km.

MEANDER
To follow a winding path, like a river does as it nears the sea.

Lakes are temporary gatherings of water that have not found their way to the sea.

Waterfalls are made where hard rock forms part of the riverbed. The flowing water cannot erode the hard rock, but does wear away the soft rock around it, forming a step in the river where the water drops over the edge.

RIVERS OF ICE

A glacier is a vast body of frozen water that flows downhill, like a river. There's one important difference though – glaciers move sooooo slooooowly that you could sit and stare at one for ages, and not spot any change.

When a glacier moves, its great weight melts the ice at its bottom, so it actually glides along on a thin film of water, like an ice skater. These rivers of ice are big and tough. Glaciers grind away at rocks, creating U-shaped valleys and collecting a heavy load of rocks and pebbles. When a glacier melts, piles of pebbles might be one of the few signs that it ever existed!

SLOW MOTION

Glaciers move very, very slowly. A glacier that travels a mile (1.6 km) in a month is considered to be moving at high speed. Each snowfall adds another layer to a glacier's surface and increases the pressure on the ice beneath. The ice at the bottom of a glacier is so compressed that it looks blue.

DANGER ZONE

Cracks in a glacier, called crevasses, can be deeper than 30 m and have steep, straight sides. Mountaineers must take care not to fall into them. That sounds easy, but sometimes a crevasse can be hidden by a snow bridge that looks safe to walk across.

True blue

This beautiful, crystal-clear pool on top of a glacier is water, not ice. The sun gets hot enough to melt the surface snow and ice and create a pool on top of the frozen layer.

SO COOL

On Greenland and Antarctica, there is so much ice, and so many glaciers, that they have joined together into vast "seas" of ice that are known as ice-sheets.

Some mountain glaciers in European ski resorts are wrapped in reflective foil to stop them from melting in summer.

A melting iceberg makes a fizzing sound, known as 'Bergie Seltzer'. It is caused by trapped air bubbles that pop as they are released.

An Arctic iceberg was seen at latitude 28°22' – that's just south of Daytona Beach in Florida.

There is a small glacier inside the crater of the extinct volcano Mount Kilimanjaro, located only 3 degrees south of the Equator in East Africa

Twist it!

CALVING

Large chunks of ice may 'calve' (break away) from a glacier and float out to sea as an iceberg. Some icebergs are huge: as big and heavy as two Statues of Liberty. Smaller, car-sized icebergs are known as growlers. Blue stripes may form if the ice freezes super fast and contains no air bubbles.

>> Berg boarding <<

Wakeboarding is a mixture of surfing, snow boarding and water skiing. Boarders are towed along on a cable and perform jumps and tricks. In July 2008, extreme wakeboarders from Florida made the trip to the Arctic to test their skills on the enormous icebergs there.

FROZEN WILDERNESS

The Earth's extremes are five times colder than the inside of a freezer. These poles are places where only the strongest survive.

More than 90 per cent of the world's fresh water is permanently frozen into ice at the poles. Around the North Pole there is no land, only frozen water that covers around 10 million square km in the winter. The continent of Antarctica covers the South Pole, and has an area of 14 million square km. It's almost entirely buried beneath snow and ice up to nearly 5 km thick.

SLEEPING ON ICE

Several hotels north of the Arctic Circle make the most of the freezing conditions to attract visitors. The hotels are built from ice and snow, with beds lined with reindeer fur to keep guests cosy at night. The hotels have to be rebuilt every year.

The polar bear is the world's largest land predator.

The term Arctic is derived from the Greek arktos, meaning bear. It was named for the polar bear.

Superhuman

Lewis Gordon Pugh, a British endurance swimmer and explorer, loves the cold. In July 2007 he swam just over half a mile across the Arctic Ocean from the geographic North Pole in only 18 minutes and 50 seconds. Wearing only briefs, a cap and goggles, the temperature ranged between freezing −1.6°C and 0°C – brrr!

Polar bears are found only in the Arctic region.

There are seven countries with parts inside the Arctic Circle: Russia, Finland, Sweden, Norway, Greenland, Canada and the USA (Alaska). Most of the area known as the North Pole is frozen sea, not land.

NORTH POLE

N

NW

NE

Arctic Circle

Tropic of Cancer

Equator

Freezing sea

Sea ice grows in stages. Small ice needles get together as mushy grease ice. Waves and wind squash this into pancake ice. Gradually, the pancakes freeze together and become permanent pack ice. This can attach itself to land, or move around the ocean.

PANCAKE ICE

PACK ICE

Antarctica is a continent, but not a country. Nobody lives there permanently. It has no cities or towns, but it does have many research stations for scientists.

The coldest recorded natural temperature was -89°C in Antarctica in July 1983.

Antarctica is the windiest place on Earth. At Commonwealth Bay, wind speed regularly reaches 320 km/h.

>> See through <<

Wright Valley in Antarctica's McMurdo Dry Valleys is home to Lake Vanda. Parts of Lake Vanda are warm and unfrozen, but the ice that forms around the edge is said to be the clearest ice in the world.

GOING TO EXTREMES

US explorer Richard Byrd (1888–1957) spent six months of an Antarctic winter living alone in a shack only 2.7 m by 4 m buried beneath the snow.

A dog named Scooter had to be rescued from an ice floe after chasing a coyote and becoming stranded. The foxhound was carried away to sea in a blizzard and travelled 70 km over five days.

Bouvet Island is probably the world's most remote place. No one lives there, and it is 1,690 km from its nearest neighbour, Queen Maud Land in Antarctica.

The lowest point on Earth's land surface is the Bentley Trench in Antarctica, and it is completely covered by ice. The bottom of the trench is more than 2,500 m below sea level.

twist it!

DRY AS A BONE
DESERTS

Water is a very precious thing in a desert. These arid places get fewer than 250 mm of rain in one year, but in reality many get far less than that. Just 25 mm of rain falls in Africa's Sahara Desert in an average year!

Imagine a desert and visions of golden dunes, palm-fringed oases and cloudless skies come to mind. In fact, while some deserts have perfect fields of sand dunes, called ergs, many more are vast, windswept plains covered with stones, gravel, dried-out mud and salt. About 21 million square km (or 14 per cent) of the Earth's land is desert, and the animals, plants and people that live here battle for survival in one of Earth's harshest habitats.

The Sahara is the largest desert in the world. It has a total area of about 9.1 million square km – about as big as the USA. Every year, around 700 people enter the Sand Marathon, which takes place in the Moroccan part of the desert. Competitors race 240 km across sand dunes, through sandstorms, and in temperatures of 50°C.

Some sand dunes grow up to 215 m high.

The only deserts larger than the Sahara are cold deserts: the Arctic and the Antarctic.

The Sahara crosses 11 countries.

Desert temperatures are hot in the day but fall to below freezing at night.

The word 'Sahara' comes from the Arabic for 'desert'.

Ripley's Believe It or Not!®

Hot hideaway

The Sonoran Desert is home to the Couch's spadefoot toad. This clever creature stays underground, only emerging in July when the rainy season comes.

BLOWN AWAY

As the wind blows across the 'Empty Quarter' desert on the Arabian Peninsula, it creates sand dunes. Many dunes are crescent-shaped, but sometimes changes in wind direction form these unusual dot-shapes.

BIG WORD ALERT

WADIS
Dried up riverbeds in the desert. If it rains they fill with water and become rivers again for a short time.

Twist it!

HOT STUFF

Deserts shrink and grow in size over time — at present, the Sahara Desert is gradually expanding southwards. As the Sahara Desert grew northwards, towards the Mediterranean, it swallowed up hundreds of ancient Roman cities.

There are parts of the Atacama Desert in Chile where no rainfall has been recorded for more than 20 years.

The Simpson Desert in Australia is closed in summer! Authorities stop tourists from going there to allow it time to regenerate, and to prevent the many accidents and deaths that happen in the hottest months.

The camel is known as the 'ship of the desert' because it can travel for days in desert conditions without eating or drinking.

Plane graveyard

The Sonoran Desert in the southwest US is home to a graveyard with a difference: it's where old planes go to die. Rows of them are kept at the Davis-Monthan Air Force Base in Tucson. The dry conditions help to preserve the planes in case they are needed for spare parts, or even to fly again.

Side step

Sidewinder snakes leave distinctive J-shaped tracks in the desert sand. They move sideways and are very fast.

Life support

An oasis is a rare place in a desert where water is close enough to the surface to form springs, streams and small lakes. However, around three quarters of the oases in the Sahara Desert are man-made. Water is directed to chosen places to allow trees to grow, giving valuable shade from the non-stop sunshine.

PASTURES NEW

GRASSLANDS

Grass is one of nature's top success stories – it's almost indestructible! This hardy plant can survive wildfires, and being grazed, mown, frozen, scorched, trampled, and blasted by high winds.

Grass grows shoots at ground level, so even if its long, narrow leaves are damaged, it can recover. It grows where there is too little rain for trees, and too much rain for deserts to form. In warm temperate zones, grasslands are called prairies, steppes, veldts and pampas. In the hot tropics, grasslands are called savannas and some types of savanna grasses can grow up to 7.6 m high.

Zebras eat only the top part of grass stalks, leaving the rest for different types of animals.

No flight zone

Ratites are a family of flightless birds that live in grassland areas of the world. The ostrich lives in Africa, the emu lives in Australia, and the rhea lives in South America. An ostrich eye measures almost 5 cm across and is as big as its brain – about the size of a walnut.

"Are you saying I'm nutty?"

Savanna is grassland with a few trees that provide valuable food and shade for animals.

Mighty mound

The savanna is home to huge termite mounds and acacia trees. Clay mounds of up to 3 m are common, but some giants reach 9 m high. Acacia trees provide food for many animals — even the roots are eaten by porcupines. The trees have sharp thorns to protect them, but a giraffe's tongue is so leathery it can eat the leaves without feeling pain.

HOME ON THE RANGE

In 1800, the prairies of North America were home to herds of wild bison (buffalo) that contained up to 30 million animals. In 2010, the Bridges' family house in Texas is home to a single buffalo called Wildthing! He is allowed into their house, except when he is in a bad mood, when his 900-kg bulk makes him too dangerous to live in a small space.

MUCHAS GRASSES

The elephant grass that grows on the savannas of India can reach 8 m in height.

A large swarm of locusts can strip an area of grassland the size of 150 square km – twice the size of Manhattan – in a day, eating about 20,000 tonnes of vegetation.

The savannas in the *cerrado* region of Brazil and Paraguay are home to about 5 per cent of the world's animal species.

Savannas have long, dry winters with about 10 cm of rain, and shorter summers with up to 65 cm of rain each month.

twist it!

Natural grasslands cover nearly 10 million square km of Earth's surface.

>> Hiding space <<

When baobab trees lose their leaves in the dry season they look as if they are stuck upside down in the ground! The massive trunk becomes hollow as the tree gets older. These hollow spaces have been made into homes, chapels, a post office, a pub, and even a toilet!

WILD WOODLANDS

CONIFEROUS AND TEMPERATE FORESTS

Life is harsh near the North Pole, and plants struggle to survive when temperatures drop. Conifer trees, however, can cope with the cold, and grow in enormous forests that stretch around the globe. Also known as needle-leaf trees, conifers cover around 16.6 million square km through North America, Europe and Asia.

Moving south, the weather warms up. Here in the wet and mild temperate zone deciduous trees grow and create a habitat for woodland life such as deer and foxes. When winter approaches, the trees lose their leaves, settle down for a long nap, and wait for spring.

CONIFEROUS

The Siberian larch is probably the world's most widespread conifer.

The trees' sap contains 'antifreeze' so water inside the tree doesn't freeze.

Coniferous trees have thin needle-shaped leaves that generally remain on the tree throughout the year. They do not have flowers, but produce their seeds inside cones. These open in dry weather so that the seeds can be blown away by the wind, and close in damp conditions to keep the seeds safe.

Nature's giant

The largest single living thing on Earth is a coniferous tree. The Giant Sequoia known as 'General Sherman' in California is nearly 84 m high and weighs an estimated 2,250 tonnes. Usually, these trees grow to at least 50 m: the height of 40 ten-year-olds standing on top of each other!

Green, Amber, Red

Deciduous trees go through a yearly cycle. In spring and summer, buds unfurl, blossoms bloom, and the tree sports its full crowning glory of leaves. In autumn, the trees start to lose their leaves ready to preserve energy in the cold winter months. Many trees are famous for their glorious autumn colours of red, orange, and gold.

TREETIME

Siberia contains 20 per cent of the world's forests, and 50 per cent of the world's coniferous forests.

Miners in Hungary in 2007 were digging for coal but found instead an eight-million-year-old forest! The 16 trees they discovered were all fossilised but were still wood, instead of turning to stone as trees often do when buried.

A sycamore tree in Scotland has handlebars! The tree has gradually 'swallowed' a bicycle that was left against it for years, and grown around the metal with its trunk.

Around 200 petrified trees were discovered by Clyde Friend on his land in Washington State. The forest contained maple, elm, hickory and sweetgum trees, and was preserved over 15 million years ago when it was covered by lava.

DECIDUOUS

A 200-year-old chestnut tree in Dorset, England, had to be chopped down in 2007 because of wood rot. Amazingly, the tree surgeons found the image of a tree in one of the branches! The shape was caused by the disease in the wood.

Tree people

This man is actually a living, growing tree! He was created by Peter and Becky Cook of Queensland, Australia. They carefully grow and graft trees into their chosen design, and have also made a growing chair strong enough for you to sit on.

The root of the problem

A pine tree stump in Michigan has been left high and dry by erosion. The tree was felled and after 40 years of being blown by the wind, the roots were left exposed 2 m above the ground.

STEAMY SURROUNDINGS

TROPICAL RAINFORESTS

Trekking through a warm, wet tropical rainforest is tough. Enormous trees, hanging vines, and large, lush leaves fill every available space and it can be a battle to make any headway.

Rainforests contain a bigger range of animals and plants than anywhere else on Earth. Just half a hectare might contain up to 120 different types of tree. Because the rainforest floor is dark, the trees have tall, straight trunks so their upper branches can reach the sunlight, and create a canopy 45 m high.

GREEN SCENE

The tallest rainforest trees are known as emergents because they emerge above the canopy. In Sarawak, Malaysia, the species *Koompassia excelsa* grows to heights of more than 80 m.

The rainforest talipot palm blooms with over 20 million individual flowers.

A quarter of the medicines we have today owe their existence to rainforest plants.

The canopy trees are packed so closely together that it can take ten minutes for rain to get through and reach the ground.

twist it!

Several rainforest frogs use their bright colours to warn off hungry predators. Certain species ooze poison through their skin. Many are called 'poison dart frogs' as some rainforest tribes were said to smear the poison on the tips of their darts for hunting – although they are far more likely to use poisonous plants for this.

The hot lips plant has special leaves that look – you guessed it – just like bright red lips. It grows in the rainforests of Ecuador in South America.

The Rafflesia plant of the Sumatran rainforest bears a single flower that measures up to 1 m in diameter and smells like rotting meat.

THE WANDERER

The wandering spider lives in Brazil, and is responsible for more human deaths than any other spider. This one is eating a termite. Its name comes from its habit of wandering through the forest rather than making webs.

The monkey slug caterpillar has pairs of hairy 'legs' that make it look more like a tarantula than a caterpillar. Underneath, it has normal legs, body, and head. The fake legs can sting for added protection.

Larger than life

The longest stick insects in the world live in the rainforests of Borneo and can be 50 cm long. Many rainforest species grow extremely large. The titan beetle of the Amazonian rainforest (see below) is one of the biggest insects in the world, reaching lengths of 16.5 cm.

Tropical rainforests cover about 11.4 million square km of the Earth's surface. The largest is the Amazon rainforest with an area of about 6 million square km, across nine countries. More than half the world's rainforests are found in just three countries: Brazil, Democratic Republic of the Congo and Indonesia.

Actual size!

EARTH IN DANGER

TIME IS RUNNING OUT

Twenty thousand years ago the Earth was in the grip of an Ice Age, and massive sheets of ice reached as far south as London and New York. Since then, the world has been slowly but gradually getting warmer.

The Earth's climate has been changing for billions of years; sometimes it's hotter than today, sometimes it's colder. However, scientists believe that the global warming we are experiencing now is not just a natural phenomenon. It's thought we humans are making it worse by putting more carbon dioxide (CO_2) gas in the atmosphere, by burning fossil fuels.

Man-made climate change is having such an effect on the world's plants and animals that a quarter of all species could die out in years, not centuries. Some scientists suggest that Australia could lose more than half of its types of butterfly by 2050.

Going under

The city of New Orleans is on the shifting delta of the Mississippi River, and its highest point is only 1.8 m above sea level. Its residents have always lived in fear of hurricanes and flooding. Now scientists are warning that rising sea levels will surround the city and cut it off from the mainland, probably within 100 years.

Hurricane Katrina in 2005 caused over 125 billion dollars-worth of damage and left tens of thousands of people with no home.

Heating up

Global warming has one certain effect: ice begins to melt. At both poles, the ice sheets are getting smaller. Large chunks fall into the sea. Scientists have recorded rising sea levels of about 0.25 cm each year, and are worried that they may be nearly 1 m higher by the end of the century.

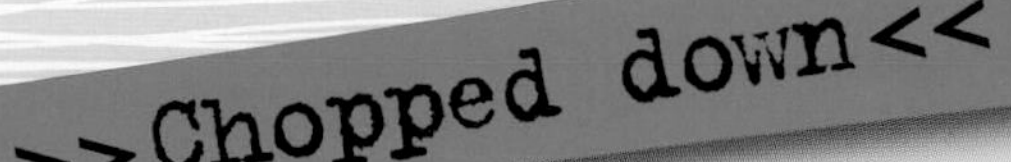

>>Chopped down<<

Massive parts of the world's rainforests are being cut down to make room for farms and roads, and to provide timber. An area of rainforest the size of two soccer pitches is destroyed every second. This leaves local people, and some of the world's rarest animal species, with nowhere to live.

>>Bottles banked<<

Not everyone throws away their rubbish. Maria Ponce of El Salvador has built a whole house out of empty plastic bottles!

SAY WHAT?

Mount Rumpke is the highest point in Hamilton County, Ohio, (305 m) and is completely made of rubbish.

Filling up

Our planet is getting full: full of people, homes, farms, cars, cities...we're running out of space. The more people crowd onto our planet, the harder it is for the Earth to supply the food, fuel, and land we need. One billion people (a sixth of the world's population) live in shanty towns, which are made up of thousands of shelters built from scraps, squashed into dangerously small, unhealthy spaces.

Thrown away

More people make more waste. We now know that it's better to reuse whatever we can, instead of filling our bins or making new things. Burying our rubbish underground can be bad for the environment, and producing new cars, TVs, and all the items we use in modern life takes up valuable energy and materials.

ACKNOWLEDGEMENTS

COVER (sp) © Tanguy de Saint Cyr/Fotolia.com, (c) © Andrew Evans/iStock.com; **2** (b) Action Press/Rex Features, (t) Patrick Landmann/ Science Photo Library; **3** Dan Belcher www.ampersandworkshop.com; **4** (b/l) © Andrew Evans/iStock.com; **4–5** (t) ©Suzannmeer.com/ Fotolia.com; **5** (b) Yang Fan/ChinaFotoPress/Photocome/Press Association Images; **6** (b) © Eric Isselée/Fotolia.com, (b/c) AFP/Getty Images, (b/r) © iStock.com; **6–7** (dps) © Srecko Djarmati/Fotolia.com; **7** (t/l, t, t/r, b/l, b, b/r) © iStock.com; **8** (c) © Lorelyn Medina/ Fotolia.com, (b) Mikkel Juul Jensen/Bonnier Publications/Science Photo Library, (b/r) Patrick Koster/Barcroft Media Ltd; **8–9** © Jan Rysavy/iStock.com; **9** (t/r) David Parker/Science Photo Library, (b) Patrick Koster/Barcroft Media Ltd; **10** (sp) Reuters/Masaharu Hatano, (t/r) © iStock.com; **11** (t/l) Sipa Press/Rex Features, (b/r) Stringer Shanghai/Reuters, (b/c) Photolibrary.com; **12** (b) © Peter McBride/ Aurora Photos/Corbis; **12–13** (dps) Ethel Davies/Robert Harding/Rex Features, (b) Camera Press; **13** (b, b/r) Sergio Pitamitz/Robert Harding/Rex Features; **14** (b) Alex Sudea/Rex Features; **14–15** (sp) Marco Fulle/GB/Barcroft Media; **15** ((b/c) I.B.L./Rex Features, (b/r) Image Courtesy of the Image Science & Analysis Laboratory, NASA Johnson Space Center, (t/r) Kirk Lee Aeder/Barcroft Media Ltd; **16** (l) © iStock.com; (b) © Shaun Lowe/iStock.com **16–17** (c) © Surpasspro/Fotolia.com; **17** (sp) Dr Juerg Alean/Science Photo Library, (t/r) Yang Fan/ChinaFotoPress/Photocome/Press Association Images; **18** (sp) Javier Trueba/Msf/Science Photo Library; **19** (sp) © Cathy Keifer/Fotolia.com, (c) Brian Brake/Science Photo Library, (t/r) Gary Berdeaux/AP/Press Association Images, (b/r) Sam Tinson/Rex Features; **20** (t) © Usefulebooks4u/Fotolia.com, (c) © Tom Bean/Corbis, (b) Alan Blacklock NIWA; **20–21** (sp) © Bsilvia/Fotolia.com; (t) © Stas Perov/Fotolia.com, (b) © Kimberly Kilborn/Fotolia.com; **21** (b/r) © Eric Nguyen/Corbis; **22** (t) © Dan Lockard/Fotolia.com, (b) Kenneth Libbrecht/Barcroft Media; **22–23** Mike Stanford WSDOT; **23** (t) Action Press/Rex Features (c) Photograph by Ray Asgar www. austinhelijet.com, (b) Eric Gay/AP/Press Association Images; **24** (b) © iStock.com, (t/l) Michael Patrick O'Neill/Science Photo Library, (t/r) Norbert Wu/Minden Pictures/FLPA; **25** (b/l) Barcroft Media via Getty Images, (c, t/r) © NHPA/Photoshot, (b/r) Christopher Griner, Woods Hole Oceanographic Institution; **26–27** (b, dps) © iStock.com; **27** (c) © Doug Perrine/naturepl.com, (t/l) Georgette Douwma/ Science Photo Library, (t/r) © David Fleetham/naturepl.com; **28** (sp) © David Woods/iStock.com, (b) Jim Denevan; **29** (b/l) Dan Belcher www.ampersandworkshop.com, (t/r) Reuters/Anwar Mirza, (r) Reuters/Ho New; **30** (b/l) Getty Images; **30–31** Hans-Peter Merten; **31** (l) www.amazonswim.com; **32** (l) © iStock.com, (r) Roberto Rinaldi/Bluegreenpictures.com; **33** (l) © Martin Harvey/Corbis, (b/r) Christian Pondella/Barcroft Media Ltd, (t/r) © iStock.com; **34** (sp) Larry Broder, (b/l) Kev Cunnick, (t/r) Ho New/Reuters; **34–35** © iStock.com; **35** (sp) Geoff Renner, (b/l) © iStock.com, (b/c) © Staphy/Fotolia.com, (t/r) George Steinmetz/Science Photo Library; **36** (sp) AFP/Getty Images, (b/r) Rodger Jackman; **37** (t/l) © George Steinmetz/Corbis, (t/r) Getty Images, (c) © NHPA/Photoshot, (b) © BasPhoto/Fotolia. com; **38** (b/l) © Irina Igumnova/iStock.com, (t/r) © Nyiragongo/Fotolia.com; **38–39** © Markus Divis/iStock.com; **39** (t) Sherron Bridges, (c) Photolibrary.com, (b) © iStock.com; **40** (sp) © Marco Maccarini/iStock.com, (b/l) © Dmitry Naumov/Fotolia.com, (b/c) © Fantasista/ Fotolia.com, (b/r) © Urosr/Fotolia.com; **41** (sp) © Stephan Levesque/iStock.com, (t/l) © iStock.com, (tr) © Olga Shelego/Fotolia.com, (t/bl) © Rxr3rxr3/Fotolia.com, (t/br) © Sean Gladwell/Fotolia.com, (c) Bournemouth News & Pic Service/Rex Features, (b/r) Pooktre. com; **42** (l) © iStock.com, (b/c) Dr Morley Read/Science Photo Library, (b/r) © Dejan Suc/iStock.com; **42–43** (dps) © iStock.com; **43** (t/l) Dr Morley Read/Science Photo Library, (t/r) © Pete Oxford/naturepl.com, (r) Hunter Stark by Tanja Stark (photographer), (b/r) Patrick Landmann/Science Photo Library; **44** (l) © PSD Photography/Fotolia.com; **44–45** (c) David J. Phillip/AP/Press Association Images; **45** (c) © Alberto L. Pomares G./iStock.com, (r) Phil Noble/PA Archive/Press Association Images, (t/r) AFP/Getty Images

Key: t = top, b = bottom, c = centre, l = left, r = right, sp = single page, dp = double page, bgd = background
All other photos are from Ripley Entertainment Inc. All artwork by Rocket Design (East Anglia) Ltd.

Every attempt has been made to acknowledge correctly and contact copyright holders and we apologise in advance for any unintentional errors or omissions, which will be corrected in future editions.

TWISTS

Ripley's
DINOSAURS
Believe It or Not!®
Ripley
PUBLISHING
a Jim Pattison Company
TWISTS

Written by Rupert Matthews

Consultant Steve Parker

Publisher Anne Marshall

Editorial Director Rebecca Miles
Project Editor Lisa Regan
Editor Rosie Alexander
Assistant Editor Charlotte Howell
Picture Researchers James Proud, Charlotte Howell
Proofreader Judy Barratt
Indexer Hilary Bird

Art Director Sam South
Senior Designer Michelle Cannatella
Design Rocket Design (East Anglia) Ltd
Reprographics Juice Creative Ltd

www.ripleys.com/books

First published in Great Britain in 2010 by Random House Books, Random House, 20 Vauxhall Bridge Road, London SW1V 2SA www.rbooks.co.uk

Addresses for companies within The Random House Group Limited can be found at: www.randomhouse.co.uk/offices.htm

The Random House Group Limited Reg. No. 954009

ISBN 978-1-60991-227-7 (USA) | ISBN 978-0-09954-445-6 (UK)

10 9 8 7 6 5 4 3 2 1
The Random House Group Limited supports The Forest Stewardship Council (FSC), the leading international forest certification organisation. All our titles that are printed on Greenpeace approved FSC certified paper carry the FSC logo. Our paper procurement policy can be found at www.rbooks.co.uk/environment

A CIP catalogue record for this book is available from the British Library

Printed in China January 2018
2nd Printing

WARNING
Some of the activities in this book are undertaken by experts and should not be attempted without adequate training and supervision.

PUBLISHER'S NOTE
While every effort has been made to verify the accuracy of the entries in this book, the Publishers cannot be held responsible for any errors contained herein. They would be glad to receive any information from readers.

CONTENTS

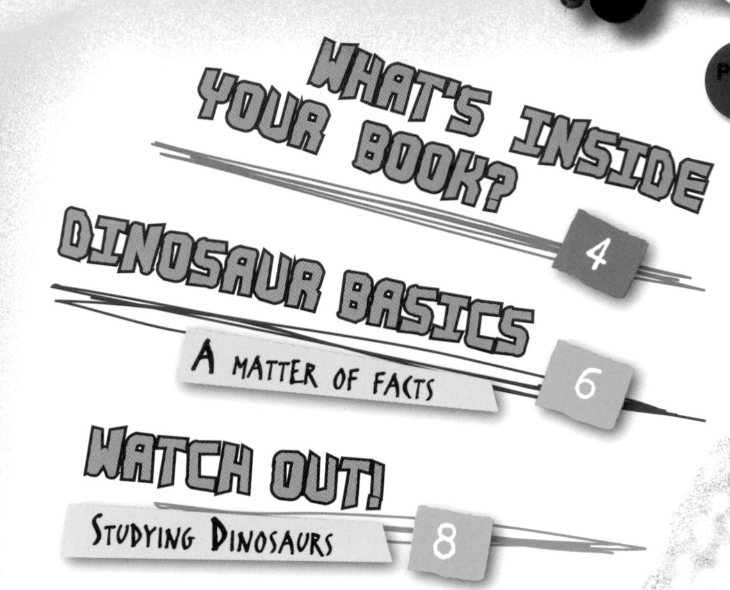

DINOSAUR DAYS

PREHISTORIC PLANET

Could you have survived living with the dinosaurs? Would you have managed to escape the terrifying teeth of the *Tyrannosaurus*, or avoid the slashing claws of a *Velociraptor*? Even if you did, would you have been happy eating moss or ferns in this strange and bizarre place? Or could you have captured a baby dinosaur – and then roasted it for your supper? In this book you will learn all you need to know about the world of the dinosaurs.

WHAT'S INSIDE YOUR BOOK?

Millions of years ago the world was a very different place. Dinosaurs stalked the Earth, other reptiles flew in the skies and swam in the seas, and the largest mammal around was the size of a badger.

Do the twist

This book is packed with cool pictures and awesome facts. It will teach you amazing things about dinosaurs, but like all Twists books, it shines a spotlight on things that are unbelievable but true. Turn the pages to find out more...

Spinosaurus

THE GREAT DEATH

Sixty-five million years ago, all the dinosaurs died out, along with many marine reptiles, flying reptiles and other types of animal. However, a few creatures survived, including lizards, birds, insects, and our own ancestors – the early mammals. Which is just as well for us!

PRIZE FIGHTERS
Whip crack away
Seismosaurus and other sauropods had enormously long, whip-like tails that were controlled by powerful muscles. They could have used these tails to lash each other into defeat. Sauropods may also have used their neck to swing their head and butt each other, in a similar way to giraffes today.
Yee-HAA!
twist it!
One family of dinosaurs had enormously thick bony domes on top of their skull that were up to an incredible 20 cm thick. The family was given the name of pachycephalosaurs, which means 'thick-headed-reptiles'.
Daspletosaurus was a slightly smaller relative of Tyrannosaurus that had a gaping mouth filled with huge sharp-tipped teeth. In battles, these dinosaurs would try to bite each other's face, often inflicting deep gashes, which have been found on some fossils.
Torosaurus had the largest frilled dinosaur skull, which was more than 2.4 m long.
COME HERE AND SAY THAT!
Ripley's Believe It or Not!
WHAT'S THE POINT?
Stegosaur tails all had a tip armed with long, sharp spikes called a 'thagomizer'. This unusual name was originally part of a joke in a 1982 cartoon by Gary Larson in which an unfortunate caveman called Thag has been killed by such a weapon. It is now used as an official term by paleontologists worldwide!
Triceratops means 'three-horned face'.
One of the most recognisable of all the dinosaurs, Triceratops was a plant-eating whopper that stood up to 3 m tall and 9 m in length. Its enormous skull could be one third the length of its body and its famous horns were probably used in mating rituals as well as for defence.
Triceratops had no front teeth, so its mouth looked like a turtle's beak.

BIG WORD ALERT

PALEOICHNOLOGIST
A scientist who studies fossils of things left behind by animals, such as footprints and nests.

Found a new word? Big word alerts will explain it for you.

A pterosaur becomes lunch!

These books are all about 'Believe It or Not!' — amazing facts, feats, and things that will make you go 'Wow!'

Don't forget to look out for the 'twist it!' column on some pages. Twist the book to find out more fascinating facts about dinosaurs.

Learn fab fast facts to go with the cool pictures.

Go to page 44 for more facts about the crazy creatures in this book

DINOSAUR BASICS

A MATTER OF FACTS

Striding across the ground, some of the largest, most incredible animals ever to walk the Earth made the ground shake with every thundering footstep. For over 160 million years, the dinosaurs were one of the most successful groups of animals our planet had ever seen...then they vanished.

The dinosaurs were a huge group of reptiles that lived all over the world. There were more than 700 different types of dinosaur. Some were enormous, but others were tiny. Many were slow and clumsy, a lot were fast and agile. Dinosaurs included several types of animal that looked utterly bizarre, and some that might not look unusual if they were alive today.

TOTAL TYRANNOSAURUS

- Tyrannosaurus had very short arms with powerful two-clawed fingers. These were probably used to seize prey, but were too short to reach its mouth.
- The closest living relative to Tyrannosaurus is the plain old chicken!
- Tyrannosaurus could eat up to 225 kg of meat in one sitting — that's equivalent to 2,000 burgers!

DINO FACTS

- The word 'dinosaur' means 'terrible lizard'.
- The tallest dinosaurs were over 15 m in height – that's as high as a five-storey building – and weighed as much as ten elephants.
- The smallest dinosaurs were about the size of a chicken.
- The fastest dinosaurs could run at about 70 km/h – that's faster than a racehorse.

HOW TO SPOT A DINOSAUR

Dinosaurs shared the following features, which helped to make them undisputed rulers of the Earth:

- A long tail for balance that made it easier for them to run quickly.
- Straight legs that tucked underneath their body, making moving more energy efficient.
- A prong on the astragalus (a bone in the ankle) that allowed for the attachment of strong tendons to aid agile movement.
- A bulge on the humerus (a bone in the upper leg) that allowed for powerful muscles to be attached to aid fast running.

WATCH OUT!

Studying Dinosaurs

Scientists studying dinosaurs are constantly making new discoveries about these amazing creatures. Only recently they concluded that birds probably evolved from one dinosaur group, and that several groups of dinosaurs had feathers!

Looking at fossils can be a confusing business, especially as most dinosaur fossils found are not complete. But, as more and more fossils are unearthed, we learn more about dinosaurs and the world in which they lived. These incredible creatures were around for such a long time that some evolved and others became extinct millions of years apart.

MESOZOIC ERA
The time in which the dinosaurs lived, made up of the Triassic, Jurassic and Cretaceous periods.

Pterosaur

Dinosaurs lived only on land, but they shared their world with flying reptiles called pterosaurs (see page 38) and several groups of water-dwelling reptiles (see page 40).

Diplodocus

This was one of the sauropod group of dinosaurs (see page 14). All sauropods were four-legged plant-eating giants and many had long whip-like tails.

The Time Lords

First signs of life 3.5 bya

First dinosaur 230 mya

First pterosaurs 220 mya

Diplodocus 155 mya

Stegosaurus 150 mya

Triassic period

Jurassic period

251 mya

bya = billion years ago
mya = million years ago

200 mya

145 mya

MESOZOIC ERA

HIP-HIP-ARRAY!

All dinosaurs belonged to one of two groups, based on the shape of their hip bones. One group had hips shaped like those of a modern reptile. These are called lizard-hipped dinosaurs, or saurischians. The other group had hips shaped like those of a modern bird, and are called bird-hipped dinosaurs, or ornithischians.

The bird-hipped dinosaurs were all plant-eaters. The lizard-hipped dinosaurs were divided into two further groups – theropods, who were all meat-eaters, and the sauropods, who were all plant-eaters with long necks and long tails.

Surprisingly, many scientists believe that birds today are descended from the lizard-hipped theropods, not from bird-hipped dinosaurs as you might expect.

Stegosaurus

Stegosaurus is famous for having a very small brain. Despite not being the brightest of dinosaurs, it was around for many millions of years.

Triceratops

Arriving on the scene just 3 million years before the dinosaurs' mass extinction, Triceratops is recognised by the shape of the horns and large bony frill on its head.

What's the Evidence?

The dinosaurs lived many millions of years ago. Not a single one is alive today, so there is no chance to study them in the wild or look at them in a zoo.

We know about dinosaurs only because scientists have found their remains buried in rocks. These remains are known as fossils and are usually the imprint of bones, teeth and other hard parts of a dinosaur body. Muscles, organs and other soft parts do not often get preserved as fossils. Scientists use the fossils to try to work out what the dinosaur looked like when it was alive. They study details on the dinosaur's bones to decide where its muscles, eyes, stomach and other missing parts would have been.

I'm back!

When scientists reconstruct dinosaurs, they often have very little evidence to work with, but meat-eating Afrovenator, here, was found as a single almost complete skeleton. The dinosaur was 9 m long from its nose to the tip of its tail.

Ripley's Believe It or Not!®

Bone home

Bone Cabin near Medicine Bay, Wyoming, is built completely from dinosaur bones. Thomas Boylan began collecting discarded bone fragments from a nearby dinosaur dig in 1916. By 1933, he had gathered 5,796 bones, which he then decided to use to construct a lodge measuring 8.8 m long and 5.8 m wide – that's the length of a Stegosaurus.

Saving Its Skin

Dinosaur skin was often scaly, as indicated by this fossil from the hindquarters of a *Triceratops* that died 65 million years ago in Hell Creek, Montana. Fossils rarely record accurate colour, so scientists in the past guessed that dinosaur skin was dark green or brown, like crocodile or alligator skin. More recently, they have changed their minds and now think dinosaurs may have come in a rainbow of colours – some green, some red, and some even sporting spots or stripes!

Feathered friends

In 1997, Chinese scientists in Liaoning Province found the fossilised remains of a small hunting dinosaur named Caudipteryx. They were astonished to see that the dinosaur had been covered in feathers. This led many scientists to believe that birds evolved from dinosaurs.

What's in a name?

If scientists discover an entirely new type of dinosaur, they are allowed to give it a name. Most scientists use names from ancient Greek or Latin that describe a feature of the fossil, such as Triceratops, which means 'three-horned face'. Other scientists use the name of the place the fossil was found, the name of the person who found it, or even what the weather was like at the time!

Dig that

In 1909, scientist Earl Douglass discovered some dinosaur fossils near Jensen in Utah, USA. He began digging, and scientists haven't stopped since – they are still finding fossils there today. More than 10,000 dinosaur fossils have been discovered at this one site, which is now preserved as the Dinosaur National Monument.

HOW TO MAKE A FOSSIL

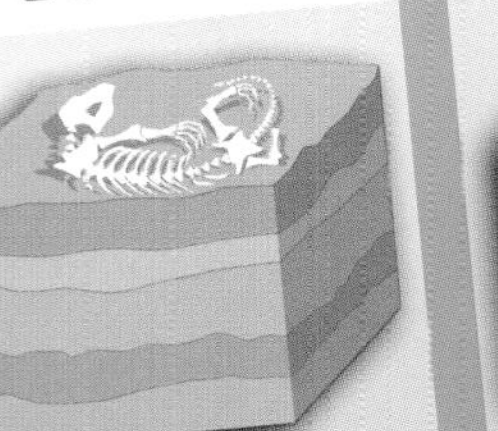

Take one newly dead dinosaur.

Leave for 1,000 years until its skeleton has been covered by deposits of mud or sand.

Allow layers of rocks, minerals, and even oceans to build up on top of the dinosaur, preserving its skeleton deep beneath the Earth's surface.

After 80 million more years the landscape changes and the rocks containing the dinosaur's fossilised remains are exposed once more.

SUCH A SOFTY

In 1981, an amateur paleontologist discovered this 113-million-year-old fossilised *Scipionyx* dinosaur in Italy. What makes it unique is that 85 per cent of its body is intact, including its windpipe, muscles, intestines and other internal organs.

BIG WORD ALERT

PALEONTOLOGIST
A scientist who studies fossils, animals and plants.

HOME SWEET HOME

DINOSAUR WORLD VIEW

BIG WORD ALERT

CONTINENT
Any of the world's main continuous areas of land, such as Africa or Asia.

The world the dinosaurs inhabited was very different from our own. Strange plants grew on the ground and bizarre creatures swam in the seas or flew in the skies. Even the continents were in different places.

During the Triassic period, dinosaurs inland coped with throat-drying desert zones, while, during the Jurassic period, they enjoyed a warm, wet climate. The Cretaceous period had both warm and cool times, and huge, shallow seas spread over the planet. Their warm waters evaporated and fell as heavy rain on land. Vast forests started to grow. Some plants and insects we see today existed back then and provided dinosaurs with a variety of foods, such as leafy ferns, pine trees, mushrooms, magnolias, dragonflies and tasty termites.

ONE WORLD

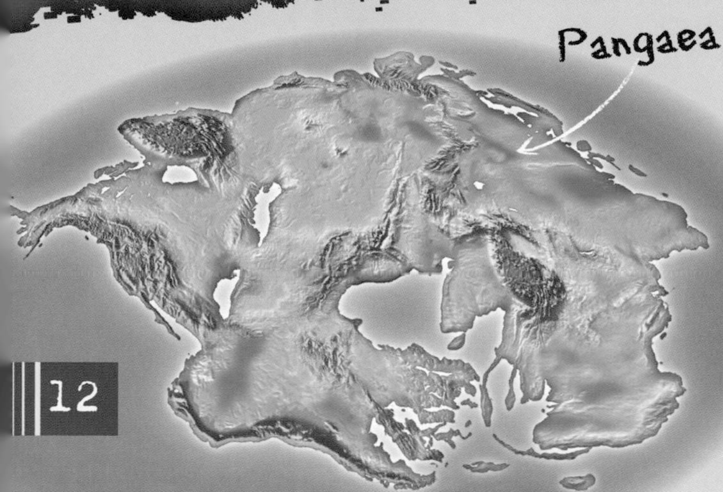

When the age of dinosaurs began, all the continents on Earth were joined together into a vast landmass that scientists call Pangaea, which means 'all of earth'. About 170 million years ago, Pangaea split in two, forming Laurasia and Gondwanaland. About 130 million years ago, Gondwanaland began to split up to form South America, India, Africa, Australia and Antarctica. Laurasia divided about 50 million years ago into North America and Europe-Asia.

WHAT A STINK!

In Kawah Ijen, Indonesia, miners cover their mouths to protect against choking on sulphurous gas, as they pull stinking sulphur from a volcanic crater.

The air dinosaurs breathed often must have been just as bad. Volcanic eruptions during the Mesozoic era pumped out huge amounts of sulphur and other evil gases. In wet areas, swamps containing rotting vegetation would have stunk. And don't even think about the terrible-smelling breath of the carnivorous dinosaurs, with rotten meat festering in their teeth.

Some of today's flora and fauna would have been known to the dinosaurs.

MAGNOLIA

HORSETAIL FERN

CYCAD

CALLING PLANET EARTH

The very first flowering plants appeared about 125 million years ago in eastern Asia, during the early Cretaceous period. Some 25 million years later, flowering plants suddenly spread right across the world and took over from earlier types of plants.

The climate of the world was at its hottest about 110 million years ago, when it was around 5°C warmer than it is today.

In the later Cretaceous period vast volcanic eruptions spurted molten rock across India. An area of land about 1.5 million sq km was covered in lava about 2 km thick.

Where did you come from?

When fossils of the same animal are found on different continents it suggests that those continents were once joined together. This is because large land animals couldn't get across oceans and only travelled around by walking.

Fossils of the crocodile-like reptile Uberabasuchus – seen here having a dinosaur for dinner – have been found in South America, Africa and Madagascar, suggesting how these landmasses were joined together about 100 million years ago.

HOW BIG?

Super Sauropods

Imagine if the sauropods – the biggest of all the dinosaurs – roamed our streets today. These gentle giants would be able to peer into windows five floors up and crush cars as if they were toys. They were the largest animals that have ever walked the Earth.

Sauropods swallowed stones and pebbles that remained in their stomach. As the stomach muscles churned the food about, the stones pummelled the leaves and twigs to a mushy liquid that could be more easily digested in their huge intestines.

Argentinosaurus
About 30 m long (head to tail)
Weighed a colossal 80 tonnes

Mamenchisaurus
About 13 m long
Had a neck that was half its total body length

The sauropods were a group of plant-eating dinosaurs that had long necks and long tails. They had small mouths, so they had to eat almost continuously to consume enough food. They couldn't chew, so they had huge stomachs and intestines – filling most of their body – to process the leaves and twigs on which they fed. Sauropods first appeared about 200 million years ago and by 150 million years ago were the most important types of plant-eating dinosaurs.

Brachiosaurus
About 24 m long
Could raise its neck 2–3 times higher than a giraffe

In the case of some sauropods, their head could be 8 m above their heart. So they needed a large, powerful heart, weighing about 400 kg – that's the weight of four average adult men – to pump blood up to the head.
Agustinia
About 15 m long
Had bony spikes down its back, unlike most other sauropods

SMALL AND SAVAGE

MINI DINOSAURS

Some of the earliest dinosaurs were no larger than chickens! *Eoraptor* from the Triassic Period was about 1 m long, and half of that was its tail. Some dinosaurs did evolve to be bigger and stronger, but others remained small. *Compsognathus*, from the Jurassic Period, was even smaller than *Eoraptor*.

Often running together in savage packs, the smaller hunters of the dinosaur world were deadly and terrifying. Armed with razor-sharp claws and teeth, they could run faster than anything else on Earth and bring down prey much larger than themselves with startling speed.

Velociraptor was one of the most intelligent dinosaurs. Its brain was relatively large in comparison to its body size.

Velociraptor was a smart turkey-sized predator. Although many images of this deadly hunter show it as a scaly reptile, we now know that it was actually covered in feathers and bird-like in appearance.

Velociraptor could run at speeds of up to 65 km/h for short bursts.

Deadly battle

Velociraptor was not afraid to attack larger animals. In 1971, fossils were found in Mongolia that showed a *Velociraptor* and a *Protoceratops* buried together. They had been fighting and the *Protoceratops'* beak had bitten deep into the *Velociraptor*, which had been attacking the *Protoceratops* with its claws. They may have died in a sudden sandstorm or when a sand dune collapsed.

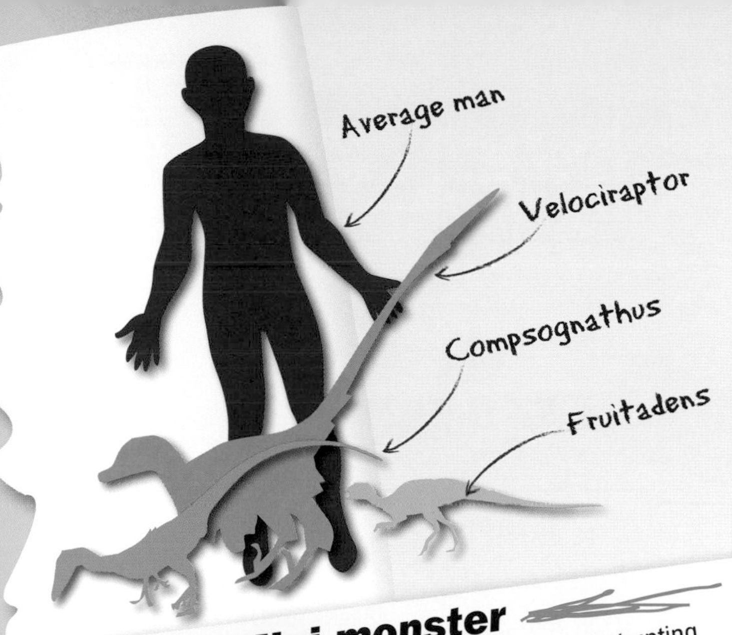

Mini monster

Microraptor got its name because it is one of the smallest hunting dinosaurs known – only 38 cm long. It had flight feathers along both its arms and on its legs, so it probably climbed trees and glided from one to another. It may have pounced on prey by gliding onto it.

Dozy dino

The dinosaur with the shortest name is 60-cm-long *Mei*. This little hunting dinosaur lived about 130 million years ago in eastern Asia. Its name means 'sleepy' because the first fossil found of this dinosaur is in the pose of a sleeping bird with its head tucked under its arm.

Insect picker

Patagonykus was 1.8 m long and had only one claw on each arm. Powerful muscles were attached to its arms and scientists think that *Patagonykus* may have used its claw to rip open termite mounds so that it could feed on the insects.

Sniff sniff

Byronosaurus had nasal bones that show it was very good at smelling things. Perhaps this 1.5-m-long dinosaur hunted at night and used its sense of smell to find food.

HIGH FLYER

One of the most successful agile early hunters was *Coelophysis* (see page 25). Scientists have found hundreds of fossils of this dinosaur buried together. The skull of one *Coelophysis* was taken into space in 1998 by the space shuttle *Endeavour*.

Ripley's Believe It or Not!®

Tiny tot

Fruitadens was a dinosaur so small and fast that it could dart between the legs of giant dinosaurs. Measuring just 30 cm tall and 60 cm from head to tail, it weighed the same as a guinea pig, and ate small animals, bugs and plants for its dinner.

KNIGHTS IN ARMOUR

POWERFUL PROTECTION

Encased in almost as much armour as a modern battle tank, and bristling with spikes, horns and clubs, armoured dinosaurs were awesome animals. Even the most ferocious hunter would think twice about launching an attack on them.

The bony armour that covered so many different types of dinosaurs – mainly the ankylosaur and stegosaur groups – was so protective that often the only way a predator could cause injury was by flipping the dinosaur over and exposing the soft belly. Judging by the size and shape of these beasts, that would not have been easy!

Scary tail

Ankylosaurus had a massive double-headed club on its tail. It may have used this to bash away at the armoured backs of rivals in disputes over territory or status. This 6-m-long chunky reptile was a herbivore and had to eat a huge amount of plant material to sustain itself, so its gut was very large. It probably had a fermentation chamber in its gut to aid in the digestion process. This offered another form of protection – enormous amounts of gas!

On a plate

All armoured dinosaurs belong to one large group called the Thyreophora. Within the Thyreophora are the stegosaurs, ankylosaurs, scutellosaurs and emausaurs. Many fossils of these dinosaurs are found upside down, as if a hunter had flipped them over to get to their less protected underbelly, and then used the shell as a plate from which to eat the juicy meat.

A LOT ON ITS PLATE

One of the earliest known armoured dinosaurs, *Scutellosaurus*, lived about 200 million years ago in the early Jurassic period. Only 1.2 m long, it had more than 300 plates of bony armour – called scutes – set into its skin.

Blinking hard

Euoplocephalus was so heavily armoured that even its eyelids were covered in bone. If provoked, all its armour may have filled with blood and turned pink.

twist it!

KEEP OUT!

Given the weight of all that armour, ankylosaurs and stegosaurs were slow-moving creatures that walked on four legs. However, with all that protection, there was little need to be able to run away from predators.

Ankylosaurs and stegosaurs all belonged to the larger Thyreophora group of dinosaurs, all of which only ate plants. Thyreophora means 'those who carry large shields'.

Yingshanosaurus was a stegosaur with a pair of huge spikes on its shoulders, each about 1.2 m long. Unfortunately, the Chinese scientist who found the fossil has now lost it, so nobody can be certain what the dinosaur looked like.

Sharp practice

Chialingosaurus was a smaller relative of *Stegosaurus*. It had bony plates on its neck and upper back, and spikes on its lower back and tail. As it was modestly sized, weighing just 180 kg and measuring 4 m in length, it might have been able to rear up on its hind legs and present a wall of spikes.

PRIZE FIGHTERS

Power Struggles

Take a ringside seat at this fight of the era. Charging towards each other at top speed, a pair of *Triceratops* clash with a resounding 'thwack'. Horns lock together, the ground vibrates, as each uses its strong shoulder muscles to try to wrestle the other backwards into defeat. Battles between rival dinosaurs would have been terrifying.

It was not only meat-eating hunters that needed to fight. Many plant-eaters had to fight other dinosaurs of the same species over territory, food or status. Some used displays of frills or feathers to scare off rivals, others had real weapons to use in their battles. Not every contest ended with serious injury, but some dinosaurs would have died in these fights.

COME HERE AND SAY THAT!

One family of dinosaurs had enormously thick bony domes on top of their skull that were up to an incredible 20 cm thick. The family was given the name of pachycephalosaurs, which means 'thick-headed-reptiles'.

Daspletosaurus was a slightly smaller relative of *Tyrannosaurus* that had a gaping mouth filled with huge sharp-tipped teeth. In battles, these dinosaurs would try to bite each other's face, often inflicting deep gashes, which have been found on some fossils.

Torosaurus had the largest frilled dinosaur skull, which was more than 2.4 m long.

Whip crack away

Seismosaurus and other sauropods had enormously long, whip-like tails that were controlled by powerful muscles. They could have used these tails to lash each other into defeat. Sauropods may also have used their neck to swing their head and butt each other, in a similar way to giraffes today.

Stegosaur tails all had a tip armed with long, sharp spikes called a 'thagomizer'. This unusual name was originally part of a joke in a 1982 cartoon by Gary Larson in which an unfortunate caveman called Thag has been killed by such a weapon. It is now used as an official term by paleontologists worldwide!

Triceratops means 'three-horned face'.

One of the most recognisable of all the dinosaurs, *Triceratops* was a plant-eating whopper that stood up to 3 m tall and 9 m in length. Its enormous skull could be one third the length of its body and its famous horns were probably used in mating rituals as well as for defence.

Triceratops had no front teeth, so its mouth looked like a turtle's beak.

PALEOICHNOLOGIST
A scientist who studies fossils of things left behind by animals, such as footprints and nests.

FINDING YOUR FEET

Ferocious footwear

Equipped with vicious claws, curving talons or ponderous pads, dinosaur feet came in a variety of shapes and sizes. The design of their feet and legs was essential to the dinosaurs' success and made them the rulers of the world.

Dinosaur legs were positioned directly under their body, so the weight of the animal rested on the bones. In other reptiles, the legs splayed sideways, so the animal used more energy to work its muscles to lift its body off the ground. This meant that dinosaurs could move more efficiently than other animals when looking for food or escaping from danger, and this was enough to give them control of the Earth.

Big foot!

The feet of the biggest dinosaurs needed to be absolutely huge to support their massive weight. This scaled-down drawing shows how they compared to creatures of today.

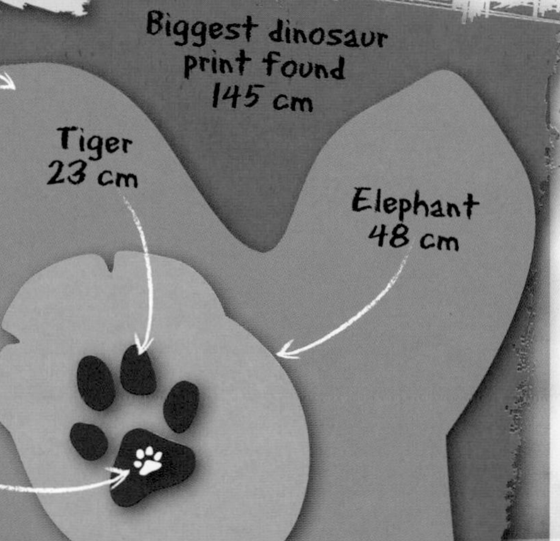

That's gotta hurt

The thumb of the plant-eater Iguanodon *took the form of a stout, very sharp spike. It may have been used in fights between rival* Iguanodon*.*

Gone fishing

The front foot of Baryonyx *carried a huge, curved claw. This may have been used to help the dinosaur catch fish from rivers or lakes.*

Take cover!
Imagine this huge claw bearing down on your flesh. It sat, ready to rip, on the hind leg of Deinonychus. Only when the fossils of this dinosaur were discovered in the 1960s did scientists wise up to the fact that some dinosaurs had been fast, agile and lethal. Before this, they thought dinosaurs had all been slow, lumbering beasts.

The sauropod group of giant dinosaurs was named because of the arrangement of the bones inside their feet. 'Sauropod' means 'lizard foot'.

Claws call

The hind legs of **Allosaurus** *and some other hunters carried three large claws, which were connected to powerful muscles. These may have been used to kick victims to death.*

No escape

The gigantic, grasping hands of **Deinocheirus** *were tipped with terrible 25-cm-long claws. On the end of 2.4-m-long forelimbs, they were the ultimate far-reaching weapon.*

Utterly useless

The front legs of **Tyrannosaurus** *were so small that they could reach neither the ground nor the mouth. They could not even have been used to scratch itches.*

Some dinosaurs had feet or claws designed for very specific purposes. Others, such as the mighty *Tyrannosaurus*, had powerful hind legs but surprisingly useless front legs.

ARMED TO THE TEETH

OPEN MOUTHS

Sharper than a steak knife and bigger than a dagger, the teeth of the immense hunter dinosaurs were ferocious weapons. Other dinosaurs had broad, flat teeth that were able to crush bones to powder. Plant-eaters had teeth designed for slicing, chopping and grinding.

We can use fossilised teeth to discover what sort of food a dinosaur ate. If the jaws are found intact, they can show how the teeth were used when the dinosaur was feeding. Dinosaur teeth can also show who ate who in the dinosaur world. Scientists have found marks that match the teeth of a *Tyrannosaurus* on the bones of a *Triceratops*. And the broken off tip of an *Allosaurus* tooth has been found stuck in a sauropod bone.

TROODON TOOTH

HUMAN INCISOR

SMALL TYRANNOSAURUS TOOTH

LION TOOTH

SMALL MEGALOSAURUS TOOTH

LARGE MEGALOSAURUS TOOTH

LARGEST DINOSAUR TOOTH EVER FOUND

ALL TEETH ACTUAL SIZE

Your point is?

One of the largest dinosaur teeth ever discovered was 28 cm long. It was found in North America and had a sharp point as it came from a meat-eater. Because the tooth was found on its own, nobody can be certain what type of dinosaur it came from.

SMILE PLEASE

The huge sauropod *Supersaurus* was one of the largest dinosaurs ever, but it had very small teeth. The adult animal was about 32 m long, but each tiny tooth was only 3 cm long. That's like an adult human having teeth no thicker than a grain of rice.

Hadrosaurs had massive rows of grinding teeth in their jaws to chew the tough plants that they ate. On average, each hadrosaur had about 4,000 teeth in its jaws.

The largest dinosaur tooth found still in its owner's jaws belonged to a *Daspletosaurus*. The tooth was 21.8 cm long and 3 cm wide. Slightly curved and found at the front of the mouth, it was probably used to tear lumps of meat from a victim.

Tyrannosaurus had teeth up to 30 cm long. Each tooth was narrow and edged with serrations that would have torn through flesh like a meat knife.

twist it!

Tusk force

Heterodontosaurus had two pairs of long, sharp tusks near the front of its mouth, and smaller, grinding teeth at the rear of the jaws. It is thought that it used the tusks to dig up roots that were then chewed by the rear teeth.

Toothless

The fast-running ornithomimid dinosaurs had no teeth at all! Instead they had a beak, like that of a modern bird. It is thought that they ate lizards, beetles and small animals.

Duck!

Gryposaurus had a giant, duck-like bill packed with hundreds of teeth. The 9-m-long plant-eater had 300 teeth inside its beak, with a further 500 in its jaw ready to grow as replacements.

Jagged edge

Coelophysis was one of the earliest dinosaurs and lived in the late Triassic period. It was an excellent hunter that could run fast and dart from side to side. Its sharp, curved, jagged teeth were perfect for gripping and eating small animals.

ON THE MENU

DINOSAUR DINNERS

Gobbling up everything in sight, the giant dinosaurs stomped across the world consuming enormous amounts of food. They then deposited great big, stinking droppings behind them.

It is very difficult for scientists to estimate just how much different dinosaurs ate. The amount eaten would depend on the nutritional value of the food available, how efficient the dinosaur's body was at digesting the food, and how active they were. Fortunately, some dinosaur droppings have been fossilised and can be studied. They are known as coprolites.

Little taste

The alvarezsaurid family of dinosaurs may have eaten termites, ants and other insects. They would have needed to eat several thousand every day.

CARNIVORE CUISINE

COCKTAIL OF THE HOUR
Swamp water at sundown

STARTER
Mixed mammal salad drizzled with blood

TODAY'S CATCH
Sea-trawled Elasmosaurus neck fillets, on a bed of volcanic ash

MAIN COURSE
Sauropod steak topped with an Oviraptor egg

DESSERT
Fried dragonflies with termite sauce

Spinosaurus was a large deadly meat-eater that grew over 18 m in length and hunted alone. It had a preference for enormous fish and delicious fleshy chunks that it tore from the flanks of big dinosaurs with its crocodile-like jaws.

How rude!

Some animals regurgitated and spat out indigestible parts of food that they ate. Hunters may have eaten small animals whole, then spat out the bones. When these items are found as fossils they are known as 'regurgitaliths'.

GOING VEGGIE

APERITIF

Freshly squeezed moss juice, served with pine pretzels

SOUP OF THE SEASON

Sun-roasted fern

MAIN COURSE

Fungal flambée, sulphur-smoked cycad cones, with a side order of tossed horsetails

DESSERT

Stripped twig roulade with magnolia flower garnish

Stones will be provided for swallowing and aiding digestion

What tickled the fancy of Stegosaurus were ferns, mosses, cycads and baby evergreen trees. Good job, its neck was too short to reach any tall plants. These were nutritiously poor plants so Stegosaurus would have had to spend all day grazing in order to get enough nutrients to survive.

Puzzling flavour

Monkey puzzle trees evolved about the same time as the earliest plant-eating dinosaurs. They produce a fruit about the size of a football that is filled with tasty, nutritious seeds.

A pile of dinosaur dung 130 million years old was sold at a New York auction for $960 in 2008. The fossilised dung, from the Jurassic period, was bought by Steve Tsengas of Ohio, USA.

Christmas lunch

The Picea spruce tree evolved about 100 million years ago and was probably a favourite food of the crested hadrosaur dinosaurs. It is still around today, but is better known as the Christmas tree.

Poo goes there?

Coprolites from many different dinosaur species have been found, but scientists find it very difficult to work out which dinosaur the poo originally came from, unless the coprolite was found inside a particular dinosaur's skeleton.

A street in the town of Felixstowe in England is called Coprolite Street!

COPROLITE

RIP ROARERS

PRIZE PREDATORS

Talons outstretched to slash at prey, the hunter raced across the landscape with its eyes focused on its intended victim. Once the prey was reached, a rip with the claws brought it down, after which it was quickly killed. Then the great teeth began to tear into the flesh.

Allosaurus grew up to 12 m long – that's the size of a school bus!

Some of the hunting dinosaurs combined large size and immense strength with the ability to run quickly and change direction with extreme agility. They had long hind legs, powered by strong leg and hip muscles, as well as large, curved claws on their small front legs.

This baby sauropod didn't stand much chance against these lethal predators.

PREY
An animal that is hunted and killed by another animal for food.

JURASSIC LUNCH

This mighty mean *Allosaurus* doesn't look like he wants to share his lunch with the group of *Ceratosaurus* that have joined him in the late Jurassic forests of North America. Although *Allosaurus* hunted large plant-eating dinosaurs, such as the sauropod here, scientists think it may also have preyed on other predators, including *Ceratosaurus* – so these guys had better watch out!

RUUUUUN!

More than 50 *Allosaurus* skeletons have been found – this is one of the highest numbers of fossil skeletons for any Jurassic dinosaur. About 70 per cent of all big dinosaur hunters in North America 155 million years ago are believed to have been *Allosaurus*.

The hunter *Saurophaganax* is the state mascot of Oklahoma, where it was found. It was similar to *Allosaurus*, but even bigger.

Dinosaur footprints found at Glen Rose in Texas show a pack of four *Acrocanthosaurus* hunters stalking a herd of sauropods. There is even a track indicating that one of the hunters kicked at a prey with its hind leg.

A piece of fossilised skin from the hunter *Carnotaurus* shows that it had round, pebble-like scales interspersed with bony cones on its body.

TWIST IT!

With razor-sharp teeth and horns, Ceratosaurus was just as scary as its deadly rival.

Ceratosaurus had a horn on the end of its nose and two smaller ones above its eyes. It grew to be 5.5 m long and had a flexible tail that it could lash about.

BEAUTY AND THE BEASTS

SHOW-OFFS

It is safer for any animal to frighten off a rival or an attacker, rather than to fight. Even a strong beast might get hurt in a battle. By looking as big and as tough as possible, a dinosaur could frighten off a predator or challenge a rival of the same species.

Some dinosaurs were real show-offs, sporting wonderful, colourful plates, gigantic head crests, and multicoloured tails. But these flourishes weren't just for fun. Dazzling dinosaurs wanted to bully and intimidate other animals, to protect themselves, get food, or attract a mate.

Moody Beast

The large bone plates on the back of *Stegosaurus* were covered in skin carrying large numbers of blood vessels. It is thought that the *Stegosaurus* could have changed the colours of the large plates to show what kind of mood it was in.

Twin Peak

Dilophosaurus was a 6-m-long hunter that lived in North America about 190 million years ago. On top of its head the dinosaur had twin crests of paper-thin bone. These may have been brightly coloured to act as signalling devices.

FAN TAIL

Nomingia had a flesh-covered bone protrusion on the end of its tail, just like that of a modern peacock. Scientists think that it had a large fan of brightly coloured feathers that it could lift up and wave around in a threatening manner.

CROWNING GLORY

Styracosaurus, a large plant-eater that lived in the Cretaceous period, had a massive six-spiked frill projecting from the back of its skull, which might have been used in mating rituals and for scaring off rivals. These rivals could have included the mighty meat-eaters *Albertosaurus* and *Daspletosaurus*, who were around at the same time as *Styracosaurus*.

FLAG WAVERS

Several types of hadrosaur, such as this *Parasaurolophus*, had bone crests that pointed back from their head. Some think that flaps of brightly coloured skin connected the crest to the neck. By waggling its head, the dinosaur could wave these flaps as if they were flags.

Fancy Flyers

Some scientists think that the wings of pterosaurs may have been brightly coloured. Reptile skin can take on shades of red, blue or green, so the wings may have been as showy as those of modern parrots.

Boat or Dinosaur?

Spinosaurus (see page 26) had a sail of skin about 1.5 m tall along its back. The dinosaur could have turned sideways to face a rival, flashing its brightly coloured sail to make itself look as big as possible.

Big Head

Torosaurus had the largest skull of any land animal that ever lived. It was over 2 m long, and most of the skin covering it was made up of a neck frill, which would have been brightly coloured.

ON THE MOVE

HERDS AND MIGRATION

Plodding along in vast herds, scampering in the undergrowth alone, or waiting in ambush for a victim, dinosaurs were active animals leading dangerous lives in hostile places.

All dinosaurs had to find food, escape enemies, seek shelter from weather, and find mates. Most did not live alone, but moved about their environment in different ways. Some lived in huge herds, such as the duck-billed dinosaur *Maiasaura*, whose fossils have been found in groups of about 10,000 animals. Others, like *Deinonychus* and *Velociraptor*, may have hunted in deadly packs, attacking even gigantic sauropods. Family groups were common, among *Centrosaurus* for example, while *Allosaurus* and other species may have lived solitary lives for much of the time.

WALL WALKING

Near Sucre, Bolivia, a vertical wall of limestone contains over 5,000 fossilised footprints left by some 250 dinosaurs.

The footprints were left in the mud around the edge of a lake about 70 million years ago.

Over time, the mud turned to rock, which was then twisted upright as the Andes mountains formed.

Now it looks as though the dinosaurs were walking up a wall.

Herd this?

About 68 million years ago, dozens of Centrosaurus were drowned trying to cross a flooded river. The bodies of the drowned herd were covered by mud and later became fossils. The archaeologists who discovered the fossils, at Alberta's Dinosaur Provincial Park in Canada, found the remains of the dinosaurs spread over an area about the size of a football field.

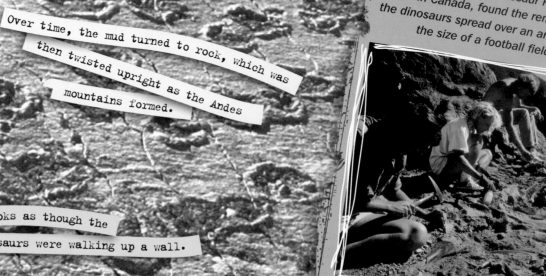

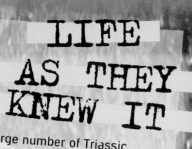

LIFE AS THEY KNEW IT

A large number of Triassic plant-eater *Plateosaurus* died crossing a desert that existed around what is now Trossingen, Germany. They were probably migrating from one food-rich area to another when they died.

Muttaburrasaurus is thought to have migrated 800 km between its winter and summer grazing lands, in modern-day Australia.

In 2008, more than 1,000 dinosaur footprints were found on a 3,000-sq-m site on the border of Utah and Arizona. Around 190 million years ago the area would have been a welcome watery oasis among hot, windswept sand dunes.

Twist it!

Baby Comes Too

A set of fossil footprints found at Culpeper in Virginia, USA, showed a number of huge sauropods walking in a small group. The adults were on the outside of the group and the young on the inside. It seems the adults were protecting the young from some threat.

Ripley's Believe It or Not!®

Death by footprint

About 160 million years ago, a huge sauropod walking across a swamp in China left footprints 1.8 m deep. Lots of smaller animals, including little Limusaurus dinosaurs, fell into the footprints, couldn't climb out, and died. Nine Limusaurus fossils were found in one of the footprints alone.

BIG WORD ALERT

MIGRATE To move regularly between two or more different places, either to find food or to find safe places to bring up young.

STOP THE DINOSAUR!

BUILT FOR SPEED

Dinosaurs were not all lumbering beasts that just plodded around their world. The swiftest of the dinosaurs could give the cheetahs and antelopes of today a run for their money. With pounding feet and awesome power, running dinosaurs could disappear into the distance in seconds.

Speed is useful for any animal, whether it's trying to catch prey or escape from a hunter. Most swift animals live on open plains with few hiding places, so they need to move quickly. Fast dinosaurs probably lived in dry, open areas with no trees and little vegetation.

The fastest dinosaurs were the ornithomimosaurs, such as 3.6-m-long *Dromiceiomimus*.

No way!

At this site near Cameron, Arizona, one man tries unsuccessfully to match the fossilised stride of a dinosaur predator that was as fast as an Olympic athlete.

LONG-LEGS

The ornithomimosaurs were large ostrich-like creatures, some of which ate meat.

Speed check

Cheetah
96 km/h

Dromiceiomimus
80 km/h

Tyrannosaurus
40 km/h

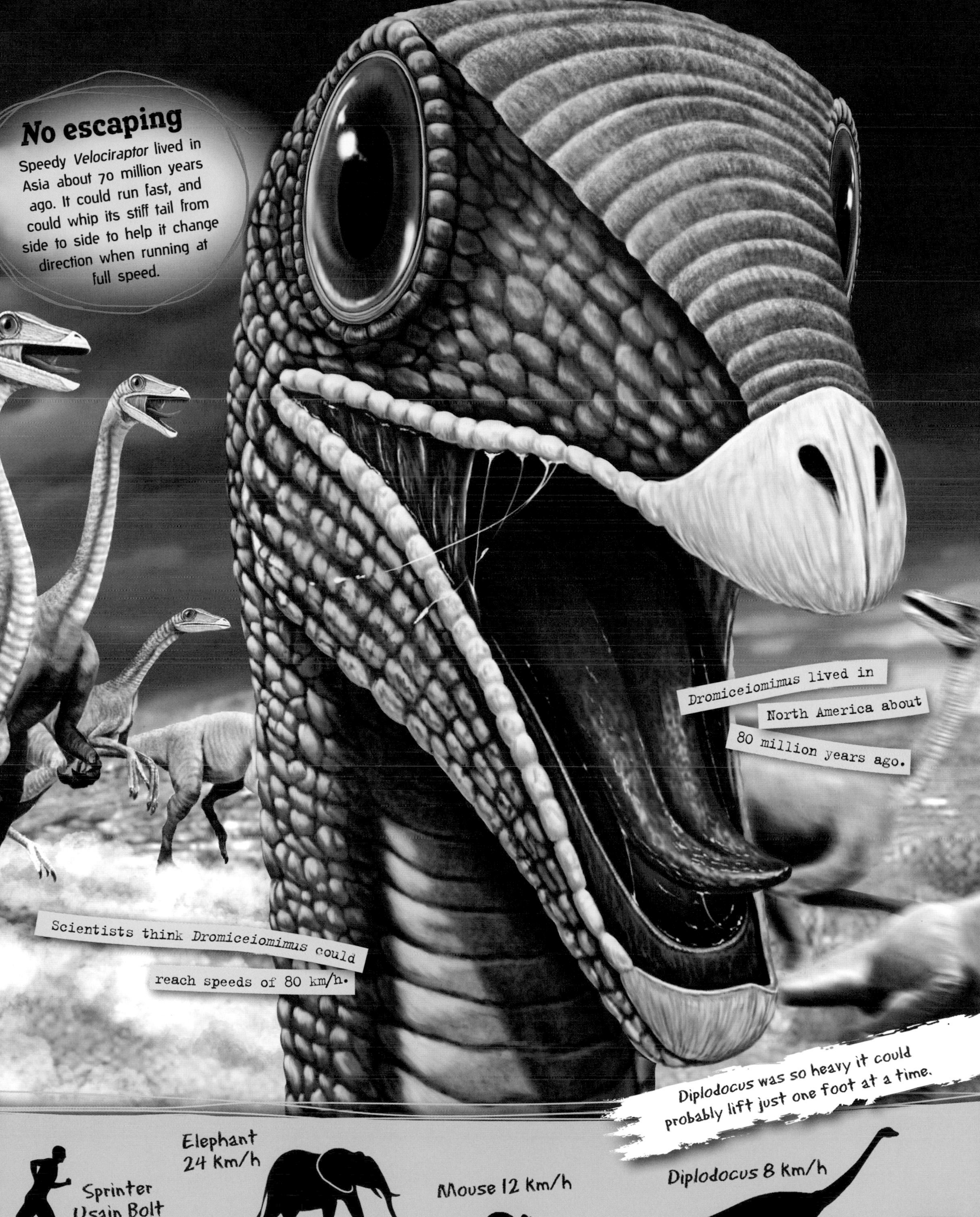
No escaping
Speedy Velociraptor lived in Asia about 70 million years ago. It could run fast, and could whip its stiff tail from side to side to help it change direction when running at full speed.
Dromiceiomimus lived in North America about 80 million years ago.
Scientists think Dromiceiomimus could reach speeds of 80 km/h.
Diplodocus was so heavy it could probably lift just one foot at a time.
Sprinter Usain Bolt 37.5 Km/h
Elephant 24 Km/h
Mouse 12 Km/h
Diplodocus 8 Km/h

BIG MAMA

Newborns

All dinosaurs laid eggs, but working out their nesting behaviour is difficult. Scientists need to find fossils of a dinosaur's nest, eggs and young to study, and, even then, it can be hard to piece together the mother's behaviour.

Some dinosaurs built very carefully constructed nests in which to lay their eggs, and would have worked hard to find the ideal spot. Once the eggs were laid, some mothers would have guarded them against dangers, fed the babies when they hatched, and may even have looked after their young for months or years to come. Others walked away and let the hatchlings take their chances.

Giant egg nest

Seen here with an ordinary-sized chicken's egg, this is a nest of fossilised dinosaur eggs that was found in France. It isn't known which dinosaur the eggs belonged to, but it looks like it must have been a lot bigger than a chicken!

BIG WORD ALERT

INCUBATE
To keep eggs warm while the babies develop inside.

Dinosaur auction

A nest of dinosaur eggs dating back 65 million years was sold at auction in Los Angeles in 2006 for $420,000. The nest, which was discovered in southern China in 1984, held 22 broken eggs, with some of the tiny unhatched dinosaurs clearly visible curled up inside. It was arranged in a circular pattern with the eggs placed along the edge. Scientists think it belonged to an oviraptor.

Baby dinosaurs grew very quickly and in some cases increased in size 16,000 times before reaching adulthood.

Triceratops laid its eggs in a spiral, *Maiasaura* in a circle. Sauropods left them in a row, as though the dinosaur laid them as she walked.

The smallest dinosaur eggs were about 2.5 cm across. They came from the small plant-eater *Mussaurus*.

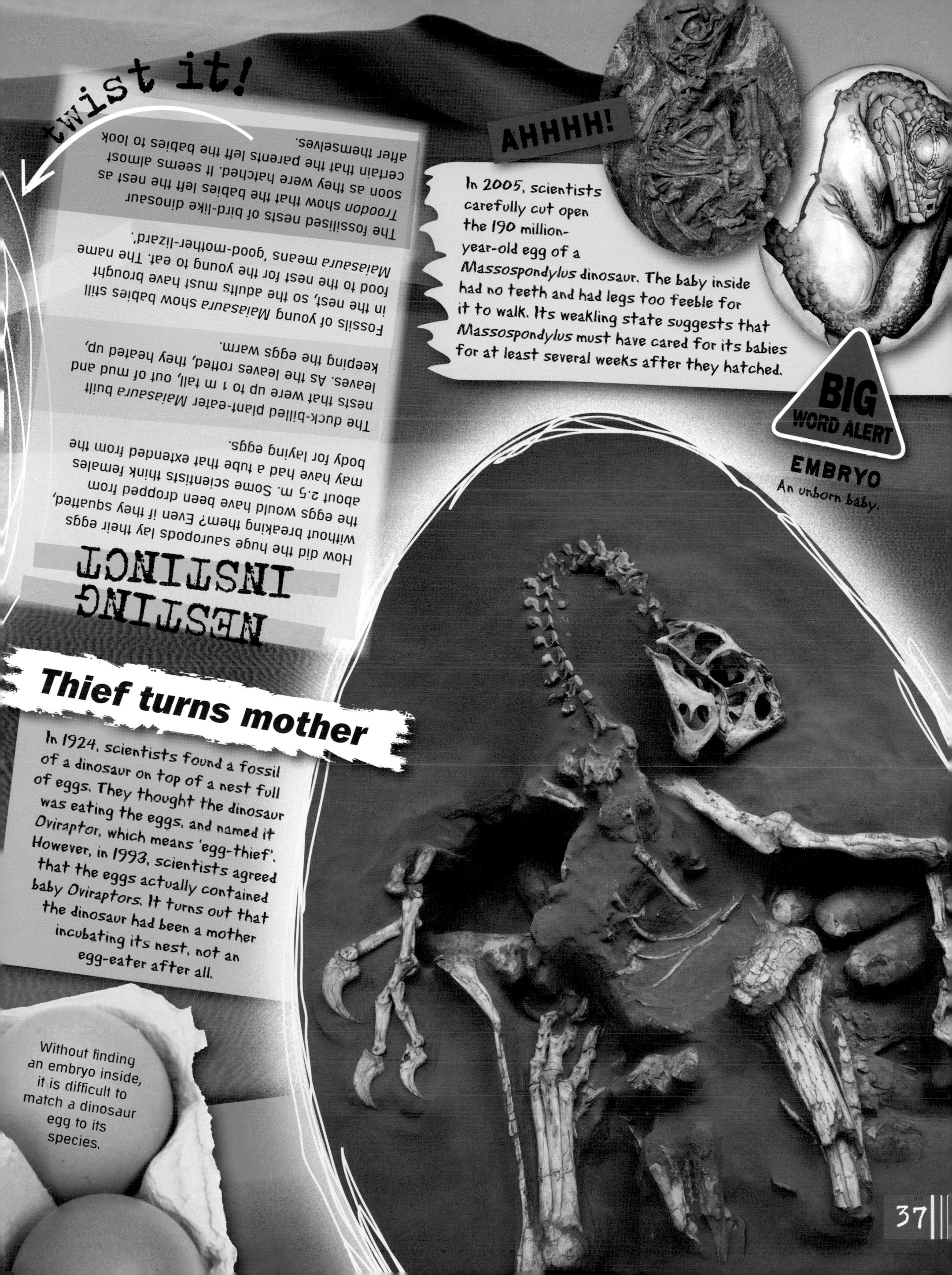

twist it!

NESTING INSTINCT

How did the huge sauropods lay their eggs without breaking them? Even if they squatted, the eggs would have been dropped from about 2.5 m. Some scientists think females may have had a tube that extended from the body for laying eggs.

The duck-billed plant-eater *Maiasaura* built nests that were up to 1 m tall, out of mud and leaves. As the leaves rotted, they heated up, keeping the eggs warm.

Fossils of young *Maiasaura* show babies still in the nest, so the adults must have brought food to the nest for the young to eat. The name *Maiasaura* means 'good-mother-lizard'.

The fossilised nests of bird-like dinosaur *Troodon* show that the babies left the nest as soon as they were hatched. It seems almost certain that the parents left the babies to look after themselves.

AHHHH!

In 2005, scientists carefully cut open the 190 million-year-old egg of a *Massospondylus* dinosaur. The baby inside had no teeth and had legs too feeble for it to walk. Its weakling state suggests that *Massospondylus* must have cared for its babies for at least several weeks after they hatched.

BIG WORD ALERT

EMBRYO
An unborn baby.

Thief turns mother

In 1924, scientists found a fossil of a dinosaur on top of a nest full of eggs. They thought the dinosaur was eating the eggs, and named it *Oviraptor*, which means 'egg-thief'. However, in 1993, scientists agreed that the eggs actually contained baby *Oviraptors*. It turns out that the dinosaur had been a mother incubating its nest, not an egg-eater after all.

Without finding an embryo inside, it is difficult to match a dinosaur egg to its species.

SKY PATROL

FLYING REPTILES AND BIRDS

The pterosaurs were a large group of flying reptiles that lived at the same time as the dinosaurs. They came in all shapes and sizes, ranging from gigantic gliders to small, agile flappers.

Soaring high above the ground, these flying reptiles twitched their great wings to swoop in a giant circle through the sky. Scanning the ground for the carcass of a dead dinosaur, the pterosaurs sniffed the air for the tell-tale stink of rotting flesh.

About 150 million years ago, the first birds evolved and began to take to the air. They gradually replaced the pterosaurs as the most important flying creatures, until only a few pterosaurs were left alive by the time of the great extinction 65 million years ago.

Feathered friends

The fossil of a strange, feathered dinosaur from the middle to late Jurassic period – just before birds evolved – has been discovered in China. The pigeon-like creature, called Epidexipteryx, had four long ribbon-like tail feathers, which were probably used for display, but had no flight feathers. This fossil suggests that feathers were probably used for decoration millions of years before they were modified for flight.

The pterosaur Pterodaustro had over a thousand bristle-like teeth in its jaws – about 25 per cm. It used these to filter tiny food particles from water.

These *Pteranodon* pterosaurs had huge, toothless bills, with which they caught their fish dinners, and wingspans of up to 9 m.

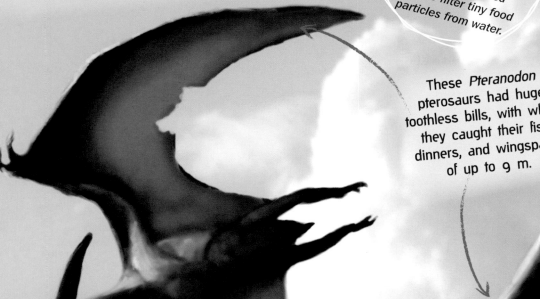

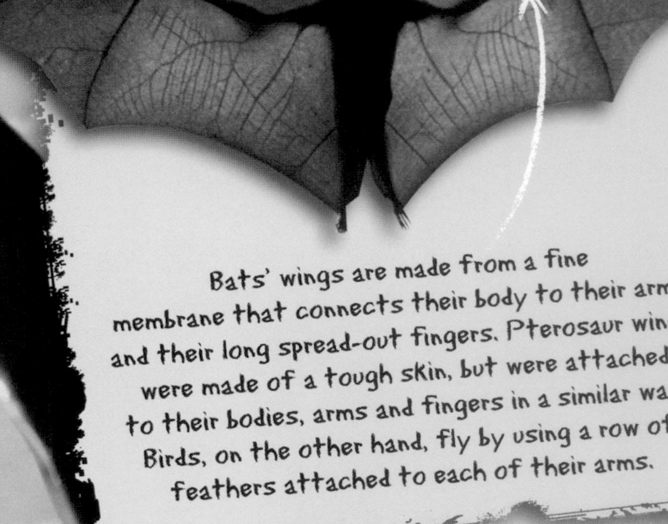

The modern-day bat is the only mammal around today that is capable of sustained flight, and its wings share many of the characteristics of a pterosaur wing.

Bats' wings are made from a fine membrane that connects their body to their arms and their long spread-out fingers. Pterosaur wings were made of a tough skin, but were attached to their bodies, arms and fingers in a similar way. Birds, on the other hand, fly by using a row of feathers attached to each of their arms.

The smallest known pterosaur was Nemicolopterus, which lived in forests in eastern Asia about 120 million years ago. It was about the size of a modern blackbird with a wingspan of just 23 cm.

Ripley's Believe It or Not!®

Giant glider

One of the largest of the pterosaurs was Quetzalcoatlus, which lived in North America about 72 million years ago. It had a wingspan of 11 m – that's the same as some small aircraft.

One of the early birds

Confuciusornis was a primitive bird that lived about 120 million years ago in eastern Asia. It was about the size of a modern crow and had long tail feathers that ended in wide flags. Its fossils provide evidence of a strong link between dinosaurs and birds.

WILD WATERS

Sea Monsters

Fossils of ichthyosaurs sometimes contain round, black pebbles near the rear of the body. It is thought that these are fossilised droppings and they are coloured black by the ink found in the squid that the ichthyosaurs ate.

Help!

The dinosaurs also shared their world with several groups of water-dwelling reptiles, some of which were almost as big as them. These hungry sea giants powered their way through the waves snapping up fish, squid, ammonites and other creatures in their tooth-fringed jaws. Some could even reach up into the air to grab flying pterosaurs on the wing.

Sea-going reptiles from the Mesozoic era included placodonts, ichthyosaurs, mosasaurs, plesiosaurs and turtles. Some of these large water-dwelling reptiles died out before the dinosaurs did, others became extinct at the same time. There was one exception that lives on today: the turtles.

Living fossil?

A modern-day frill shark was found by a fisherman in Numazu, Japan, in 2007. Rarely seen out of its depth of 600 m, this ancient-looking creature's body has many similarities to fossils of sharks that lived 350 million years ago.

Anyone for a swim?

A giant fossil sea monster found in the Arctic in 2008 had a bite that would have been able to crush a car. The marine reptile, which patrolled the oceans some 147 million years ago, measured 15 m long and had a bite force of around 16,000 kg.

Big flipper

The fossils of the giant sea turtle *Archelon* date to around 75–65 million years ago, when a shallow sea covered most of North America. The largest specimen ever found is 4.1 m long and 4.9 m wide from flipper to flipper.

Underwater flying

The plesiosaurs were a group of sea reptiles with stout bodies and four powerful flippers. They flapped their flippers in a similar way to how birds' wings work. *Pliosaurs* were massive plesiosaurs with short, powerful necks and sharp teeth. Some were more than 10 m long and might have been able to rear up to catch passing pterosaurs or birds.

Supersize!

The biggest ichthyosaur was *Shonisaurus*, which grew more than 21 m long. Scientists found the fossils of 37 of these monsters in one small area in Nevada. Perhaps a family group had become stuck on a prehistoric beach and died.

The 13.7-m-long plesiosaur *Elasmosaurus* had more bones in its neck than any other animal that has ever lived – 72 in all.

Amazingly, no complete fossil has been found that is as big as the blue whale that lives on Earth with us today.

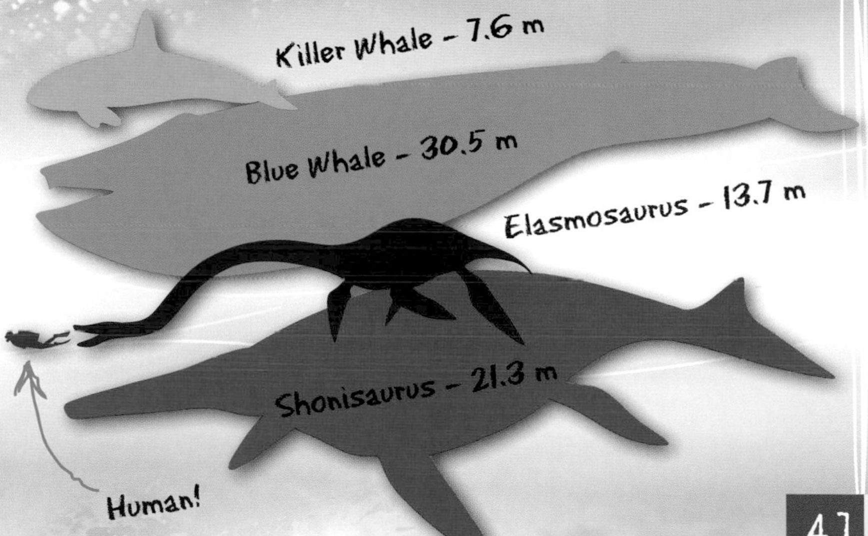

Killer Whale – 7.6 m
Blue Whale – 30.5 m
Elasmosaurus – 13.7 m
Shonisaurus – 21.3 m
Human!

DINO DT TIMES

WORLDWIDE EVENTS COMING TO YOU www.dinotimes 65 MILLION YEARS AGO

MASSIVE METEORITE HITS EARTH!

Scientists are agreed. Our planet has suffered a catastrophic meteorite hit in the Gulf of Mexico. Although reports are sketchy, as there is no sign of life in the immediate area, news is filtering through that the asteroid was about 10 km wide and slammed into Earth at 69,200 km per hour.

Reports suggest that, in just 30 seconds, the meteorite drilled a crater in Chicxulub, on the Yucatán Peninsula in Mexico, that was 39 km deep and 200 km wide. The meteorite collision has been compared to a blast from 100 megatonnes of high explosives.

Where is the sun?

Dust thrown up from the meteorite impact is starting to block out sunlight. As a result, in many parts of the world, temperatures have dropped. Our dinosaur in the field has seen trees that are wilting and dying from lack of light. A *Triceratops* that depends on foliage for food moans, "We always have to eat a lot and now there's just not enough to go round."

Sightings of *Tyrannosaurus* and other meat-lovers gorging on weakened herbivores are becoming increasingly rare. "When the dark days first set in, forests began to die and dying herbivores were everywhere. Frankly, times were good," explains one. "But now their carcasses are starting to go off and we're panicking that fresh meat could be a thing of the past."

Hard to Breathe

Air quality is poor, as poisonous volcanic gases are becoming trapped under the dust clouds and ash continues to rain down. In some areas, gases have been acting like a lid on the world's atmosphere and have trapped in heat from volcanic activity. Rivers have dried and deserts are growing – all presenting more problems for plants and animals.

WEATHER WARNING!

Tsunamis, earthquakes and hurricane winds imminent.

Today's Horoscope

Those born in the Mesozoic era will be confronting new challenges. Hold tight on booking next year's holiday.

JOKE OF THE DAY

What comes after extinction?

Y-stinction, of course!

Obituaries: Extinction has been announced of the following dinosaurs: Every single one.

DINO STATS

All the facts and figures on the main dinosaurs you'll find in this book.

KEY TO SYMBOLS

L = Length *H* = Height *W* = Weight

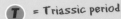

Herbivore (a plant-eating dinosaur)

Carnivore (a meat-eating dinosaur)

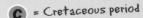

Omnivore (a plant- and meat-eating dinosaur)

T = Triassic period

J = Jurassic period

C = Cretaceous period

AFROVENATOR
say *af-ro-vee-nay-tor*
'African hunter'
Type theropod
L 9 m ***H*** 3 m ***W*** 1,400 kg

AGUSTINIA
say *ah-gus-tin-ee-ah*
'for Agustin'
Type sauropod
L 15 m ***H*** 4.5 m ***W*** 9,000 kg

ALLOSAURUS
say *al-oh-saw-russ*
'different lizard'
Type theropod
L 12 m ***H*** 4.5 m ***W*** 3,000 kg

ANKYLOSAURUS
say *an-key-low-saw-rus*
'fused lizard'
Type ankylosaur
L 6 m ***H*** 3 m ***W*** 3,600 kg

ARGENTINOSAURUS
say *are-jen-teen-owe-saw-rus*
'silver lizard'
Type sauropod
L 40 m ***H*** 11 m ***W*** 72,500 kg

BARYONYX
say *ba-ree-on-ix*
'heavy claw'
Type theropod
L 10 m ***H*** 4.5 m ***W*** 2,000 kg

BRACHIOSAURUS
say *brack-ee-oh-saw-rus*
'arm lizard'
Type sauropod
L 24 m ***H*** 13 m ***W*** 70,000 kg

CERATOSAURUS
say *see-rat-oh-saw-rus*
'horned lizard'
Type ceratosaur
L 5.5 m ***H*** 3 m ***W*** 1,400 kg

CHIALINGOSAURUS
say *chee-ah-ling-oh-saw-rus*
'Chialing lizard'
Type stegosaur
L 4 m ***H*** 1.5 m ***W*** 225 kg

COELOPHYSIS
say *see-low-fy-sis*
'hollow form'
Type theropod
L 3 m ***H*** 1 m ***W*** 45 kg

COMPSOGNATHUS
say *comp-sog-nay-thus*
'pretty jaw'
Type theropod
L 70 cm ***H*** 0.25 m ***W*** 3 kg

DEINOCHEIRUS
say *dine-oh-kir-us*
'terrible hand'
Type ornithomimosaur
L 7–12 m ***H*** 3 m ***W*** 9,000 kg

DEINONYCHUS
say *die-non-i-kuss*
'terrible claw'
Type dromeosaur
L 3 m ***H*** 1.5 m ***W*** 80 kg

DIPLODOCUS
say *dee-plod-oh-cus*
'double-beam'
Type sauropod
L 27 m ***H*** 5 m ***W*** 12,000 kg

DROMICEIOMIMUS
say *droh-mee-see-oh-my-mus*
'emu mimic'
Type ornithomimosaur
L 4 m ***H*** 2 m ***W*** 115 kg

EUOPLOCEPHALUS
say *you-oh-plo-sef-ah-lus*
'well-armoured head'
Type ankylosaur
L 7 m ***H*** 2.5 m ***W*** 1,800 kg

FRUITADENS
say *fruit-ah-denz*
'fruita tooth'
Type heterodontosaur
L 60 cm ***H*** 30 cm ***W*** 1 kg

GRYPOSAURUS
say *grip-oh-saw-us*
'hook-nosed lizard'
Type hadrosaur
L 9 m ***H*** 4 m ***W*** 2,700 kg

IGUANODON
say *ig-wah-no-don*
'iguana tooth'
Type iguanodont
L 9 m ***H*** 4 m ***W*** 4,500 kg

MAMENCHISAURUS
say *mah-men-chee-saw-rus*
'mamen lizard'
Type sauropod
L 23 m ***H*** 9 m ***W*** 14,000 kg

MASSOSPONDYLUS
say *mass-oh-spon-dye-luss*
'massive vertebra'
Type prosauropod
L 5 m ***H*** 2 m ***W*** 135 kg

Nomingia

say *no-ming-ee-uh*
'Nomingiin' (part of the Gobi desert)
Type oviraptor
L 2 m ***H*** 75 cm ***W*** 32 kg

Oviraptor

say *ov ee rap tor*
'egg thief'
Type theropod
L 2.5 m ***H*** 1 m ***W*** 34 kg

Protoceratops

say *pro-toe-sair-ah-tops*
'first horned face'
Type ceratopsian
L 2.5 m ***H*** 1 m ***W*** 410 kg

Scipionyx

say *sip-ee-on-ix*
'scipio's claw'
Type theropod
L 2 m ***H*** 0.75 m ***W*** 11 kg

Scutellosaurus

say *skoo-tel-o-saw-us*
'little shield lizard'
Type thyreophora
L 1 m ***H*** 50 cm ***W*** 11 kg

Seismosaurus

say *size-mow-saw-rus*
'earthquake lizard'
Type sauropod
L 40 m ***H*** 5.5 m ***W*** 30,000 kg

Spinosaurus

say *spy-no-saw-rus*
'spiny lizard'
Type spinosaur
L 18 m ***H*** 7 m ***W*** 9,000 kg

Stegosaurus

say *steg-oh-saw-rus*
'roofed lizard'
Type stegosaur
L 9 m ***H*** 3 m ***W*** 2,700 kg

Styracosaurus

say *sty-rak-o-saw-us*
'spiked lizard'
Type ceratopsian
L 5.5 m ***H*** 2 m ***W*** 2,900 kg

Triceratops

say *tyr-seer-ah-tops*
'three horned face'
Type ceratopsian
L 9 m ***H*** 3 m ***W*** 10,000 kg

Tyrannosaurus

say *tie-ran-oh-saw-rus*
'tyrant lizard king'
Type tyrannosaur
L 12 m ***H*** 5.5 m ***W*** 6,350 kg

Velociraptor

say *vel-oh-see-rap-tor*
'speedy thief'
Type theropod
L 2 m ***H*** 1 m ***W*** 30 kg

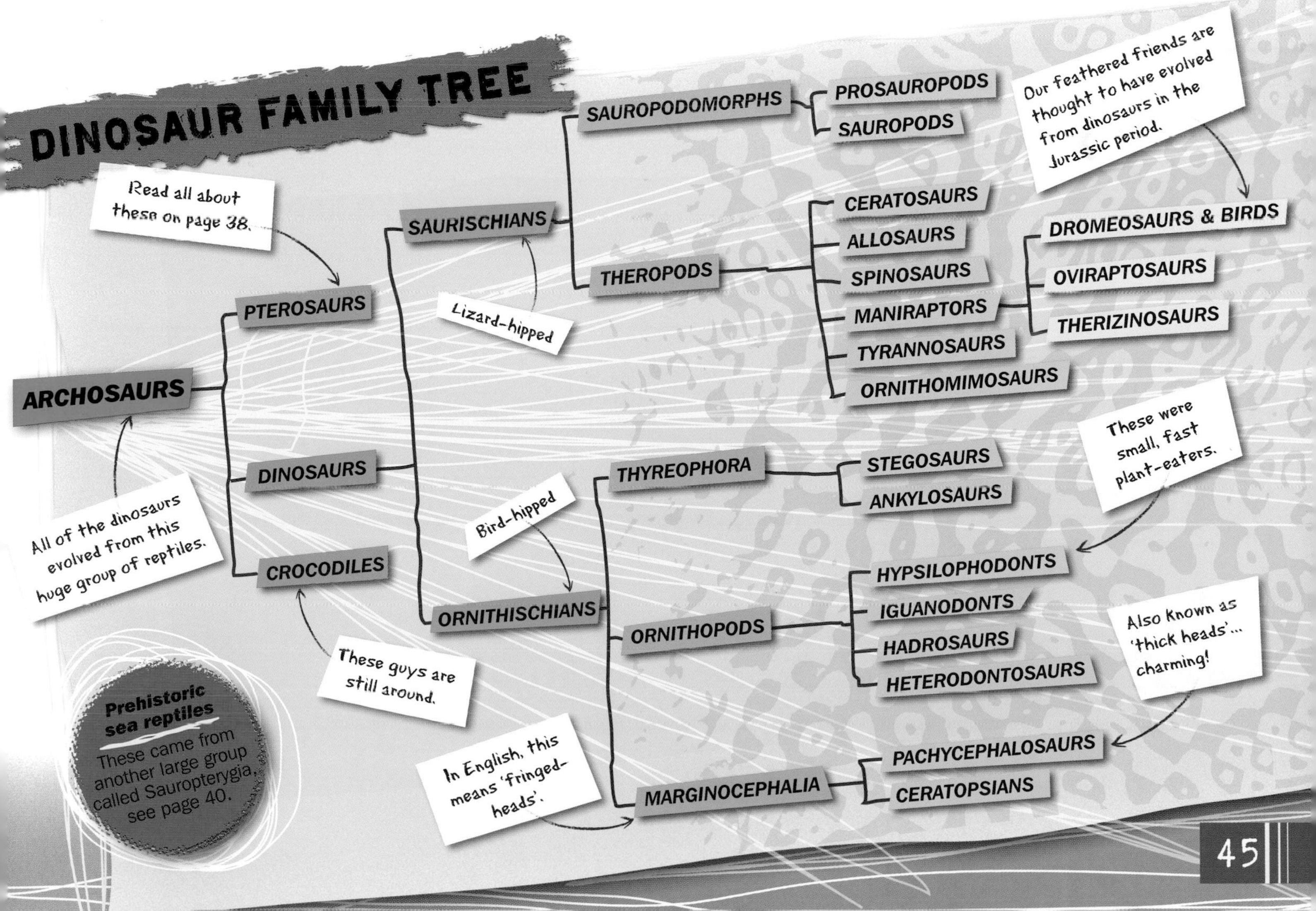

DINOSAUR FAMILY TREE

- ARCHOSAURS
  - PTEROSAURS
  - DINOSAURS
    - SAURISCHIANS
      - SAUROPODOMORPHS
        - PROSAUROPODS
        - SAUROPODS
      - THEROPODS
        - CERATOSAURS
        - ALLOSAURS
        - SPINOSAURS
        - MANIRAPTORS
          - DROMEOSAURS & BIRDS
          - OVIRAPTOSAURS
          - THERIZINOSAURS
        - TYRANNOSAURS
        - ORNITHOMIMOSAURS
    - ORNITHISCHIANS
      - THYREOPHORA
        - STEGOSAURS
        - ANKYLOSAURS
      - ORNITHOPODS
        - HYPSILOPHODONTS
        - IGUANODONTS
        - HADROSAURS
        - HETERODONTOSAURS
      - MARGINOCEPHALIA
        - PACHYCEPHALOSAURS
        - CERATOPSIANS
  - CROCODILES

Read all about these on page 38.

Our feathered friends are thought to have evolved from dinosaurs in the Jurassic period.

Lizard-hipped

Bird-hipped

All of the dinosaurs evolved from this huge group of reptiles.

These were small, fast plant-eaters.

Also known as 'thick heads'... charming!

These guys are still around.

In English, this means 'fringed-heads'.

Prehistoric sea reptiles
These came from another large group called Sauropterygia, see page 40.

ACKNOWLEDGEMENTS

COVER (dp) © zsollere – Fotolia.com, (r) Leonardo Meschini Advocate Art **2** (b) © Ralf Kraft – Fotolia.com; **2–3** © Robert King – Fotolia.com; **3** (t) © Fabian Kerbusch – iStock.com; **4** (b/l) © Sergey Drozdov – Fotolia.com; **5** (t/r) © Klaus Nilkens – iStock.com; **6** Mark Garlick/Science Photo Library; **6–7** © Metin Tolun – Fotolia.com; **7** (sp) © Alwyn Cooper – iStock.com, (t/l) © Bill May – iStock.com, (r) © Todd Harrison – iStock.com; **8** (l) © Ericos – Fotolia.com, (r) © Olga Orehkova-Sokolova – Fotolia.com; **8–9** (b) © zobeedy – Fotolia.com; **9** (t) © Metin Tolun – Fotolia.com, (t/r) Laurie O'keefe/Science Photo Library, (l) © Olga Orehkova-Sokolova – Fotolia.com, (r) © Ericos – Fotolia.com; **10** (t/l) © Didier Dutheil/Sygma/Corbis, (r) Photo courtesy of Charlie and Florence Magovern; **10–11** (c) © Metin Tolun – Fotolia.com; **11** (t/r) Reuters/STR New, (t) © Bill May – iStock.com, (b/r) © Didier Dutheil/Sygma/Corbis; **12** (b/l) Mikkel Juul Jensen/Bonnier Publications/Science Photo Library, (c) © Robert King – Fotolia.com, (t) © Fabian Kerbusch – iStock.com, (t/r) Eightfish; **13** (t) © Fabian Kerbusch – iStock.com, (t/r) © greenmedia – Fotolia.com, (c/r) © LianeM – Fotolia.com, (r) © Duey – Fotolia.com, (b/r) Reuters/Sergio Moraes, (sp) © Czardases – Fotolia.com; **14–15** Leonardo Meschini Advocate Art; **16** (sp) Roger Harris/Science Photo Library **17** (b/l) © Metin Tolun – Fotolia.com, (b/cl) © Bill May – iStock.com, (t) Christian Jegou Publiphoto Diffusion/Science Photo Library, (b) Reuters/STR New; **18** (t) De Agostini/Getty Images, (t/l) © Paul Moore – Fotolia.com, (b) © Metin Tolun – Fotolia.com, (b/r) Highlights for Children (OSF)/www.photolibrary.com; **18–19** (sp) © Ivan Bliznetsov – iStock.com, (r, l) © Steven van Soldt – iStock.com; **19** (t) Photoshot, (t/l) © Joonarkan – Fotolia.com, (c) © Sabina – Fotolia.com, (b) De Agostini/ Getty Images; **20–21** Leonardo Meschini Advocate Art; **21** (t/r) © Olga Orehkova-Sokolova – Fotolia.com; **22–23** Leonardo Meschini Advocate Art; **24** (sp) Colin Keates; **25** (t/l) © Michael S. Yamashita/Corbis, (t/r) Ken Lucas, (b) Dea Picture Library; **26** (c) © Ralf Kraft – Fotolia.com (b/l, t/r) © Serhiy Zavalnyuk – iStock.com, (b/r) © Little sisters – Fotolia.com; **26–27** © klikk – Fotolia.com; **27** (t/l) © Little sisters – Fotolia.com, (t/r) © Olga Orehkova-Sokolova – Fotolia.com, (b) Peter Menzel/Science Photo Library; **28–29** Leonardo Meschini Advocate Art; **30** (b/c) Leonardo Meschini Advocate Art, (b) © Metin Tolun – Fotolia.com; **30–31** © Petya Petrova – Fotolia.com; **31** (t/l) Jeffrey L. Osborn, (t, b) © Metin Tolun – Fotolia.com, (b/r) Joe Tucciarone/Science Photo Library; **32** (t/r) Nigel Tisdall/Rex Features; **32–33** (dp) © Louie Psihoyos/Science Faction/Corbis; **33** (r) Christian Darkin/Science Photo Library; **34** (l) © Louie Psihoyos/Science Faction/Corbis, (b/l, b/r) © zobeedy – Fotolia.com, (b/c) © N & B – Fotolia.com; **34–35** Leonardo Meschini Advocate Art; **35** (b/l) © Pawel Nowik – Fotolia.com, (b/c) © N & B – Fotolia.com, (b/cr) © a_elmo – Fotolia.com, (b/r) © zobeedy – Fotolia.com; **36** (t) © Louie Psihoyos/Science Faction/Corbis, (b/r) © Chris Hepburn – iStock.com; **36–37** (dp) © Vladimir Wrangel – Fotolia.com; **37** (t/r) Reuters/Ho New, (b) © Louie Psihoyos/Corbis; **38** (t/l) © Gijs Bekenkamp – iStock.com; **38–39** Jaime Chirinos/Science Photo Library; **39** (t/l) Joe Tucciarone/Science Photo Library, (t) © Hypergon – iStock.com, (t/r) Richard Bizley/Science Photo Library; **40** (c) Getty Images, (b) search4dinosaurs.com; **41** Reuters/Ho New; **42** (b/r) © Darren Hendley – iStock.com, (c/r) © nikzad khaledi – iStock.com, (t/l) D. Van Ravenswaay/Science Photo Library, (t) Mauricio Anton/Science Photo Library; **43** Mark Garlick/Science Photo Library

Key: t = top, b = bottom, c = centre, l = left, r = right, sp = single page, dp = double page, bgd = background

All other photos are from Ripley's Entertainment Inc. All other artwork by Rocket Design (East Anglia) Ltd.

Every attempt has been made to acknowledge correctly and contact copyright holders and we apologise in advance for any unintentional errors or omissions, which will be corrected in future editions.

Ripley's SPACE

Believe It or Not!®

a Jim Pattison Company

Written by Dr. Mike Goldsmith
Consultant Clint Twist

PUBLISHING

Publisher **Anne Marshall**

Editorial Director **Rebecca Miles**
Picture Researcher **James Proud**
Editors **Lisa Regan, Rosie Alexander, Charlotte Howell**
Proofreader **Judy Barratt**
Indexer **Hilary Bird**

Art Director **Sam South**
Design **Rocket Design (East Anglia) Ltd**
Reprographics **Juice Creative Ltd**

www.ripleys.com/books

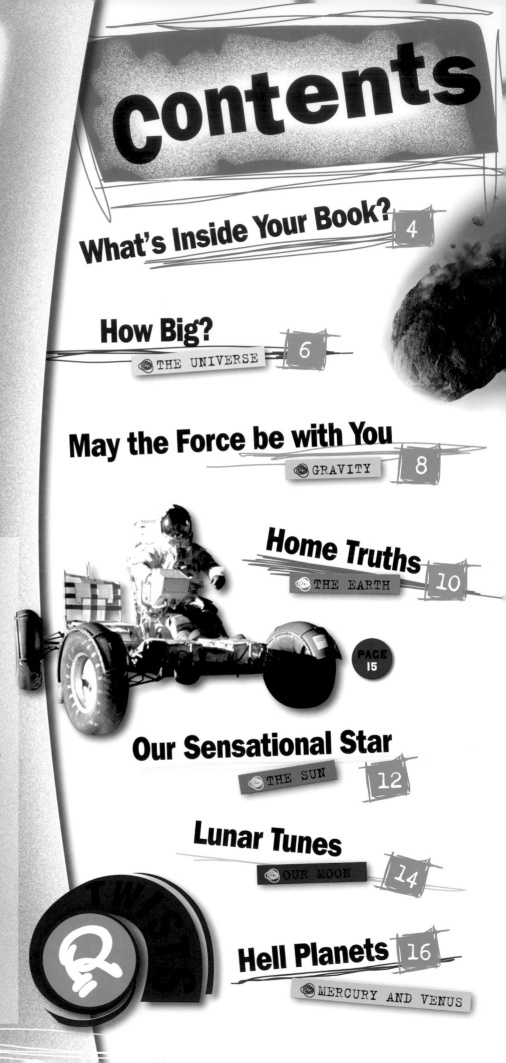

First published in Great Britain in 2009 by Random House Books, Random House, 20 Vauxhall Bridge Road, London SW1V 2SA www.randomhouse.co.uk

This edition 2013

Addresses for companies within The Random House Group Limited can be found at: www.randomhouse.co.uk/offices.htm

The Random House Group Limited Reg. No. 954009

ISBN 978-1-60991-236-9 (USA) | ISBN 978-0-09956-815-5 (UK)

10 9 8 7 6 5 4 3 2 1

A CIP catalogue record for this book is available from the British Library

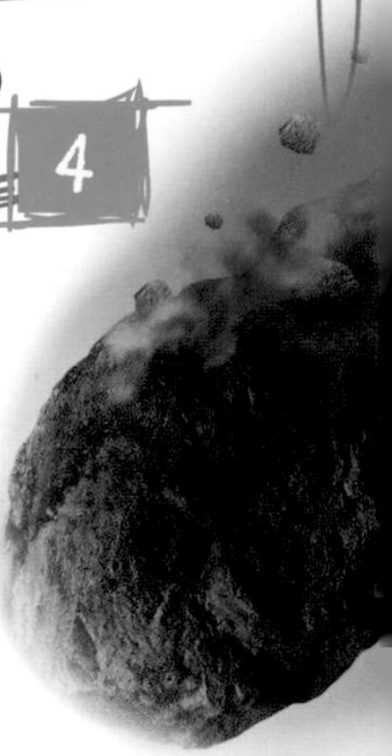

Printed in China
January 2018
2nd Printing

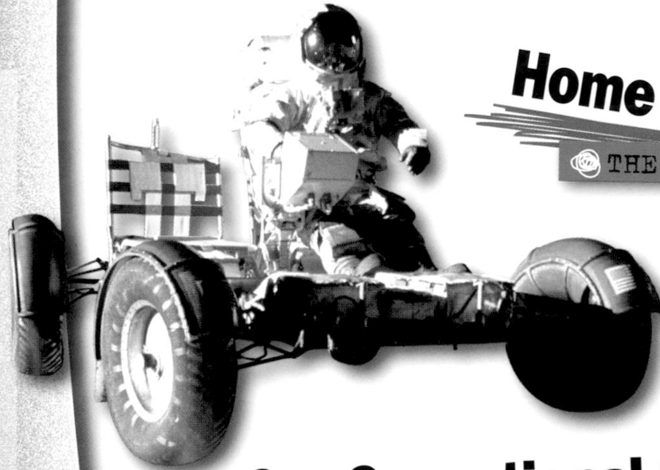

Contents

PAGE 24
PAGE 22
PAGE 44

Universally Speaking

TOTALLY OUT THERE

WHAT'S INSIDE YOUR BOOK?

Space is fascinating, and huge, and complicated. It's full of things you can see, like stars, and satellites, and the Sun. It's even more full of things you can't see, like black holes and wormholes and dark energy. Scientists have spent lifetimes trying to make sense of what's out there. How big is the Universe? How did it all begin? Where will it all end?

Found a new word? We will explain it for you.

24

This book shows you some of space's best bits: shuttles and space stations, planets and probes, meteorites and moons, asteroids and astronauts. Every page is packed with out-of-this world info, with special Ripley's fascinating facts and amazing 'Believe It or Not!' stories. Are you ready to read on? 5-4-3-2-1...

It's not enough for some astronauts to go into space in a spaceship – they want to take a walk while they're there! A special protective suit (see page 40) allows EVA (extra-vehicular activity). The longest EVA was done in 2001 by two astronauts who stayed outside the International Space Station (see page 42) for nearly 9 hours.

TWISTS

Look for the Ripley R to find out even more than you knew before!

Danger Zone

ASTEROIDS AND COMETS

Comets are like giant dirty snowballs. Usually comets are pretty happy orbiting far out at the edge of the Solar System, about seven trillion kilometres from Earth, but sometimes they swoop in towards the Sun, growing tails of gas and dust as they warm up.

If you've ever seen a comet, you probably weren't afraid – after all, it was just a whitish streak in the sky. Don't be fooled, though: comets can kill. In fact, it was probably a comet (or perhaps an asteroid) that wiped out the mighty dinosaurs 65 million years ago. It crashed into the Earth and the dust it threw up froze the planet, which killed the dinosaurs. And it could happen again – to us.

amazing!!

This colossal crater, seen here from space, in Australia's Northern Territory is called Gosses Bluff and is about 4.5 km wide. It was made by an asteroid or comet about 1 km across that crashed into Earth around 142 million years ago.

SAY WHAT?

ASTEROID

small rocky body in orbit [around] the Sun. Many asteroids [are l]ocated between the orbits of [Mar]s and Jupiter. These are the [buil]ding blocks of a planet that failed to form there.

In 2000, Comet Hyakutake had a tail 550 million km long – nearly four times longer than the distance from the Earth to the Sun!

Comets are made of ice, dust and rocky material that came from the Solar System when it was first created about 4.5 billion years ago.

The centre of a comet is called its nucleus.

...osh...

twist it!

In 1908, a strange explosion flattened 2,150 sq km of forest in Siberia. It was probably caused by a comet exploding in the air.

If you had been around in 1910, when the Earth passed through the tail of a comet, you could have tried some of the anti-comet pills that were on sale. But they wouldn't have done you any good!

Halley is a comet that reappears every 75.3 years. There are records of its visits that go back to 25 May, 240BC.

A comet called Shoemaker-Levy 9 crashed into Jupiter in 1994. It hit the planet on the side that was facing away from Earth, so the impact itself wasn't seen, but huge marks could be seen in Jupiter's atmosphere for several months afterwards.

A comet or asteroid the size of a city crashed into Mexico's Yucatan Peninsula 65 million years ago.

WATCH I...

25

Ripley's Believe It or Not!®

Who'd have thought it? Read all about some totally out there (but totally true) stories – like the teddies sent into space. Members of Cambridge University space-flight club launched four teds on a weather balloon. The teddies wore suits made of foil, foam, plastic bottles and tape, which had been designed by schoolchildren to protect their furry friends from the -58°F temperatures.

Learn fab fast facts to go with the cool pictures.

Do the twist

This book is packed with superb sights from the Known Universe. It will teach you amazing things about space, but like all Twists books, it shines a spotlight on things that are unbelievable but true. Turn the pages and find out more...

Twists are all about Believe It or Not: amazing facts, feats, and things that will make you go 'Wow!'.

Don't forget to look out for the 'twist it!' column on some pages. Twist the book to find out more fast facts about the Universe we live in.

Everything that exists is part of the Universe, and that's a big, big, big place. HUGE! In fact, the distance across the Universe is at least a whopping 900 billion trillion kilometres. Many scientists think that it's larger than this: it may even go on for ever!

The Universe contains at least a billion trillion stars, yet it is mostly empty space. All the stars and planets and other things we can see only make up about 5% of the Universe – the rest is called 'dark energy' and 'dark matter' – and no one knows what they are!

These smudges of light are groups of millions of stars, billions of trillions of kilometres away. The time taken for their light to cross the Universe means this picture is a few billion years out of date!

If you travelled through the Universe in a spaceship, you would never reach an edge, no matter how fast or far or long you travelled!

The Universe is expanding (getting bigger) every second.

The Universe has no centre.

How big?

JUST HOW BIG IS 900 BILLION TRILLION KILOMETRES? EVEN ON THE PAGE IT'S AN ENORMOUS NUMBER:

900,000,000,000,000,000,000,000!

seeing stars

Fancy waking up and seeing the stars above you? You don't need to sleep outdoors – artist Rip Read can paint a StarMural on your ceiling. The painting is only visible in the dark, so the 'Startist' has to work at night, with the lights out!

OUT OF THIS WORLD

The temperature of most of the Universe is −270°C, much colder than the coldest freezer on Earth, and only 3 degrees warmer than the coldest possible temperature.

Three-quarters of the known Universe (that is, other than dark matter and dark energy) is hydrogen.

Even on the clearest, darkest night you can see fewer than 1/100,000,000,000,000,000 (one-one hundred thousand trillionth) of the stars in the Universe.

On average, the Universe contains only one atom in every four cubic metres. This is like one lump of sugar in a box with sides 10,000 km long.

twist it!

It is possible that before our Universe existed there was another one, and another one before that, and another before that...

Ripley's Believe It or Not!®

UP, UP AND AWAY

SpaceShipOne was the first private manned spacecraft in space (exceeding an altitude of 100,000 m). In 2004, it was successfully launched twice within a two-week period, claiming the Ansari X prize of $10 million. The competition's aim was to boost civilian-led (rather than military-led) spaceflight. The team have joined forces with Virgin Galactic, intending to send customers into space on short trips.

SAY WHAT?

BILLION AND TRILLION

A billion is one thousand million, or 1,000,000,000. A trillion is even bigger: one million million, or 1,000,000,000,000. A billion trillion has 21 zeros on the end!

May the Force be with You

GRAVITY

Gravity, the force that holds you to the ground, also stops the Earth falling apart, keeps the Moon going around the Earth, and the Earth going around the Sun.

The more massive the planet you stand on, the stronger gravity becomes, and the more you weigh. If you could stand on Jupiter you would weigh more than twice as much as on Earth, and on the Sun you would weigh a thundering 2 tonnes. On the Moon you would weigh so little that you would be a super-Olympian, jumping about four times higher than on Earth. In deep space, far from any star or planet, you would weigh zilch, zero, nothing at all.

Everything in the Universe pulls on everything else with the pull of gravity – even you and this book are strangely attracted to each other!

Near a black hole (see page 30) the gravity is strong enough to tear you apart.

When you are falling, you don't feel the pull of gravity – which is why astronauts in orbit are weightless, even though the Earth's gravity is nearly as strong in orbit as on the surface of the Earth. The astronauts are in a constant state of falling – but so is their spacecraft, so the astronauts float around inside.

>> space surgery >>

In 2006, surgeons from Bordeaux University carried out an operation under weightless conditions, to practise for surgery in space.

FORCEFUL STUFF

If you could survive the heat in the centre of the Earth, you would find that you weighed nothing there and could float around, because the gravity would pull you equally in all directions.

Time slows down where gravity is strong. So, if your parents spent a few decades near a black hole, they could be younger than you when they came home. This also means that people who live on mountains age faster than those living at sea level.

Neurolab was a 1998 space shuttle experiment to test the reactions of living creatures to weightless conditions. It contained 1,500 crickets, 230 swordtail fish, 130 water snails, 150 rats and 18 pregnant mice.

The gravity on some asteroids (see page 24) is so low you could jump off them.

twist it!

You weigh more at the Poles and less at the Equator, due partly to the Earth's shape and partly to its spin.

Albert Einstein discovered that gravity is a warp (bend) in time and space. Einstein was one of the world's most famous scientists. He lived from 1879 to 1955 and developed the Theory of General Relativity, about how gravity works.

SAY WHAT?

ORBIT The path of one object around another in space.

Ripley's Believe It or Not!®

Paralympian Wojtek Czyz set a new long jump record in 2008, wearing a prosthetic leg made of space materials! The same material was used in his leg and in a spectrometer to b90e mounted on the ISS (International Space Station), as both items need to be extremely strong and light.

SAY HI to a robot Einstein! This US robot can act like a human in certain ways, such as having a conversation, recognizing faces, changing facial expressions and mimicking emotions.

FASCINATING FACT

Vesta (asteroid) 62.2 metres

JUMP AROUND>>

Want to break the world high jump record? All you have to do is go to the Moon: our space-neighbour is much less massive than the Earth, which means the pull of gravity there is less, and so is your weight, so you could jump much higher than at home. To really impress the spectators, try jumping on an asteroid like Vesta. Don't forget to take some air with you.

Pluto 24.1 metres

Moon 9.2 metres

Mars 4.5 metres

Earth 2.4 metres

Home Truths

THE EARTH

As far as we know, Earth is the only place in the Universe where life exists. Though we live all over the place, some of our planet isn't too friendly: 71% is covered in water, and 97% of that water is too salty to drink. Temperatures at the Poles fall as low as –89°C, and in deserts they can rise to a blistering 58°C.

That's just on the surface. Inside the Earth, it gets hotter as you go deeper. It reaches about 6000°C in the core – about as hot as the surface of the Sun. In the other direction, up in the air, the temperature falls fast and you would freeze to death just a few kilometres up.

OLD TIMER

Planet Earth is roughly a third of the age of the Universe (making Earth about 4.5 billion years old).

The Earth is carrying you with it round the Sun at 107,000 km/h.

251 million years ago, most species (kinds) of living thing died out, including 96% of all water species and 70% of land species. No one is sure why this happened.

If you travelled back to a time before life existed on Earth, you would be killed by the deadly atmosphere. Without plants, the air would still be unbreathable today.

Ripley's Believe It or Not!®

No one knows exactly how many individual living things there are on Earth, but it is at least 5 million trillion trillion – almost all of which are too small to see without a microscope.

5 MILLION TRILLION TRILLION IS WRITTEN LIKE THIS **5,000,000,000,000,000,000,000,000,000,000,000** **THAT'S A WHOLE LOT OF ZEROS!**

IN THE KNOW... ...THE EARTH

- Diameter: 12,742 km (on average)
- Mass: 6 trillion trillion kg
- Goes around the Sun in: one year (365.24 days)
- Spins on its axis in: 24 hours
- Made mostly of: iron
- Atmosphere made mostly of: nitrogen

FASCINATING FACT! FASCINATING FACT!

>>all around the world>>

40-year-old Jason Lewis from Britain was the first man to travel around the world using only muscle power. It took him 13 years to complete the journey on roller blades, bicycle and a pedal-powered boat on his 'Expedition 360'.

Photographs taken by satellites and from the International Space Station (ISS) show huge differences in the landscapes around our planet.

If all the ice on the Earth melted, the sea would rise by 100 m.

The Earth's Poles are about 21 km closer to the centre of the Earth than the Equator.

If you stood on the Earth's Equator, you would be spinning around with the Earth at 1670 km/h.

SAY WHAT?

POLES

The 'ends' of a planet, around which it spins.

Our sensational Star

...THE SUN

IN THE KNOW...

- Average distance from Earth: 150 million km
- Average diameter: 109 times Earth
- Mass: 333,000 times Earth

THE SUN

The Earth seems like a pretty gigantic place, but compared to the Sun it's nothing to brag about. The Sun is literally massive – 333,000 times the Earth's mass. This bulk is what makes the Sun shine – deep inside, the pressure is so enormous that nuclear reactions take place, like billions of nuclear weapons going off every second.

Even though the surface of the Sun is much cooler than the core, it's still 6,050°C: so hot that any metal on Earth would melt there. Yet, despite all that, the Sun is a very dull and ordinary star, like many of those in the sky. It is only the fact that it is 250,000 times closer to Earth than the next nearest star that makes it seem so bright.

The Sun is about one-third as old as the Universe, and about halfway through its life.

The Sun sometimes ejects (throws out) plasma. This is called a coronal mass ejection (CME).

If it were not for the Sun, Earth's surface temperature would be about -270°C.

The Earth could fit inside the Sun 1.3 million times!

Shown here is the approximate size of Earth in comparison with the Sun.

Here Comes The Sun

twist it!

If the Sun suddenly vanished, we would see it in the sky for another eight minutes. This is the time it takes for sunlight to reach the Earth.

When the Sun begins to run out of fuel, it will grow so large and hot that it will melt the surface of the Earth.

The element helium was discovered on the Sun before it was found on Earth.

In 840, Emperor Louis of Bavaria died of fright caused by experiencing an eclipse of the Sun.

The Sun gives out enough energy in one second to supply the USA with energy for 50 million years! To produce this, it burns up an incredible 4 million tonnes of its mass. However, it will take about 5 billion years to burn it all up, so we needn't worry about it running out.

The Sun is 400 times bigger than our Moon but also 400 times farther away from the Earth.

The Sun outweighs the Earth by the same amount as 175 Boeing 747 planes to one person.

Ripley's Believe It or Not!®

A pinhead-sized speck of the burning gases from our Sun could kill a man from 160 km away.

SAY WHAT?

ELEMENT

One of about 100 basic substances from which everything is made.

>> solar power >>

By harnessing the power of the Sun, a family in Montana, USA, spends only $20 a month on their fuel bills. Their aim was to build an environmentally friendly house without spending a fortune; 250 old tyres and 13,000 empty drinks cans were used in the building!

Blackout

If the Moon moves between the Earth and the Sun, a solar eclipse occurs. Total eclipses are rare, and don't last long – usually less than seven minutes. In 1973 passengers on Concorde flew along with the Moon's moving umbra (shadow) and watched the eclipse for 74 minutes!

Lunar Tunes

OUR MOON

It's around 384,000 km away in space, but the Moon is the Earth's nearest neighbour – though it's as far away from home as humans have managed to get. It is an airless, lifeless ball of rocky mountains and plains of old lava but its effect on the Earth is massive – literally. Together with the Sun, it moves billions of tonnes of water each day, making the tides that wash every shore.

IN THE KNOW... ...OUR MOON

* Average distance from Earth: 384,000 km
* Average diameter: 27% Earth
* Mass: 1.2% of Earth
* Length of day: 27 Earth days

There are dozens of seas on the Moon, but no liquid water. The seas are areas of solidified lava (melted rock).

The beginning of the Moon was almost the end of the Earth: about 4.5 billion years ago, a planet-sized object smashed into our newly born world, and fragments from both planets made the Moon. If the object had been a little bigger, you wouldn't be here to read about it.

The Moon is getting farther away from you all the time: each full moon is about 2 mm further away than the last one.

Ripley's Believe It or Not!®

Because there is no weather on the Moon, astronauts' footprints will survive for decades.

twist it!

FULL OF MOONS

The far side of the Moon was not seen until 1959, when a spacecraft sent a photo of it back to Earth. The Moon turns as it circles the Earth, always keeping the same face toward us.

In 1968, Russian tortoises flew around the Moon before returning safely to Earth in the *Zond 5* spaceship.

The Moon contains mysterious areas called 'mascons', which generate gravity strong enough to pull satellites off course.

If something happens 'once in a blue moon' it could be more often than you think: a blue moon is the second of two full moons in one month, and occurs about once every $2\frac{3}{4}$ years. Don't get too excited – the Moon doesn't actually change colour!

Wish you were here!

The US has successfully put people on the Moon six times. The first was in 1969 and the last was in 1972. Twelve astronauts have walked on the surface. Neil Armstrong was the first person to set foot on the Moon.

The massive costs involved in putting people on the Moon have prevented further government-funded missions. However, the Google Lunar X Prize offers $20 million to the first privately funded team to land a robotic probe on the Moon.

GLITTER BALL

In 1992 the *Galileo* spacecraft, on its way to Jupiter, took pictures of the Moon using special colour filters to record different substances making up the surface. When all the images are put together they give quite a different view – something more like a festive decoration than the Moon we see at night!

GETTING AWAY FROM IT ALL

Dutch architect Hans-Jurgen Rombaut has designed the first hotel intended for the Moon. It is supposed to be finished by 2050 and will have two tall, thin towers, extra-thick walls, and an insulating layer of water to keep out dangerous cosmic rays and regulate the temperature indoors.

Hell Planets

MERCURY AND VENUS

Imagine a world where the Sun is six times brighter than usual, the sky is black, and the weather is hot enough to melt lead during the day and colder than a freezer at night. There is almost no air at all... This is what it is like on Mercury, the closest planet to our Sun.

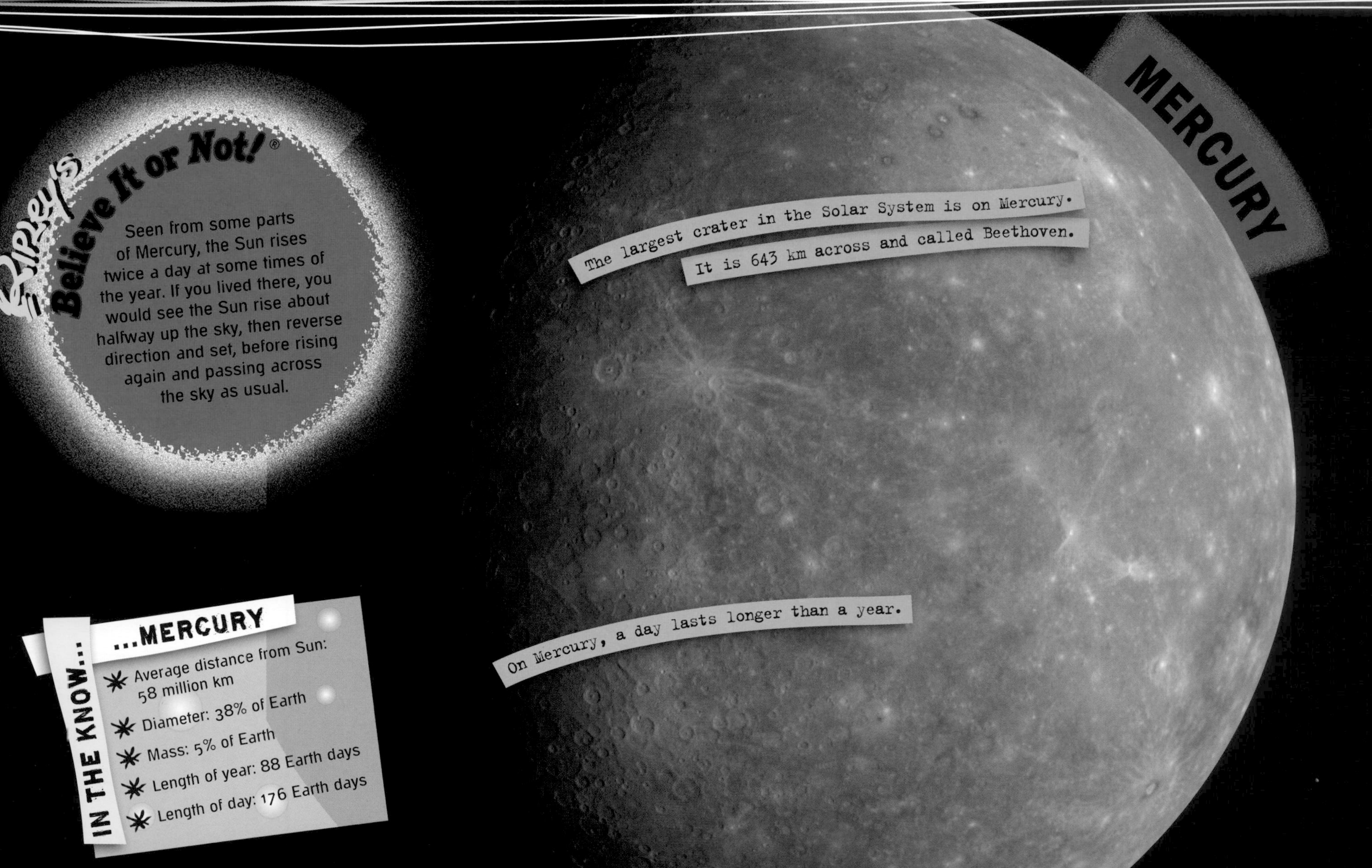

MERCURY
The largest crater in the Solar System is on Mercury.
It is 643 km across and called Beethoven.
On Mercury, a day lasts longer than a year.

Ripley's Believe It or Not!®

Seen from some parts of Mercury, the Sun rises twice a day at some times of the year. If you lived there, you would see the Sun rise about halfway up the sky, then reverse direction and set, before rising again and passing across the sky as usual.

IN THE KNOW... ...MERCURY

* Average distance from Sun: 58 million km
* Diameter: 38% of Earth
* Mass: 5% of Earth
* Length of year: 88 Earth days
* Length of day: 176 Earth days

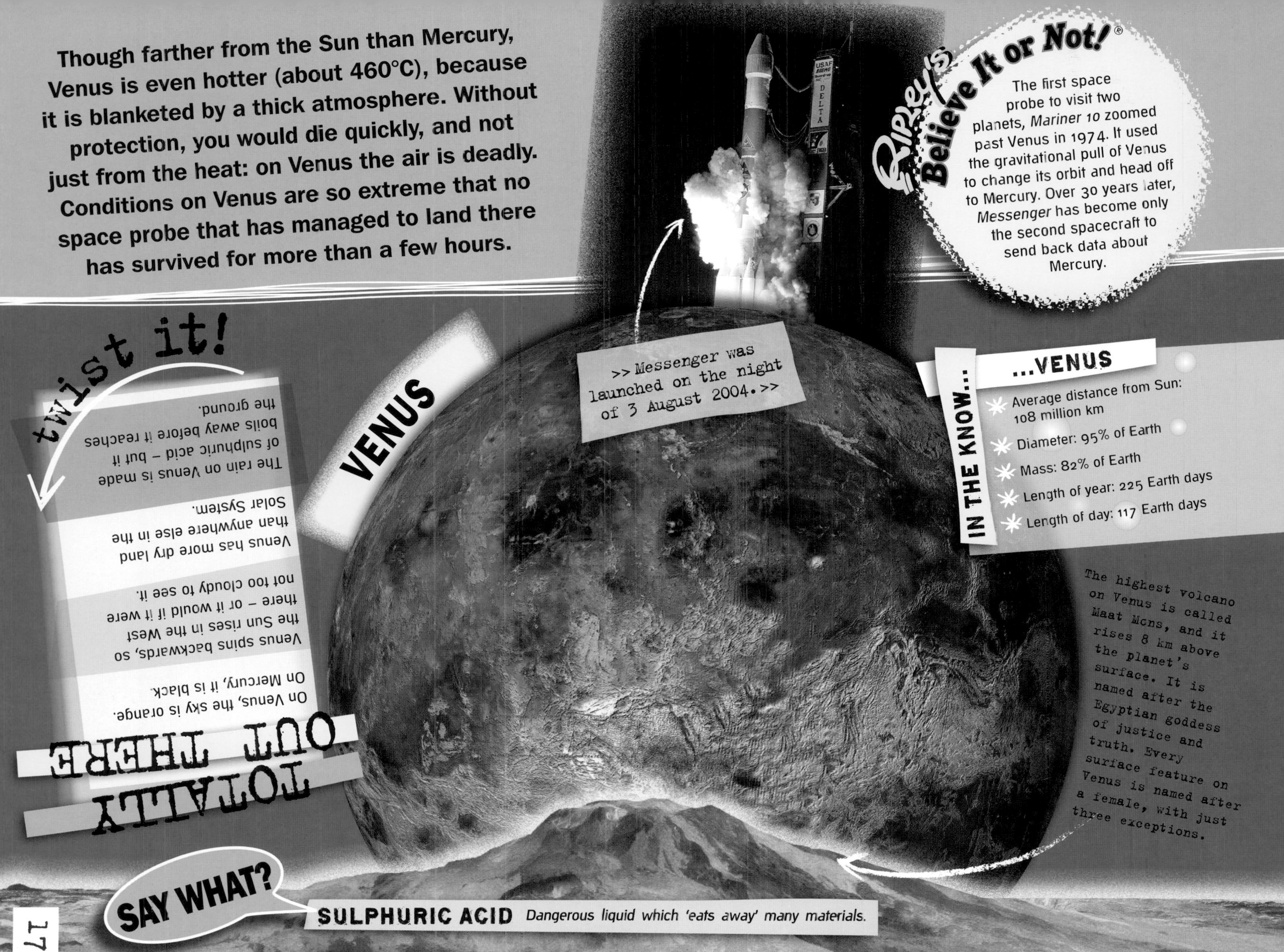

VENUS

Though farther from the Sun than Mercury, Venus is even hotter (about 460°C), because it is blanketed by a thick atmosphere. Without protection, you would die quickly, and not just from the heat: on Venus the air is deadly. Conditions on Venus are so extreme that no space probe that has managed to land there has survived for more than a few hours.

Ripley's Believe It or Not!®

The first space probe to visit two planets, *Mariner 10* zoomed past Venus in 1974. It used the gravitational pull of Venus to change its orbit and head off to Mercury. Over 30 years later, *Messenger* has become only the second spacecraft to send back data about Mercury.

>> Messenger was launched on the night of 3 August 2004.>>

IN THE KNOW... ...VENUS

- Average distance from Sun: 108 million km
- Diameter: 95% of Earth
- Mass: 82% of Earth
- Length of year: 225 Earth days
- Length of day: 117 Earth days

The highest volcano on Venus is called Maat Mons, and it rises 8 km above the planet's surface. It is named after the Egyptian goddess of justice and truth. Every surface feature on Venus is named after a female, with just three exceptions.

TOTALLY OUT THERE

On Venus, the sky is orange. On Mercury, it is black.

Venus spins backwards, so the Sun rises in the West there – or it would if it were not too cloudy to see it.

Venus has more dry land than anywhere else in the Solar System.

twist it!

The rain on Venus is made of sulphuric acid – but it boils away before it reaches the ground.

SAY WHAT?

SULPHURIC ACID *Dangerous liquid which 'eats away' many materials.*

Red Planet

MARS

Mars is a harsh world of deserts and dust, red with rusted iron, but it would still win a 'most similar planet to Earth' competition, with its icy poles, seasons and 24.6-hour day. It used to be even more like home, with a thick atmosphere. Rivers once ran across the surface – and maybe living creatures did, too.

Since *Mariner 4* flew past in 1965, over 40 probes have been sent to explore Mars (more than to any other planet), and it is the next destination for human explorers. Despite the thin air on Mars, it does have weather – clouds, frost and dust-storms – but the last rainy day there was more than a millicn years ago.

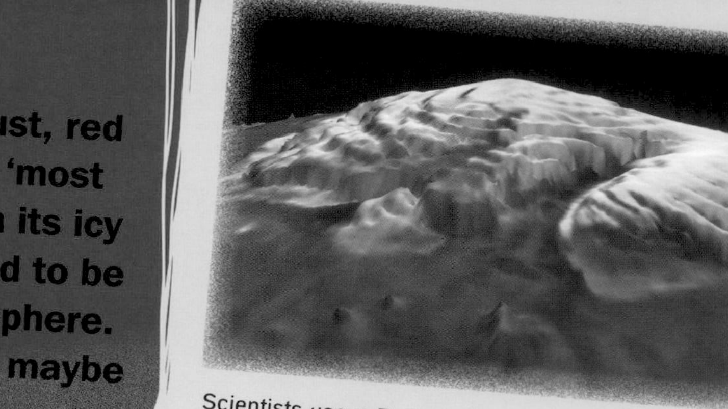

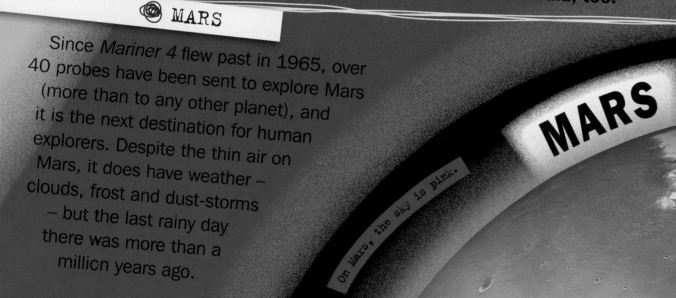

Scientists use 3-D pictures like this one of the North Pole of Mars to work out the amount of water or ice there, and to study the surface and clouds.

MARS

On Mars, the sky is pink.

In the 19th century, creatures from Mars were usually called Martials.

Dust storms on Mars sometimes cover the whole planet.

Viking - landed here in 1976 and took photos of the surface of Mars.

IN THE KNOW... ...MARS

* Average distance from Sun: 228 million km
* Diameter: 53.2% of Earth
* Mass: 11% of Earth
* Length of year: 687 Earth days
* Length of day: 24.6 hours

WHEELIES!

In 1997 the first ever 'thinking' robot to be sent into space arrived on Mars. The *Pathfinder* rover *Sojourner* was equipped with laser 'eyes' and automated programming so it could find its own way across the rocky surface of the planet without bumping into anything. During its travels it sent over 17,000 photos back to scientists on Earth.

Ripley's Believe It or Not!®

Scientists are keen to find out about water and ice on Mars as it may hold the key to whether life has existed (or could exist) on the planet. NASA's 2003 rovers, *Spirit* and *Opportunity*, are still exploring the Martian surface and sending back information. The cost of making and sending the rovers was said to be $820 million for the first 90-day planned mission!

Spirit on the surface of Mars.

twist it!

LIFE ON MARS

In 1938, the radio play *War of the Worlds* tricked people in the USA into believing Martians were invading Earth. Thousands of people fled the danger area.

Mars has the deepest canyon and the largest volcano in the Solar System. This volcano, Olympus Mons, is three times higher than Mount Everest and big enough to fit all of Hawaii's volcanic islands inside.

In 1911 a meteorite from Mars killed an Egyptian dog!

Phobos, one of Mars' moons, orbits only 9,377 km from the planet – only 2.4% the distance at which the Moon orbits Earth.

Around 5,000 people (many of them NASA employees) belong to the Mars Society. They practise life on Mars by spending time in remote places, simulating the conditions they would expect on the red planet. Apparently, they wear helmets made from dustbin lids and plastic light fixtures!

Planet GIANTS

JUPITER AND SATURN

Jupiter and Saturn are the overweight giants of the Solar System – Jupiter is heavier than all the other planets put together. It has an enormously deep atmosphere full of multicoloured storm clouds. It has 63 moons and is surrounded by a system of rings made of millions of pieces of rock.

- Jupiter gives out more heat than it gets from the Sun.
- In 1609, Italian scientist and astronomer Galileo Galilei used his new telescope to discover the four largest of Jupiter's moons.
- Many of Jupiter's moons orbit in the opposite direction to the planet's spin.
- Europa, a moon of Jupiter, is the smoothest world we know, with no hills or valleys.

Jupiter's Red Spot is a hurricane that has lasted for centuries. It is the biggest storm in the Solar System.

The Red Spot is 24,800 km across – almost twice as wide as Earth. Wind speeds inside the storm reach 435 km/h.

Ripley's Believe It or Not!®

Volcanoes on Jupiter's moon Io can spew out hot material at speeds of 1 km/second. That's 20 times faster than the average volcano on Earth.

Io is the most volcanic place in the Solar System.

IN THE KNOW... ...JUPITER

- Average distance from Sun: 778 million km
- Average diameter: 10.9 times Earth
- Mass: 318 times Earth
- Length of year: 12 Earth years
- Length of day: 9.9 hours

SATURN

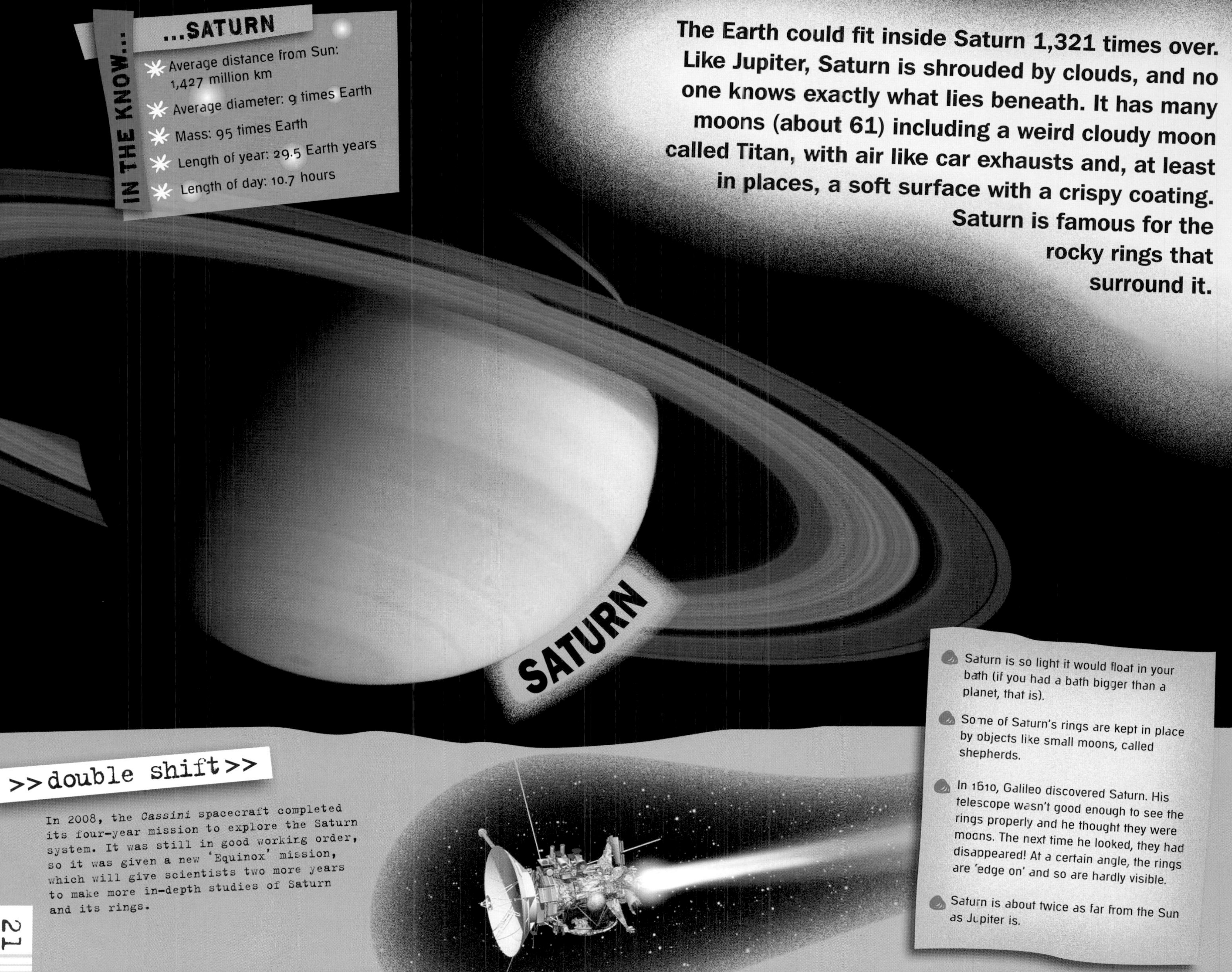

IN THE KNOW... ...SATURN

* Average distance from Sun: 1,427 million km
* Average diameter: 9 times Earth
* Mass: 95 times Earth
* Length of year: 29.5 Earth years
* Length of day: 10.7 hours

The Earth could fit inside Saturn 1,321 times over. Like Jupiter, Saturn is shrouded by clouds, and no one knows exactly what lies beneath. It has many moons (about 61) including a weird cloudy moon called Titan, with air like car exhausts and, at least in places, a soft surface with a crispy coating. Saturn is famous for the rocky rings that surround it.

- Saturn is so light it would float in your bath (if you had a bath bigger than a planet, that is).
- Some of Saturn's rings are kept in place by objects like small moons, called shepherds.
- In 1610, Galileo discovered Saturn. His telescope wasn't good enough to see the rings properly and he thought they were moons. The next time he looked, they had disappeared! At a certain angle, the rings are 'edge on' and so are hardly visible.
- Saturn is about twice as far from the Sun as Jupiter is.

>>double shift>>

In 2008, the *Cassini* spacecraft completed its four-year mission to explore the Saturn system. It was still in good working order, so it was given a new 'Equinox' mission, which will give scientists two more years to make more in-depth studies of Saturn and its rings.

Ice Worlds

URANUS, NEPTUNE AND PLUTO

Neptune is also huge and cold, about –210°C, and is blue, with white clouds and the fastest winds in the Solar System (over 2,000 km/h).

Uranus is an ice giant. It is so far from the Sun that it is always colder there than the coldest Earth winter: about –200°C. A greeny blue planet, it spins on its side following a collision (crash) with an unknown object billions of years ago.

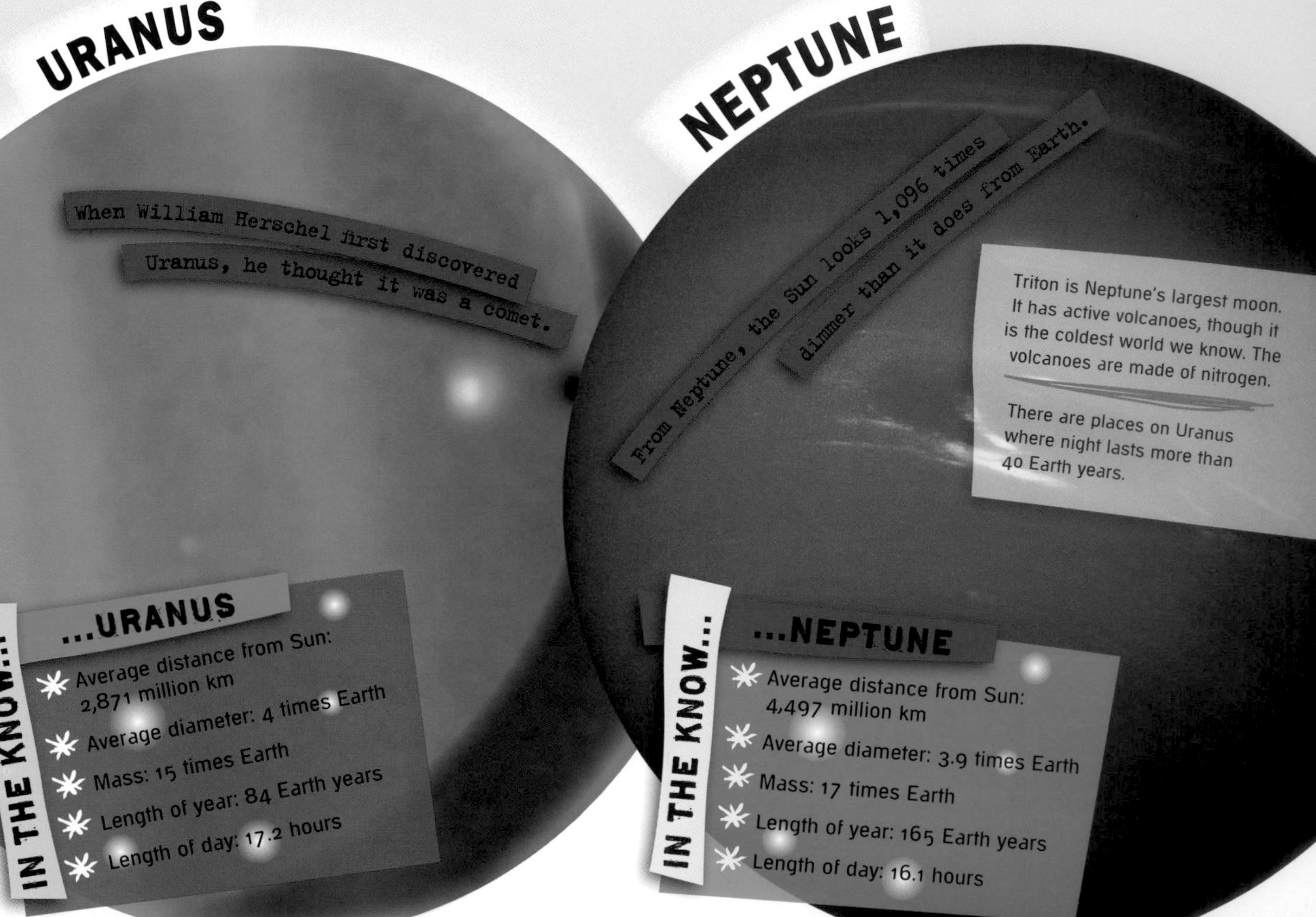
URANUS
When William Herschel first discovered
Uranus, he thought it was a comet.
IN THE KNOW...
...URANUS
Average distance from Sun: 2,871 million km
Average diameter: 4 times Earth
Mass: 15 times Earth
Length of year: 84 Earth years
Length of day: 17.2 hours
NEPTUNE
From Neptune, the Sun looks 1,096 times
dimmer than it does from Earth.
Triton is Neptune's largest moon. It has active volcanoes, though it is the coldest world we know. The volcanoes are made of nitrogen.
There are places on Uranus where night lasts more than 40 Earth years.
IN THE KNOW...
...NEPTUNE
Average distance from Sun: 4,497 million km
Average diameter: 3.9 times Earth
Mass: 17 times Earth
Length of year: 165 Earth years
Length of day: 16.1 hours

FAR OUT

The ice giants are so dim that Uranus was only discovered by accident in 1781.

Neptune, the outermost planet in the Solar System, was tracked down through the effect of its gravity on the way Uranus moved, and not found until 1846.

If you visited either of these planets and looked back towards the Sun, it would simply look like a bright star.

William Herschel wanted to call Uranus 'George's Star', in honour of the king, George III.

Neptune is so far from the Sun that it takes 165 Earth years to make one orbit, so if you were born there, you would not live long enough to celebrate your first birthday.

Neptune has still not been around the Sun once since it was discovered in 1846. It will finally complete its first orbit on 8 June 2011.

If you can't imagine Uranus spinning on its side (rather than like a spinning top, like the other planets) then try to imagine it like a ball rolling along.

twist it!

amazing!!

This colossal crater, seen here from space, in Australia's Northern Territory is called Gosses Bluff and is about 4.5 km wide. It was made by an asteroid or comet about 1 km across that crashed into Earth around 142 million years ago.

Comets are made of ice, dust and rocky material that came from the Solar System when it was first created about 4.5 billion years ago.

Ripley's Believe It or Not!®

Most comets have two streaming tails – a blue one made of gas and a white one made of dust.

WATCH IT!

In 1908, a strange explosion flattened 2,150 sq km of forest in Siberia. It was probably caused by a comet exploding in the air.

If you had been around in 1910, when the Earth passed through the tail of a comet, you could have tried some of the anti-comet pills that were on sale. But they wouldn't have done you any good!

Halley is a comet that reappears every 75.3 years. There are records of its visits that go back to 25 May, 240BC.

A comet called Shoemaker-Levy 9 crashed into Jupiter in 1994. It hit the planet on the side that was facing away from Earth, so the impact itself wasn't seen, but huge marks could be seen in Jupiter's atmosphere for several months afterwards.

A comet or asteroid the size of a city crashed into Mexico's Yucatan Peninsula 65 million years ago.

twist it!

Rubbish!

SPACE RUBBLE AND JUNK

Building a solar system isn't a tidy job: after gravity pulled together our Sun and the planets, trillions of grains of dust and lumps of rock were left hanging about in space. There is a ring of scattered rubble between Mars and Jupiter called the asteroid belt, and even more rubble beyond Neptune.

There are thousands of pieces of space junk in orbit around Earth. Space junk includes items such as broken satellites, parts of rockets, and even rubbish thrown from space staions. There are also around 6,000 artificial satellites.

Most of this rubble keeps itself to itself, but some of it falls through our atmosphere. If it is small enough, it drifts down to Earth and just makes everything a bit dustier. Bigger chunks burn up as meteors (shooting stars), and a few reach the ground as meteorites.

The first TV satellite was launched in 1964 to allow the Tokyo Olympics to be transmitted around the world.

Ripley's Believe It or Not!®

Think you've seen a flying saucer? It could just be the reflection of the Sun off a satellite!

This artist's impression shows all the satellites (drawn larger than actual size) orbiting Earth.

METEORIC!

The *Skylab* space station created a spectacular meteor shower over Australia when it crashed to Earth in 1979.

The oldest man-made debris hurtling around our planet is the US satellite *Vanguard*. It was launched in 1958 and is still up there today.

For centuries, people living in Greenland made their tools out of three large meteorites, which were almost pure iron.

Asteroids were once thought to be fragments of an exploded planet.

About 500 meteorites crash to Earth each year, but only about five of these are found and reported to scientists. So you'll be fairly famous if you find one and hand it in.

Some meteorites began life on the Moon or Mars and were thrown into space by volcanoes before drifting through space to land on Earth.

twist it!

ACTUAL SIZE!

Scientists have only three rock samples from other objects in our Solar System – they are from the Moon, Mars and this piece of the asteroid Vesta, which fell to Earth as a meteorite.

TRASH CRASH

The first major collision between two satellites happened in February 2009, when an old Russian satellite crashed into a working US satellite and created at least 600 more pieces of space junk.

LETHAL CLOTHING

In 1965 the US astronaut Edward White lost a glove while on a space walk from Gemini 4. It remained in orbit for a month, reaching speeds of 28,000 km/h, and posed a lethal danger to spacecraft.

PUTTING OUT THE TRASH

The Mir space station threw more than 200 rubbish bags into space over ten years. They are all still in orbit.

POW!

Space junk travels extremely fast, which makes it highly dangerous. At a speed of 27,400 km/h a tiny speck hitting an astronaut on a space walk would have the same impact as a bullet.

Mrs Hewlett Hodges from Alabama, USA, has actually been hit by a meteorite! It crashed through her roof, bounced off a radio and hit her on the hip. Ouch!

>>shooting from the hip>>

Looking Up

STARS

How many stars do you think you can see in the night sky? A million? A billion? Actually, even on the darkest, clearest night, fewer than 3,000 are visible. This is only a tiny fraction of the mind-numbing total number, which is at least 70 billion trillion – said to be more than all the grains of sand on all the beaches in the world.

Some stars you can see are as big and bright as our Sun – and some are much bigger. Many stars are double, each spinning around the other. Many stars have planets, too. Stars usually last for billions of years – but the more massive they are, the brighter they burn and the shorter they live.

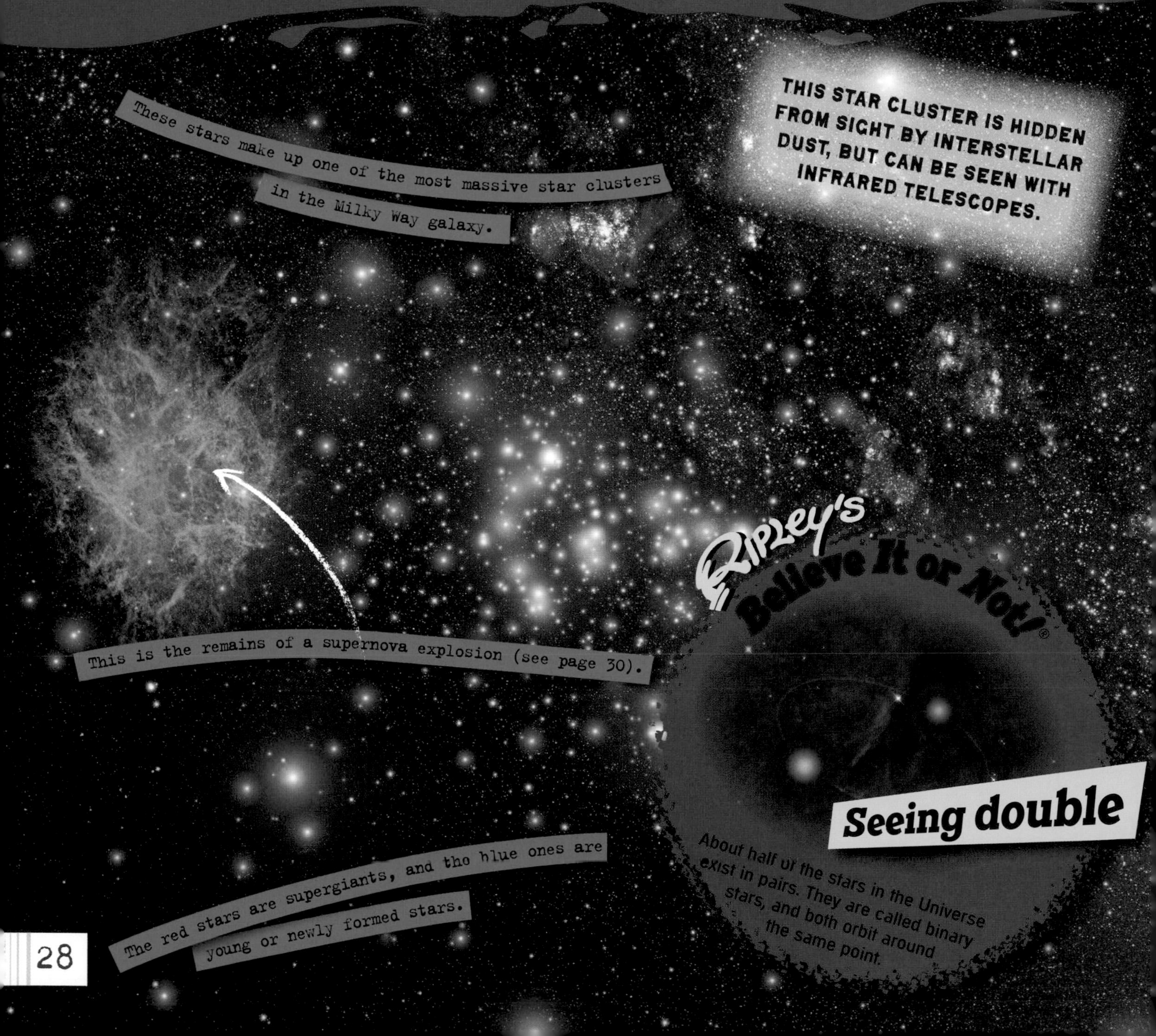

These stars make up one of the most massive star clusters in the Milky Way galaxy.

THIS STAR CLUSTER IS HIDDEN FROM SIGHT BY INTERSTELLAR DUST, BUT CAN BE SEEN WITH INFRARED TELESCOPES.

This is the remains of a supernova explosion (see page 30).

Ripley's Believe It or Not!®

Seeing double

About half of the stars in the Universe exist in pairs. They are called binary stars, and both orbit around the same point.

The red stars are supergiants, and the blue ones are young or newly formed stars.

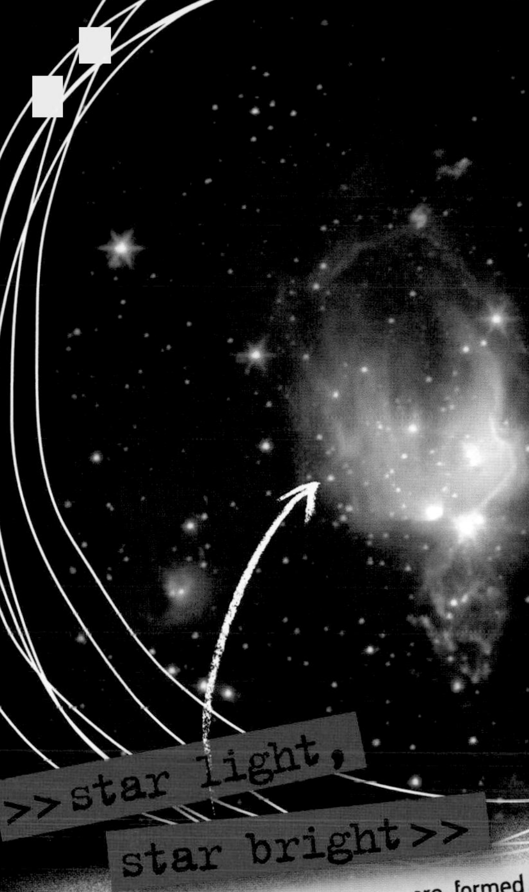

>>star light, star bright>>

Scientists think that new stars are formed inside nebulae (the plural of a nebula) such as this one. A nebula is a cloud full of dust and gas; when it gets squashed, parts of it get so hot that they become newborn stars.

STAR TURNS

The largest known star, VY Canis Majoris, is large enough to contain about 100 billion objects the size of the Sun.

If the Earth were the size of a marble, the nearest star would be 30,000 km away.

The star with the longest name is Shurnarkabtishashutu, which is Arabic for 'under the southern horn of the bull'.

Some brown dwarf stars are cooler than burning houses.

The light from most stars you can see takes decades to get to the Earth – which means you are seeing them as they were before you were born.

star stories

CANIS MAJOR

GEMINI

TAURUS

Constellations are groups of stars that, from the Earth, look close to each other. They may really be huge distances apart in space, but they line up to form patterns that have been given names through history.

Orion, or The Hunter, is instantly recognisable by the three central stars making his 'belt'.

Canis Major, one of Orion's 'hunting dogs', contains Sirius, the brightest star in our sky. It is about 25 times brighter than the Sun.

The constellation of **Gemini** is one of the signs of the zodiac. It looks like a pair of twins and can be seen around the world between December and March.

Taurus is also known as The Bull. It contains the Pleiades (say 'ply-uh-dees') star cluster and is visible between November and February.

Celebrities as diverse as Britney Spears, Harrison Ford, Bruce Lee and even the whole of Arsenal FC have had stars named for them! Scientists give stars a name made up of letters and numbers (such as HD172167) but fans and celebrities themselves can pay to have their name given to a specific star.

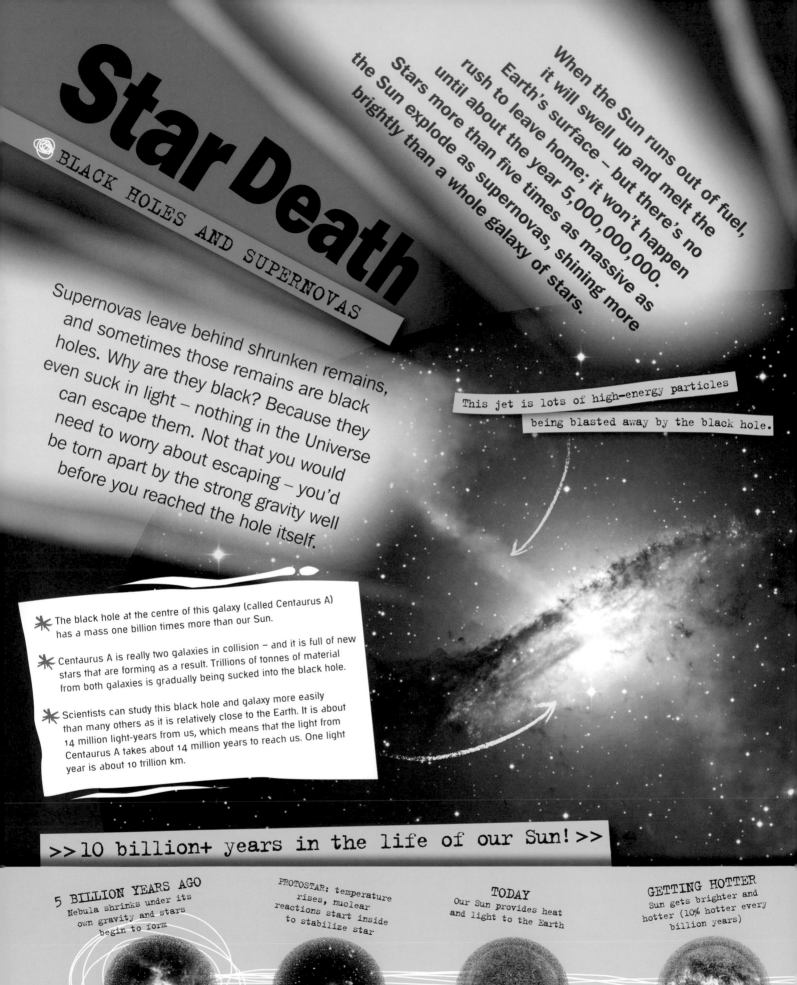

Star Death

BLACK HOLES AND SUPERNOVAS

When the Sun runs out of fuel, it will swell up and melt the Earth's surface – but there's no rush to leave home; it won't happen until about the year 5,000,000,000. Stars more than five times as massive as the Sun explode as supernovas, shining more brightly than a whole galaxy of stars.

Supernovas leave behind shrunken remains, and sometimes those remains are black holes. Why are they black? Because they even suck in light – nothing in the Universe can escape them. Not that you would need to worry about escaping – you'd be torn apart by the strong gravity well before you reached the hole itself.

This jet is lots of high-energy particles being blasted away by the black hole.

- The black hole at the centre of this galaxy (called Centaurus A) has a mass one billion times more than our Sun.
- Centaurus A is really two galaxies in collision – and it is full of new stars that are forming as a result. Trillions of tonnes of material from both galaxies is gradually being sucked into the black hole.
- Scientists can study this black hole and galaxy more easily than many others as it is relatively close to the Earth. It is about 14 million light-years from us, which means that the light from Centaurus A takes about 14 million years to reach us. One light year is about 10 trillion km.

>> 10 billion+ years in the life of our Sun! >>

5 BILLION YEARS AGO
Nebula shrinks under its own gravity and stars begin to form

PROTOSTAR: temperature rises, nuclear reactions start inside to stabilize star

TODAY
Our Sun provides heat and light to the Earth

GETTING HOTTER
Sun gets brighter and hotter (10% hotter every billion years)

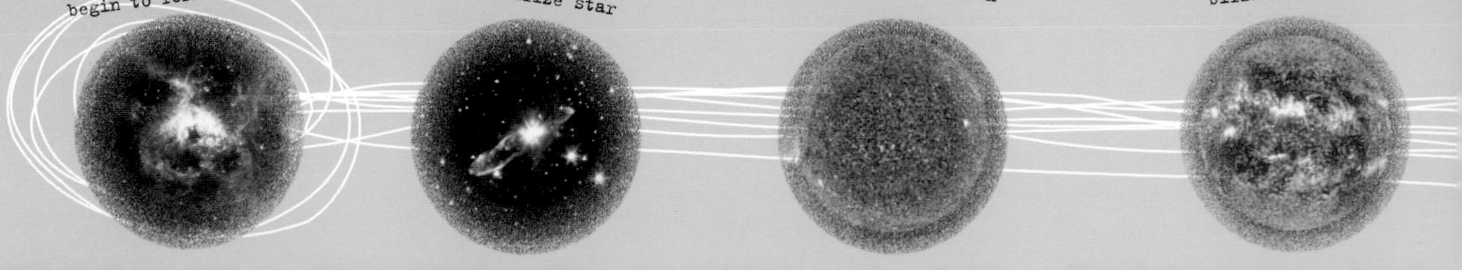

SUPER STATS

Some of your body was formed in a supernova: to be precise, all the atoms of carbon and oxygen inside you.

A supernova was seen by Chinese astronomers in AD1054. Actually, it exploded in about 4000BC, but the light took 5,000 years to get here.

It is just possible that spinning black holes might allow astronauts in the far future to travel back in time.

A supernova releases more energy over a few months than the Sun will over its entire lifetime.

Supernovas can cause the birth of new stars and planets when their explosions disturb nearby dust clouds.

Supernovas can also be caused by one star dumping material onto a companion star.

twist it!

Ripley's Believe It or Not!®

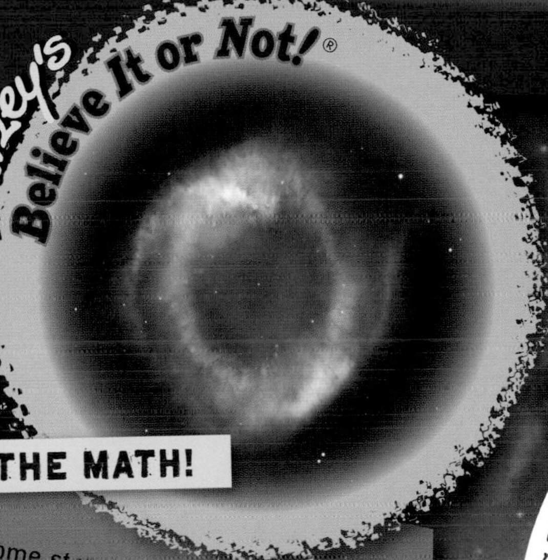

YOU DO THE MATH!

- After some stars run out of fuel and collapse, what is left of them is a shrunken massive object called a neutron star, where the gravity is so strong that you would weigh over 100,000 million kg there.
- A single spoonful of material from a neutron star would weigh a billion tonnes on Earth!
- Neutron stars are so compressed that they squeeze a tenth of the matter that made up the original giant star (before it imploded) into a ball that is 1.5 billion times smaller.
- Some neutron stars send beams of radio waves sweeping through space. If they sweep across the Earth, the radio waves can be detected as short pulses. Neutron stars like this are called pulsars.

STARTING SOMETHING

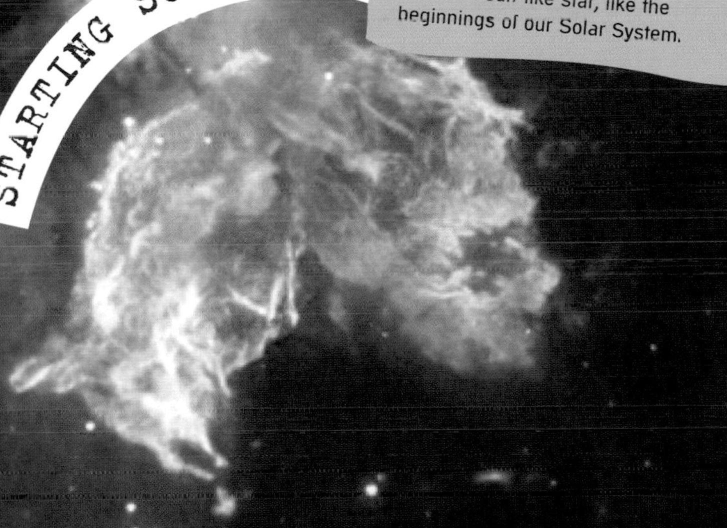

This picture of a supernova remnant was taken by the Hubble Space Telescope (see page 35). It is made up of gas and dust. In a few million years, it could form new planets around a sun-like star, like the beginnings of our Solar System.

SAY WHAT?

ATOMS

Tiny objects, much too small to see. All solids, liquids and gases are made of them.

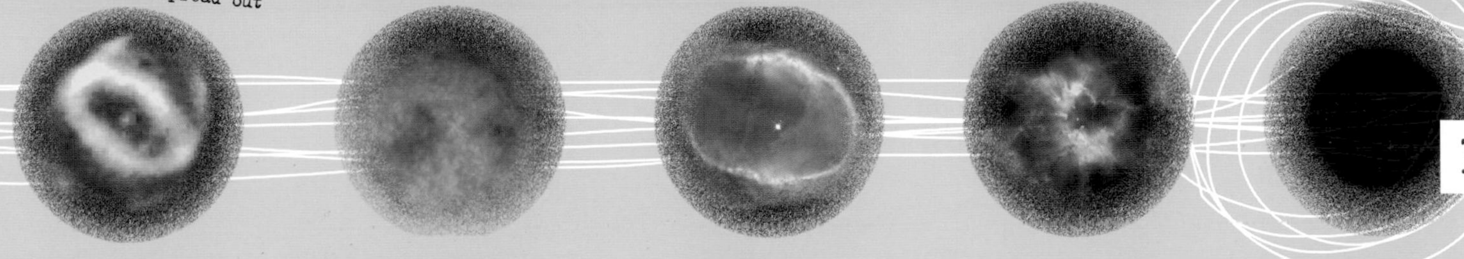

5 BILLION YEARS FROM NOW
Sun's core collapses and outer layers spread out

RED GIANT:
Sun swallows up Mercury, Venus and maybe Earth

PLANETARY NEBULA:
Sun throws off a cloud of gas

WHITE DWARF:
nebula cools and fades

BLACK DWARF:
Sun is no longer visible

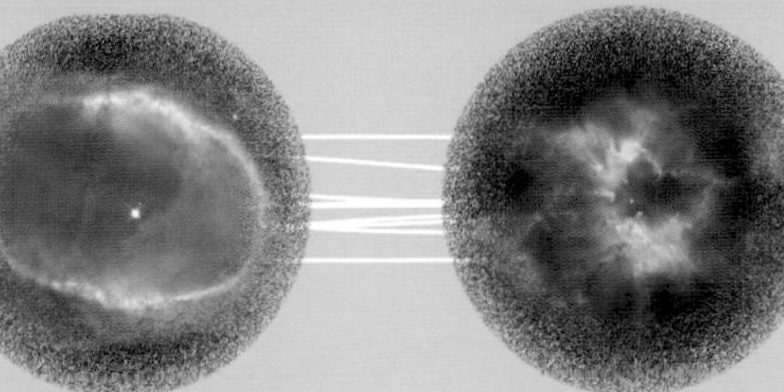

Getting Together

GALAXIES AND THE BIG BANG

Stars are gathered together throughout the Universe in groups called galaxies. Our own one is the Milky Way and it is made of about 300 billion stars (give or take a hundred billion) – so all the stars you can see on the darkest night add up to less than 0.000001% (or one-ten-millionth) of the whole thing.

Last century, astronomers noticed something very odd – most other galaxies are hurtling away from ours, and from each other too. They realised that the whole Universe is getting bigger every second, and that everything in the Universe must have been crunched up together long ago. Very, very long ago (13.7 billion years to be precise), when it all began as a sudden expansion – the Big Bang.

- Our Solar System is perched between two arms of the Milky Way.
- If you counted one star a second and never slept, it would still take you about 3,000 years to count the stars in our galaxy.
- Long ago, most galaxies were blue, because of all the young stars being born in them.
- There are different types of galaxy, named according to their shape. The Milky Way is a spiral galaxy – it's not hard to see why.

NO PLACE LIKE HOME

Our Solar System is here.

INTO GALACTIC

The nearest large galaxy to the Milky Way is the Andromeda galaxy: it is so far away that its light takes 2.5 million years to reach us, and it is the furthest thing you can see with your naked eye.

Our galaxy is on a collision course with the Andromeda galaxy; but the galaxies won't meet until after our Sun has died.

You, along with the rest of our galaxy, are being dragged through space at about 2 million km an hour by a mysterious unknown object called the Great Attractor. It's hidden from us by dust clouds.

It takes about 225 million years for our Sun to revolve (move in a circle) once around the centre of the galaxy.

twist it!

RIPLEY'S Believe It or Not!®

the Milky Way

The Milky Way looks brighter from the Southern Hemisphere, because the southern part of our planet points roughly towards the star-packed centre of our Galaxy. We live out in the suburbs, near the galactic edge, and can look out on the stars around us. If we lived near the centre, the sky would be packed with stars, and the starlight would be brighter than the light of the full Moon. But, as there is a massive black hole in those parts, you might not have long to enjoy the view.

>>what happens next?>>

Most scientists think the expansion will go on for ever, even after the stars have all died and the Universe is cold. They call this the Big Chill. But some scientists think that, in about the year 50,000,000,000, everything will fall apart. First galaxies will be torn apart, then stars, then planets, then you (if you're still around, which is a bit unlikely) and finally atoms – the Big Rip.

BIG BANG FACTS

Astronomers see back to almost the beginning of time when they look at quasars. Quasars are very bright objects (caused by various things falling into supermassive black holes) that can be seen across vast distances. To cross those distances, their light takes nearly as long as the age of the Universe.

For hundreds of thousands of years after it formed, the Universe was dark.

The Big Bang wasn't an explosion – space was only created when it happened, so there was nowhere for it to explode into!

Most of the atoms in your body are hydrogen, which formed very soon after the Big Bang – so most of you is almost as old as the Universe.

The most distant objects in the Universe are moving away from us at over 280,000 km/second.

The Universe is more than a hundred million times older than the oldest person.

Star Gazing

TELESCOPES

Telescopes allow astronomers to see objects so far away that their light takes billions of years to reach us. Many telescopes gather light using huge mirrors, which is then focused by a lens. Some of these mirrors are ten million times the size of your pupils, which are what you use to gather light. They can collect light for hours on end (which your eyes can't).

There are also telescopes that detect 'light' that we can't see at all – like radio waves, infra-red, ultraviolet, X-rays and gamma rays. So, if you want to have a good look round outer space, take some advice – use a telescope.

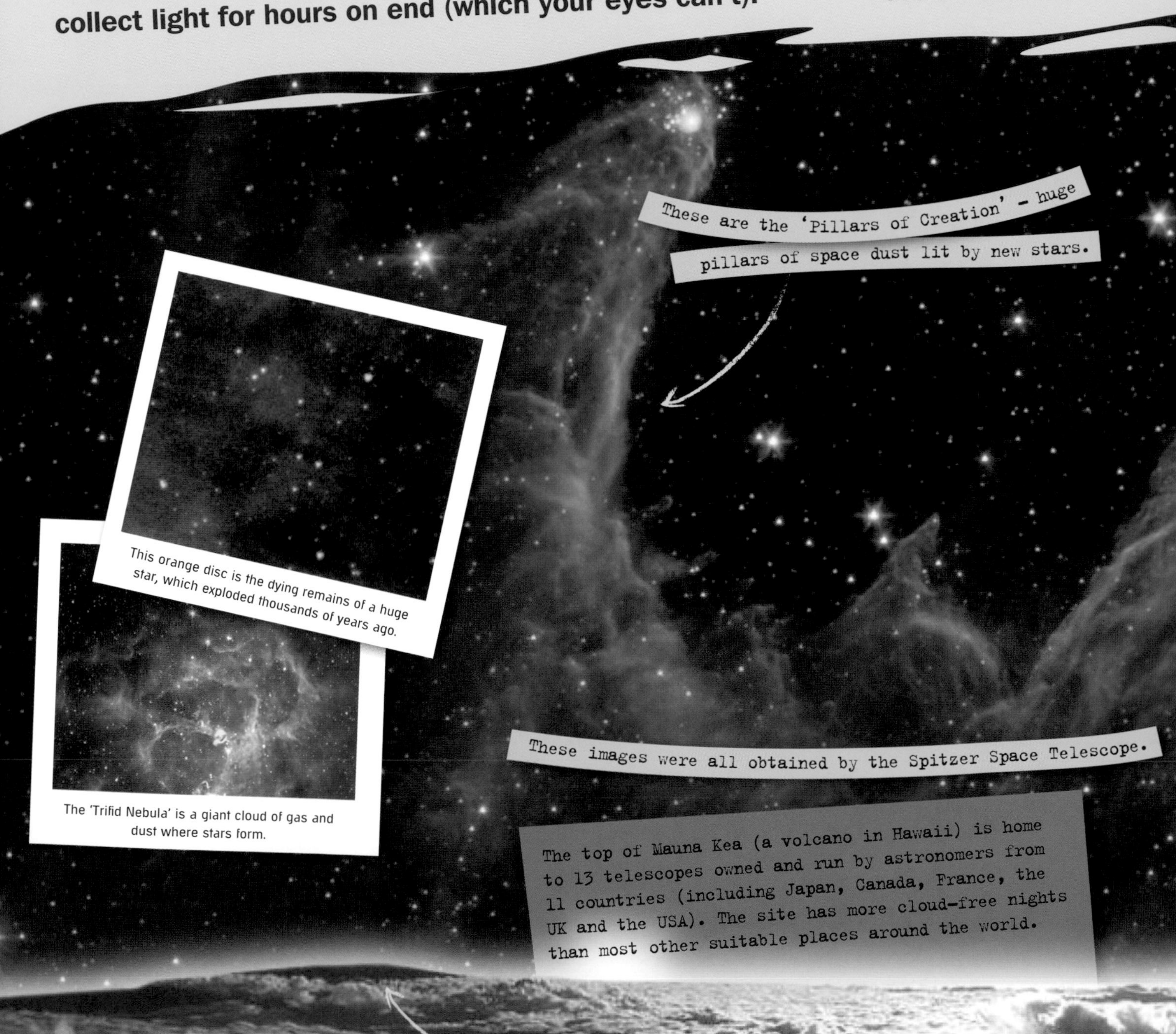

These are the 'Pillars of Creation' – huge pillars of space dust lit by new stars.

This orange disc is the dying remains of a huge star, which exploded thousands of years ago.

The 'Trifid Nebula' is a giant cloud of gas and dust where stars form.

These images were all obtained by the Spitzer Space Telescope.

The top of Mauna Kea (a volcano in Hawaii) is home to 13 telescopes owned and run by astronomers from 11 countries (including Japan, Canada, France, the UK and the USA). The site has more cloud-free nights than most other suitable places around the world.

This is Mauna Loa, the world's largest volcano.

LOOK OUT!

The most powerful telescopes can see so far away, the light started travelling billions of years ago. They show us galaxies as they looked less than one billion years after the beginning of the Universe.

The largest radio telescope dish in the world is at Arecibo, Puerto Rico. It is 305 m across.

Italian scientist Galileo Galilei built one of the first telescopes in 1609. Within a few nights he had discovered mountains on the Moon, four moons of Jupiter and hundreds of unknown stars.

The nearest star is about one million times further from Earth than the nearest planet.

twist it!

The highest speed in the Universe is the speed of light, which is 299,792 km/second. It would take over four years to reach the nearest star even at this speed. But don't bother trying to go that fast – the faster you go, the more massive you get, and you would weigh more than the Universe by the time you got close to light speed.

Ripley's Believe It or Not!®

The Hubble Space Telescope (HST) orbits the Earth so that its view of the Universe is not interrupted by the atmosphere (like ground-based telescopes). It can see a coin 700 km away!

SAY WHAT?

PUPIL

The dark hole in the middle of each eye, through which light enters.

STARING INTO SPACE

The Spitzer Space Telescope was launched in 2003 and orbits the Earth, taking infrared pictures to help scientists study how galaxies are formed and develop. Infrared is heat radiation, so the telescope has to be kept cool so that its own heat doesn't interfere with the signals it receives from space.

The Very Large Array (VLA) is an arrangement of 27 large radio telescopes in New Mexico, USA. Each one measures 25 m across (about the size of a house). They are all mounted on tracks so they can be moved into different positions, but work together to act like one large radio telescope.

Observatories with telescopes inside.

Into the Unknown

THE 'SPACE RACE'

Looking at the stars, it's hard to imagine what it's like in space. Telescopes allow us to see what's up there in much more detail. But there's nothing like getting up close and personal, and that's what the invention of spaceships has done for humans – and for the various animals that have been blasted into space for research purposes.

The first space orbit was by the Russian artificial satellite, *Sputnik*, in 1957. The first human in space was also Russian, Yuri Gagarin, who orbited the Earth in 1961. The rivalry between the USA and Russia (then called the Soviet Union) drove both countries on in the 'Space Race' to achieve milestones in all areas of space exploration. Many people think that putting man on the Moon, in 1969, made the US the ultimate winners. Nowadays, international cooperation allows us to find out more about our Universe than ever before.

IN THE KNOW... ...SATURN V

- First manned flight: December, 1968
- Last flight: December, 1972
- Total launches: 13
- Total made: 15 (2 were unused)

- **The Saturn V rockets** used to launch the Apollo craft on their Moon missions were the biggest and most powerful launch vehicles ever used.
- Each Saturn V rocket carried enough fuel to fill an Olympic swimming pool, and used it up in 2.5 minutes.
- There were three stages in a Saturn V rocket. Each stage separated and fell away after use. The third stage fired twice: to enter orbit and to change its path to head toward the Moon.

Saturn V Rocket

111 m tall (including *Apollo* spacecraft).

As tall as St Paul's Cathedral in London; higher than the Statue of Liberty!

USA
Base has five engines, positioned like the five dots on dice.
10 m across.

The 2008 movie *Space Chimps* was based on a true story! Well, kind of – the main character, Ham III, is the supposed grandson of a real chimp called Ham, who was launched into space in 1961. Ham was sent up in a *Project Mercury* capsule as part of the research needed for human space travel. He landed successfully in the ocean after the flight, and lived until 1983 at North Carolina Zoo.

Ripley's Believe It or Not!®

>> FIRSTS >>

In 1961, Yuri Gagarin (USSR) became the first human being ever in space, and the first to orbit the Earth. The first people to see him upon his return were two Russian farm workers, Anna and Rita Takhtarov, who must have been quite surprised to see him emerge into a field from his landing craft.

The Russian *Soyuz* series of spacecraft first flew in 1966 and is still operating today, carrying astronauts to the International Space Station. *Soyuz* rockets have launched more human spaceflight missions than any other space program.

To Boldly Go

EXPLORATION

All modern spaceships are launched from Earth using liquid-fuelled rockets. The first of these took off in 1926 and reached a height of 12 m. Impressive? No, but 43 years later, a liquid fuel rocket carried three men 30,000 times further – to the Moon. The 1960s and 1970s was an era of giant rockets, with giant pricetags, and they could be used only once. From the 1980s a cheaper vehicle has been used and re-used: the space shuttle.

A space shuttle does exactly what it says – shuttles satellites to space and people to the International Space Station (ISS). Russian *Soyuz* spacecraft go there, too, and one *Soyuz* craft is always docked at the ISS just in case an emergency getaway is needed.

KEY FACTS

- After launch, the shuttle starts to twist into an arc ready to enter orbit.
- 126 seconds after launch, the thin white rocket boosters are pushed away from the shuttle.
- Next, the brown fuel tank falls away and burns up as it re-enters the Earth's atmosphere.
- When the mission ends, the shuttle orbiter glides back to Earth and lands like an aeroplane.

The space shuttle blasts off.

The spent fuel tank falls away.

The shuttle lands back on Earth.

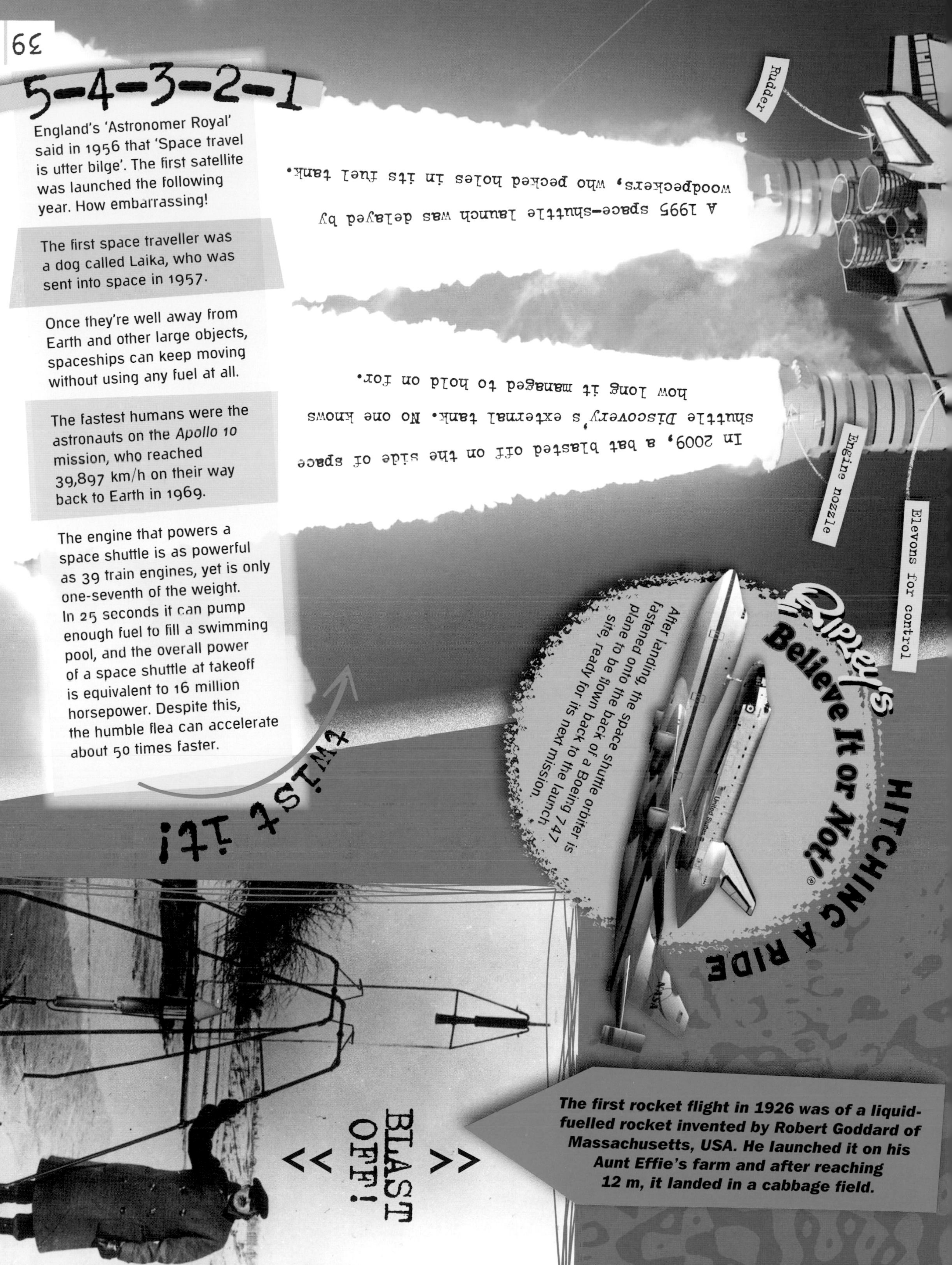

5-4-3-2-1

England's 'Astronomer Royal' said in 1956 that 'Space travel is utter bilge'. The first satellite was launched the following year. How embarrassing!

The first space traveller was a dog called Laika, who was sent into space in 1957.

Once they're well away from Earth and other large objects, spaceships can keep moving without using any fuel at all.

The fastest humans were the astronauts on the *Apollo 10* mission, who reached 39,897 km/h on their way back to Earth in 1969.

The engine that powers a space shuttle is as powerful as 39 train engines, yet is only one-seventh of the weight. In 25 seconds it can pump enough fuel to fill a swimming pool, and the overall power of a space shuttle at takeoff is equivalent to 16 million horsepower. Despite this, the humble flea can accelerate about 50 times faster.

twist it!

A 1995 space-shuttle launch was delayed by woodpeckers, who pecked holes in its fuel tank.

In 2009, a bat blasted off on the side of space shuttle *Discovery*'s external tank. No one knows how long it managed to hold on for.

Ripley's Believe It or Not!® HITCHING A RIDE

After landing, the space shuttle orbiter is fastened onto the back of a Boeing 747 plane to be flown back to the launch site, ready for its next mission.

<< BLAST OFF! >>

The first rocket flight in 1926 was of a liquid-fuelled rocket invented by Robert Goddard of Massachusetts, USA. He launched it on his Aunt Effie's farm and after reaching 12 m, it landed in a cabbage field.

Sky Workers

ASTRONAUTS

Space is a dangerous place: there's no air there, and it's full of deadly radiation. In the sunlight, it's hotter than an oven; in the shadows it's colder than a freezer. An unprotected person would be dead in seconds.

So, to venture into space, people have to be sealed into spacesuits, and the suits have to be warmed, cooled, pressurised and supplied with fresh air. It's no wonder that a spacesuit takes over six hours to put on, and costs well over a million dollars.

SUITS YOU!

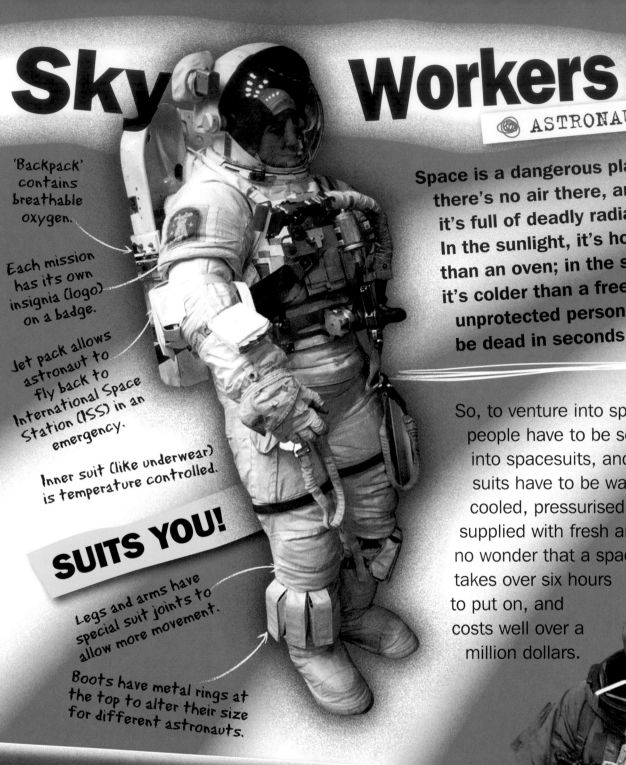

'Backpack' contains breathable oxygen.

Each mission has its own insignia (logo) on a badge.

Jet pack allows astronaut to fly back to International Space Station (ISS) in an emergency.

Inner suit (like underwear) is temperature controlled.

Legs and arms have special suit joints to allow more movement.

Boots have metal rings at the top to alter their size for different astronauts.

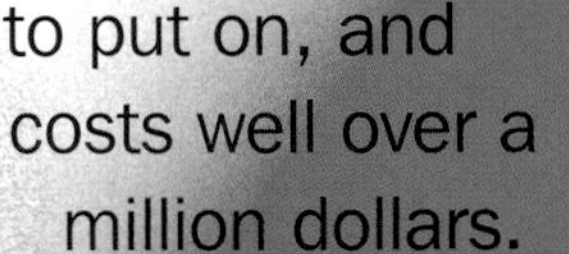

Astronauts wear this orange suit for launch and landing. It's called an LES: Launch and Entry Suit.

- Living in weightless conditions for weeks and months takes its toll on the human body. Astronauts have to exercise every day to keep their muscles strong.
- It can be tricky using a toolbox in space – your screwdriver floats away! To help with ordinary maintenance, astronauts use velcro belts to keep their tools on hand, and hook their feet under straps or bars to stop themselves from drifting around.
- Astronauts only wear special spacesuits for take off and landing, or when they leave the ISS. The rest of the time, they wear normal clothes like shorts and T-shirts.

Space Diary

Get up at 6am GMT. We're allowed 90 minutes' 'post-sleep' to wash, dress, eat breakfast, maybe exercise, and be ready to start work.

DPC (daily planning conference) with ground control centre for 15 mins, to confirm the day's actions. My job today is unpacking supplies brought by the shuttle. I think tomorrow will be science experiments, and at the weekend I get time to myself. Will hook up with my family on a video link (until the signal dies!). Most mornings I manage to use the treadmill or the exercise bike, too.

Lunch break is an hour, and the crew all eat together. Warm up my food and take the chance to take photos out of the Service Module windows. Earth looks amazing from up here!

More ground support links in the afternoon to check that all is going to plan. Have to do our chores even up in space! We have a new toilet system for one of the guys to activate, and I need to finish that unpacking. Everything has its proper place!

Finish work at 6pm and unwind over dinner with the others. Time to catch up on some reading, emails or just gazing at the views. We have movies for the weekends, and tuck ourselves into bed about 9.30 (although sometimes we stay up later!).

It isn't easy using the toilet in space! The waste gets sucked away and put in bags for disposal. On spacewalks, astronauts wear adult nappies as they can be outside the ISS for hours.

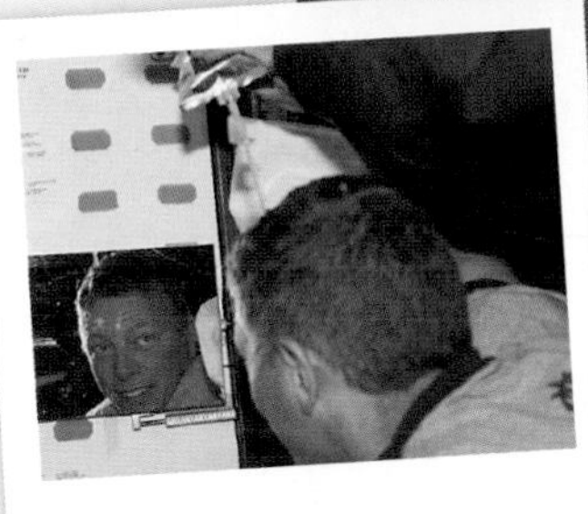

Astronauts often wash with a damp cloth to reduce the amount of water used on the ISS.

When it's bedtime, astronauts climb into sleeping bags, which are fixed to the wall, and hook their arms into restraints to stop them from floating around in their sleep.

Food is often warmed in a microwave and eaten from a special tray that stops everything from floating away.

twist it!

SPACED OUT

There is no up (and no down) in space.

If you were an astronaut in orbit, you would see the Sun rise and set 15 times a day, because of your speedy motion around the Earth.

Astronauts can't shed tears in space, so it's an ideal place to peel onions!

In 2001, orbiting astronauts took delivery of a pizza! It wasn't delivered by a person on a moped though...

The longest spacewalk was in 1992 and took 8 hours and 29 minutes. It was made by shuttle astronauts who were dealing with a faulty satellite.

Astronauts grow 5 cm when they are in space, because their backbones are no longer squashed by the Earth's gravity.

Half of all space-travellers get space-sick.

Ripley's Believe It or Not!®

FOR SALE

During a spacewalk to retrieve two broken satellites, American astronaut Dale Gardner had his photo taken offering to sell them to anyone interested! The picture was taken by his fellow astronaut Joseph Allen, who can be seen in the reflection on Gardner's visor.

SPACE AGE

John Glenn was the first American to orbit the Earth, in 1962. He went back into space in 1998 onboard the shuttle *Discovery*, making him the oldet person (aged 77) to fly in space.

Action Stations

It's a long, long, way to the stars: if you were at the wheel of the fastest racing car there is, and if it could drive to the stars, how long do you think it would take to get there? A year? A century? How about 4 million years! That's just to the nearest star – most of the ones you can see are much farther away.

LIFE IN SPACE

The International Space Station (ISS), currently being built 350 km above the Earth by 16 nations, will be the size of a football pitch when it is finished.

Three to four times a year, the unmanned Progress robot vehicle docks with the ISS to deliver food, water and fuel, and take away the trash. It burns up as it re-enters Earth's atmosphere – true waste disposal!

Flying High

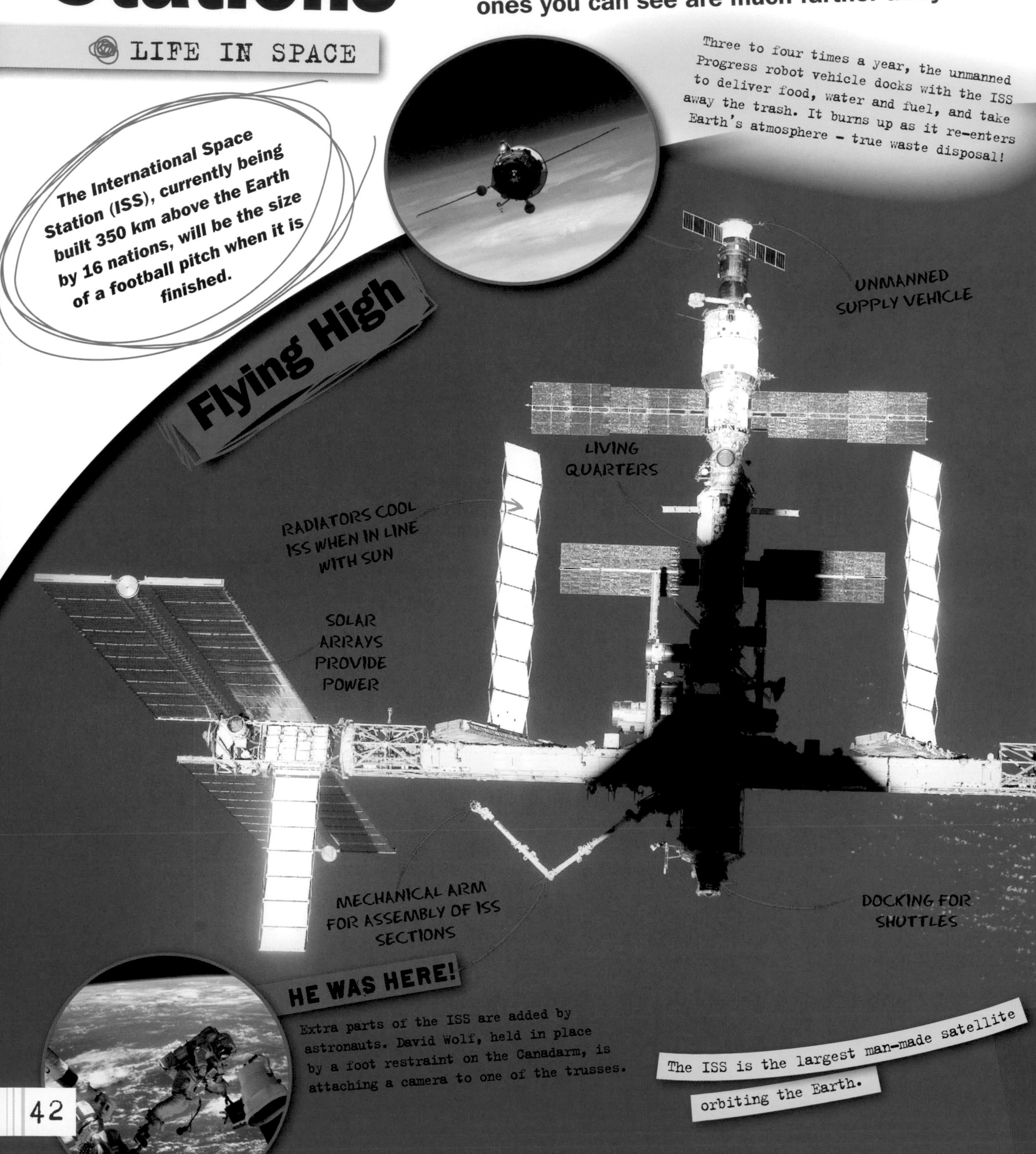

HE WAS HERE!

Extra parts of the ISS are added by astronauts. David Wolf, held in place by a foot restraint on the Canadarm, is attaching a camera to one of the trusses.

The ISS is the largest man-made satellite orbiting the Earth.

However, that doesn't mean people will never reach them. The plans for the first starship have already been made: a spaceship the size of a city, that will fly for a hundred years. In the meantime, astronauts can live in space for months at a time, on the International Space Station (ISS) that is being constructed in space over years and years.

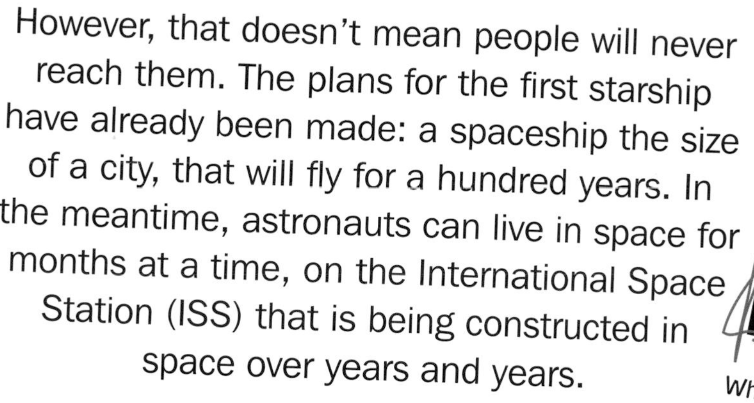

>> web of light >>

What's this? Believe it or not, it's a photo of London at night, taken from the ISS. The wiggly line around the bottom edge is the M25, and the dark patches just below and left of the central bright section are Hyde Park and Regents Park.

IN THE KNOW... ...ISS

- Width: approx. 100 m
- Length: approx. 75 m
- Mass when finished: about 450,000 kg
- First launch: 20 November 1998
- Number of orbits per day: 15.7
- Travelling speed: 27,700 km/h

Ripley's Believe It or Not!®

In a Spin

Two spiders called Arabella and Anita were kept on the *Skylab* space station to study the effect of weightlessness on their ability to spin webs. It obviously took its toll, as the spiders spun uneven webs that weren't as strong as the ones they spun before take off.

NO SPACE LIKE HOME

Prior to the ISS, both the USA and Russia had working space stations orbiting the Earth. *Skylab* (USA) in the 1970s had three crew visits, while Russia's *Salyut* (1971–82) led to the more successful *Mir* space station.

In 1869, the first story was published about a space station – made of bricks! It was *The Brick Moon* by Edward Everett Hale.

The longest spaceflight was by the Russian cosmonaut Valeriy Polyakov, who stayed on space station *Mir* for 437 days.

twist it!

Sections of the ISS are taken into space on board the shuttles *Endeavor*, *Atlantis* and *Discovery* and the Russian crafts *Proton* and *Soyuz*. The first stages were joined together in orbit in 1998.

LONG SHOT

In 2006, a golf ball hit by cosmonaut Mikhail Tyurin entered Earth's orbit. It may still be travelling around the Earth even now! If not, it will fall towards Earth and burn up when it enters the atmosphere. It was hit off the ISS from a special tee attached to a platform, and will probably cover a distance of a billion miles. Now THAT'S a long shot!

Aliens are Coming!

REALLY?

Do aliens exist? If so, they might have heard from us by now – radio and TV signals that were broadcast 50 years ago, and are travelling out from the Earth at 299,792,458 m/second, have already reached more than 130 stars. Roughly 10% of those stars are likely to have planets – maybe inhabited ones.

Several specially designed radio messages have been sent out into space, in the hope that someone will answer. So why haven't they? Well, perhaps they have – in 1977 a radio signal was received that no one has been able to explain in any other way – it was so surprising that the scientist who received it wrote 'Wow!' on the printout.

Wow!

EXTRA TERRESTRIALS

Launched in 2009 from Cape Canaveral in Florida, the Kepler telescope is on the lookout for planets in other systems. It will spend at least 3.5 years staring at 100,000 stars in a section of the Milky Way. It's hoped that it will confirm the existence of planets like Earth that are capable of sustaining life.

FOR REAL?

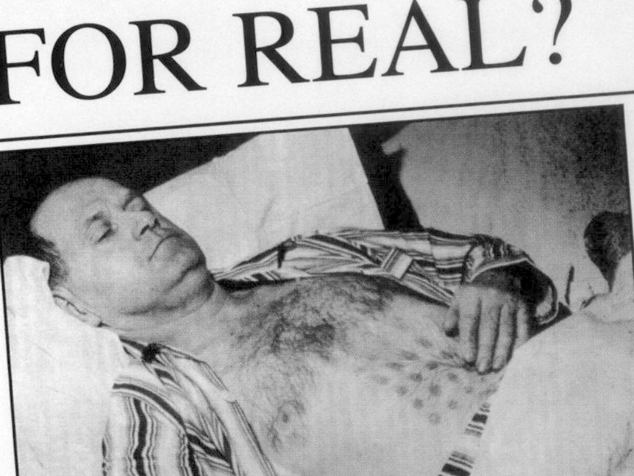

Stephen Michalak said he found a UFO at Falcon Lake, Manitoba, Canada, in 1967. As he got closer he appeared to have been burned with a pattern of dots on his chest.

Signs of life

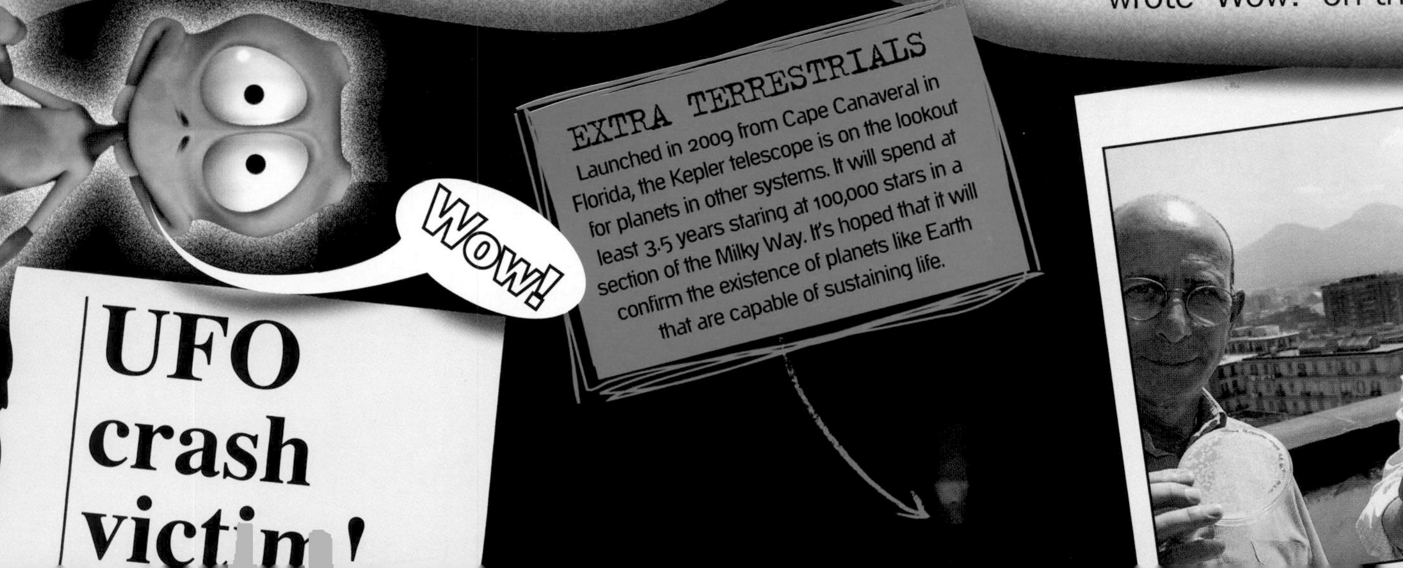

Two Italian professors have found signs of life from outer space! These micro-organisms were discovered concealed inside meteorites, and when put under lab conditions, they began to move and reproduce. Can it be the proof needed for those who believe life exists elsewhere in the Universe?

UFO crash victim!

TALK TIME

In 1967, a ticking radio signal from space was detected. The project to explain it was called 'LGM' for 'Little Green Men'. The source turned out to be a type of spinning star called a pulsar.

Some scientists think that there may be thousands of intelligent civilisations in our galaxy.

In 1960, radio messages were sent to two nearby stars in the hope that intelligent aliens might reply.

More than 30 planets have so far been found in orbit around other stars.

Chatting to aliens on a planet going around another star would need a lot of patience. The nearest such planet goes around a star called Epsilon Eridani, and to send a message there and get a reply back would take 21 years.

twist it!

Alien found in Israel!

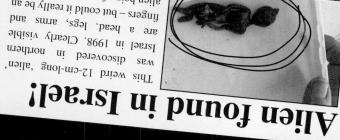

This weird 12-cm-long 'alien' was discovered in northern Israel in 1998. Clearly visible are a head, legs, arms and fingers – but could it really be an alien being from another world?

erghh!

CODED MESSAGE

The two Voyager spacecraft, both on their way to the stars, are carrying golden discs containing messages for any aliens that might encounter them.

The Voyager and Pioneer space probes should eventually reach other stars, after journeys lasting more than 80,000 years. Plenty of time for them to bump into other beings along the way!

Location of our Sun

Diagram of hydrogen atom

Shows direction of scan needed to play disc

Video recording shown as waves

Image of record being played

Claims that this photograph show an alien recovered from a crashed UFO have been put under scrutiny. The crash was said to have taken place in New Mexico in 1950. The picture was sent to Germany for examination and it is believed to be a hoax.

Acknowledgements

COVER (l) © dieter Spears – istockphoto.com, (r) Geoffrey Robinson/Rex Features; **2** Courtesy NASA; **3** (l) © Iuliia Kovalova – fotolia.com, (t/c) Courtesy NASA, (b/c) © Darren Hester – fotolia.com; **4** (c) © Dieter Spears – istockphoto.com; **5** (c) Geoffrey Robinson/Rex Features; **6** (sp) R. Williams (STScI) the Hubble Deep Field Team and NASA; **7** (l) Reuters/Mike Blake, (t/l, t/r, c/l c/r) Rex Features; **8** (t) Courtesy NASA, (b/l) © mario beauregard – fotolia.com, (b/r) Reuters/Ho New; **9** (l) Courtesy of David Hanson, (c) STR/AP/PA Photos, (r) © treenabeena – fotolia.com; **10–11** (c) © suzannmeer – fotolia.com; **10** (l) © icholakov – fotolia.com, (b/l, t/r) Geoeye; **11** (t/l, c, b/r) Geoeye, (t/r) Lewis Whyld/PA Archive/PA Photos; **12** (sp) ESA, (b/r) © suzannmeer – fotolia.com; **13** (c) Courtesy of Yohkoh Project ISAS/Lockheed–Martin Solar and Astrophysics Laboratory/National Astronomical Observatory of Japan/University of Tokyo/NASA, (b/r) © Ekaterina Starshaya – fotolia.com; **14** (sp, b/l) Courtesy NASA; **15** (c/l) Courtesy NASA, (b/r) Courtesy NASA/JPL–Caltech/Galileo Project, (t/l, t/r, t/b/l, c, t/b/r) Courtesy NASA; **16** NASA/Johns Hopkins University Applied Physics Laboratory/Carnegie Institution of Washington; **17** (l) Courtesy NASA, (c) Riedrich Saurer/Science Photo Library, (r) Courtesy NASA; **18–19** (sp) Detlev Van Ravenswaay/Science Photo Library; **18** (t/l) NASA; Greg Shirah, SVS, (b/r) Courtesy NASA; **19** (t) NASA/JPL, (r) NASA/JPL–Solar System Visualization Team; **20** (l) A. Simon-Miller/GSFC/NASA/ESA/STScI/Science Photo Library, (r) Copyright Calvin J. Hamilton; **21** (sp) NASA/JPL/Space Science Institute, (r) David Ducros/Science Photo Library; **22** (t) NASA/ESA/L. Sromovsky, U. WISC/STScI/Science Photo Library, (b) Courtesy NASA; **23** (sp) Chris Butler/Science Photo Library, (b/r) NASA/Kim Shiflett; **24** (l) © Jess Wiberg – istockphoto.com, (r) © Iuliia Kovalova – fotolia.com; **25** (l) © Dennis di Cicco/Corbis, (r) AFP Photo/NASA; **26** (l) © Dragos Constantin – fotolia.com (c, t) ESA; **27** (l) © Bettmann/Corbis, (r) Courtesy NASA; **28** NASA, ESA and A. Schaller (for STScI); **29** (t) NASA/JPL–Caltech/T. Megeath (Harvard-Smithsonian CfA); **30** (sp) X-ray: NASA/CXC/CfA/R.Kraft et al.; Submillimeter: MPIfR/ESO/APEX/A.Weiss et al; Optical: ESO/WFI, (b/l) NASA/JPL–Caltech/B. Brandl (Cornell & University of Leiden), (b/r) NASA/JPL–Caltech/A. Noriega-Crespo (SSC/Caltech), Digital Sky Survey (b/l, b/r) Courtesy of SOHO/[instrument] consortium. SOHO is a project of international cooperation between ESA and NASA; **31** (t/l) NASA, NOAO, ESA, Hubble Heritage Team, M. Meixner (STScI) and T.A Rector (NRAO), (r) NASA, ESA, HEIC and The Hubble Heritage Team (STScI/AURA), (b, l–r) Matt Bobrowsky (CTA INCORPORATED) and NASA, NASA/JPL–Caltech, The Hubble Heritage Team (STScI/AURA/NASA), H. Bond (STScI), R. Ciardullo (PSU), WFPC2, HST, NASA; **32–33** (sp) Mark Garlick/Science Photo Library; **33** (l) Allan Morton/Dennis Milon/Science Photo Library; **34–35** (dp) NASA/JPL-Caltech/L. Allen (Harvard-Smithsonian CfA), (b) Jean-Charles Cuillandre (CFHT), Hawaiian Starlight, CFHT; **34** (t/l) NASA/JPL–Caltech/P. Morris (NASA Herschel Science Center), (b/l) NASA/JPL–Caltech/J. Rho (SSC/Caltech); **35** (l) NASA/STScI, (r) © Jonathan Larsen – fotolia.com; **36–37** (dp) Courtesy NASA; **37** (l) Courtesy NASA, (r) Rex Features, (b) ESA – S. Corvaja; **38** (sp) © Scott Andrews/Science Faction/Corbis, (l, t, r) Courtesy NASA; **39** (l) Courtesy NASA/Carla Thomas, (t) Courtesy NASA; **40** (l, r) Courtesy NASA; **41** (t/c, t/l, c/l, t/r, b/r, l) Courtesy NASA; **42–43** (sp) Courtesy NASA; **42** (b, t/l) Courtesy NASA; **43** (c) Courtesy NASA, (t/r) Image courtesy of Earth Sciences and Image Analysis Laboratory, NASA Johnson Space Center, ISS Crew, JSC, NASA, (b) © altec5 – fotolia.com; **44** (l) © Snaprender – fotolia.com, (c/l) Mary Evans Picture Library, (c/r) AFP/Getty Images; **45** (t/l) AFP/Getty Images, (l) FPL, (c/l) Courtesy NASA, (c/r) Voyager Project, JPL, NASA, (r) © Darren Hester – fotolia.com

Key: t = top, b = bottom, c = centre, l = left, r = right, sp = single page, dp = double page, bgd = background

Every attempt has been made to acknowledge correctly and contact copyright holders and we apologise in advance for any unintentional errors or omissions, which will be corrected in future editions.

DON'T MISS VOLUME 1!

Ripley's Believe It or Not!®

100 YEARS

TWISTS EDITION

DON'T MISS ALL THE EXCITING FACTS, PLUS UNBELIEVABLE, WEIRD, AND WONDERFUL STORIES FROM *RIPLEY'S BELIEVE IT OR NOT!*

IRON MAIDEN
RIPLEY'S EXHIBIT
CAT. NO. 6720

ADORNED WITH SPIKES ALIGNED TO
PIERCE THE EYES, THROAT, AND HEART.
ORIGIN: NUREMBERG, GERMANY

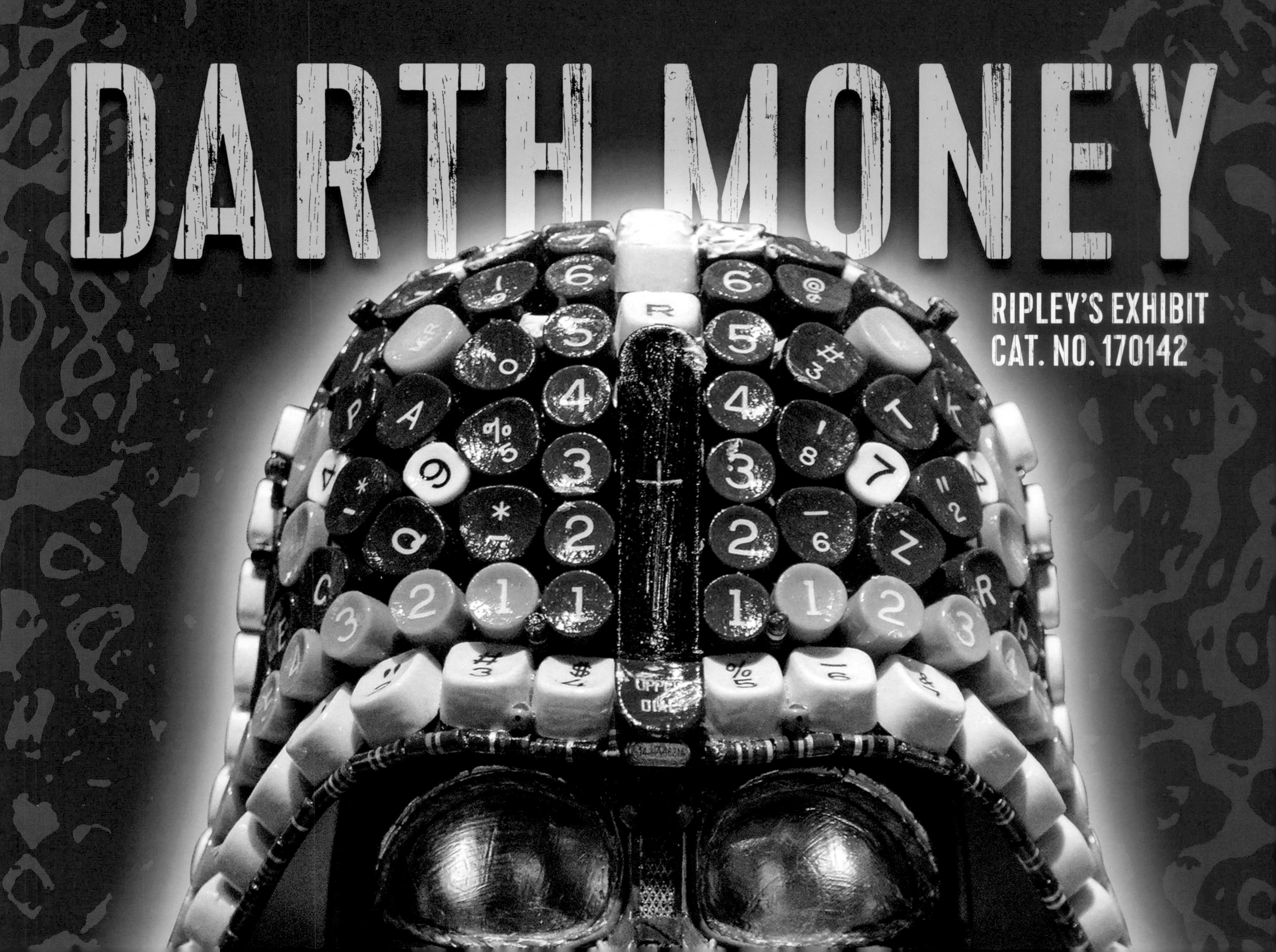
DARTH MONEY
RIPLEY'S EXHIBIT
CAT. NO. 170142

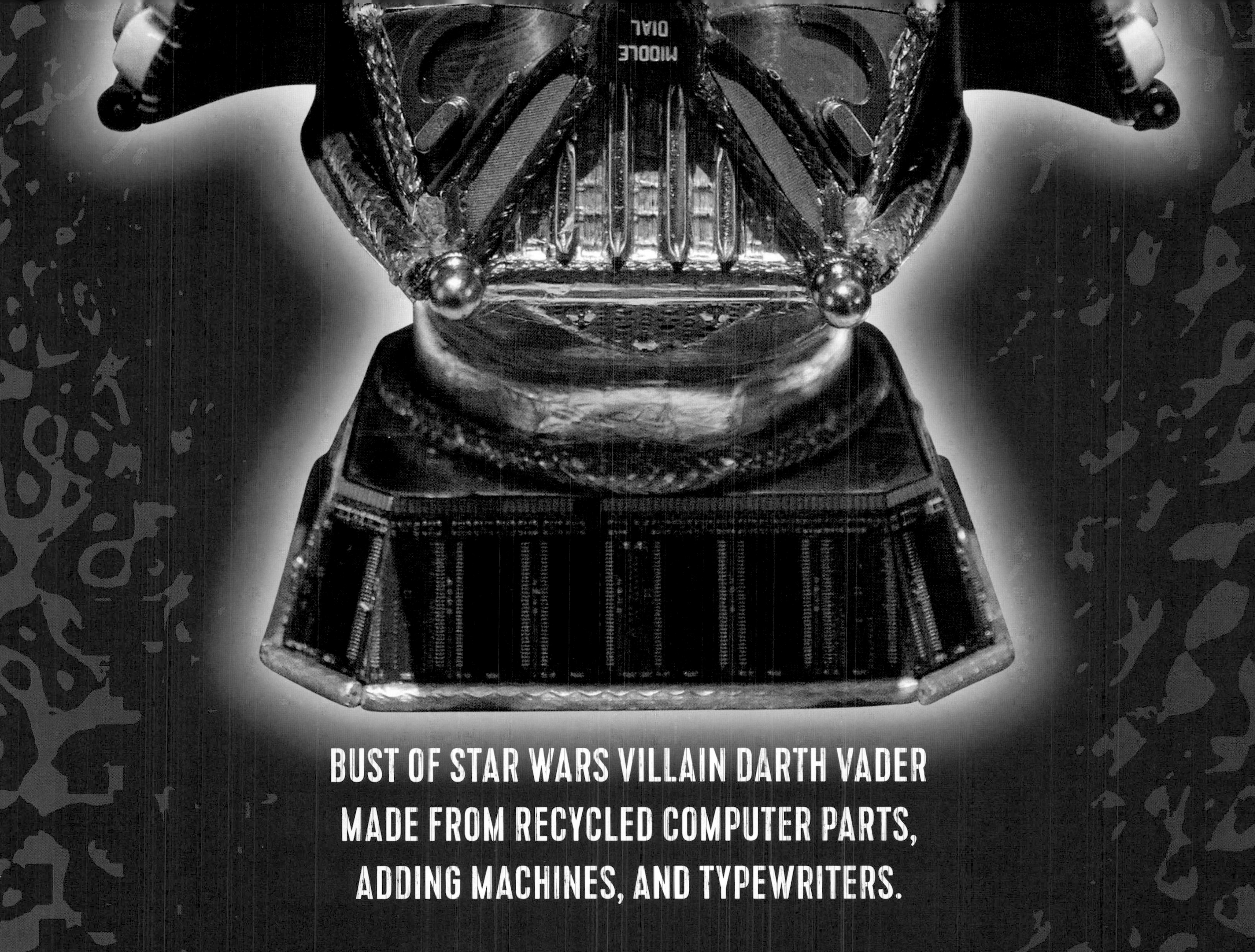

BUST OF STAR WARS VILLAIN DARTH VADER MADE FROM RECYCLED COMPUTER PARTS, ADDING MACHINES, AND TYPEWRITERS.

Ripley's Believe It or Not!®

ALL NEW BOOKS!

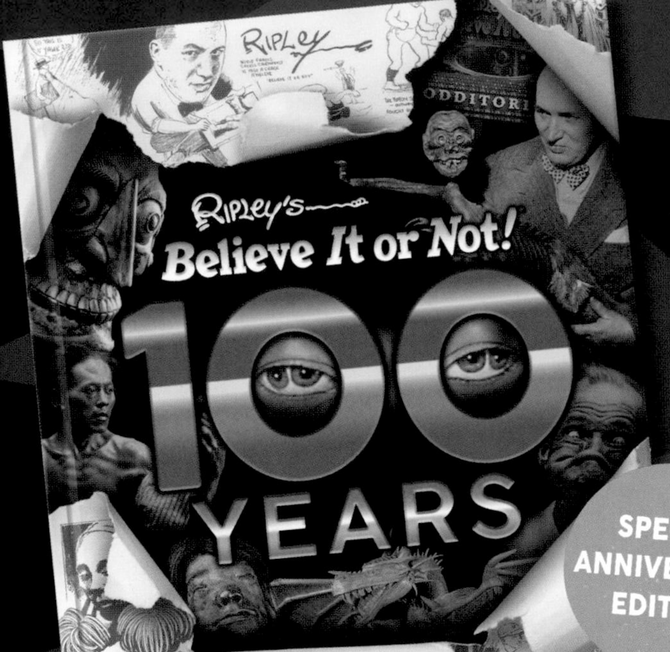

100 YEARS

Celebrate 100 years of the unbelievable through never-before-seen photos, anecdotes, stories, and images!

TIME WARP

All-true facts comparing events, inventions, and people that you would never believe existed at the same time in history!

ODD IS ART

A visually stunning display of unusual art that will delight and amaze art lovers and Ripley fans alike.

TO ORDER COPIES, GO TO WWW.RIPLEYS.COM/BOOKS

COLORS AND SHAPES

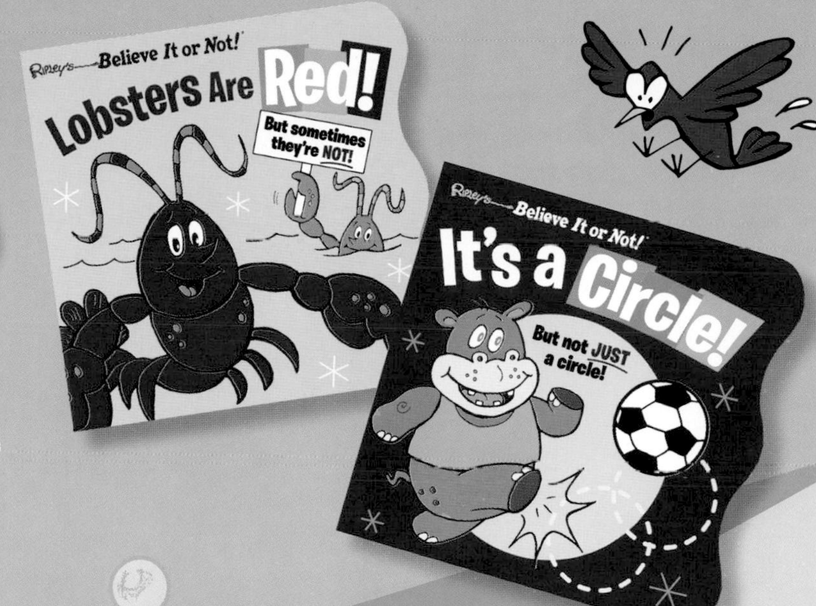

Learning colors and shapes has never been so much fun with these two new board books featuring easy-to-understand, real-life examples, silly characters, and colorful, engaging illustrations!

SHARKEE
the Teddy Bear
ca Firpi • Illustrated by John Graziano
BREMNER
and the Party
Carrie Bolin and Jessica Firpi • Illustrated by John Graziano

SHARKEE AND BREMNER

Captivating new picture books feature two favorite Ripley's Aquarium mascots—Sharkee the sand tiger shark and Bremner the puffer fish. Filled with expressive illustrations, silly situations, and lovable characters, kids and parents alike will be enchanted by each of these charming "tails"!

PLAY IT LOUD!

The newest edition to the best-selling Fun Facts & Silly Stories series is packed with amazing stories, unbelievable facts, eye-catching photos, and wacky games and puzzles.

UNBELIEVABLE!

FUN FACTS
Ripley's Believe It or Not!
Kids
& SILLY STORIES
PLAY IT LOUD!

SILLY!

RIPLEY'S BELIEVE IT OR NOT! ODDITORIUMS

Ripley's legacy lives on today with 30 Ripley's Odditoriums all around the world, the greatest collection of oddities ever assembled. The Ripley's team continue to search the globe, hunting for the oddest, most unusual, and the most unbelievable artifacts ever seen.

JEJU ISLAND, KOREA

GATLINBURG, TENNESSEE

NIAGARA FALLS, CANADA

BALTIMORE, MARYLAND

NEW YORK CITY, NEW YORK

Connect with Ripley's Online or in Person

There are 30 incredible Ripley's Believe It or Not! Odditoriums all around the world, where you can experience our spectacular collection during our century of strange!

Amsterdam
THE NETHERLANDS

Atlantic City
NEW JERSEY

Baltimore
MARYLAND

Blackpool
ENGLAND

Branson
MISSOURI

Cavendish
P.E.I., CANADA

Copenhagen
DENMARK

Gatlinburg
TENNESSEE

Genting Highlands
MALAYSIA

Grand Prairie
TEXAS

Guadalajara
MEXICO

Hollywood
CALIFORNIA

Jeju Island
KOREA

Key West
FLORIDA

Mexico City
MEXICO

Myrtle Beach
SOUTH CAROLINA

New York City
NEW YORK

Newport
OREGON

Niagara Falls
ONTARIO, CANADA

Ocean City
MARYLAND

Orlando
FLORIDA

Panama City Beach
FLORIDA

Pattaya
THAILAND

San Antonio
TEXAS

San Francisco
CALIFORNIA

St. Augustine
FLORIDA

Surfers Paradise
AUSTRALIA

Veracruz
MEXICO

Williamsburg
VIRGINIA

Wisconsin Dells
WISCONSIN

Stop by our website daily for new stories, photos, contests, and more! **www.ripleys.com**
Don't forget to connect with us on social media for a daily dose of the weird and the wonderful.

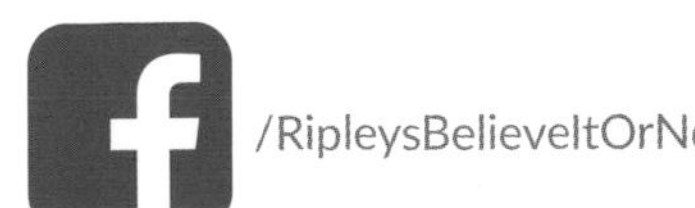 /RipleysBelieveItOrNot

 @Ripleys

youtube.com/Ripleys

 @RipleysBelieveItorNot

Ripley's

Believe It or Not!®